**PUBLIC OPINION IN
SEMISOVEREIGN GERMANY**

Office of West European Studies

Published in conjunction with the

OFFICE OF INTERNATIONAL
PROGRAMS AND STUDIES

PUBLIC OPINION IN SEMISOVEREIGN GERMANY

The HICOG Surveys, 1949-1955

Edited by
ANNA J. MERRITT and RICHARD L. MERRITT

With a Foreword by
LEO P. CRESPI

UNIVERSITY OF ILLINOIS PRESS
Urbana Chicago London

© 1980 by the Board of Trustees of the University of Illinois
Manufactured in the United States of America

Library of Congress Cataloging in Publication Data

Merritt, Anna J
  Public opinion in semisovereign Germany.

  Part 2 consists of summaries by the authors of the unpublished reports prepared by the Reactions Analysis Staff, Office of the U. S. High Commissioner for Germany.
  Continues the authors' Public opinion in occupied Germany.
  Includes bibliographical references and index.
  1. Public opinion--Germany, West. I. Merritt, Richard L., joint author. II. United States. Office of High Commissioner for Germany. Reactions Analysis Staff. III. Title.
HM261.M49   301.15'4'0943   78-20995
ISBN 0-252-00731-X

For Christopher, Geoffrey, and Theo
—continuing their multicultural journey

CONTENTS

Acknowledgments	xxi
Foreword by Leo P. Crespi	xxiii
List of Abbreviations	xxvii

PART I: POLITICAL PERSPECTIVES IN SEMISOVEREIGN GERMANY

THE HICOG SURVEYS	4
COMING TO TERMS WITH NAZISM	6
Views of the Nazi Past	6
Nazi System	7
World War II	8
Treatment of Jews	9
Removing the Remnants of Nazism	10
War Crimes Trials	10
Denazification	11
Organizations	11
FROM FOREIGN OCCUPATION TO INDEPENDENCE	12
Federal Republic	12
Federal Government	13
Parties and Elections	15
Konrad Adenauer	17
Rearmament	19
Militarism	19
An Independent German Military	20
Atlantic Pact	20
West European Army	22
Rearmament under NATO	23
GERMANY IN THE WORLD	23
West German Foreign Relations	23
Between East and West	24
Reunification	25
West Europe	30
East German Perspectives	31
Interviewing East Germans	32
Life in the GDR	33
The West	34
American Information Policy	35
Press	37
Radio	38
U.S. Information Centers	39
POLITICAL PERSPECTIVES IN SEMISOVEREIGN GERMANY: A BALANCE SHEET	40

PART II: THE HICOG SURVEYS

1. The State of German Nationalism Following the Founding of the West German Republic (30 December 1949) — 53
2. Readers' Evaluation of the U.S. Overt Publications (6 January 1950) — 55
3. West German Republic vs. East German Government: Some Evaluations and Comparisons (18 January 1950) — 55
4. RIAS and Its Listeners in Western Berlin (8 February 1950) — 56
5. West Berliners Appraise Present Economic and Political Situation (20 February 1950) — 57
6. The German Public Views the Conduct of the U.S. Occupation Forces (6 March 1950) — 58
7. The German Public Views the CARE Organization (6 March 1950) — 58
8. Reactions toward the Württemberg-Baden Denazification Affair (17 March 1950) — 59
9. German Attitude toward an Army and Military Training (17 March 1950) — 59
10. Germans View the U.S. Reorientation Program: I. Extent of Receptivity to American Ideas (30 March 1950) — 60
11. Germans View the U.S. Reorientation Program: II. Reactions to American Democratization Efforts (30 March 1950) — 61
12. Germans View the U.S. Reorientation Program: III. Opinions on the Cultural Exchange Program (30 March 1950) — 62
13. Implications of the H-Bomb in the East-West Struggle (1 April 1950) — 62
14. Readership of *Heute* and Other Illustrated Periodicals (4 April 1950) — 63
15. The German Public Assays Political Democracy (24 April 1950) — 64
16. Reactions and Recommendations of West Berliners in Face of Prospective Whitsuntide March (28 April 1950) — 64
17. Attitudes of Students at Erlangen and Munich Universities (30 April 1950) — 65
17-S. Trends in German Public Opinion: 1946 through 1949 (May 1950) — 66
18. West Germans View the East-West Struggle: I. General Evaluations and Extent of Allegiance to the West (19 May 1950) — 68
19. West Germans View the East-West Struggle: II. Trends and Current Attitudes on Withdrawal of the Occupying Powers (22 May 1950) — 69
20. West Germans View the East-West Struggle (25 May 1950): III. Defense of Western Germany — 70
21. Views of the German Public in the U.S. Zone on Chancellor Adenauer's Proposal of a Franco-German Union (31 May 1950) — 71

Contents/ix

22.	The Problem of Unemployment in Western Germany: I. German Appraisal of Its Causes and Consequences (5 June 1950)	71
23.	The Problem of Unemployment in Western Germany: II. Comparative Views of the Bavarian Unemployed and the Bavarian and U.S. Zone Public (5 June 1950)	72
23-S.	Reactions of a Munich Movie Audience to an Animated Film Based on the *Races of Mankind* (14 June 1950)	73
24.	German Youth in Five Cities Give Their Impression of the Supplement *Jugend in der Freien Welt* (30 June 1950)	73
25.	Post Mortem on the Whitsuntide March: A Survey of West Berliners' Evaluations (6 July 1950)	74
26.	Trends and Current Attitudes Regarding the "Voice of America" Broadcasts (26 July 1950)	74
27.	Trend in German Opinions on Socialization of Industry (27 July 1950)	75
28.	Trends in Opinions on the West German Federal Republic (31 July 1950)	76
28-S.	Rumors in West Germany Following the Korean Outbreak (31 July 1950)	77
29.	German Reactions to the American-Sponsored Newsreel *Welt im Film* (4 August 1950)	77
30.	Have the Western Occupying Powers Furthered or Hindered German Reconstruction? (8 August 1950)	78
31.	Trends in Awareness and Patronage of the U.S. Information Centers in the U.S. Zone, West Berlin, and Bremen (8 August 1950)	78
32.	Germans View the Korean Outbreak: I. Urban Trends in U.S. Occupied Areas (14 August 1950)	79
33.	Germans View the Korean Outbreak: II. Urban Opinions in West Germany (23 August 1950)	80
34.	A Summary of Trends in Radio Listening in West Berlin (28 August 1950)	81
34-S.	Further Study of Post-Korean Rumors in Germany (29 August 1950)	81
35.	Observers Evaluate Effectiveness of Communist Press in West Germany (8 September 1950)	82
36.	The Question of Remilitarization in Western Germany (15 September 1950)	82
37.	Germans View the Korean Outbreak: III. Overall Opinions and Group Differences in the U.S. Occupied Areas (28 September 1950)	83
38.	German Youth View the American Program: I. Some General Evaluations (9 October 1950)	84
39.	The Effectiveness of the ERP Information Program in Western Germany (12 October 1950)	85
40.	German Youth View the American Program: II. American Reorientation Efforts (23 October 1950)	86
41.	German Youth View the American Program: III. The "Voice of America" and General Radio (23 October 1950)	87
42.	German Youth View the American Program: IV. Awareness and Patronage of Amerika Häuser among Youth (25 October 1950)	87

43. German Youth View the American Program: V. Audience of U.S. Overt Magazines and U.S. Documentary Film Program (25 October 1950) ... 88
44. German Youth View the American Program: VI. The German-American Exchange Program (30 October 1950) ... 88
45. Trend in Opinion on West German Remilitarization (31 October 1950) ... 89
46. Germans View the Remilitarization Issue: Urban Opinion in Western Germany (10 November 1950) ... 89
47. Germans View the Remilitarization Issue: Further Findings and Some Limitations on Majority Approval (18 November 1950) ... 90
48. An Analysis of Possible Determinants of Opposition to German Participation in the Defense of Europe (22 November 1950) ... 91
49. A Test of Reader Reaction to Third Reich and Defeatist Articles (27 November 1950) ... 93
50. German Youth View the American Program: VII. Acceptance of Democratic Responsibility and Related Political Issues (30 November 1950) ... 94
51. Germans View the Remilitarization Issue: Pre-Election Trend and Further Findings (1 December 1950) ... 95
52. Germans View the Remilitarization Issue: New Korean Trend and Further Analysis of Opposition (7 December 1950) ... 96
53. Germans View the Remilitarization Issue: Reactions to Korean Reverses and Associated Issues (14 December 1950) ... 97
54. German Youth View the Adult Education System (21 December 1950) ... 98
55. Germans View the Remilitarization Issue: Year-End Developments and the Present Status of Neutralism (28 December 1950) ... 98
56. West German Opinions on Political Parties and Election Issues (29 December 1950) ... 99
57. Germans View the Remilitarization Issue: Has Western Policy Changed on German Militarism?--and Present-Day Attitudes on Nuremberg (12 January 1951) ... 101
58. Germans View the Remilitarization Issue: Further Trends on Neutralism, Defense Participation, and Associated Issues (18 January 1951) ... 102
59. Public Appraisal of Effectiveness of Communist Activity in West Germany (25 January 1951) ... 103
60. New Light on German Neutrality Sentiments (31 January 1951) ... 103
61. Defense Participation Sentiments and the Extent of "Ohne Mich": With Other Current Developments on Issues Related to German Defense Participation (22 February 1951) ... 104
62. Franco-German Relations as Viewed by Residents of the U.S. Zone, Berlin, and Bremen (28 February 1951) ... 105

63.	West German Reactions to the Landsberg Decisions (6 March 1951)	106
63-S.	Attitudes behind the Iron Curtain: A Survey Approach to East German Thinking: I. General Mood and Resistance Sentiments (9 March 1951)	107
64.	German Attitudes on Eve of Paris Deputies Conference (14 March 1951)	108
65.	Frankfurt School-Children React to the Booklet *Eight Great Americans* (14 March 1951)	109
66.	Ruhr Miners Specify Their Housing Wants (20 March 1951)	109
67.	Survey Studies among German Opinion Leaders: I. German Bürgermeisters Evaluate the Landsberg Decisions (21 March 1951)	110
68.	Survey Studies among German Opinion Leaders: II. A Note on Bürgermeisters' Reactions to a Four-Power Conference (22 March 1951)	111
69.	The West German People View Defense Participation, Neutrality, and Related Issues (29 March 1951)	111
70.	Some Further Findings on West German Reactions to the Landsberg Decisions (30 March 1951)	112
70-S.	A Note on the Communist Projected Plebiscite on West German Defense Participation (2 April 1951)	112
71.	West German Reaction to the Schuman Plan (5 April 1951)	113
71-S.	Attitudes Behind the Iron Curtain: II. Current Views on Unity, Neutrality, and Related Issues (10 April 1951)	114
72.	West German Reactions to Increased Occupation Costs (12 April 1951)	114
73.	Do Germans Want a Single Youth Organization in West Germany? (13 April 1951)	115
74.	West German View on Two Current Issues: The Proposed Four-Power Conference and the Revised Occupation Statute (16 April 1951)	115
75.	German Reactions to Three Current Economic Issues: Codetermination, Decartelization, and Freedom of Enterprise (18 April 1951)	116
76.	Continuing Trends in Awareness and Patronage of the Amerika Häuser in the U.S. Zone (24 April 1951)	117
77.	Initial Reactions of Urban West Germans to the Recall of General MacArthur (24 April 1951)	117
78.	U.S. Zone Germans View the Kreis Resident Officers (14 May 1951)	118
79.	Attitudes behind the Iron Curtain: III. A Preliminary Exploration of Attitudes among East Zone Male Youth (17 May 1951)	118
80.	Current Trend on Defense Participation: With West German Reactions to the Communist Remilitarization "Plebiscite" (28 May 1951)	119
81.	The Effectiveness of Recent Informational Efforts on the Schuman Plan (30 May 1951)	120

82.	Does East or West Really Want a Four-Power Conference? (31 May 1951)	120
83.	The Present State of West German Confidence in the West: With Reactions to General MacArthur's Recall (12 June 1951)	121
84.	Guns or Butter? West German Opinion on the Use of Marshall Plan Funds (14 June 1951)	122
85.	The Impact of the Europa Train: A Preliminary Study on a Mainz Audience (15 June 1951)	122
86.	The East-West Trade Issue as Viewed by the West German People (21 June 1951)	123
87.	West Germans View the Socialist Reich Party: With a Preliminary Analysis of SRP Attitudes (29 June 1951)	123
88.	Current Thinking on West German Defense Participation: With Projected Reactions to a Possible Bonn Agreement (6 July 1951)	124
89.	Urban West German Reactions to the Kemritz Case (13 July 1951)	126
90.	Attitudes behind the Iron Curtain: IV. Radio Listening in the East Zone (25 July 1951)	126
91.	West German Attitudes on Some Current Political Issues (6 August 1951)	127
92.	West German Reactions to the Korean Armistice Negotiations (20 August 1951)	128
92-S.	A Note on West German Reactions to Ending the State of War (23 August 1951)	128
93.	West German Reactions to the Projected American-Spanish Military and Economic Pact (24 August 1951)	129
94.	The Views of West Germans on the Defense of West Europe (27 August 1951)	129
95.	Germans View the "Voice of America": I. The Extent and Characteristics of the VOA Audience in West Germany and West Berlin (28 August 1951)	131
96.	How Do West German Youth React to American History? A Preliminary Study of Stuttgart Pupils' Appraisal of *An Outline of American History* (30 August 1951)	131
97.	Germans View the "Voice of America": II. Some Technical Factors in VOA Listenership (31 August 1951)	132
98.	Reactions of the Berlin Audience to the Train of Europe (13 September 1951)	132
99.	West German Reactions to a "Preservation of Democracy" Clause in the Projected Contractual Agreement (21 September 1951)	133
100.	Program Tastes of West German and West Berlin Radio Listeners: And Tabular Summary (27 September 1951)	133
101.	Attitudes of East German Youth: I. Evaluations of the Berlin Youth Festival and Impressions of West Berlin (29 September 1951)	134

Contents/xiii

102.	Attitudes of East German Youth: II. What Young Germans Would Like to Ask Mr. McCloy (29 September 1951)	135
103.	The Current State of German-American Relations (12 October 1951)	136
104.	Germans View the "Voice of America": III. Program Preferences and Evaluations of VOA Listeners (17 October 1951)	137
105.	Germans View the "Voice of America": IV. The Question of Effectiveness (17 October 1951)	137
106.	Some Evaluations of the Bonn Government: With Current Thinking on the Issue of New Federal Elections (22 October 1951)	138
107.	A Balance Sheet on Western Information Efforts: Extent of German Accord with Western Viewpoints on Some Major East-West Issues (30 October 1951)	139
108.	Attitudes of East German Youth: III. Reactions to Eastern versus Western Propaganda (31 October 1951)	141
108-S.	A Note on the Representativeness of German Listener Letters to VOA (7 November 1951)	142
109.	Attitudes of East German Youth: IV. Radio Evaluations and Recommendations of East Zone Youth (19 November 1951)	142
110.	Are East Zone Youth Spreading the Message of West Berlin? A Study of the Effects of the Berlin Youth Festival on the East Zone Population (26 November 1951)	143
111.	West German Thinking on a Federation of Europe (28 November 1951)	144
112.	West German Views on Veterans' Organizations and Their Role in Political Life (30 November 1951)	145
113.	German Opinions on Jewish Restitution and Some Associated Issues (5 December 1951)	146
114.	The July 20 Plot on Hitler's Life: Does It Afford a Rallying Point for Rightist Groups? (5 December 1951)	147
115.	Some Further Soundings of West and East German Opinions on Unity Issues (19 December 1951)	147
116.	Are East Zone Youth Resisting Totalitarian Education? (19 December 1951)	148
117.	Current German Views on a National versus a European Army (21 December 1951)	149
118.	The Present Status of "Neo-Nazism" in West Germany (10 January 1952)	150
119.	The German Appraisal of the Allied Forces in West Germany: With Recommendations for Improved Citizen-Soldier Relations (28 January 1952)	151
120.	German Evaluations of NATO: With Other Opinions on European Defense Issues (29 January 1952)	153
121.	Anxieties and Aspirations of East Zone Youth: A Study in Certain Morale Factors as Reported during the Communist Youth Rally (29 January 1952)	154

122. Progress toward Political Equality and Economic 154
Well-Being (31 January 1952)
123. West German Reactions to the West's Disarmament 155
Proposals at the Paris Meeting of the United
Nations (11 February 1952)
124. Repercussions in West Germany of the French Ambas- 155
sadorial Appointment to the Saar (26 February 1952)
125. The Current State of West Berlin Morale (29 Feb- 156
ruary 1952)
126. East Zone Youth's Appraisal of Western Political 158
Pamphlets: With Sidelights on Penetration of
Printed Matter into East Germany (29 February 1952)
127. An Appraisal of the Impact of the Berlin Cultural 158
Festival (10 March 1952)
128. Current Trends in West Berlin Opinions on Issues 159
Related to the East-West Struggle (29 March 1952)
129. West German Public Opinion on Defense Participa- 160
tion Following the Formal Bundestag Debate: I.
Impact of the Bundestag Debate (31 March 1952)
130. West German Public Opinion on Defense Participa- 161
tion Following the Formal Bundestag Debate: II.
Current Support and Resistance--and Some of the
Factors Related Thereto (31 March 1952)
131. West German Public Opinion on Defense Participa- 162
tion Following the Formal Bundestag Debate: III.
National versus Integrated Army (31 March 1952)
132. East Zone Farmers' Reactions to RIAS Farm Broad- 162
casts: With Sidelights on the Extent of VOA
Listenership (10 April 1952)
133. Are East German Farmers Resisting Collectivism? 163
A Study of Farmers' Evaluation of East German
Agriculture (10 April 1952)
134. How Are West Berliners Reacting to the Economic 164
Blandishments of East Berlin? (29 April 1952)
135. Contractual Agreement versus Russian Unity Pro- 165
posal: A Preliminary Report on West German Views
(30 April 1952)
136. Hard Core Refugees Evaluate Their Situation: A 166
Study of Camp Inmates in Western Germany (16
May 1952)
137. Follow-up Study of German Views on the Contractual 167
Agreement versus the Russian Unity Proposal (21
May 1952)
138. East Zone Thinking on the Russian Unity Proposal 168
versus the Contractual Agreement: With Comparisons
to West Berlin and West German Reactions (23 May
1952)
139. Do the West German People Believe the U.S. Is for 169
German Unity? With Comparative Judgments about
the British and French (27 May 1952)
140. How Do Germans React to East-West Trade Restric- 171
tions? (30 May 1952)

Contents/xv

141.	Initial West German Reactions to the Soviet War of Nerves (May 1952)	171
142.	First Reactions of West Berliners to the Current Soviet Pressure Campaign (11 June 1952)	172
143.	Some Basic Guides to Predicting the Future Behavior of West Germany (30 June 1952)	174
144.	German Views on the Contractual Agreement Following Initialing and Publication (8 July 1952)	175
145.	A Further Assessment of German Reactions to the Soviet War of Nerves (10 July 1952)	176
146.	How Strong Is Resistance Morale in West Berlin Today? (28 July 1952)	177
147.	The Basic Economic Orientations of the West German People: I. General Views on Socialism, Capitalism, and Communism (April 1952)	179
148.	The Basic Economic Orientations of the West German People: II. The Status of Trade Unions and the Question of Codetermination (7 August 1952)	180
149.	A Note on Receptivity and Resistance to Introducing American Working Methods into German Industry (8 August 1952)	181
150.	The Korean Record in German Eyes: And Some Comparisons with British, French, Dutch, and Italian Views (13 August 1952)	182
151.	West German Receptivity and Reactions to the Exchange of Persons Program (25 August 1952)	183
152.	West German Public Opinion in re the Latest Russian Note (2 September 1952)	184
153.	Current West German Views on the War Criminals Issue (8 September 1952)	184
154.	West German Evaluation of the U.S. Air Force in Germany (15 September 1952)	185
155.	Present Level of West German Political and Economic Satisfaction: With Current Standings of the Major Political Parties (22 September 1952)	186
155-S.	An Experimental Audience Reaction Study on the "Voice of America" (22 September 1952)	188
156.	West German Reactions to Visit of East Zone Delegation: With an Appraisal of Current Temper on the Unity Issue (3 October 1952)	188
157.	Are the Difficulties of Recent East Zone Refugees Breeding Disaffection with the West? (13 October 1952)	189
158.	West Germans Appraise Their Present Day Press: I. Newspaper Readership and Preferences (14 October 1952)	190
159.	West Germans Appraise Their Present Day Press: II. Evaluations and Recommendations (15 October 1952)	191
160.	West Germans Appraise Their Present Day Press: III. Readership and Evaluations of the *Neue Zeitung* (16 October 1952)	193

161.	The Impact of the BDJ Affair upon American Prestige in Germany (30 October 1952)	194
162.	Have East Zone Catholics Been Demoralized by Communist Pressure? (5 November 1952)	194
163.	West German Reactions to the American Presidential Elections (15 November 1952)	195
164.	West German Audience Potential for a Projected Atomic Energy Exhibit (17 November 1952)	196
165.	An Appraisal of Pamphlets as a Medium of Influence in West Germany (22 December 1952)	196
166.	An Evaluation of the Effectiveness of the Marshallhaus Exhibit (23 December 1952)	197
167.	A Year-End Survey of Rightist and Nationalist Sentiments in West Germany (12 January 1953)	197
168.	The Year's Trends in West German Thinking on the Peace Contract and Political Party Preferences (15 January 1953)	199
169.	The Year-End Status of West German Confidence in the Strength of the Western Powers (28 January 1953)	200
169-S.	Public Opinion in Western Europe: Attitudes toward Political, Economic, and Military Integration (January 1953)	201
170.	RIAS Coverage and Programming as Evaluated by East Zone Listeners (10 February 1953)	204
171.	How Do Germans Feel about an American Informational Operation in West Germany? (11 February 1953)	204
172.	Note on Year-End Trends in West German Attitudes toward the United Nations (14 February 1953)	205
173.	Some Early West German Reactions to the New American Administration (24 February 1953)	206
174.	The American Soldier as Appraised by the West German People: A Continuing Study of Civilian-Troop Relations (5 March 1953)	207
175.	A German Audience Evaluation of the Film *Without Fear* (20 March 1953)	208
176.	Green Week Visitors Appraise the Marshall House Exhibit "Agriculture in the Free World" (27 March 1953)	208
177.	Current Appraisal of West Berlin Morale, with Reactions to the Refugee Influx (20 April 1953)	209
177-S.	West German Public Opinion in the Wake of Stalin's Death and the Soviet "Peace Offensive" (30 April 1953)	210
178.	German Impact and Evaluations of President Eisenhower's Foreign Policy Address (14 May 1953)	212
179.	Current West German Political Trends and Projected Reactions to Possible Russian Proposals (15 June 1953)	213

180.	German Political Trends Following Recent Soviet Concessions and Subsequent East Zone Riots (6 July 1953)	214
181.	The America House Evaluated: A Study of the Effectiveness of the U.S. Information Centers in West Germany (17 July 1953)	215
182.	The Current Standing of RIAS among West Berlin Radio Listeners: I. Reactions and Evaluations (31 July 1953)	216
183.	Some Clues to the Effectiveness of a Productivity Film Program among German Factory Workers (14 August 1953)	216
183-S.	German Thinking on a Four-Power Conference (24 August 1953)	217
184.	West Berlin Subscribers Appraise the *Neue Zeitung* (27 August 1953)	218
185.	East Zone Views on the June Riots, Food Aid, and Current Political Issues (27 August 1953)	219
186.	Further Soundings of East German Opinions on Current Political Issues (18 September 1953)	220
187.	An Evaluation of Audience Reactions to the U.S.I.A. Film *Magic Streetcar* (7 October 1953)	221
188.	The Current Standing of RIAS among West Berlin Radio Listeners: II. Comparative Indices of Station and Program Popularity (29 October 1953)	221
189.	East Zone Radio Listening: Trend and Current Evaluations of RIAS (30 October 1953)	222
190.	The Marshall House Exhibit at the 1953 Berlin Industrial Fair: An Evaluation of West Berlin and East German Reactions (16 November 1953)	222
191.	A Survey Analysis of the Factors Underlying the Outcome of the 1953 German Federal Elections (11 December 1953)	223
192.	West German Reactions to U.N. Airing of Korea Atrocities (28 December 1953)	225
192-S.	International Survey on President Eisenhower's U.N. Speech (German Results)	225
193.	German Public Opinion on the Four-Power Conference: With Latest Trends in EDC Thinking (18 January 1954)	226
194-I.	Public Opinion during the Four-Power Conference: I. West German Views on Eve of Four-Power Conference (24 January 1954)	227
194-II.	Public Opinion during the Four-Power Conference: II. West German Reactions to Initial Developments (31 January 1954)	228
194-III.	Public Opinion during the Four-Power Conference: III. Flash Reactions to Eden and Molotov Plans (3 February 1954)	229
194-IV.	Public Opinion during the Four-Power Conference: IV. West German Reactions to Western versus Soviet Proposals (7 February 1954)	230

194-V.	Public Opinion during the Four-Power Conference: V. East German Reactions to Western versus Soviet Proposals (8 February 1954)	231
194-VI.	Public Opinion during the Four-Power Conference: VI. West German Opinion on Molotov's European Security Proposal and Other Late Conference Developments (15 February 1954)	232
195.	Who Won the Four-Power Conference? The West German Public State Their Views (11 March 1954)	233
196.	Current West German Political Opinions and Reactions to Recent Developments (12 April 1954)	234
196-S1.	The Status of Red-White-Red among Austrian Radio Listeners: I. Preliminary Report for Vienna and Lower Austria (17 May 1954)	236
196-S2.	The American and West German Aid Program in the Eyes of West Berliners: With General Indications of Current West Berlin Morale (25 May 1954)	236
197.	The Impact of American Commercial Films in West Germany (14 June 1954)	237
198.	Trends in West German Appraisal of the United States Forces in Germany (15 June 1954)	238
199.	West Germans State Their Views on the Role of Atomic Weapons in Western Defense (18 June 1954)	239
200.	Current Trends in West German Opinions on Major Political Issues: With Reactions to Bonn-Moscow Overtures and the Geneva Conference (28 June 1954)	241
201.	Estimates of Soviet Zone Audiences of RIAS Program Features (20 August 1954)	242
202.	German Reactions to the John Affair and Other Recent Political Events: With Trends on EDC, Further European Conferences, and Related Issues (8 September 1954)	242
202-S.	Post-EDC Climate of West European Opinion: With Reactions to the London Conference (2 November 1954)	244
203.	East Zone Refugees Report on Their Radio Listening Habits (10 November 1954)	245
204.	Radio Diary Study in West Germany and West Berlin, May 1954 (29 November 1954)	246
205.	The Berlin Atomic Energy Exhibit: West and East German Reactions (1 December 1954)	246
206.	Current German Opinion on the Saar (Following the Paris Agreement) (6 December 1954)	247
206-S.	The Current State of Morale among Youth in West Berlin (4 February 1955)	248
207.	Public Opinion in Western Germany on the Reestablishment of Military Forces (4 February 1955)	250
208.	Frankfurt Visitors Appraise the Atomic Energy Exhibit "Atoms for Peace" (15 February 1955)	250
209.	German Attitudes toward France and the French: A Program Guidance Study on Franco-German Rapprochement (11 March 1955)	251

209-S.	West European Public Opinion on Current Issues (23 March 1955)	252
210.	An Appraisal of the America Houses in Germany: A Program Guidance Study on Effectiveness of the U.S. Information Centers (15 April 1955)	254
211.	Reunification: West German Aspirations and Expectations (9 May 1955)	255
212.	West German Radio Listening during February 1955 (13 May 1955)	256
213.	Sovereign Germany Speaks: Reactions to Sovereignty, Austria Solution, and Coming Four-Power Conference (1 July 1955)	257

Appendix: List of U.S. Embassy Survey Reports — 259

Index — 263

FIGURES

1. Satisfaction with Governmental Performance — 14
2. Identification with Political Parties — 16
3. West German Participation in the Defense of West Europe — 21
4. Preferences for Alliance with the West vs. Neutrality — 26
5. Preferences for Alliance with the West vs. Reunification — 27

TABLE

1. Reunification at What Price? — 29

ACKNOWLEDGMENTS

Several individuals and institutions provided important assistance in the preparation of this volume. Copies of reports were provided by Donald V. McGranahan of the United Nations Research and Development Branch, Leo P. Crespi of the United States Information Agency, Harold Hurwitz of the Free University of Berlin, and the Political Science Research Library of Yale University. Karen Fletcher provided technical assistance at the very outset, and Judith Graham prepared first drafts of numerous summaries. The manuscript was typed by Carolyn Foster, Ruth Gartner, and Judith Holt. Financial support came from several sources within the University of Illinois at Urbana-Champaign. The Research Board of the Graduate College and the Institute of Communications Research financed the summarizing and analysis, and the Department of Political Science provided the typing. For all this friendly assistance, we are very grateful.

Urbana, Illinois   A.J.M. & R.L.M.

FOREWORD

As far back as the Declaration of Independence, America committed itself to pay a decent respect to the opinions of mankind. Nowhere had this Jeffersonian commitment been more honored than in the remarkable opportunity to voice their sentiments given by America as an occupying power to the German people following their defeat in World War II.

"*Was sind momentan Ihre grössten Schwierigkeiten und Sorgen?*"--"What are your greatest cares and worries at the present time?"--was an inquiry that, from the earliest days of the German occupation, prefaced the efforts of a busy corps of interviewers to find out from the German people their opinions on the significant political, economic, and social issues of the day.

In the good democratic tradition, occupation officials were quick to perceive the value of knowing how their charges--the German people--reacted to the measures being taken to restore their economic well-being and to bring their country back within the community of nations. Occupation leaders turned to the relatively new science of public opinion surveying to provide them with a thermometer, so to speak, by which they could chart the hoped-for recovery of the German body politic.

The German people, despite their unfortunate experiences with spies and informants, reacted most favorably to the opportunity to voice their views. From the beginning of the occupation, the great bulk of those interviewed evidenced appreciation of the opportunity to tell their story; only a negligible proportion expressed the feeling that no good was served by such public opinion inquiries.

That appreciation was widespread is perhaps not astonishing, for surely it was extraordinary for an occupied people--even the meanest among them--to be cordially invited by their occupiers to express their views and criticisms on current problems and even on the policies of the occupying powers.

But what assurances are there that the German people under such extraordinary circumstances were truthfully answering the questions put to them? This is a fair inquiry, since the Germans, having had unfortunate experiences with questioners and questioning generally, might be expected to be somewhat less than candid with interviewers, particularly representatives of the current authority, the American occupation.

From the beginning of the survey program, however, the German interviewers of the survey staff took pains to assure their fellow countrymen that the survey inquiries were entirely anonymous and that a candid expression of opinion would give their views a hearing in the establishment of occupation policies.

Both survey results and specific methodological studies have indicated that the German people took the interviewers at their word; in fact, far from having difficulty getting respondents to talk, the problem was often to get them to stop. And from the opening surveys there was never any dearth of criticisms of Allied policies, often stated in the strongest possible terms, thus suggesting that respondents were reacting to the interviewing situation as one in which they might candidly express their real sentiments.

For more specific assurances of candor, a study was conducted wherein the same questions were put to comparable samples, in one case under the usual conditions of open American sponsorship and in the other under purely German sponsorship.[1] It was found that, in the majority of inquiries, answers under the two sets of sponsorship conditions did not differ significantly, thus suggesting that the fact of American military government sponsorship was not for the most part introducing any material deviation of the results from those that would be obtained under more conventional native auspices.

On a few questions, particularly those touching directly upon American prestige, and, to a less extent, those bearing on militarism or National Socialism, favorable responses were somewhat more frequent with American than with German sponsorship. While the differences were not large, they did suggest that, in interpreting results to questions of these types, allowance should be made for the possibility of some favorable bias.

It was the hope of those of us engaged in public opinion research in Germany during the OMGUS and HICOG years that this enterprise would not only be of value to the guidance of American policy, but would also contribute to the development of German democracy. This hope was based on the conviction that polling and authoritarianism do not mix well. When people begin to learn that their opinions are important and begin to like giving their opinions and finding out what their fellows are thinking, it becomes more difficult for a government to force arbitrary measures on the populace. Moreover, the experience of being polled and of reading about public opinion issues of the day helps to build the interest in political participation that was at so low an ebb in postwar Germany and that is so fundamental to the success of democracy.

We at HICOG therefore welcomed the opportunity to contribute what inspiration we could to the development of a thriving public opinion research community in West Germany. I remember with pleasure a milestone in this development: a

---

[1] Leo P. Crespi, "The Influence of Military Government Sponsorship in German Opinion Polling," *International Journal of Opinion and Attitude Research* 4:2 (Summer 1950), 151-178.

research convocation amid the picturesque surroundings of
Weinheim on the Bergstrasse in the winter of 1951. This convocation, the culmination of two years of HICOG effort, brought
together under one roof an illustrious company of German empirical social researchers who were interested in promoting the
development of the infant science of public opinion research
on the German scene. The thoughtful and constructive German
contributions to this conference[2] provided, I believe, a major
impetus to the establishment of German survey research.

With this opportunity to review some of the history of
survey research in Germany, I treasure the thought that the
present flourishing state of this discipline derives in some
small part at least from the efforts of a group of dedicated
social scientists with whom I had the pleasure and the privilege to be associated. They are too numerous to mention by
name in this brief foreword, but each of them, I hope, is enjoying the satisfaction of a job well done.

It is not only my less than disinterested judgment that
I am drawing upon for a favorable evaluation of the German
surveys but also the assessment of such distinguished reviewers of the communication research literature as Bruce Lannes
and Chitra Smith, who in their definitive 1956 overview of
the field[3] were kind enough to characterize the HICOG surveys and the OMGUS surveys that preceded them as "immensely
impressive" and of "great substantive value and major scientific caliber."

I am thus reassured that the German surveys deserve the
audience that this book and its predecessor *Public Opinion in
Occupied Germany* strive to achieve; and I am sure that interest in the survey indications will be stimulated in no small
part by the masterful summary of the HICOG series drafted by
those devoted students of German survey research, your editors
Anna and Richard Merritt.

> Leo P. Crespi
> Senior Research Advisor
> Office of Research and
>   Evaluation
> International Communication
>   Agency

---

[2]*Empirische Sozialforschung: Meinungs- und Marktforschung
Probleme und Methoden* (Frankfurt am Main: Institut zur
Förderung öffentlicher Angelegenheiten e.V., 1952).

[3]Bruce Lannes Smith and Chitra M. Smith, *International Communication and Political Opinion: A Guide to the Literature,*
Bureau of Social Science Research, The American University,
Washington, D.C. (Santa Monica, Calif.: The RAND Corporation,
Report R-285, January, 1956), p. 8.

LIST OF ABBREVIATIONS

AFN	American Forces Network
AMZON	American Zone of Occupation
BDJ	League of German Youth
BHE	League of Expellees and Those Deprived of Their Rights (Refugee party)
CDU	Christian Democratic Union
CSU	Christian Social Union
DIVO	Deutsches Institut für Volksumfragen
DRP	German Reich party
ECSC	European Coal and Steel Community
EDC	European Defense Community
ERP	European Recovery Plan (Marshall Plan)
FDJ	Free German Youth (GDR)
FDP	Free Democratic party
GDR	German Democratic Republic
HICOG	High Commission for Germany
KPD	Communist Party of Germany
NATO	North Atlantic Treaty Organization
NSDAP	National Socialist German Workers party (Nazi party)
NWDR	Northwest German Radio
OEEC	Organization for European Economic Cooperation
RIAS	Radio in the American Sector (Berlin)
SED	Socialist Unity party (GDR)

SPD	Social Democratic party
SRP	Socialist Reich party
VOA	Voice of America

PART I

POLITICAL PERSPECTIVES IN SEMISOVEREIGN GERMANY

PART I: POLITICAL PERSPECTIVES IN SEMISOVEREIGN GERMANY

The rise of the German phoenix from the ashes of World War II has been a topic of never-ending scholarly fascination. During the war itself, some Allied writers and statesmen had called for the destruction, or at least dismemberment and pastoralization, of the country from which three major wars had sprung in less than three generations. Final wartime decisions nonetheless foresaw the eventual resumption of its rightful place in the comity of nations by a peaceful, democratic, united Germany. Deepening hostility among the victors was to frustrate this goal. By mid-1949 the country had indeed been dismembered: Poland and the Soviet Union had incorporated some of it into their own territory, and the remainder had been divided into two states, with the tiny enclave of West Berlin left under Western Allied control but surrounded by the hostile German Democratic Republic (GDR).

The areas of prewar Germany (excluding Berlin) occupied by the American, British, and French military were merged in 1949 to form the Federal Republic of Germany (FRG). Initial antagonisms among the three Western Allies had ultimately, in the face of a perceived Soviet threat, given way to a willingness both to cooperate with each other and to reconstruct the western rump of Germany as a bulwark against the new enemy. In 1946 the Americans and British merged their zones of occupation into what came to be called "Bizonia," and with the London agreements of 1947-48 came the addition of the French Zone and a general currency reform for "Trizonia." The London agreements also called for a constituent assembly that would draft a constitution for the trizonal area. This constitution--or "Basic Law," as the West Germans termed it to indicate that it was only a provisional document--provided the basis for the promulgation, in September 1949, of the Federal Republic.

Although nominally sovereign, the Federal Republic continued under the tutelage of the Western Allies until May 1955. American, British, and French military governments were replaced by High Commissions, which retained certain rights of occupation, most notably in the areas of foreign policy and defense.[1] Along with these rights came a deeply felt responsibility to see to it that the FRG would develop into a strong but peaceful ally. This meant pumping vast sums into West Germany to build up its economy. It meant laying the groundwork for West German defense forces that could contribute to Western defenses. And it meant creating a set of institutional bonds in the field of politics and economics that would tie the FRG inextricably to its West European neighbors.

The half-dozen years of semisovereignty comprised a period of immense growth for the FRG. Political stability reigned at home under the firm (or, in the view of opponents, sometimes authoritarian) hand of Konrad Adenauer, the FRG's first federal chancellor. The country's economy was still in ruins in 1949, but by 1955 it had achieved full employment as well as a moderate level of prosperity. It was well on its way to becoming the economic giant that it is today. The FRG had joined with France, Italy, and the Benelux countries to form the European Coal and Steel Community, which by 1955 was moving toward a more general European Economic Community. Moreover, despite the dashed hopes for a European Defense Community, a way had been found to permit the FRG to rearm under the aegis of the North Atlantic Treaty Organization. Functioning democracy in West Germany itself and such international measures as the decision to pay reparations to Israel for the crimes committed against Jews by the Nazi régime allayed at least the Western world's fears about the future of the country.

In short, by late 1954 only the permission of the Western Allies was lacking to permit the Federal Republic to assume full sovereignty over its own affairs. The Paris agreements of that October paved the way, and in May 1955 the FRG launched its course of independence. Under Adenauer's continued leadership, it moved even more toward West European economic union, took the steps necessary to set up a new military establishment (albeit under strict controls to maintain its democratic character, and fully integrated into the NATO concept), and undertook new diplomatic initiatives, almost always, to be sure, in full consultation with the former occupying powers.

THE HICOG SURVEYS

The general historical lines of the period of semisovereignty are well known.[2] What is less understood is the set of perspectives--values, beliefs, and attitudes--that moved the West German population during these difficult years. To what extent had they really thrown off the yoke of Nazism? How much legitimacy did they accord the new federal government? What did they think about their country's future rearmament, its economic ties with France and the rest of West Europe, or the threat to its security ostensibly posed by the Soviet Union? How important to them was the eventual reunification of all Germany? What hopes did they entertain that the eastern territories would be restored to Germany, that the FRG and GDR could in fact come to terms on a plan for merger?

All these questions and more are the stuff of which the West German domestic political scene was made. Public opinion might not be able to forge new policies for the FRG, but it could at least tell leading statesmen what the sources and limits of their public support were. Politicians, especially in the conservative Christian Democratic Union (CDU), were quick to recognize the value of public opinion surveys, even if they often did not heed their findings on matters of policy. It is no small wonder, then, that surveying organizations flourished during the early 1950s in the Federal Republic.³

Very early in their occupation, American officials in Germany had understood the usefulness of public opinion surveys for their own purposes. Even before fighting had died down in some instances, social psychologists and sociologists in the Psychological Warfare Division of the U.S. Army entered towns to survey their populations' potential for resistance, attitudes toward Nazism, and expectations about the pending military occupation. By October 1945 informal surveying had been institutionalized by the Opinion Survey Section of the Information Control Division, Office of Military Government (U.S.), which subsequently conducted seventy-two major surveys in the American Zone of occupation. Topics explored by these OMGUS surveys were as diverse as attitudes toward Hitler, bathing habits, the growing split among the wartime Allies, and readership of newspapers and magazines.⁴

With the formal end of the military occupation in September 1949, the U.S. High Commission for Germany (HICOG) replaced the Office of Military Government, and the Opinion Survey Section became the Reactions Analysis Staff within the HICOG Office of Public Affairs. Surveying operations, under the direction of Dr. Leo P. Crespi, continued unabated. By the end of 1950 the Reactions Analysis Staff had both expanded its sample to include the whole of the Federal Republic and engaged the newly formed Deutsches Institut für Volksumfragen (DIVO) to conduct the fieldwork. The Reactions Analysis Staff later became part of the Research Staff of the Office of Public Affairs, United States Embassy, when the Federal Republic attained virtually complete sovereignty in May 1955.

The HICOG Reactions Analysis Staff carried out more than one hundred surveys of West German public opinion during its five and a half years of existence. The surveys were mainly of two types. The first type were regular monthly surveys, requiring about three weeks of fieldwork, and based on interviews with approximately 3,000 adults in the territory that had formerly comprised the American Zone of occupation, 500 in West Berlin, and 300 in the American-held enclave of Bremen in the former British Zone. They generally used a "split-sample" approach, giving slightly different questionnaires to the two halves of each sample. The second type, "flash" surveys introduced in October 1950, sought to ascertain very quickly the views of a relatively small number of people (about 640) living in major cities *throughout* the Federal Republic and not just in the American Zone. The flash survey was replaced in March 1951 by an intermediate sample of 800 West Germans, selected *nationwide* on the basis of stratified probability procedures.⁵ At the same time, the regular surveys were broadened to include a representative sample from the whole of West Germany and West Berlin. Occasional surveys of special samples, such as West Berliners or youth, also took place. Some of these, to be discussed in greater detail below, interviewed GDR citizens attending public events in West Berlin or else former GDR citizens who had fled into the Federal Republic.

The data, whether stemming from surveys conducted directly under the auspices of HICOG officials or those developed by DIVO, were analyzed and presented in periodic reports published by the Reactions Analysis Staff. Most of the data cards themselves have disappeared--lost, some say, when the Rhine River overflowed its banks, or, alternatively, destroyed when American archivists made an administrative decision that IBM cards were not worth preserving once they had been analyzed by the appropriate government agencies, or, perhaps, still packed in boxes in a corner of some forgotten warehouse.[6] What remains is a set of 237 reports prepared from September 1949 to May 1955 and ranging in length from 4 to 369 pages (with the average 33 pages long.)

The present volume summarizes each of these reports. In the summaries the reader will find indications of West German public perspectives on matters as diverse as adult education, massive retaliation, West European unity, and agricultural exhibits arranged by the United States Information Service (USIS). This is not the place to analyze in detail the full set of reports or even their summaries. Nor can this brief introduction go into differences in attitudes expressed by various segments of the population. Men, the more highly educated, urban dwellers, and those with higher incomes, for instance, almost invariably demonstrated more knowledge about and interest in political affairs than did women, the less well educated, country folk, and the less wealthy respondents. Similarly, West Berliners almost always took a much firmer stance against the Soviet Union than did their compatriots in the Federal Republic.

The following pages will merely point to some of the main dimensions of German public opinion from 1949 to 1955. One set of attitudes of particular interest to HICOG pollsters and later scholars deals with the West Germans' transition from Nazi domination, through a decade of occupation by foreign powers, to substantial independence. How did they view their Nazi past, Allied programs designed to bring democracy to their country, their new federal government? A second set centers on three aspects of Germany's position in the world: the FRG's foreign policy, views held by East Germans, and the effects of United States information programs in the Federal Republic. The interested reader will find more information on these topics in the summaries comprising the second part of the volume, still more in the HICOG reports themselves.

COMING TO TERMS WITH NAZISM

Views of the Nazi Past[7]

The intent of the Allied occupation of Germany after World War II was to ensure that the country would never again become a threat to its European neighbors and the peace of the world. To that end the Allies destroyed the Nazi military machine and punished those guilty of setting it into motion, broke up the industrial and other organizations they felt had helped create a climate conducive to the Nazi takeover, and undertook a broad program to "re-educate" the Germans to democracy. This last point was particularly important. Until Germans themselves realized how basically evil National Socialism really was, Allied officials reasoned, they might be tempted to recreate it. To convince Germans of this fact, they initiated extensive information programs, rewrote textbooks, published photographic records and conducted tours of the infamous death camps, started a spectacular year-long trial of the major war criminals at Nuremberg, and much more.

Germans, for their part, had only to look around them to know that National Socialism had failed. Hitler's government had collapsed ignominiously; aerial bombardment had severely damaged their cities, industrial capacity, and communication and transportation networks; the much feared *Wehrmacht* had gone down to defeat in the field on both the eastern and western fronts; and once again foreign troops occupied the country. About three and a half million Germans had lost their lives as a direct consequence of the war. And every day brought refugees streaming into the West from Soviet-occupied territories. Was all this a necessary consequence of National Socialism, or was it due merely to bad judgment on the part of its leaders?

Nazi System. The four occupation years revealed considerable retrospective antipathy to the Nazi system.[8] Few had much sympathy for Hitler and his closest associates. Only one in eight (12%) recalled trusting Hitler as a leader up to the end of the war; over half claimed either never to have trusted him (35%) or to have lost faith in him by the time war had broken out in 1939 (16%). Large majorities thought the Nuremberg defendants guilty of the charges leveled against them. Based on a wide range of findings presented by OMGUS pollsters, only about one in six adults in the American Zone of occupation could have been termed a hardcore Nazi.

Closer analysis in the 1950s nonetheless revealed considerable differentiation in attitudes. Surveys throughout the occupation years found a declining percentage of American Zone respondents, averaging only about a third, who rejected National Socialism outright. An increasing percentage, averaging about a half, thought it merely a good idea badly carried out. In November 1949 the figures were 30 and 59 per cent respectively, with 11 per cent expressing no opinion (#17).[9] In eight nationwide surveys conducted from May 1951 to December 1952, an average of 41 per cent saw more good than evil in Nazi ideas, and 36 per cent more evil than good (#87, 118, 167). Only a tiny minority (4%) thought that all Germans bore "a certain guilt for Germany's actions during the Third Reich" although many more (21%) felt some responsibility for rectifying these wrongs (#113).

Regardless of how they evaluated National Socialism as a whole, West Germans agreed strikingly on its good and bad aspects. To be sure, those who found Nazism generally objectionable were able to cite more negative than positive features, and the reverse was true for those who found more good than evil in it (#87, 118). More interesting is the fact that their rankings within each category were quite similar. The population as an aggregate was of two minds on issues such as compulsory labor service; and what some saw as the maintenance of law and order, others termed the absence of freedom. Equally significant, however, is the fact that not a single respondent reported that the persecution of Jews was good or that Nazi social welfare policies were bad.

What did postwar Germans see as good or bad in Nazism? Chief among the positive points offered by respondents were good job opportunities and living standards, good social welfare, and, a distant third, good organization, discipline, and security. The negative aspects most frequently mentioned were preparation for war, rearmament, and the war itself; absence of freedom, dictatorship; racial policy, persecution of Jews; and violence, cruelty, and concentration camps. Only a third of a total sample of respondents (35%) indicated any willingness to try to reduce unemployment in the early 1950s by reintroducing measures used by the Nazis (#22). When unemployed Bavarians were asked, however, HICOG surveyors found over half (55%) willing to introduce such measures, especially public works programs (#23).

Whatever the good aspects of the Nazi party may have been, few wanted a new party like it to take power in the FRG. About an eighth of nationwide samples said they would welcome such an event, but only a quarter of these added that they would do everything they could to support it; by contrast, 20 to 25 per cent reportedly would have done everything possible to prevent a new Nazi takeover (#118, 167). Even the percentage favoring "a single strong national party which really represents the interests of all classes of our people" dropped from 44 per cent in December 1952 to 25 per cent in March 1956, while opposition to this notion climbed from 37 to 47 per cent (#230). In the latter year, only one in six saw any need to "have, as before, a national leader who rules Germany with a strong hand for the welfare of all" in contrast to well over half (55%) who felt no such need.

World War II. Although few West Germans accepted collective responsibility for crimes committed during the Nazi era, fewer still accepted such responsibility for the outbreak of World War II. Several surveys conducted during the occupation years produced steady and solid majorities, averaging more than 70 per cent, who denied that "the entire German people are responsible for the war because they let a government come to power which plunged the whole world into war." Those accepting this responsibility numbered a quarter as many.[10] If not the German people as a whole, who, then, was to blame for the most destructive war in modern times?

Germans were far from agreed upon responsibility for the outbreak of World War II (#1). A sizable percentage of American Zone residents in late 1949 blamed Germany (37%) or Hitler and the Nazi government (4%). One in six (17%), however, blamed foreign countries exclusively, and an equal percentage thought the fault lay on both sides.[11] By the mid-1950s, there was an emerging consensus on Germany's guilt. In May 1955, 43 per cent and in April 1956 47 per cent put the blame on Germany, and far smaller numbers named other countries (14 and 12 per cent respectively) or both sides (15 and 11 per cent respectively).[12] In all these surveys, by the way, a small percentage attributed the war to international capitalism or simply to fate.

Similarly, consensus was growing on the main reason for the Third Reich's defeat: The material superiority of its enemies (#154).[13] Even so, in the early 1950s, about a quarter saw treason or sabotage as the main cause for German defeat, although it must be added that a substantially greater portion of the German population explicitly denied this view, particularly as it concerned the men who had organized the July 20, 1944, plot against Hitler's life (#114).[14]

Treatment of Jews. Asked what National Socialism had done that was wrong, large numbers of postwar Germans pointed to the persecution of Jews and other minorities. This does not mean, however, that they felt much personal responsibility for what had, in fact, happened (#167). In choosing among three alternative expressions of viewpoints on this issue, only 5 per cent acknowledged a sense of collective guilt, 29 per cent saw a responsibility to right the wrongs that Germany did to the Jews, and 59 per cent saw no need for guilt or responsibility except for "those who really committed something." A fifth (21%) were even willing to argue that "the Jews themselves were partly responsible for what happened to them during the Third Reich" (#113). The main reasons given for this view were that the Jews had pursued unfair business practices (10%), pushed themselves into positions of power and influence (4%), or agitated against the Third Reich (4%). Well over half (53%) of the nationwide sample nonetheless denied that the Jews were at fault.

As far as postwar behavior was concerned, a large part of the West German population saw the need for restitution (#113). Given a list of five categories of victims--war widows and orphans, those who had suffered bombing damage, refugees and expellees, relatives of people executed because of their participation in the July 1944 plot against Hitler's life, and Jews who had suffered because of the Third Reich and the war--respondents were least responsive to the needs of the Jews. Even so, over three times as many (68%) favored such assistance as opposed it (21%). There was also substantial support for legislation designed to protect Jews still living in West Germany, although many Germans (27%) felt that it would be best for the remaining Jews to emigrate (#113). And two out of three West Germans with opinions on the subject urged the Bundestag to reject an agreement of August 1952 according to which the Federal Republic was to pay $715 million to Israel as restitution for what had happened to Jews during the Third Reich (#167).

Data on their views of the Nazi system, World War II, and treatment of Jews suggest that by the mid-1950s West Germans had come to terms with their Nazi history, at least as far as their publicly expressed perspectives are concerned. It was not Nazism itself that distressed them, for indeed most respondents had some positive recollection of its potential and policies; rather, its leaders and party machinery had both failed to realize this potential and, in the process, had committed heinous crimes. West Germans deplored these crimes but felt little sense of personal or collective responsibility for them. What Germans thought about as they lay in bed trying to go to sleep, or what they discussed in the family circle or over a glass of beer at the local pub, cannot be determined through public opinion analysis. But, for the public record, most felt that the Nazi régime had ultimately failed.

If the aim of the Allied occupation was to turn Germans against the entirety of the National Socialist era, to force individuals to recognize the part they had played in bringing the régime to power or sustaining it, then surely the Allies' reeducation program must be deemed a failure. Perhaps it was sufficient, however, to provide documentary information and arguments that reinforced their antipathy to that régime. If the occupation years and those of semisovereignty also strengthened the democratic tendencies in German society, then so much the better. But did they? The answer to this question rests in part on how West Germans perceived and accepted Allied policies aimed at democratizing Germany.

Removing the Remnants of Nazism[15]

One of these policies aimed at foreclosing any possibility that those whom the Allies saw as responsible for Nazism should ever again hold positions of influence. To this end they tried and meted out punishment to "war criminals," held denazification hearings to remove from responsible positions both former Nazis and those who had actively aided them, broke up the large industries and banks, which many saw as the chief supports of National Socialism, and banned organizations and publications tainted with Nazism. The task was Herculean: to sweep the last remnants of Nazism from German stables, to do for German democrats what they themselves had been unable to accomplish after World War I.

Without German support, carrying out such policies would have been at best very difficult. As long as Allied troops remained in Germany, of course, some progress was ensured. But what about afterwards? Would Germans permit "reactionary" forces to undo the "democratic" gains made during the occupation? How Germans viewed these various programs initiated by occupation authorities and what impact they were likely to have on Germans' attitudes and behavior after the Allied troops went home became highly significant questions, not only in gauging the effectiveness of the programs themselves but also in setting the course of the FRG's future.

War Crimes Trials. Although the initial German response to the trial in 1945-46 of major war criminals such as Göring, Hess, and Speer was quite positive,[16] observers at the time wondered what German views would be several years hence. The early 1950s revealed three trends. The first was growing disenchantment with justice as dealt out by the occupying powers at Nuremberg and subsequent war crimes trials. Most important, there was growing sentiment (rising from 6 per cent in October 1946 to 30 per cent four years later) that the trials had been unfair (#57), the verdicts too severe (increasing from 9 to 40 per cent), or that, by failing to prosecute Allied officers accused of war crimes, the entire notion of justice was aborted (#157).

A second development was the notion that the time had come to terminate trials based on wartime acts. In mid-1952 only 10 per cent of a national sample approved and six times that number (59%) disapproved of the way in which the Western Powers were handling the problem of war criminals (#153). Asked directly what should be done with the remaining prisoners, about half of the critics called for their outright release, the others for legal review by Allied or German courts.[17]

Implicit in the above was a third trend: a growing feeling that the sole purpose of even the original trials was something less than an attempt to apply evenhanded justice. Respondents saw political motives driving the hands of the judges (#153). Bolstering this perception was resentment that commando raiders who had killed German prisoners, pilots who had bombed Dresden and Hiroshima, and those who had committed the Katyn Forest massacres were never prosecuted (#167).[18] When the Allies commuted some sentences in the early 1950s, the bulk of Germans with opinions viewed these decisions as pure opportunism aimed at placating Germans so as to draw them into the Western camp in the struggle against the Soviet Union (#63, 67, 70).

Denazification. German attitudes on denazification followed much the same course as those on war crimes trials,[19] and by the early 1950s the whole idea had fallen into disrepute (#87).[20] This did not mean, however, that Germans were enthusiastic about putting former Nazis into positions of power. They simply did not perceive such a development, should it have occurred, as a threat to the new democratic state. Two of three respondents with opinions (58 to 29 per cent) thought that former members of the Nazi party should have the same opportunities for advancement in business and politics as other Germans (#167). Somewhat fewer (42%) felt that German generals whom the Allies had convicted of war crimes had experience and capabilities entitling them to hold high positions in a new German army (#153). (The predominant sentiment among the 27 per cent who opposed this notion was that the generals would be too old and broken in spirit by the prison terms or were to blame for Germany's current misery and might repeat their earlier mistakes.) An even smaller number (36 per cent in favor, in contrast with 48 per cent opposed) was willing to give the same equality of opportunity to those who had held high positions in the Third Reich.

Organizations. The Allies had flatly banned the National Socialist German Workers' (or Nazi) party, along with its ancillary bodies. They also broke up various rightist organizations, such as veterans' associations, which had set a political tone conducive to Nazism, as well as the institutions of "big business," which many in East and West alike held responsible for easing Hitler's way into power. HICOG surveys revealed a lack of awareness in the German mass public about the means and effects of decartelization (#75). Nor did many respondents express concern when war veterans began to organize in mid-1951 (#112). And, as noted earlier, only about an eighth expressed any willingness to take an active part in recreating the old Nazi party.

The real danger, as many observers saw it, was the threat of a *new* Nazi party. Actually, Article 9 (2) of the Basic Law forbade the formation of any such party, but some continued to fear that Nazism would simply reemerge in a different guise. The test came with the Socialist Reich party (SRP), which made a spectacular debut in the national political arena in May 1951, when it captured 11 per cent of the vote in the Lower Saxony state election. Even so, by November of that year only two in five respondents (41%) claimed to be aware of the SRP (#87, 118). Those citizens who knew of the party were by and large against banning it as unconstitutional. Those who favored such a ban (22 per cent in May 1951) were fairly clear about the SRP's Nazi orientation; those opposed (25%) argued that declaring it illegal would violate democratic principles, be counterproductive by making the party more attractive to dissidents (even if driving it underground) and thereby strengthening it, or make it more difficult to control the party's activities (#87).[21]

In one sense the data summarized in this section support the point made earlier: by the mid-1950s West Germans had, for the most part, rejected the formal trappings of Nazism. These organizations and their leaders--not the German people--had thrust their country into a devastatingly destructive war. The population was in no mood to make the same mistake again. Even if some attitudes associated with Nazism might remain, politicians and parties identifying themselves too closely with the repudiated past had little future in the Federal Republic.

The data also underscore a second and equally important point: West Germany wanted the books closed on the Nazi era. Since those responsible for the war and the major crimes had been punished adequately (if sometimes unfairly), they argued in effect, it was time for the Western Allies to quit imposing their restrictions upon German politics and society. This was particularly the case, in the West German view, if the West seriously wanted the Federal Republic as an ally in the struggle against "international communism." "The war is over," West Germans were saying; "Let's get on with the fight for peace with justice."

FROM FOREIGN OCCUPATION TO INDEPENDENCE

Federal Republic

Views of the past aside, the critical question facing Allied officials was how the population would respond to its new political system. Prognostications ranged from bleak to euphoric, with most recognizing a democratic tendency that only time and constructive participation could make firm. It would require the entrenchment of certain kinds of habits--assuming civic responsibilities, becoming informed, voting, obeying just laws, paying taxes, making occasional short-term sacrifices in the community interest, and the like. HICOG officials could observe progress made (or not made) in many of these areas. What they also wanted to know was how West Germans *felt* about the polity developing around them.

Federal Government. West Germans were by and large satisfied with the new federal government created under the Basic Law. Approval in principle rose from 62 per cent among American Zone respondents in September 1948, when the constituent assembly began meeting, to 78 per cent in November 1949, two months after the FRG's promulgation, while disapproval dropped from 16 to 5 per cent (#3). This is not to say that no complaints were heard. Seven in ten (70%) felt in late 1949 that West Berlin should have been included as a state (or *Land*) in the federal system; two fifths (42%) thought that the Western Powers exerted too great an influence on the FRG's decisions (in fact, more than a third of these, or 15 per cent of the total sample, even agreed with the assertion that the West German government was only a "puppet" government!), in contrast with only 28 per cent who thought that the FRG was independent enough; and well over half (55%) argued that the Western Powers should have transferred more rights to the West German government.

Subsequent surveys revealed that confidence in the FRG grew steadily. Figure 1 shows that the ratio of those satisfied with governmental performance to those dissatisfied increased substantially between late 1949 and early 1955; and, interestingly enough, the number of those unwilling or unable to express an opinion declined markedly. Other more isolated findings support this basic trend. In May 1950, for instance, over half (52%) of American Zone respondents felt the Bonn government was keeping the public welfare rather than partisan politics uppermost in mind, although a third (32%) thought the opposite (#28). Respondents seemed particularly pleased with the progress being made in the economic sphere. Two other major points of contention, remilitarization and reunification, will be discussed below.

Moreover, West Germans generally felt that democracy had taken root in German soil. In September 1953, 44 per cent were of the opinion that democracy in West Germany had become stronger in the course of the few years previous (5 per cent thought it weaker and 18 per cent about the same), and over three-quarters of those with opinions believed that the Germans could govern themselves democratically (#191). Surveys in mid-1954 revealed that, by a ratio of more than five to one, West Germans were satisfied with the progress that the FRG was making on the road to freedom and independence (#202). Such sentiments bolstered the government's efforts to terminate the military occu-

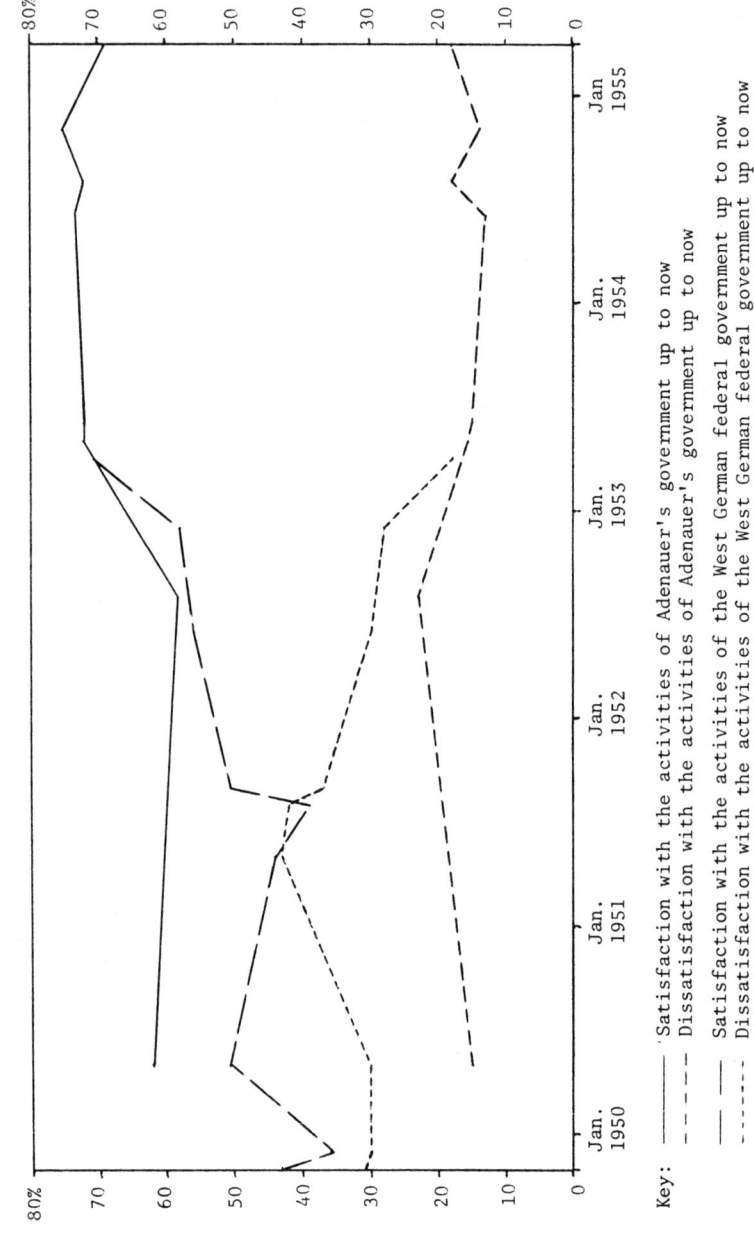

FIGURE 1. SATISFACTION WITH GOVERNMENTAL PERFORMANCE

Key: ———— Satisfaction with the activities of Adenauer's government up to now
 ———— Dissatisfaction with the activities of Adenauer's government up to now
 ———— Satisfaction with the activities of the West German federal government up to now
 ········ Dissatisfaction with the activities of the West German federal government up to now

Note: Data from November 1949 through May 1950 are for the American Zone of Occupation only.

pation of West Germany.

Implementation of the Paris accords in May 1955, which provided virtually complete sovereignty to the FRG, was welcomed by the overwhelming majority of those West Germans who expressed opinions (#213). But only 13 per cent believed these accords provided complete independence. Some 60 per cent were aware that the Western Powers had retained certain rights (particularly with respect to internal security and West Berlin) --and, it may be added, most of these respondents, evidently feeling that sovereignty is as indivisible a concept as honor or virginity, disapproved of the reservations. When the Federal Republic rejoined the powers in mid-1955 then, it was more autonomy in decision making that its population called for, not revolution or the restoration of some previous régime. The FRG had attained widespread legitimacy in the eyes of its citizens.

Parties and Elections. The proliferation of political parties during the Weimar era and their subsequent collapse in the face of Nazism did not give the occupying powers in 1945 much cause for hope, nor were Germans completely sure of what kind of party system they wanted for the future. The Allies, for their part, initially prohibited any kind of party activity whatever. Before a year was over, however, the organization of democratic parties was permitted first at the local level, then for each occupation zone, and finally across zonal boundaries.

The bulk of voters quickly aligned themselves behind two major political parties.[22] The larger of these was the Social Democratic party of Germany (SPD), which could trace its history back to 1875. A centrist coalition--the Christian Democratic Union (CDU) and its Bavarian ally, the Christian Social Union (CSU)--replaced the more Catholic-oriented Center party of Weimar years. There were also, on the left, the Communist party (KPD) and, on the right, the liberal Free Democratic party (FDP) and a number of small parties. After the 1949 parliamentary election, the CDU/CSU, with a slight plurality (31 per cent, as opposed to the SPD's 29 per cent), forged a governing coalition with the FDP and the slightly nationalist German party (DP).

The subsequent years of semisovereignty saw two dominant trends. The first was the consolidation of party groupings. Figure 2 shows that the smaller parties declined in popular support from an average of 25.3 per cent in seven national surveys conducted in 1951 to 19.6 per cent in seven surveys carried out in early 1953. (For the 24 times between March 1951 and September 1953 questions about preferred parties were asked, an average of one in five interviewees or 19.6 per cent gave no response whatever; and of the remainder, 27.6 per cent reported no preference. The comments here and in Figure 2 are based upon that 58.2 per cent of the total samples which named a preferred party.) In terms of parliamentary seats, these parties dropped from 132 in 1949 (33%) to 93 in 1953 (19%) and still further to 58 in 1957 (12%). By 1961 only the CDU/CSU, SPD, and FDP remained as serious contenders in the national political arena--

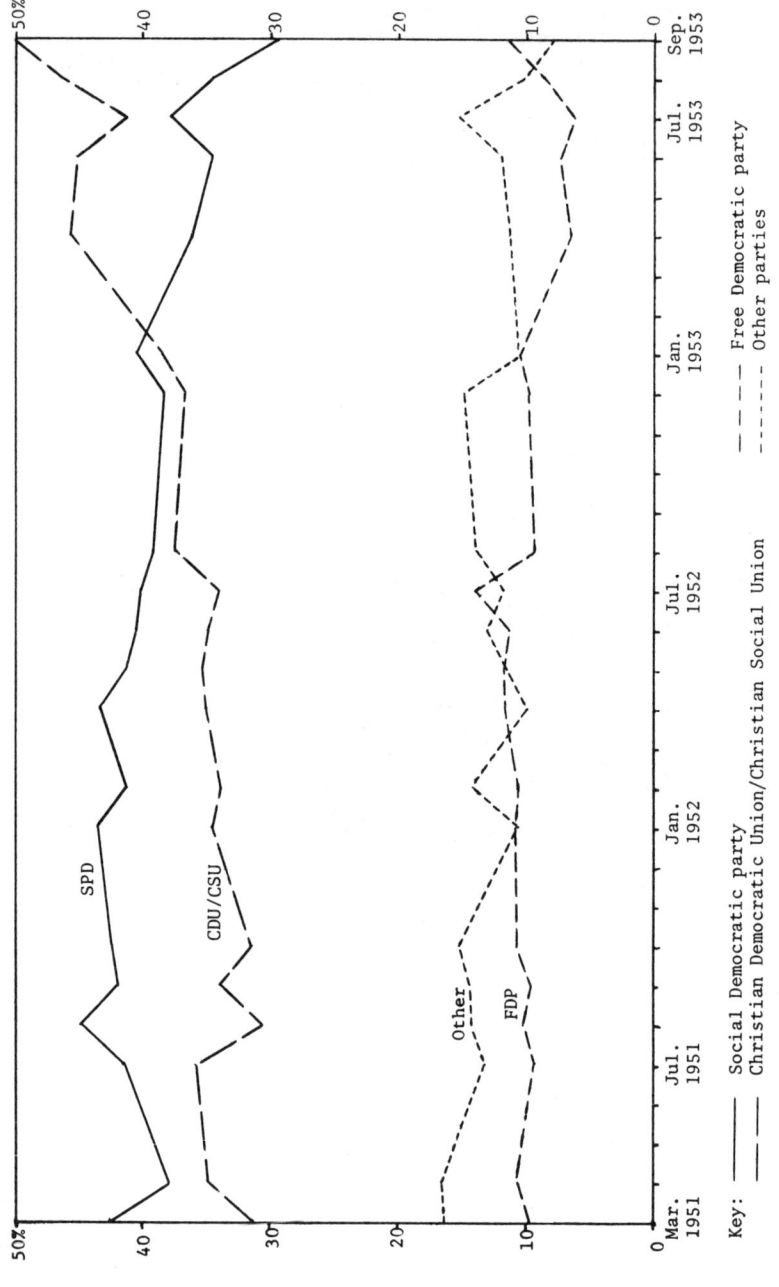

FIGURE 2. IDENTIFICATION WITH POLITICAL PARTIES

Key: ——— Social Democratic party   — — — Free Democratic party
     ———— Christian Democratic Union/Christian Social Union   ------ Other parties

Note: Data in this figure exclude 41.8 per cent of the total samples, who either did not respond to the question about party preference (19.6%) or named no preferred party (22.2%).

and even the FDP threatened to fall below the percentage of votes required for representation in the Bundestag.

The second dominant trend was the entrenchment in power of the Christian Democrats under the leadership of Konrad Adenauer. As Figure 2 suggests, the point at which the CDU/CSU assumed the lead in public opinion was in early 1953--several months after the death of the Socialist leader, Kurt Schumacher, and shortly after the bitter parliamentary debate in which the SPD tried fruitlessly to halt the rearmament of the Federal Republic.[23] Subsequent surveys showed that the CDU/CSU held onto its commanding lead throughout the period up to May 1955 (and, of course, even beyond that).[24] Meanwhile, the share of Bundestag seats controlled by the CDU/CSU increased from 139 in 1949 (35%) to 243 four years later (49.9%), and the party achieved an absolute majority (54.3%) of 270 seats in 1957.

What accounts for this phenomenal success of the CDU/CSU? In part it represented an unwillingness by many--even nominal Social Democrats --to place much trust in the SPD, both because of the lack of visible, highly qualified leadership and because of the party's rigid stand against rearmament, which many Germans of all parties saw as a path toward independence (see below). In part, too, the electoral outcomes and public opinion findings reflected a vote of confidence in the past accomplishments and leadership of the dominant party. Asked why they had voted the way they did in the 1953 parliamentary election (#191), some main reasons given by CDU/CSU voters were religious (cited by 21 per cent, especially devout Catholics), the economic gains achieved during the previous four years of the CDU/CSU-dominated coalition (19%), and satisfaction with the achievements of the party (17%). But the reasons mentioned most frequently (30%) were Adenauer's personality and worldwide prestige. Thus Adenauer, the party he headed, and economic and political progress in the Federal Republic were closely associated in the minds of many West German voters.

Konrad Adenauer. Sixty-nine years old when the war ended, apparently in frail health, and known more than anything else only for having been mayor of Cologne before the Nazis took over in 1933, Adenauer hardly seemed destined to play a great role in Germany's future. Those who doubted his capabilities were nonetheless surprised. With foresight, hard work, wiles, and a certain audacity, he took over the incipient Christian Democratic Union and molded it in his own image. The election of 1949 and strenuous efforts to build a coalition yielded a majority of a single parliamentary vote that put Adenauer into the chancellorship. For the next fourteen years Konrad Adenauer dominated the West German political scene.

Adenauer soon became the Federal Republic's best-known politician. In November 1949, two months after he assumed office, 44 per cent of an American Zone sample gave his name when asked who the federal chancellor was; by May 1950 the number had increased to 62 per cent; and in September 1951, 81 per cent of a national sample gave the correct response (#28, 106). (In contrast, only 55 per cent could say in September 1951 what political party was the leading one in the West German federal government.) In August 1953, 99 per cent recognized Adenauer's name and knew that he was an FRG politician; and 87 per cent could even correctly identify the party of which he was a member.[25] Konrad Adenauer's name had truly become a household word in postwar Germany.

More than being merely known, Adenauer was widely respected in semisovereign Germany. Asked which German had done most for Germany, not a soul mentioned Adenauer in January 1950, but four years later 17 per cent did so--a figure second only to Bismarck.[26] In four surveys conducted in 1954, an average of 59 per cent said that Adenauer enjoyed high to very high prestige with them personally, and 6 per cent accorded him low or very low prestige (#206)--a ratio of almost ten to one. By April 1955, it must be added, the number ranking him high or very high diminished to 47 per cent, and those rating his prestige with them personally as low or very low grew to 9 per cent (#211), still a ratio of over five to one in his favor.

This last finding suggests that Adenauer's popularity had peaked sometime before 1955. Other survey data, collected during the years before and after that date, confirm such an impression. In response to a question about whom they considered to be Germany's most capable politician, the number naming Adenauer rose from 5 per cent in October 1948 to 19 per cent in November 1951 and reached a high point of 62 per cent in November 1953. Surveys in January and September 1955 found 55 and 60 per cent, respectively, naming him; but by June 1959 the figure had dropped to 28 per cent and still further by August 1961 to 26 per cent.[27] Similarly, asked to select from a list of twenty-nine attributes with which to characterize Adenauer, the number selecting each positive adjective (except one, "genius," which remained the same) declined from January 1955 to November 1959, while the number selecting pejorative adjectives rose in almost all cases.[28] The point is not that Adenauer dropped from public favor after 1954, for indeed he did not. Throughout the late 1950s he remained the Federal Republic's most popular and revered politician. The point is, rather, that his popularity began to wane, and people began to perceive rigidity and autocratic behavior where they had once seen firmness in the face of pressure.

The data presented in this section on the federal government, parties and elections, and Konrad Adenauer suggest widespread acceptance by the West German public of their political institutions and leadership. There was, of course, a darker side. One problem, mentioned in an earlier section, was the continuing if low level of support for a new right-wing party-- a situation which, although not likely to endanger democracy in Germany, nonetheless upset the Western Allies. There was also substantial dissent on such policies pursued by the Adenauer government as those dealing with housing, the Saar, rearmament, reunification, and "reparations" to Israel. None of this proved to be divisive. On the contrary, West Germans repeatedly demonstrated that they stood behind their government whatever their personal preferences and disappointments may have been.

What seemed to bother the West German public most of all were the continued Allied controls on their government's autonomy. Even the elation occasioned by the promulgation in May 1955 of the Paris accords, which ended the occupation, was tempered by the realization that the Allies retained some residual rights, that the FRG was not truly independent. Achieving this level of autonomy had been no mean task. And, ironically, given the Allies' earlier insistence on German disarmament, the most significant stumbling block was the way in which an independent West Germany should defend itself. Should Germany be rearmed, and, if so, how?

Rearmament[29]

Uppermost in the minds of the wartime Allies was the final destruction of Germany's military potential. At their meeting in Potsdam in mid-1945, Attlee, Stalin, and Truman agreed on "the complete disarmament and demilitarization of Germany and the elimination of all German industry that could be used for military production." By 1949, however, the world's climate had changed. American military officials, impressed by their view of the Soviet threat to West Europe, were agitating for a West German contribution to the Western defense structure. And, in December of that year, in an interview with an American journalist, Chancellor Adenauer let it be known that he would favor participation by German military units in some type of Western defense system but not a separate West German army. After the outbreak of the Korean War in 1950, the answer to the question of German rearmament was a foregone conclusion. The salient issues were timing and form.

Militarism. Given these dramatic shifts in Allied policy, the analysis of public opinion data is especially relevant to an understanding of postwar West German society. Early polls focused less on aspects of a defense establishment than on detecting the extent to which Germans harbored a "militaristic" mentality. The questions were consistent with the notion that some sociopsychological characteristic of Germans might be responsible for their country's propensity to get involved in wars.

For whatever reason--vivid memories of the recent war, basic antipathy toward militarism, poorly worded questions, or, less likely, an unwillingness to reveal true feelings[30]--respondents expressed highly nonmilitaristic views.[31] In 1946-47, for instance, 96 per cent of respondents in the American Zone of occupation agreed that "the human spirit is not glorified by war alone," 94 per cent felt that "war does not pay," 90 per cent refused to accept the proposition that "a civilian is a less worthy person than a soldier," and five of six respondents (82%) denied that "in all probability, foreign nations and races are enemies; therefore one should be prepared at all times to attack them first."

Such consistent views did not mean that Germans in the American Zone saw no need for a German army. In fact, they were about evenly split on the issue. Surveys in April and August 1946, asking whether or not "Germany should be allowed to have an army in order to defend herself against aggression from other European nations," found 45 and 44 per cent, respectively, answering positively, while 46 and 47 per cent, respectively, saw no such need.

An Independent German Military. By late 1949 the question of a German army had moved from the realm of sociopsychological investigation to that of high international politics. Polled immediately after Adenauer's press statement in December 1949, a solid majority (62%) of respondents in the American Zone said they opposed the establishment of any army in West Germany, and only 26 per cent favored such an idea (#9). By spring, however, the ratio of those opposed to those favoring had dropped to 56 to 39; and shortly after the outbreak of hostilities in Korea, it dropped still further to 45 to 43--a slim majority still opposed to an independent West German army (#36). Reasons given for favoring an army centered on security (16%) and, more specifically, on protection against the Soviet Union (14%). Those opposing expressed an antipathy toward war (15%), fear based on "loss of loved ones in the last war" (8%), and the observation that, given Allied controls, the FRG could not organize an army (8%).[32]

Any indecisiveness or division implicit in these findings was more apparent than real. For one thing, a clear-cut majority (63%) of American Zone respondents felt that West Germany could not be defended without German help (#36). For another, almost half (47%) of those opposing an army in August 1950 were willing to accept it if it were part of a more general West European army--or a total of 64 per cent of the sample amenable to *some* form of rearmament. The point at issue in West German public opinion was the organizational framework for rearmament.

Atlantic Pact. By this time, of course, the main line of discussion among the Allies and in the FRG focused on integrating German units into a broader, supranational military arrangement. Whether out of conviction or practical necessity, the West German public accommodated itself quickly to this new idea. To return again to the survey of August 1950 (#36), those who had approved of the creation of a West German army indicated by a ratio of almost two to one, when asked further, that they preferred West German units to be part of a broader Western defense arrangement rather than independent.[33]

One prominent proposal in 1950-51 was that the Federal Republic would participate in the North Atlantic Treaty Organization (NATO) and, through it, would contribute to a general army for the defense of Europe. Figure 3 shows that, in twenty-one surveys between August 1950 and late February 1952 an average of 52 per cent of those interviewed favored this idea while 35 per cent opposed it. The trend of responses lends itself to several interpretations, none of which can be explored here, since it would take us too far afield. High points in the curve occur, for instance, after the initial phase of the Korean War and shortly after the Chinese army began to push United Nations

FIGURE 3. WEST GERMAN PARTICIPATION IN THE DEFENSE OF WEST EUROPE

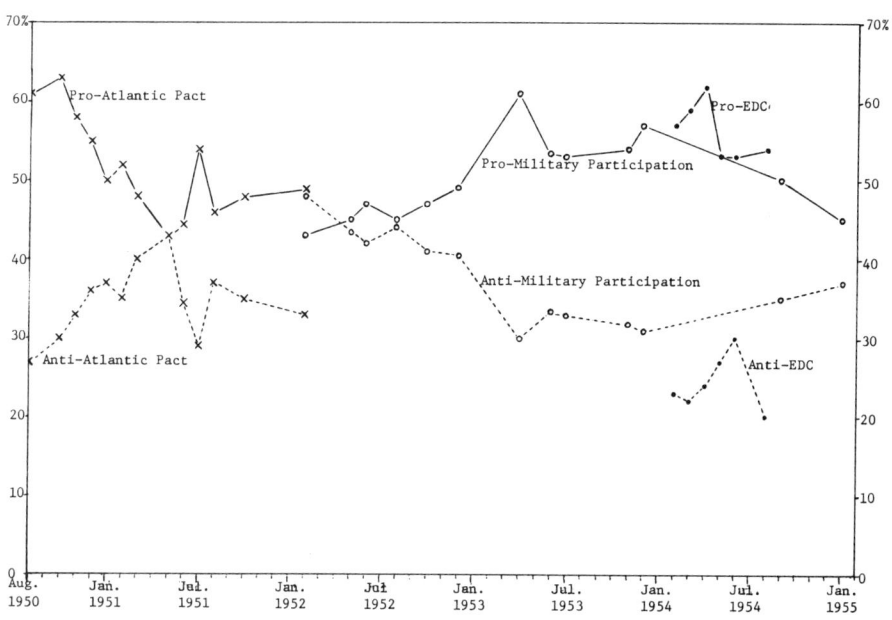

Questions and Key:

August 1950 to February 1952: "Some time ago, several West European nations and America signed a defense pact, the so-called Atlantic Pact. Supposing West Germany would join the Atlantic Pact and be asked in connection with it to participate in a general army for the defense of Western Europe. Would you then be for or against such a participation in a defense army?"

x———x———x———x   in favor of participation in the Atlantic Pact
x----x----x----x   opposed to participation in the Atlantic Pact

February 1952 to January 1955: "Are you, in general, for or against West Germany's military participation in the defense of West Europe?"

o———o———o———o   in favor of participation in the defense of West Europe
o----o----o----o   opposed to participation in the defense of West Europe

February 1954 to August 1954: "In general, are you for or against West Germany's participation in the EDC, that is, the West European Defense Community? Very much for it or somewhat for it? Very much against it or somewhat against it?"

•———•———•———•   very much or somewhat in favor of participation in EDC
•----•----•----•   very much or somewhat opposed to participation in EDC

Note: Multiple surveys conducted in a single month are averaged for the month as a whole.

troops southward, suggesting that fear of communist aggression underlay support for a strengthened NATO. Alternatively, the overall trend of declining support for a tie to NATO may be attributed to increasing Social Democratic opposition to any German rearmament whatever (although, it may be added, substantial numbers of respondents who identified themselves as Social Democrats continued to support all such plans), or else growing interest in a West European rather than Atlantic defense structure.

West European Army. During most of the early 1950s solid majorities of West German respondents favored some form of participation by FRG troops in the defense of West Europe (Figure 3). But in what form? The plan capturing most attention called for the formation of a European Defense Community (EDC), which would have integrated twelve West German divisions into a European army. Proposed by René Pléven in late 1950 and subsequently endorsed by American leaders, the EDC took shape in an agreement initialed in May 1952. The Bundestag ratified the agreement in March 1953; but after the French parliament refused to do so in August 1954, the EDC died quickly.

West Germans had mixed emotions about EDC. On the one hand, it would have provided a framework within which to create a military--which many saw as vital to the attainment of full sovereignty. But, on the other hand, they suspected that the original proposals for EDC were really designed to keep West Germany perpetually under Allied (i.e., in this case, French) controls, that the FRG would not have a position of full equality. Chancellor Adenauer fought hard to secure, in May 1952, a contractual agreement with the three Western Powers that would ensure this equality. Even so, throughout the period when EDC was a live issue, the bulk of West Germans with views on the topic expressed a preference for a West German national army that would participate in the defense of West Europe (averaging 44 per cent in eight surveys from November 1951 to August 1954) over the integration of German divisions in a general West European army (averaging 25 per cent), with a sizable number (31%) declining to give an opinion (#117, 131, 196, 200, 202).

Before the contractual agreement was signed, suspicion manifested itself in the form of generalized opposition to participation in West European defense (Figure 3). Indeed, in the three months beforehand, an average of 45 per cent opposed such participation, while 44 per cent favored it (#141, 180). During the negotiations, 55 per cent reported that they would favor some form of participation, provided that it guaranteed equality of treatment for the FRG; and a quarter that many (14%) indicated continued opposition (#135). Afterwards, support for defense participation edged up to a high point in April 1953, when 63 per cent favored and only 28 per cent opposed it (#177-S); then support declined fairly steadily to a low point of 45 per cent in favor and 37 per cent against in January 1955 (#207).

The decline after mid-1953 coincided with the growing intensity of debate in France on the advisability of not only EDC but any plan whereby West Germany would be rearmed. But to this observation must be added two facts. First, even at the end of the decline, a majority of those with opinions favored some form of participation by West Germany in West European defense. Second, EDC itself received high marks after the Bundestag ratification--in part, no doubt, because the population looked favorably on any policy adopted by the government,[34] and also in part because respondents saw it as a means to accomplish full sovereignty for the FRG. Even this support declined in the months before the French parliament defeated EDC (Figure 3).[35]

Rearmament under NATO. The failure of EDC sent statesmen in search of a new plan for West German rearmament. In October 1954, conferring in Paris, they agreed on ending the occupation of West Germany, revitalizing the Western European Union, and permitting the creation of a virtually independent West German defense force under NATO command. The new plan, it may be noted, corresponded closely to the expressed German preference for a national army that would participate in the defense of West Europe rather than the integration of German divisions in a general West European army (e.g., #202).

Subsequent surveys found continued support among West Germans for some kind of military establishment. Asked in January 1955 how necessary they considered it for the FRG to have an army, regardless of whether or not they personally liked it, 60 per cent saw it as necessary and only 25 per cent did not (#207).[36] Moreover, although differences in age, party identification, religion, and other attributes seemed to make a difference in the way people responded to this question, majorities in each of the fifty-one categories of respondents listed in HICOG survey reports recognized this necessity. This was the case even for the Social Democrats, 54 per cent of whom saw the necessity for such a military establishment and 40 per cent of whom saw none. Similar although smaller majorities in all categories (except those expressing no party preference) thought the federal government should have the right to draft men, if necessary, for service in the new army.

With the promulgation, in May 1955, of the Paris agreements, the Federal Republic of Germany was well on its way toward rearming--bolstered by the explicit blessing of the Western occupying powers and the support of its own population (#213). What had been unthinkable ten years earlier was now accomplished fact.

GERMANY IN THE WORLD

West German Foreign Relations

The Occupation Statute of 1949 left ultimate responsibility for the conduct of West Germany's foreign relations with the Western Allies. The years between 1949 and 1955 were, nonetheless, ones in which the Federal Republic was fashioning its future foreign affairs environment. By and large, Adenauer's government pursued a policy of firm alliance with the West, eschewing détente with the East temporarily, in the hope that strength in the West would force the Soviet Union to adopt a more conciliatory policy. German rearmament, then, was tied closely to East-West relations in Europe and the world, the question of German reunification, and steps toward economic and even political integration in West Europe.

Between East and West. The very notion that the Western Powers should rearm the Federal Republic assumed that a rearmed West Germany would ally itself with the West and participate in Western defense efforts. This is certainly what Chancellor Adenauer agreed to in signing the contractual agreement of 1952. Moreover, data reviewed earlier also indicate a strong strain within the West German public pushing for precisely such a link. What was the motive behind such sentiments? There is no particularly good reason to think that it was anything other than what it appeared to be--a sincere desire to share in the burdens and benefits of a multifaceted Western alliance.

Let us assume for the moment, however, that something else was afoot: that West Germans were merely using the defensive alliance as a springboard to full autonomy, neutrality, and eventual political and economic dominance over Europe.[37] The continued presence, after May 1955, of Allied troops might have guarded against this eventuality, but, then again, maybe not. Could not the citizenry have bridled against foreign troops, demanding their ouster? Could not the country's leaders have reached an understanding with the Soviet Union--a new Rapallo, if you will--that would have worked to the detriment of Western (and particularly American) interests?

Answers to such questions hinge on the extent to which West Germans truly felt allied to the West or, alternatively, the degree to which they harbored thoughts of a neutralist future. Determining this is by no means simple. On the one hand, West Germans had little use for the Soviet Union. Asked whether they would prefer to ally with the East or the West, at no point during the early 1950s did more than one in a hundred choose the former (#213). In survey after survey the Soviet Union emerged as the culprit--in Berlin, Korea, the German Democratic Republic, various foreign ministers' conferences, and elsewhere. This hostility toward the USSR continued long past the point at which other West European populations began to adopt a more moderate attitude.[38]

West Germans expressed an attachment to the West, especially the United States, almost as strong as their antipathy to the East. The number opting to ally with the West, given a choice, rose from 35 per cent in May 1952 to 72 per cent a year later before dropping off (#213). Even after the Paris agreements went into effect in mid-1955, the number choosing the West over the East or remaining neutral stood at 52 per cent. As far as the United States was concerned, the ratio of those according it high or very high prestige to the number rating it of low or very low prestige grew from four to one in late November 1953 to twice that high in the following June (#200). In October 1954 and February 1955, over three in five (61%) expressed a good or very good opinion of the United States, while only 4 and 2 per cent respectively had a bad or very bad opinion of America (#202-S, 209-S). West Germans did not don rose-colored glasses when they looked at the West; but, particularly when given a choice between East and West, their sentimental ties were clear.

On the other hand, West Germans were capable of putting aside sentimental preferences when they calculated the prospects for war between East and West, and they asked themselves what role the FRG should play in the event war did break out. As Figure 4 shows, sentimental neutralism (or answering "neither" when asked to choose between alliances with the East or the West) averaged about one-third (33%) during the early 1950s. The average level of neutralism in the event of a war, by contrast, was half again higher (48%). It rose markedly from 37 per cent in September 1952 to achieve plurality status in early 1954 (46%) and majority status by October of that year (53%).[39] Substantial numbers were also willing to forego alliances if that would achieve German reunification (Figure 5). In ranking their preferences within the hypothetical world posited by public opinion surveys, West Germans simply refused to give the highest priority to their Western ties.

When they returned to their perceptions of the real world, however, West Germans were prepared to accept certain facts about the FRG's role in the struggle between East and West. As HICOG analysts noted in May 1952 (#137, p. 17), "most of the West Germans who long for neutrality have indicated in further inquiry in past surveys the impracticability of such a course, and have been inclined, however unenthusiastically, to throw their lot in with the West." Large numbers felt that the United States would not go along with the idea of a neutral Germany.[40] Moreover, if confronted with the prospect that Western guarantees of security would be withdrawn from a neutral and reunified Germany, then well over half of those who had said they would accept neutrality as the price of reunification said they would prefer to wait for more favorable conditions rather than press for immediate reunification (#202). Even after the Paris accords went into effect, few (17 per cent) felt that the FRG should revise its relationship with the Western Powers (as opposed to 57 per cent who thought not). (#213) Although they might have preferred otherwise, then, West Germans realized in the mid-1950s that they had no real choice but to go along with the West.

Reunification. A concomitant realization was that such ties affected the prospects for reunifying Germany.[41] Postwar disagreements between the Soviet Union and the Western Allies had led to separate economies in Germany by 1948 and, in 1949, the creation of separate governments in their respective zones of occupation. Territories east of the Oder and Neisse rivers formerly belonging to Germany were quietly absorbed into Poland and the Soviet Union. Not until two decades later were Western statesmen, including those of the Federal Republic, prepared to recognize formally the reality of this new status quo of a dismembered Germany. In the early 1950s, few had been ready to do so, nor was the West German public at large.

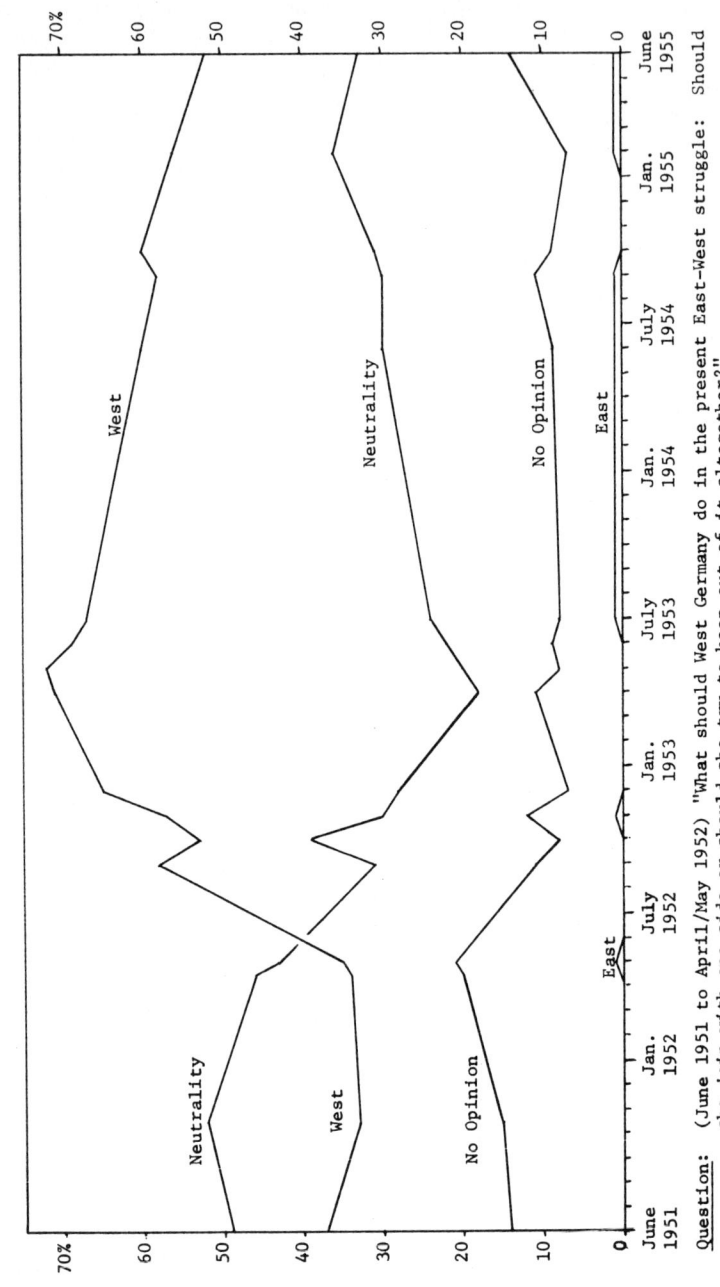

FIGURE 4. PREFERENCES FOR ALLIANCE WITH THE WEST VS. NEUTRALITY

Question: (June 1951 to April/May 1952) "What should West Germany do in the present East-West struggle: Should she join with one side or should she try to keep out of it altogether?"

(May 1952 to June 1955) "Do you personally think that West Germany should be on the side of the West at this time, on the side of the East, or not be on either side?"

FIGURE 5. PREFERENCES FOR ALLIANCE WITH THE WEST VS. REUNIFICATION

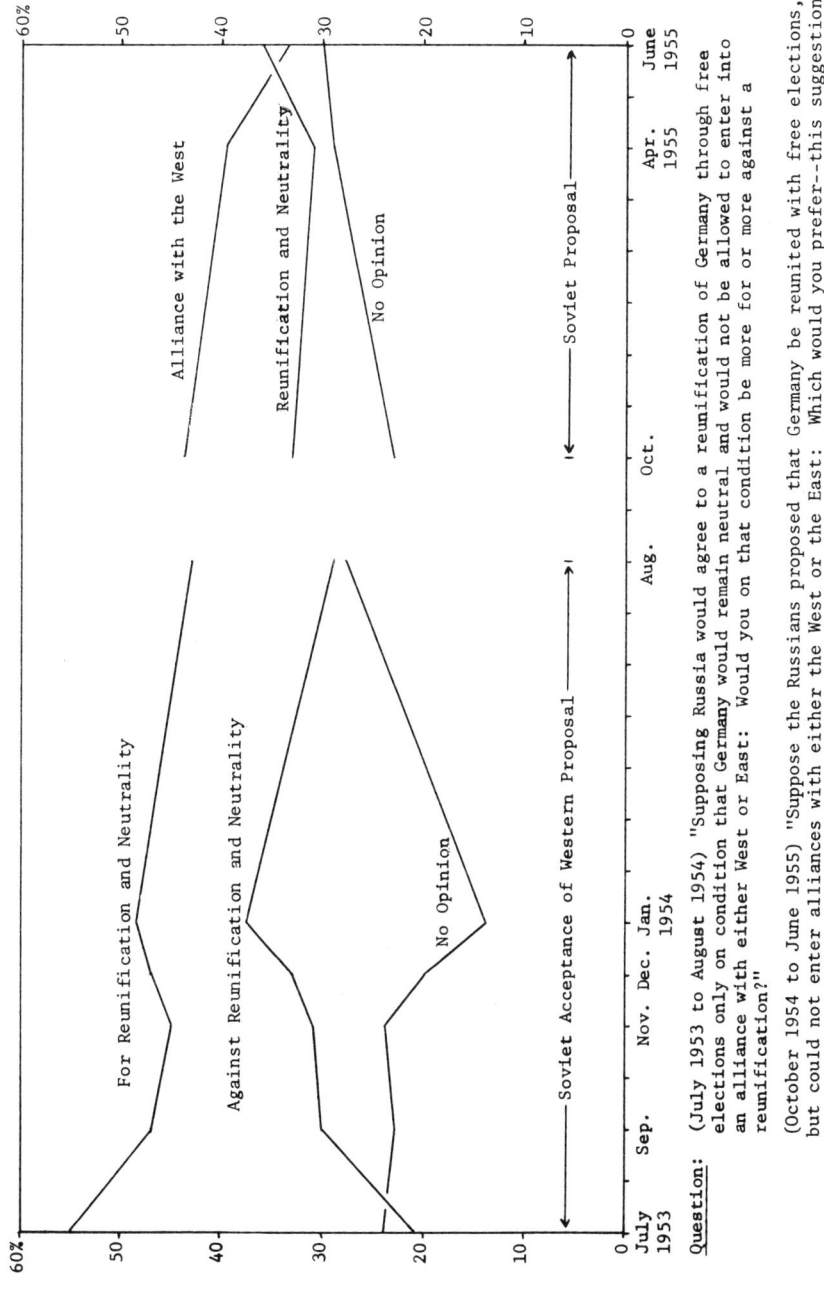

Question: (July 1953 to August 1954) "Supposing Russia would agree to a reunification of Germany through free elections only on condition that Germany would remain neutral and would not be allowed to enter into an alliance with either West or East: Would you on that condition be more for or more against a reunification?"

(October 1954 to June 1955) "Suppose the Russians proposed that Germany be reunited with free elections, but could not enter alliances with either the West or the East: Which would you prefer--this suggestion or present plans to incorporate West Germany into the Western defense system?"

From the very outset of West Germany's period of semi-sovereignty, the population exhibited attitudes that turned out to persist, albeit at diminished levels, throughout the next fifteen or twenty years. A survey in September 1949 (#1), for instance, found that 93 per cent of American Zone respondents favored a reunion of Germany (3 per cent against), two-thirds (67%) expected it to come about (22 per cent thought it unlikely), but 71 per cent felt that checking the spread of communism was more important than uniting Germany (against 25 per cent who thought reunification to be more important). Unity under an East German government was rejected by 81 per cent and favored by only 4 per cent (#3). As far as the Eastern territories were concerned, majorities thought that East Prussia (74%), Silesia (73%), and Danzig (54%) rightfully belonged to Germany, but far fewer (47, 48, and 21 per cent respectively) were prepared to accept the probability of war to regain them (#1).[42]

The years rolled by, and plan after plan for German reunification was discarded. Some called for certain Western concessions. We have also already noted a susceptibility for neutralist solutions (Figure 2)--a susceptibility that nonetheless sagged when respondents faced the prospect that such a solution might mean the withdrawal of American guarantees of security.[43] Only a small minority (10 to 15%) was willing to accept the Oder-Neisse line as the German boundary in exchange for reunification of the rest of Germany through free elections, while roughly seven in ten (69 to 72%) opposed paying this price (#193, 206, 211). Again, however, most of the proposed suggestions were in the realm of hypothesis (Table 1), not ones that negotiators on *both* sides were seriously discussing.

Reunification as an issue came to dominate German political discourse.[44] In April 1955, on the eve of the promulgation of the Paris agreements, the topic was listed by respondents as the most important issue facing their country, but they were less than sanguine about its prospects (#211). Four in five were very strongly (34%), strongly (31%), or somewhat (15%) in favor of reunification, and only 3 per cent were somewhat or strongly opposed.[45] About a quarter (27%) saw the chances for achieving it to be very good or good, about a third (35%) bad or very bad. Asked how it might come about, almost two in five (39%) could give no answer. Three in ten (29%) thought that some kind of diplomatic negotiations could achieve reunification, another sixth (16%) emphasized a Western policy of strength, including the possible use of force.

What did West Germans in mid-1955 think should be done about reunification (#211)? First of all, 55 per cent felt that the United States should do something.[46] The bulk of these respondents (39%) thought that the United States should be more forthcoming vis-à-vis the Soviet Union--adopting more agreeable attitudes, pursuing more reasonable policies. Only a sixth (17%) expressed the view that the United States should assume a firmer policy toward the USSR or else strengthen the Western alliance. A somewhat smaller number (47%) thought that the Federal

TABLE 1. REUNIFICATION AT WHAT PRICE?

Question: "Would you be willing, for the sake of reunification, to . . .

	Yes	No	No Opinion
...accept an all-German election which would not be as free as those here in West Germany?	10%	68%	22%
...accept some form of government other than democratic?	13	62	25
...accept the present leaders of the East Zone government as members of an all-German government?	18	59	23
...bear a heavier tax burden?	31	56	13
...put up with a reintroduction of food rationing?	41	49	10
...recognize the present leaders of the East Zone as conferees?	46	31	23
...put up with a shortage of consumer goods?	52	38	10
...accept withdrawal of NATO forces from Germany, which means diminished security for Germany, if Russian troops would leave East Germany at the same time?	53	25	22

Source: #211, pp. 47-48; survey dates were March 28 to April 12, 1955, with the nationwide sample comprising 843 adults.

Republic should take action (while 30 per cent felt that the FRG could do nothing). Again, specific responses emphasized a more reasonable stance (34%) rather than a firmer policy (13%). How receptive would the Soviet Union be to overtures? Most Germans (55%) expected Soviet negotiators to call for concessions in exchange for reunification. But more than four out of five of those who listed possible political and economic concessions (54 per cent of the total sample) rejected them. Among those mentioning military concessions (32%), opinion was evenly divided on accepting or rejecting them. Again, as in the case of allying with the West, the population's expressed desire for progress through conciliation was not matched by any strong willingness to accept the costs of conciliation.

West Europe. Throughout the early 1950s West Germans strongly backed steps to unite West Europe. Surveys in September 1952, March 1954, and June 1954 found an average of 74 per cent supporting such an idea and only 7 per cent opposing it (#200). Confronted with a proposal calling for a single common government to make decisions on matters concerning West Europe as a whole but permitting each country to decide on things concerning it alone, 74 per cent in September 1952 and 72 per cent in June 1954 favored it and 4 and 7 per cent, respectively, opposed it. Those accepting the proposal were then asked whether or not they would continue to support such a common West European government if its decisions, made on behalf of the whole community, should affect West Germany adversely. A hard core of 63 and 57 per cent, respectively, endorsed this "Europeanist" notion (4 and 7 per cent, respectively, opposed it; and the remaining 7 and 8 per cent, respectively, had no opinion to offer.) It may be added that the more mobilized sectors of the population (men, the more highly educated, the wealthier) were most in favor of such a political union.

The most significant concrete step during this period in the direction of West European unity was the European Coal and Steel Community (ECSC). Proposed in May 1950 by the French foreign minister, Maurice Schuman, and signed in April 1951, the agreement creating ECSC went into effect in July 1952 after ratification by the FRG (the first to do so), France, Italy, and the Benelux nations. Two months later 79 per cent of a national West German sample had heard of the Schuman plan and about two-thirds of these (53%) were aware that it dealt with coal and steel, or heavy industry in general (#169-S). Of this percentage in turn, over half (28%) favored West German participation in ECSC, and less than a third (15%) opposed it. When all respondents were informed of the nature of the plan, then half (50%) were positive and less than a quarter (22%) negative toward West German participation.

Other issues proved more thorny. The case of the European Defense Community discussed earlier led to moderate West German resentments toward France during two periods--first, the months before the contractual agreement of May 1952, when it had appeared to some that the French were planning to use EDC as a means for limiting West Germany's autonomy; and, second, from late 1953 to the summer of 1954, when the French were dragging their feet on ratifying the agreement. In fact, over half of those respondents with views on the matter (or 41 per cent of the whole sample) advocated disregarding France in future defense planning should the latter fail to ratify EDC (#200).[47] The Saar question was also somewhat divisive. An agreement signed in October 1954, which called for the area's "Europeanization" before a plebiscite rather than its outright return to Germany, was known by only half (53%) of a West German sample (#206); and over half of those who had opinions felt that the Bundestag should reject it. Over half of the total sample (53%) felt that France's claims in the Saar were not at all justified (with only 3 per cent terming them predominantly or fully justified).

Subsequent years would show that West Germany remained America's most faithful ally on the European continent, German separation became firmer (and more accepted, if not liked), and problems regarding EDC and the Saar would not stand in the way of further steps toward European unity. Western policymakers could not have known all that in 1955, of course. From their perspective, if public opinion had been their sole guide, granting West Germany virtually full sovereignty was risky (however necessary it may have been for whatever reasons). The West German population was simply not convinced of the linkage between international institution-building in the economic sphere and the Western defense alliance. Nationalistic leaders might have used this popular ambivalence as a basis for asserting a greater measure of West German independence in European and world politics. It is noteworthy, however, that the Adenauer government did not do so. It saw the somewhat unsettled state of public opinion rather as guaranteeing its freedom of action to pursue policies that strengthened Western defenses and West European integration.

East German Perspectives

Psychological support for Adenauer's policies was provided by the view that the FRG spoke for Germans on both sides of the iron curtain. The claim to "sole representation" of the German nation would later be disputed in the FRG, but during the early 1950s there were few public figures willing to accept the proposition that Walter Ulbricht and his associates truly represented the 17 million Germans in the GDR. Similarly, there was little doubt in the West that most East Germans, if they had had the choice, would clearly have opted to live in the Federal Republic. Steady refugee flows seemed to underscore this view. But what did East Germans really think?

Berlin of the 1950s provided a unique opportunity for Allied officials to gain insights into the perspectives and behavior of East Germans. When the Berlin blockade was lifted in May 1949, Germans found that their country was to all intents and purposes formally divided into the FRG in the West and GDR in the East, and so, too, was their former capital city of

Berlin. Access between East and West Berlin nonetheless remained fairly free. This situation, which ended in August 1961 with the construction of the Berlin wall, permitted HICOG officials to make direct observations in the Soviet-controlled portion of the city and allowed East Berliners and other GDR citizens to visit friends and relatives, shop, attend the theater and other public events, and even find employment in West Berlin.

In August 1950 the Reactions Analysis Staff of HICOG turned its attention for the first time to the multitude of East Germans visiting West Berlin. During the next four and a half years, in addition to its more frequent and exhaustive surveys of West Germans and West Berliners, it conducted at least nineteen separate samplings of East German views on a wide range of topics. The peculiar nature of the surveying, however, deserves some attention before getting into substantive findings.

Interviewing East Germans. Problems encountered in conducting the surveys were formidable. Not the least of these was locating East Germans. Initial efforts centered on such sites as currency exchanges and shopping areas, but by 1951 HICOG surveyors had set a pattern of interviewing East Germans attending the annual industrial fair in the early fall and agricultural fair in the late winter. Sometimes other opportunities presented themselves as well: visits to reception centers in West Berlin by young people who were attending an East Berlin youth festival in August 1951, to food distribution centers set up in West Berlin after the East German uprising of June 1953, and to the international architectural exhibit in the Hansa Quarter of West Berlin in summer 1957. Generally, the industrial and agricultural fairs were best, since the surveyors could count on visits by several hundred thousand East Germans to each during the period of one or two weeks.

Another problem was the approach to be used in soliciting interviews. Initially the German interviewers working for HICOG acknowledged United States sponsorship in some cases, but the difference that knowledge of sponsorship made in the responses was sufficiently slight that HICOG officials finally instructed their interviewers to report merely that the survey was being conducted under the (presumably neutral-sounding) auspices of the "Institute for Opinion Research." Eventually the entire task was turned over to DIVO, the same German firm that conducted HICOG surveys in the Federal Republic and West Berlin. Early surveys found between a tenth and a fifth of the prospective respondents refusing interviews, possibly because of a fear that they were being watched or that the interviewers were GDR agents in disguise, or else possibly because they feared that interviewers were Western agents, contact with whom could be compromising.[48] Conducting interviews in private rooms at a large public event, such as the industrial fair, seemed to allay such fears, producing higher response rates.

Ultimately, however, the key question for the surveyors was the validity of the sample. Once they secured reliable information on the GDR's population structure, it was possible to establish quotas (according to geographic region, sex, and sometimes age) to guide the interviewers' selection of potential respondents. What they could not control was the distribution of the respondents' attitudinal and behavioral predispositions. A survey of spectators at a pornographic movie house in an American town may well be representative of those actually attending the movie, but not all groups in the community are equally likely to attend the movie in the first place. Similarly, for whatever reasons, individual East Germans were not equally likely to visit the exhibition center in West Berlin.

HICOG officials made some attempts, if not to validate their samples, at least to determine how they compared with other samples--notably West Germans and refugees from the GDR. Comparisons with West Berliners and West Germans showed that they all focused their attention on the same things, but viewed them somewhat differently, and that, if anything, the East Germans were more pessimistic about the future of East-West relations and prospects for German reunification than were those from the West. A similar comparison with responses of refugees reveals few statistically significant differences, with most of these accounted for by the low level of the refugees' information (#157, 170, 203, 206-S). In the remaining cases, the refugees were simply more critical of the governments' behavior--East and West alike--on such questions as the reunification of Germany. These tests, however interesting, did not validate the sample of GDR respondents as being representative of the entire GDR population in terms of attitudinal and behavioral predispositions. The nagging doubt remained of how much bias the data contained. The best that HICOG reporters could say finally was that their readers had to bear in mind the limitations of the data when evaluating them.

Life in the GDR. Regardless of what one thinks of communist governments or the GDR's progress since then, it is difficult to argue that life was anything but bleak in the GDR of the early 1950s. Wartime disruptions persisted, there were shortages of most commodities, and the ruling Socialist Unity party (SED) under the leadership of Walter Ulbricht was more concerned with building socialism than such niceties as liberal concepts of civil rights.

Respondents in HICOG surveys reflected these unhappy circumstances. In December 1950, 72 per cent estimated the popular mood to be bad or very bad (#63-S), and only one in eight (13%) thought that East Germans themselves could improve their political situation. Three months later 68 per cent guessed that, should the occupying powers leave, the SED would not long remain in power (#71-S). Even so, almost as many (62%) said it would be unwise for the West to accede to Soviet proposals for troop withdrawals, since such a step could only benefit the USSR, leaving Germans worse off than ever.

East German visitors to the West demonstrated a certain pride in their antigovernment uprising of June 17, 1953 (#185, 186). A substantial majority (62%) foresaw new demonstrations stemming from the population's general discontent and unrest (20%), the government's unkept promises (19%), and intolerable political pressures (9%). The sample as a whole was by no means certain, however, that new demonstrations would benefit GDR citizens. About half (49%) argued that such demonstrations would force the Soviet Union to make concessions (27%), lead to the overthrow of Ulbricht's government (13%), or guarantee the reunification of Germany (8%). But 37 per cent anticipated negative consequences, most particularly suppression by the Red Army (20%) and intensified political oppression (10%).

Special groups had their own complaints about life in the GDR. Young people objected to the dominant position held by the Free German Youth (FDJ); 63 per cent--pointing out that people have varying opinions and interests--wanted more youth groups (#79). Pupils in public schools decried political pressure in the classroom, compulsory courses in the Russian language, and current events courses that they perceived as propagandistic in tone and substance (#116). Only one in ten claimed any willingness to express open disagreement with teachers. Farmers resisted the GDR's push toward collectivization and thought the government's land reforms to be misdirected (#133). And large majorities of GDR delegates to a Catholic convocation in West Berlin pointed to hindrances which their government placed in the way of church activity (#162). Given such malaise at home, it was perhaps natural that East Germans cast interested and sometimes envious eyes at the West.

The West. GDR respondents to surveys conducted in West Berlin had by and large a positive image of Western life, political institutions, and leaders. On the broad international level, in December 1950 almost twice as many (49%) thought that the Western Powers were stronger than the number thinking that the Communist Powers were (25%), and 11 per cent rated them equal in strength (#63-S).[49] Two and a half years later, shortly after the June 1953 uprising in the GDR, few East German respondents (3%) thought that, in the recent world situation, the Communist Powers had enjoyed more success. Three out of four cited rather the successes of the West (#185).[50] Moreover, a substantial majority (54%) expressed satisfaction with American policy toward the Soviet Union.

East German visitors to the West ranked reunification among their most important goals. In fact, a survey in September 1953 even found that 62 per cent were willing to agree to Germany's use of force, if that were the only way to secure it; 34 per cent disagreed with this proposal (#186). Soviet, not Western, intransigence was seen as blocking any progress toward reunification (#115).[51]

Western proposals for reunification generally enjoyed considerable support. In March 1951, at a time when 86 per cent felt that the Western Powers were fundamentally in favor of German reunification,[52] almost four in five (79%) nonetheless applauded Chancellor Adenauer's refusal to agree to negotiations on terms proposed by the GDR's prime minister, Otto Grotewohl (#71-S). A Soviet proposal of the following spring elicited little but scorn from an East German sample (#138). Seven out of ten (69%) considered it sheer propaganda, in contrast to a third of that number (23%) who thought the USSR was prepared to make real concessions. Five out of six with opinions (72 per cent of the total sample) called for the plan's outright rejection.

Nor did East Germans expect much to come from a quadripartite foreign ministers' conference to be held in early 1954 in Berlin (#186). Three-quarters (75%) anticipated no agreement on German reunification, and only a fifth (20%) were more hopeful.[53] Half (50%) hoped for a tough Western reaction should the Berlin conference fail (and, as noted earlier, 62 per cent were willing to entertain the use of force to obtain reunification). While the conference was in progress, 86 per cent approved (1 per cent opposed) a Western plan for reunification presented by Anthony Eden (#194-V), and almost as many (79%) rejected (2 per cent favored) the proposal made by V. M. Molotov. In fact, 69 per cent preferred that things remain as they were rather than agree to the Molotov plan (which a mere 6 per cent would have accepted in such circumstances). More generally, East Germans followed a far harder line in refusing to consider Soviet conditions for reunification than did West Germans.

This unwillingness to pay the price asked by the USSR was especially true with respect to West Germany's rearmament and integration into the Western defense system. Three in five (59%) in March 1951 (#71-S) exhorted the FRG to choose this rather than reunification based on neutrality (24%). The same point was made even more sharply after the June 1953 uprising (#185). Two-thirds (66%) saw no reason to delay EDC because of the chance that a new four-power conference might bring reunification; only 19 per cent thought the opposite.[54] The reason given for such views was most frequently that only a policy of strength by the West would force the Soviet Union to give ground on reunification or, indeed, any other issue.

On all these questions, then, East German visitors to West Berlin followed a tough line vis-à-vis the Soviet Union. To the extent that the respondents were truly representative of their compatriots, these findings bore heavy implications for Western policymakers. One point was that the West could count on considerable passive resistance in the GDR to any new moves by either Ulbricht's government or the USSR. Second, the West could be assured of substantial support from GDR citizens for its own policies--and the tougher these policies were, the better the East Germans seemed to like them! But third, by the same token, the West bore some moral obligation to East Germans not to let them down in their times of trial. The extent to which such perceptions strengthened, or at least supported the militancy of the West, including the FRG, can only be guessed. What we do know from recorded history, however, is that West German statesmen frequently mentioned such points when defending their policies privately or in public.[55]

American Information Policy

Transforming the western portion of Germany from an occupied territory into a trustworthy ally required a complex strategy on the part of the United States. During the occupation, of course, military authorities had intervened into every phase of Germans' public lives and many aspects of their private lives as well. American personnel directed public works, held denazification proceedings, issued ration cards, allocated scarce resources, limited individuals' mobility, disseminated information, reorganized schools and curricula, and much more. The Occupation Statute of 1949 brought an end to most of that. Then, too, budgetary restrictions on the United States' role in Germany, required because of the extraordinary expenditures of the Korean conflict, as well as the budget-cutting policies of the first Eisenhower administration, forced American authorities to reevaluate the scale of their operations. Withal, as the cold war deepened in intensity, the United States increasingly looked on Germans as allies and potential friends--a nation to be wooed rather than managed.

American policy toward the Federal Republic during the years of semisovereignty was accordingly a fascinating amalgam of support, encouragement, exhortation, pressure, and occasional intervention. The main lines of this policy have already been sketched: the effort to create a fully independent, rearmed West Germany tied firmly to the Atlantic alliance as well as the emerging European political and economic system. To go into all other aspects would take us too far afield in this necessarily brief introduction to the HICOG public opinion analyses.[56] Many issues, such as the disposition of confiscated German assets in the United States or patterns of American investment in German industry, were not even considered appropriate topics for public opinion surveys. A plethora of other issues we have omitted for the sake of keeping the introduction reasonably brief. They include economic assistance to West Germany through the Marshall Plan (cf. #17-S, 39, 84, 107, 169-S), support for West Berlin as a symbol of freedom (cf. #5, 16, 125, 128, 134, 142, 146, 177, 196-S-2, 206-S), and changing both the American and German images of the role of the U.S. Army in the Federal Republic (cf. #1, 6, 119, 154, 178, 194, 198).

One point that merits further attention, however, if for no other reason than that HICOG pollsters spent an increasing amount of time trying to assess its impact, but also because of its intrinsic role in the American strategy of conciliation, is information policy.

Any information program undertaken by the United States in the HICOG years was bound to face certain difficulties. Reducing the scope and range of activities could create an image of declining concern for Germany. This could, in turn, lead to misunderstandings about American intentions or, what was doubtless worse, an inclination on the part of American policy officials to over-react, to go a bit far in accommodating German sensitivities. Second, the image of military control would doubtless remain long after its last vestiges had been wiped away. We have already seen this in the case of rearmament and governance more generally, where a small but significant portion of the population persistently opined that the FRG was little more than a puppet on the Allies' strings. Similarly, in the field of communications, sizable percentages continued to think, long after licensing had been abolished in 1949, that Allied approval was required to publish a newspaper or operate a radio station, and that the Allies could exercise censorship over the content of the media (#159, 212).

Still a third problem was popular resistance to any government information programs whatever. A population that had lived through Goebbels and the technique of the "big lie" could justifiably be expected to shy away from new propagandizing. Indeed, a straightforward question in July 1952 asking if they approved "of the Americans carrying on propaganda here in West Germany" found almost equal thirds approving, disapproving, and expressing no opinion (#170). Closer examination revealed, however, that only 12 per cent both believed that the United States was engaged in propagandizing and disapproved of it. A subsequent survey in December 1952 discovered that five of six with opinions on the topic (or 39 per cent of the entire sample) regarded America's representation of its ideas and views in West Germany to be more to the FRG's advantage than disadvantage.[57] The bulk (64%) nonetheless felt that propaganda was most effective when it stuck to the truth, and substantial minorities chided Americans either for making exaggerated claims about democracy (31%) or for being insufficiently frank in discussing shortcomings in the American version of democracy (31%).

Whatever ambivalence West Germans felt about an American information program in general, they were quite receptive to its specific aspects. Here we shall focus solely upon publications, radio programming, and information centers. Similar, though in some cases less spectacular, findings also pertain to American exhibits (cf. #89, 98, 164, 166, 176, 190), information films (cf. #23-S, 29, 43, 175, 183, 187), and exchange programs (cf. #12, 44, 151).

Press. The American-operated press was, in effect, a victim of changing times. OMGUS officials had created their own newspapers and magazines to keep the German public informed and only later permitted Germans to acquire publishing licenses. The competition proved to be increasingly stiff. And, eventually, as HICOG officials also faced shrinking budgets, they felt constrained to phase out their publishing program.

Magazines suffered particularly. American magazines founded in the OMGUS years--*Amerikanische Rundschau*, *Der Monat*, *Heute*, and *Neue Auslese*--continued to appeal to certain groups of readers, especially those in high socioeconomic strata. Those who read them were usually quite positive in their evaluations (#2, 43). Although the share of the reading public that such magazines attracted was reasonably great, as early as 1950 it was clear that they would be overshadowed by German publications, most notably the illustrated weekly, *Quick*. Before the year was over *Amerikanische Rundschau* and *Neue Auslese* had been discontinued, and *Heute* followed suit a year later. Only

Der Monat remained, but it had been turned over to an independent German editorial board and publishing company (albeit with continuing financial support from the American government).

The American-owned newspaper, *Neue Zeitung*, enjoyed a longer life. Published originally in Frankfurt, Munich, and Berlin, it was continued beyond 1949 only in the last of these, where its readership actually expanded over the years. In December 1948 the *Neue Zeitung* was read by every tenth American Zone respondent and every fifth West Berliner; readership in early 1952 stood at 7 per cent nationally and 29 per cent in West Berlin (#160). Its West Berlin subscribers in March 1953 were by and large much more well-educated, wealthier, older, and more likely to be in the professions or business than were those who read other newspapers (#184). They stressed the high quality of political reporting in their evaluations. Asked whether they would like a weekly rather than daily edition, 94 per cent responded negatively and over half (55%) threatened in that event to cancel their subscriptions. Despite this kind of loyalty, American officials decided to end publication of the *Neue Zeitung* in January 1955.

Radio. American radio programming captured the attention of more West Germans than did HICOG publications. One instrument was the "Voice of America," a half-hour program (later 15 minutes) of news and commentary about the United States, that was beamed daily from West German radio stations. In May 1950, 57 per cent of the American Zone radio audience (representing 36 per cent of the total zonal population, down from 38 per cent a year earlier) and 90 per cent of those listening to radio during the hour when VOA was transmitted listened to the VOA broadcast (#26). A year later 62 per cent of American Zone radio listeners said that they heard VOA occasionally (9%), frequently (31%), or very frequently (22%), as did 38 per cent of all West German radio listeners (#95).[58] The results of more detailed radio diaries kept by samples of West German radio listeners found that 6 per cent in May 1953 and 10 per cent in May 1954 listened to at least one 15-minute segment of VOA during the week (#204).[59]

Evaluations of the "Voice of America" were generally quite positive. It was the single program most frequently heard in the American and French zones, as well as West Berlin, in mid-1951. Almost two-thirds (63%) of an American Zone sample in May 1950 considered the program good, particularly because it was informative about the American way of life or instructive and interesting in general (#26). A somewhat larger number (74%) thought that it made a favorable or very favorable impression on West Germans, a finding supported by data obtained a year later (#105). At this time, too, two-thirds (64%) thought that VOA programming demonstrated real understanding of Germany and its problems.

In West Berlin, by contrast, the United States operated its own radio station, Radio in the American Sector (RIAS), which dominated the radio-listening habits of the population. The proportion of the total West Berlin radio audience listening to

RIAS rose from 73 per cent in January 1948 to 98 per cent in November 1949, and then to 99 per cent in May 1953 before dropping slightly to 96 per cent a year later (#34, 204).[60] The average listener reported tuning in to RIAS for almost eighteen hours per week--twice as much as for the nearest competitor. As far as quality was concerned, there were very few complaints. A negligible number (3%) felt, in December 1949, that RIAS served American interests alone (#4); overwhelming majorities thought that it accurately portrayed political happenings in Berlin (95%) and the world (93%). Large numbers felt in May 1953 (#182) that RIAS had done much or very much for Berlin (69%), was effective or very effective in refuting propaganda from the East (78%), and presented reliable rather than one-sided political commentary (87%).

In the GDR, according to East German visitors to West Berlin, RIAS was by far the most popular station (#90, 109).[61] It headed the list of sources of radio news, mainly because respondents felt that RIAS told the truth. Particularly popular programs, the type of which respondents wanted more (#90, 109), were those dealing with events in the GDR ("Berlin Speaks to the Zone") and the "Voice of America." In late 1953, after the June uprising, 13 of 14 respondents asserted that RIAS had done much (37%) or very much (56%) for the people in the GDR, not only through its news and information programs but also by issuing warnings, details on informers, and suggestions about appropriate behavior (#189).

U.S. Information Centers. A third important component of the American information program in West Germany was the establishment of information centers, called Amerika Häuser (or "America Houses"), where visitors could use library facilities, attend lectures, see films, view art exhibits, and participate in other activities. By 1955 there were twenty-two such centers in major West German cities and West Berlin.

Their existence and offerings were generally well known to West Germans (#31, 76, 181, 210). Surveys conducted between May 1950 and April 1955 found that an average of 64 per cent of American Zone respondents (up from 49 per cent in October 1948) and 48 per cent of all West Germans knew that such centers existed in the larger cities. Very large and increasing numbers (78 per cent in the American Zone, 86 per cent in West Germany) of those aware of the centers could also specify some of their offerings. Only a few respondents (averaging 10 per cent in the American Zone, 9 per cent in West Germany), however, had actually visited an Amerika Haus.[62] HICOG analysts estimated that, in all, 3.25 million Germans over 15 years of age had made a total of 35.9 million visits in 1954 to U.S. Information Centers (#210).

The typical visitor to an Amerika Haus was far from being the average West German citizen. A third (34%) of the visitors were high school or university graduates (4 per cent in the general population). Visitors were far more likely to be men, in the professions, with a greater income, very active politically, and younger than were nonvisitors. Only 18 per cent had no knowledge of the English language (86 per cent nationwide). Two in five (41 per cent; 17 per cent nationally) were in contact with someone in the United States, and 7 per cent (2 per cent nationally) had themselves been in America.

Understandably, perhaps, those who visited U.S. Information Centers also evaluated them quite positively. The overall impressions of most were excellent (23%), very good (45%), or good (29%); and many more thought Amerika Haus facilities to be improving (41%) rather than deteriorating (8%), with 38 per cent seeing no significant change. The focal point of visitors' interest was each center's collection of books, mostly about the United States or activities of Americans. (We are not surprised to learn that, when asked what benefits they had obtained from their visits, the largest number mentioned increased knowledge of the United States.) As far as future governance of the Amerika Häuser was concerned, a majority (51%) preferred continued United States direction and financial support, 43 per cent wanted joint American-German control, and only 2 per cent thought it best for German agencies to take over the centers.

Viewed as a whole, the American information program in the Federal Republic presented policymakers in Washington with a dilemma. Its appeal, on the one hand, was to a relatively small percentage of West Germans; but, on the other hand, its impact on that segment, which comprised the more socially mobilized Germans, was considerable. Given the uniquely favorable conditions for the various aspects of the information program--a measure of continuing American control over semisovereign Germany, the high priority that top-level American officials gave to the task of enlisting German support for a tight Western alliance, and substantial if declining sums to spend in the pursuit of this goal--and, given both German predispositions to go along with the West (particularly if the option were falling under Soviet influence!) as well as a certain resistance to any overt propagandizing on the part of the United States, it would seem that the program fulfilled its maximum potential. The question faced by policymakers then was whether its successes justified the cost in money and time. That the program continues to the present day, albeit reduced still further in scale,[63] reflects to some measure the firm basis it attained during the HICOG years.

POLITICAL PERSPECTIVES IN SEMISOVEREIGN GERMANY:
A BALANCE SHEET

Fifty-six months of semisovereignty strengthened tendencies observable in West Germany in late 1949. First of all, West Germans demonstrated that Nazism as a movement was a thing of the past. This is not to say that all ideas associated with the movement were dead. Indeed, a review of the wide range of data presented in HICOG reports suggests that in the mid-1950s perhaps one in eight adults espoused a set of perspectives consistent with Nazism.[64] The point is, rather, that there was no significant support at the mass or elite level for any institutionalization of these notions. Political parties that tried to capitalize on such sentiments--most notably the SRP in the early 1950s and the National Democratic party of Germany (NPD) in the late 1960s, but also a number of smaller parties--never gained sufficient backing to be anything more than small black clouds on the horizon.

Another strain of opinion apparent at the birth of the Federal Republic was the desire for full autonomy. Germany had paid for the last war, people argued increasingly, and those responsible for its crimes had been punished sufficiently. There was no need for the Allies to continue using the specter of the Nazi past as justification for continued controls over West Germany. Of the three Western Allies, the United States was most anxious to establish the FRG's independence--albeit within a framework of Western unity. EDC was seen as a means to this end. The West German public, however, supported its political leaders, who delayed action on EDC until the principle of German equality could be recognized in a contractual agreement, signed in May 1952, with the Allies. As the ratification debate in France dragged on, Germans chafed even more. The Paris agreements of October 1954, which brought an independent FRG into NATO, called forth ambivalence from the population when they were put into effect in May of the following year: rejoicing over West Germany's new status, but distress that the Allies had retained some rights that, in principle at least, undercut the country's true autonomy.

As far as the domestic scene was concerned, the decision of the late 1940s to permit the elites and institutions of pre-Nazi Germany to reassert their preeminence led to an interesting self-reinforcing cycle of conservatism. The chief goals of the public and elected leadership alike were political stability and economic growth. Certainly, both were achieved by 1955. But the cost had been a willingness to tolerate a reconcentration of German industry and mass media, wage and taxation policies that increased disparity between rich and poor, the employment of some former Nazis in the government and judiciary, and the encouragement of black-white thinking in the international realm--all measures that redounded to the benefit of the governing Christian Democratic Union. That the party, under Adenauer's capable leadership, gained ever more popular support merely encouraged its conservative tendencies. Indeed, some saw its overwhelming success as a greater danger to the future of German democracy than the reemergence of Nazism.

In retrospect, it may be argued that Germans really had few options open to them. In the eyes of voters, the establishment of an effective conservative government was preferable to any number of alternatives: continued rule by foreign troops, a fractionated party system not unlike the one that had contributed to the death of the Weimar Republic, even a more moderate multiparty system that would not permit the strong measures necessary to restore the country's economic well-being. Then, too, there was a certain amount of political pragmatism. The population sensed that the Western Allies would not give up their grip on the FRG's destiny until its government paid a price, one that the conservatives were more willing than others to pay.

The price was the FRG's irrevocable integration into the Western alliance system. Without getting into the origins or merits of the cold war, the reality of its existence during the 1950s cannot be denied. Hitler's old bugbear, bolshevism, became in the eyes of Western leaders the nemesis of the free world. Accordingly, it seemed imperative to enlist at least a rump portion of Germany in the struggle against international communism. The data reviewed here reveal that the West German public was prepared to lend its moral support to this cause, even if they were less sure about offering up their bodies should war actually break out between East and West.

The decision to ally with the West meant, of course, acceptance of the prospect that Germany would not be reunited in the foreseeable future. It is impossible even at this juncture to say whether or not Soviet leaders were sincere in their desire to see a neutral, reunified Germany. What we do know is that few West Germans (and still fewer East Germans, if we may judge by attitudes expressed by those who visited West Berlin) were willing to push for such a goal if it incurred the risk that the Western Powers would withdraw their guaranties of Germany's security. What emerged was the argument--strongly felt by some, a polite fiction to others--that only by strengthening itself could the West create the political conditions that would lead the Soviet Union to "return" to the FRG the eastern portions of Germany, including the GDR. One important way to strengthen the West was to add German divisions to its defense forces.

Alliance with the West, then, promised the attainment of two goals: immediately, West Germany's freedom of action, and, at some more distant time, German reunification. This "policy of strength" found widespread endorsement among the West German public. Indeed, so deeply entrenched was this notion that it took later German leaders years before they could persuade the public that times had changed, that the FRG should be seeking ways to adapt to the new status quo rather than merely denying the legitimacy of its existence. Even Chancellor Willy Brandt's Eastern policies of the early 1970s would not still the voices of some who felt he had betrayed Germany's "true" national interests, those that had become articles of faith two decades earlier.

Popular predispositions, Allied pressures, and policies favored by the Federal Republic's elected leaders meshed neatly, if not perfectly, in the early 1950s to produce a restored Germany firmly tied to the West. There was opposition to be sure. Theirs were voices in the wilderness, however, for they seriously misjudged the mood of the times, and their effective influence soon diminished. Eventually even the major opposition party, the Social Democrats, adopted the basic understandings that had been reached by 1955 and vied with the Christian Democrats in proclaiming anticommunism as the FRG's legitimate goal.

In short, the years of semisovereignty had produced--or strengthened, if you will--a new orthodoxy. The FRG was not the model democracy for which American occupiers had initially hoped, but it was a popular, stable, and effective democracy in a formal sense. Its very strength gave the Federal Republic the breathing space that it would need to expand some of democracy's less formal aspects, such as social justice and equality. The firm hand of Adenauer, moreover, pushed the country persistently toward its rehabilitation in the world comity of nations. Even if complete independence escaped it in the early 1950s, the FRG would eventually achieve as much of it as any state has in the modern world. Whatever its more troublesome aspects, then, the political system that developed in West Germany from 1949 to 1955 provided a solid basis for autonomous and democratic growth.

NOTES

1. The last of these rights were not relinquished until mid-1968, after the FRG's parliament had passed the "emergency powers" bill. The Western Allies continue to exert occupation rights and duties in West Berlin.
2. See Karl W. Deutsch and Lewis J. Edinger, *Germany Rejoins the Powers: Mass Opinion, Interest Groups, and Elites in Contemporary German Foreign Policy* (Stanford, California: Stanford University Press, 1959); Alfred Grosser, *Germany in Our Time: A Political History of the Postwar Years* (New York: Praeger Publishers, 1971); and Manfred Knapp, editor, *Die deutsch-amerikanischen Beziehungen nach 1945* (Frankfurt and New York: Campus Verlag, 1975). More generally, see Anna J. Merritt and Richard L. Merritt, *Politics, Economics and Society in the Two Germanies, 1945-75: A Bibliography of English-Language Works* (Urbana: University of Illinois Press, 1978).
3. Among these are Emnid, K.G., in Bielefeld, which produces a monthly newsletter; DIVO, in Frankfurt, which edited three volumes of data, *Umfragen* (Frankfurt-am-Main: Europäische Verlagsanstalt, 1958-62), covering the years 1957-60; and especially Institut für Demoskopie, which continues to publish both a newsletter and occasional collections of data. For the period in question, see Elisabeth Noelle and Erich Peter Neumann, editors, *Jahrbuch der öffentlichen Meinung, 1947-55* (Allensbach am Bodensee: Verlag für Demoskopie, 1957).
4. For summaries and an analysis, see Anna J. Merritt and Richard L. Merritt, editors, *Public Opinion in Occupied Germany: The OMGUS Surveys, 1945-49* (Urbana: University of Illinois Press, 1970).
5. The summaries of individual reports presented in this volume give detailed information, when available, on samples (see particularly the full version of report no. 69 of March 21, 1951). Complete information in the files of the U.S. Department of State has not yet been released.

6. Questionnaires and IBM cards for some of the later HICOG surveys are available at the Roper Public Opinion Research Center, Yale University, New Haven, Connecticut. The reports (a total of 7,817 pages) summarized in this volume may be found in the library of the International Communication Agency (1750 Pennsylvania Avenue, N.W., Washington, D.C. 20547), Yale University's Political Science Research Library, and the Center for West European Studies at Harvard University.

7. For a fuller discussion of the data and arguments presented in this section, see Richard L. Merritt, "Digesting the Past: Views of National Socialism in Semi-Sovereign Germany," *Societas*, 7:2 (Spring 1977), 93-119.

8. Data in this paragraph are from Merritt and Merritt, *Public Opinion in Occupied Germany*, pp. 30-39.

9. Numbers in parentheses refer to HICOG reports summarized in the second part of this volume.

10. Merritt and Merritt, *Public Opinion in Occupied Germany*, p. 36.

11. A national sampling two years later produced similar results. Roughly a third (32%) cited Germany, Hitler, or the Nazis as the cause, a quarter (24%) mentioned other countries, and a sixth (18%) blamed both sides. See Noelle and Neumann, *Jahrbuch, 1947-1955*, p. 137.

12. Elisabeth Noelle and Erich Peter Neumann, editors, *Jahrbuch der öffentlichen Meinung, 1957* (Allensbach am Bodensee: Verlag für Demoskopie, 1957), p. 142.

13. Noelle and Neumann, *Jahrbuch, 1947-1955*, p. 137.

14. Cf. Noelle and Neumann, *Jahrbuch, 1947-1955*, p. 138.

15. For more details, see Merritt, "Digesting the Past."

16. Merritt and Merritt, *Public Opinion in Occupied Germany*, pp. 33-35.

17. Impatience with war crimes trials continued in the years after 1955. See Elisabeth Noelle and Erich Peter Neumann, editors, *Jahrbuch der öffentlichen Meinung, 1965-1967* (Allensbach and Bonn: Verlag für Demoskopie, 1967), p. 166; and Regina Schmidt and Egon Becker, *Reaktionen auf politische Vorgänge: Drei Meinungsstudien aus der Bundesrepublik* (Frankfurt am Main: Europäische Verlagsanstalt, 1967), pp. 113-18.

18. For later data, see Noelle and Neumann, *Jahrbuch, 1965-1967*, pp. 204, 268. See also Richard L. Merritt, "Perceived Legitimacy of Military Occupations: The United States in Germany, 1945-1949," *Sozialwissenschaftliches Jahrbuch für Politik* (forthcoming).

19. See Anna J. Merritt, "Germans and American Denazification," in *Communication in International Politics*, ed. Richard L. Merritt (Urbana: University of Illinois Press, 1972), pp. 361-83.

20. See Noelle and Neumann, *Jahrbuch, 1947-1955*, p. 142.

21. The Federal Constitutional Court banned the SRP anyway. Not too long afterward, in November 1952, 37 per cent of a national sample indicated agreement with the court order, and only 22 per cent thought it incorrect (Noelle and Neumann, *Jahrbuch, 1947-1955*, pp. 274-75). In August 1956 the Federal Constitu-

tional Court also ordered the dissolution of the KPD.

22. For public opinion data on trends from 1946 to 1949, see Merritt and Merritt, *Public Opinion in Occupied Germany*, pp. 48-49 et passim.

23. Predictions made by HICOG analysts on the basis of pre-election surveys were, for the most part, within one per cent of the actual vote totals in the 1953 election (#191); see Richard L. Merritt, "The 1953 Bundestag Election: Evidence from West German Public Opinion," *Sozialwissenschaftliches Jahrbuch für Politik* (forthcoming). For more thorough analyses of this election, see Erich Reigrotzki, *Soziale Verflechtungen in der Bundesrepublik* (Tübingen: J.C.B. Mohr [Paul Siebeck], 1956), and especially Juan J. Linz Storch de Gracia, "The Social Bases of West German Politics" (Ph.D. diss., Columbia University, 1959).

24. See Noelle and Neumann, *Jahrbuch, 1947-1955*, pp. 252-53. In personal correspondence dated June 4, 1976, David P. Conradt adds that, more generally, the electoral data throughout the 1950s showed a steady decline of support for "anti-system" parties. As the data discussed in this introduction show, the decline was not due solely to the banning of anticonstitutional parties but reflected a popular mood.

25. Noelle and Neumann, *Jahrbuch, 1947-1955*, p. 192.

26. Noelle and Neumann, *Jahrbuch, 1947-1955*, p. 132; by 1958 Adenauer had overtaken Bismarck in this historical popularity contest.

27. Noelle and Neumann, *Jahrbuch, 1947-1955*, p. 192; and particularly Erich Peter Neumann and Elisabeth Noelle, editors, *Statistics on Adenauer: Portrait of a Statesman* (Allensbach and Bonn: Verlag für Demoskopie, 1962), pp. 123-33. The June 1959 figure is technically not comparable to the others, since in this survey respondents were presented with a list of politicians, whereas the other surveys used open-end questions.

28. Neumann and Noelle, *Statistics on Adenauer*, p. 14. Respondents selected 493 positive and 165 negative terms in 1955, and 400 positive and 217 negative terms in 1959; a different categorization of terms according to their positive and negative connotations would produce slightly different results but would not change the main finding of continued but diminished respect.

29. In the strictest sense, the term "rearmament" is inaccurate here, since the FRG did not exist before 1949. Its general usage in discussing the creation of a West German military establishment after 1949 nonetheless justifies its use.

30. Subsequent tests revealed that the bias introduced by the nature of the interviewing situation (that is, occupiers or their representatives interviewing the occupied) was in the nature of 10 per cent on questions of this sort, which is to say that the number of people likely to respond in a "nonmilitaristic" fashion was increased artificially by about ten percentage points. See Leo P. Crespi, "The Influence of Military Government Sponsorship in German Opinion Polling," *International Journal of Opinion and Attitude Research* 2:2 (Summer 1950), 167-69. Even taking this bias into account leaves a strong

strain of antimilitarism in German public perspectives of the immediate postwar period.

31. Data in this and the following paragraph are from Merritt and Merritt, *Public Opinion in Occupied Germany,* passim (especially OMGUS survey #19).

32. A series of thirteen surveys conducted by the Institut für Demoskopie from November 1950 to February 1955 yielded an average of 41 per cent who favored an independent German army and 40 per cent who opposed it. The periods of ascendancy for an independent army were in the months before the adoption of the contractual agreement (see below) and the months between August 1953 and November 1954--that is, when EDC was undergoing severe criticism and eventual rejection in France. See Noelle and Neumann, *Jahrbuch, 1947-1955,* pp. 372-73.

33. In the series of questions asked in this survey, a net of only one in eight (13%) ended up favoring a completely independent West German army. In fact, as footnote 32 suggests, the percentage favoring this alternative was considerably higher.

34. In June 1951, for instance, at a time when 59 per cent favored the FRG's adherence to the Atlantic Pact and, with it, participation in a general army for the defense of Europe, and 29 per cent opposed it, a far greater number indicated that they would either welcome their government's decision to accept such a proposition (22%), accept the fact however unenthusiastically (45%), or oppose it without doing anything about it (13%)--or a total of 80 per cent who would accept the decision (or even 98 per cent, if we assume that the 18 per cent who expressed no opinion would accept their government's decision without opposition). Only two per cent said they would oppose such a decision in an active fashion (#88). Several weeks later, there were 26 per cent who were enthusiastic supporters, 45 per cent passive supporters, 14 per cent passive opponents, and 13 per cent with no opinion (again, a total of 98 per cent), with two per cent terming themselves active opponents (#94).

35. In five surveys from late February to June 1954, an average of 57 per cent favored participation in EDC (28 per cent very much and 29 per cent somewhat) and 25 per cent opposed it (14 per cent very much so and 11 per cent somewhat). In late August, just before the French parliament turned down EDC, positive and negative opinion had declined: 23 per cent favored participation very much and 31 per cent somewhat (a total of 54 per cent), and 10 per cent opposed it very much and another 10 per cent somewhat (a total of 20 per cent). The number of those expressing no opinion increased from an average of 18 per cent in the first half of 1954 to 26 per cent in August (#196, 199, 200, 202).

36. In terms of degrees, 16 per cent saw it as absolutely necessary, 16 per cent very necessary, and 28 per cent somewhat necessary; 11 per cent termed it not so necessary and 14 per cent not at all necessary.

37. See, for a somewhat extreme example, T. H. Tetens, *Germany Plots with the Kremlin* (New York: Henry Schuman, 1953), and his *The New Germany and the Old Nazis* (New York: Random

House, 1961).

38. See Richard L. Merritt, "Visual Representation of Mutual Friendliness," in *Mathematical Applications in Political Science, III,* ed. Joseph L. Bernd (Charlottesville: University Press of Virginia, 1967), pp. 96-119; for relevant data, see Richard L. Merritt and Donald J. Puchala, editors, *Western European Perspectives on International Affairs: Public Opinion Studies and Evaluations* (New York: Frederick A. Praeger, Publishers, 1968). It may not be amiss to point out here that in almost all regards West Berliners were hostile to the Soviet Union and friendly toward the United States, more in favor of a policy of strength, less willing to make concessions to the Soviet Union, and less anxious to come to terms with the prospect of a divided Germany.

39. Indeed, in February 1955, placed before the hypothetical choice between seeing the whole of Europe fall under Soviet rule or else using all means possible to defend the Western way of life, a narrow plurality (38%) opted for a vigorous defense over doing everything to avoid war (34%), with two of seven respondents (28%) expressing no opinion whatever. Noelle and Neumann, *Jahrbuch, 1947-1955,* p. 348.

40. In July 1953, 18 per cent thought that America would go along with a neutral Germany as a basis for the reunification of Germany and 43 per cent did not think so; the gap widened to 15 and 51 per cent, respectively, five months later (#193).

41. For an interesting study of German public opinion on reunification, see Gebhard Schweigler, *National Consciousness in Divided Germany* (Beverly Hills: Sage Publications, 1975).

42. Percentages feeling that areas seized by the Nazis were rightfully German were much smaller: the Sudetenland (40%), Alsace (25%), Bohemia (19%), and Austria (17%); and the willingness to accept war to regain them averaged only 11 per cent (#1).

43. Asked whether security from the Russians or the unity of Germany was the more important, substantial majorities--51 per cent in July 1952, 52 per cent a year later, and 59 per cent in October 1954--opted for the former over the latter, chosen by 33, 36, and 27 per cent respectively. Noelle and Neumann, *Jahrbuch, 1947-1955,* p. 315.

44. An interesting point that cannot be discussed here is the extent to which the Adenauer government may have encouraged such heavy emphasis for the purpose of using public opinion as a bargaining counter in its relations with West and East alike.

45. Only 16 per cent could see specific disadvantages for the FRG likely to derive from reunification, 70 per cent saw none; 62 per cent forecast specific advantages, particularly in the economic and social sectors, and 18 per cent expected none (#211).

46. There was a growing image in the FRG of Soviet-American corresponsibility for Germany's division. In October 1954, 61 per cent attributed blame solely to the East, 2 per cent to the West, and 24 per cent to both. Six months later, the corresponding figures were 43, 4, and 38 per cent (#211). In other words,

42 per cent saw the United States to be partly to blame for the division, and an even larger number thought that the United States should take some initiative to end it.

47. Should the French have turned down EDC (which they later did), then, according to the survey conducted in June 1954 (#200), another 15 per cent would have had West Germany give up all plans for Germany's remilitarization, and 18 per cent would have had West Germany make renewed efforts to induce France to give its approval to EDC.

48. Indeed, East German sources did warn that Western pollsters were espionage agents; see Henry Halpern, "Soviet Attitude Toward Public Opinion Research in Germany," *Public Opinion Quarterly*, 13:1 (Spring 1949), 117-18.

49. Comparable figures for a West German urban sample in early January 1951 were almost reversed: 24 per cent saw the Western Powers as stronger, 46 per cent the Communist Powers, and 15 per cent termed them equally strong.

50. In the FRG, 44 per cent named the Western Powers as the more successful, 10 per cent the Communist Powers.

51. At this time, respondents expressed pessimism about the prospects for reunification; 58 per cent thought the Western Powers more in favor of the idea, only 8 per cent named the USSR.

52. In September 1953, 89 per cent agreed with the statement "I'm sure the United States is for the reunification of Germany" (#186).

53. Optimism increased somewhat during the conference itself (to 27 per cent, with 69 per cent still expressing pessimism); but, of course, their hopes were dashed (#194-V).

54. Comparable figures for West Germany at the time were 48 per cent in favor of continuing efforts to establish EDC, 28 per cent opting for delaying such efforts.

55. See, for example, Konrad Adenauer, *Memoirs, 1945-1953* (Chicago, Ill.: Henry Regnery Company, 1966), pp. 189-90, 416, 417, 422. "One thing was sure," the former chancellor wrote (p. 426); "if we did not sign the [EDC and contractual agreements in 1952], we would not improve the chances of reunification in any way. I knew that the men and women in the Soviet Zone shared this view. I knew that they regarded the road taken by us as the only way that might one day lead them too out of their distress." Similarly, "everything we heard from [the GDR], especially in the statements by refugees, urged a firm policy toward the Russians" (p. 432).

56. Besides the items listed in footnote 2 above, see Harold Zink, *The United States in Germany, 1944-1955* (Princeton, N.J.: D. Van Nostrand Company, 1957); Eugene Davidson, *The Death and Life of Germany: An Account of the American Occupation* (New York: Alfred A. Knopf, 1959); and Roger P. Morgan, *The United States and West Germany, 1945-1973: A Study in Alliance Politics* (London: Oxford University Press, 1974).

57. Most (78%) of the respondents accepting the appropriateness of an American information program also believed that such ideas and views would have a lasting effect in West Germany, particularly in strengthening democratic tendencies.

58. Listeners who tuned in to VOA at least once a week numbered 53 per cent in the American Zone, 30 per cent in all of West Germany.

59. In the American Zone, the figures were 15 and 24 per cent respectively. Thus listeners in the American Zone accounted for most of the listenership in the FRG as a whole.

60. The Northwest German Radio (NWDR) began cutting into RIAS's popularity by 1953 (#182, 204).

61. Again, although the early 1950s saw no serious Western (or Eastern) competitor to RIAS's preeminence, NWDR began making serious inroads in 1953. For a detailed breakdown of estimates on what East Germans listened to, see #201.

62. The American information program also included bookmobiles and German-American reading rooms in areas where there were no Amerika Häuser. Only one in eight (13%) West Germans was aware of the former, one in nine (11%) of the latter; and only about one in a hundred used either.

63. The U.S. International Communication Agency continues to send VOA programs to West Germany, operate RIAS in Berlin (albeit with German direction and joint German-American financing), maintain Amerika Häuser or other I.C.A. posts (binational centers, reading rooms, information centers) in fifteen cities, organize exhibits, and otherwise conduct informational activities in the FRG.

64. Deutsch and Edinger, *Germany Rejoins the Powers,* p. 40, make a similar estimate. The figure was about one in six in 1949; see Merritt and Merritt, *Public Opinion in Occupied Germany,* p. 38.

PART II

THE HICOG SURVEYS

Report No. 1 (30 December 1949)

THE STATE OF GERMAN NATIONALISM FOLLOWING THE FOUNDING OF THE WEST GERMAN REPUBLIC

Sample: about 3,000 people in the American Zone, 500 in West Berlin, and 300 in Bremen.
Interviewing dates: September 1949. (40 pp.)

During the preelection campaign, in summer 1949, numerous critical comments were made about the occupying powers. Some commentators feared that this might signify a concomitant resurgence of nationalism. That these criticisms were not directed at the Americans is supported by the fact that a solid majority (65%) of AMZON Germans felt that Americans are similar to Germans; a similarly high percentage (61%) felt the same way in November 1947. Also, 50 per cent of the respondents in AMZON (59 per cent in Berlin and 64 per cent in Bremen) thought that the most important factor in American treatment of Germany was "understanding." An even higher percentage (60 per cent in AMZON, 85 per cent in Berlin, and 71 per cent in Bremen) felt that the United States had furthered rather than hindered reconstruction in Germany. Over a third of the AMZON respondents (35%) thought that American troops had become more popular in the course of the previous year, a third (33%) thought their popularity had remained the same, and only one in eight (12%) felt it had diminished; 65 per cent of West Berliners and 47 per cent of Bremen residents felt that the troops had increased in popularity.

Another campaign issue was the Ruhr statute approved in April 1949. It created a six-power Ruhr Authority to supervise the reorganization of the coal and steel industries in the Ruhr. In AMZON, awareness of the statute dropped from 46 per cent in February 1949 to 30 per cent in September. Adverse opinion also dropped sharply, from 23 per cent in February 1949 to only 7 per cent in September; the percentage of those who thought it was good rose from 7 to 9 per cent, and those with no opinion rose from 9 to 12 per cent.

Perhaps the most critical issue to which commentators turned when discussing the question of nationalist sentiment in Germany is that of racist attitudes. This survey produced no evidence of an increase in such attitudes; nonetheless they did exist, and to an appreciable degree. In December 1946, 48 per cent of the AMZON population felt that some human races are more fit to rule than others; in November 1947 this figure had dropped to 42 per cent; by March of the following year it had jumped to 54 per cent; and in October 1949 it had gone back down to 44 per cent. Although a fairly large percentage (34%) of AMZON residents felt that some races are inferior to others, over half (55%) of these thought it possible to educate the inferior races up to the level of the others. Asked whether a Jew whose parents and grandparents were born and had grown up in Germany was a real German or not, 68 per cent of AMZON Germans said that he was, whereas 28 per cent thought he was not. Interestingly enough, when the same question was asked about a person living in France whose parents and grandparents had been born and grew up in Germany, the responses were 58 per cent positive and 35 per cent negative.

The desire for German unity was considered another important factor increasing nationalist sentiment. Almost all Germans hoped for reunification, and a substantial majority (67%) felt that it would indeed come about some day. Unification, however, was not desired at any cost. When asked which was more important, reunification or checking the spread of communism, only 25 per cent of the respondents chose the former, while fully 71 per cent wanted to check the spread of communism. Closely related to the question of reunification is that of the restoration of former German territories. In AMZON almost three-quarters of the population felt that East Prussia (74%) and Silesia (73%) rightfully belong to Germany; over half had the same feeling about the Saar (59%) and Danzig (54%). Far fewer, however, would go to war to attain these goals: 48 per cent would do so for Silesia, 47 per cent for East Prussia, 28 per cent for the Saar, and 21 per cent for Danzig. In all cases the figures were much higher in Berlin and Bremen than in Bavaria, Hesse, or Württemberg-Baden.

Between November 1947 and September 1949, a growing proportion of Germans viewed their country as mainly responsible for the last war, a trend running counter to what would be expected if nationalist feelings were increasing. Whereas 26 per cent blamed Germany in 1947, 37 per cent did so in 1949; at the same time, those blaming other circumstances, primarily the world situation, dropped from 55 per cent to 36 per cent.

To see if there was any connection between growing acceptance of responsibility for the war and nationalist sentiment, the Germans were asked a number of questions concerning the military. Asked from which field the greatest Germans had come, 38 per cent replied poetry, 32 per cent music, and only 17 per cent chose the military. If Germans did ever have an army again, six out of ten AMZON residents felt that military service should not be compulsory; even in case war should come, four out of ten still insisted that service should not be compulsory. Nonetheless, fully a third of the population felt that military service ought to be required. Contrary to the traditionally high prestige of military careers, postwar Germans preferred to see their sons in other vocations than as professional officers.

Finally, AMZON residents were asked a number of questions concerning the word and concept of nationalism. For somewhat over half the population (52%) the term had no meaning whatever; the second highest proportion of responses (15%) came under the heading "attachment to and love of one's country." Among this large number of persons for whom the term had no objectionable connotation, more people felt that there was just as much nationalist sentiment in the United States as in Germany (34%) than felt there was more in Germany (26%) or less (24%).

Report No. 2 (6 January 1950)

READERS' EVALUATION OF THE U.S. OVERT PUBLICATIONS

Sample: 3,000 residents of the American Zone, 500 in West Berlin, and 300 in Bremen; also a special sample of 78 subscribers to *Der Monat* in Bavarian cities and towns.
Interviewing dates: December 1949. (22 pp.)

Only 24 per cent of the adult population in AMZON read any magazines with national circulation. The proportionate share of this total going to each of the U.S. overt publications (*Amerikanische Rundschau, Der Monat, Heute,* and *Neue Auslese*) compared favorably with that obtained by other magazines of comparable standards. With the exception of *Heute,* all appealed to approximately the same kind of audience: upper income groups, the better educated, urban upper socioeconomic groups, and men. *Heute,* a more "popular" magazine, appealed to people with attributes of magazine readers in general. The high editorial standards of *Monat, Rundschau,* and *Neue Auslese,* much appreciated by their readers, also served to limit the number of potential readers. Among *Heute* readers, 34 per cent best liked its pictures or picture stories; 19 per cent mentioned articles and stories.

Report No. 3 (18 January 1950)

WEST GERMAN REPUBLIC VS. EAST GERMAN GOVERNMENT
Some Evaluations and Comparisons

Sample: representative random sample of unspecified numbers of residents in the American Zone, West Berlin, and Bremen.
Interviewing dates: November 1949. (16 pp.)

In September 1948, 62 per cent of the AMZON population approved of the formation of a West German government; by May 1949, the figure had risen to 71 per cent; two months later, in July, it had dropped to 67 per cent; but in November it had again risen, this time all the way to 78 per cent. Only about four out of ten (43%), however, expressed satisfaction with the accomplishments of the Bonn government up to that point. The better educated and better informed were more likely than others to be critical of the government's performance.

Even after the decision to make Bonn the capital of West Germany became final, only 9 per cent of the AMZON population was satisfied with this choice; 40 per cent would still have preferred Frankfurt. In West Berlin 80 per cent would have chosen the former capital city, their own.

A large proportion (42 per cent in AMZON, 48 per cent in West Berlin) felt that the Western Powers were exerting too much influence on the West German government. Only 15 per cent, however, would go so far as to contend that the new government was nothing more than a puppet of the Western Powers.

Regarding the East German government, in November 1949 only somewhat over half (58%) of the AMZON population knew that it existed; in West Berlin 88 per cent were aware of this fact. Three-fourths (76%) of the AMZON respondents who knew about the East German government and 88 per cent of the knowledgeable West Berliners considered it to be merely a puppet government; and 66 per cent felt it more dependent on the occupation powers than was the West German government. Only 10 per cent felt that the East German government was representative of the people living in its territory.

Opinion was fairly evenly divided on the question of whether the West German government should confine its relationship with the East German government to economic matters (39%) or whether the two governments should also try to come to some political agreements (37%).

Although 53 per cent of the AMZON population felt that the creation of an East German government would widen the split between the two halves of the country, 73 per cent of the population believed that Germany would be unified at some future date. AMZON Germans did not, however, want reunification at any price. Asked if they would prefer to unite Germany under the East German government or keep the existing situation with separate East and West German governments, 81 per cent replied that they preferred the status quo. Very few (11%) felt that communist influence would spread in West Germany because of the establishment of the East German government; 17 per cent felt that such influence would decrease; and 56 per cent thought that the situation would remain unchanged.

Report No. 4 (8 February 1950)

RIAS AND ITS LISTENERS IN WESTERN BERLIN

Sample: over 300 West Berliners.
Interviewing dates: December 1949. (5 pp.)

Almost three-quarters (72%) of the West Berlin population claimed to be regular or occasional radio listeners (up from

38 per cent in September 1947). Of these 76 per cent said that RIAS was their favorite station; 95 per cent felt that RIAS correctly portrayed political events in Berlin and only slightly fewer (93%) said the same of the world news reports.

Report No. 5 (20 February 1950)

WEST BERLINERS APPRAISE PRESENT ECONOMIC AND POLITICAL SITUATION

Sample: 300 West Berliners.
Interviewing dates: completed just before 25 December 1949.
(20 pp.)

Two-thirds (67%) of the West Berlin population said they were not able to meet all necessary expenses with their incomes (up from 56 per cent in April 1949). Three in ten of those interviewed said that someone in their family was looking for a job; the high level of unemployment was blamed on the general lack of money. Two-thirds (67%) were aware that Berlin was receiving Marshall Plan aid, and 23 per cent of these thought this would bring a great improvement; a further 22 per cent felt it would bring a satisfactory improvement.

Although the economic situation in Berlin at the time of the survey was critical, 80 per cent said they were better off than before the blockade was lifted and 93 per cent felt they would get through the coming winter better than they had the previous one. Only 13 per cent said they had expected progress in Berlin to be more rapid than it in fact was after the blockade was lifted.

In July 1948, shortly after the start of the blockade, West Berlin morale was very low, as indicated by the fact that 43 per cent of the population said they would leave the city if given a chance to do so; by October 1948 this figure had dropped to 30 per cent; but in January 1949 it had again risen, but only to 39 per cent. After the blockade, the percentage of those wanting to leave dropped again; by December 1949 the figure stood at 20 per cent.

Over half (53%) of the West Berliners said they thought there was less threat of a Soviet takeover than previously. The most frequently cited reason for this view was that, in the balance of power between East and West, the Western Powers were stronger.

American prestige in West Berlin was extraordinarily high: 99 per cent of those surveyed even felt that this prestige had grown during the previous year. Nonetheless, a third of the population felt that the Western Powers could do more than they already had done to relieve distressed conditions in Berlin.

Report No. 6 (6 March 1950)

THE GERMAN PUBLIC VIEWS THE CONDUCT OF THE U.S. OCCUPATION FORCES

Sample: 1,500 persons in the American Zone, 250 in West Berlin, and 160 in Bremen.
Interviewing dates: December 1949. (10 pp.)

Six in ten (59%) of the AMZON population and 53 per cent of the West Berliners interviewed said they did not see any American troops during the course of an average day. In addition, 68 per cent of those surveyed in AMZON and 72 per cent of the West Berliners said they had not become acquainted with an American since the end of the war. The proportion of Germans knowing Americans was naturally greater in the urban areas frequented by soldiers; the proportion knowing Americans rose with the education, income, and social status of the respondents.

Majorities in all areas surveyed described the conduct of American occupation troops as good, with an additional six per cent in AMZON saying they thought it was very good. Of those who saw more than ten soldiers a day, 11 per cent found their behavior to be bad or even very bad, but 66 per cent of this group felt it was good or very good. In addition, with the exception of Bavaria, majorities in AMZON and West Berlin felt that the soldiers' behavior had improved since the end of the war; and the trend was upward since the previous survey on this question conducted in 1948.

Half of the AMZON population approved of American soldiers patronizing German cafés, 39 per cent were indifferent, and only 9 per cent disapproved. Those with greater contact with Americans were less indifferent. Disapproval increased at a greater rate among these persons than approval. Most of those opposed to the presence of soldiers in German establishments, when asked why they did so, responded that it led to fights.

Report No. 7 (6 March 1950)

THE GERMAN PUBLIC VIEWS THE CARE ORGANIZATION

Sample: 1,500 people in the American Zone, 250 in West Berlin, and 160 in Bremen.
Interviewing dates: January 1950. (7 pp.)

An overwhelming majority (80%) of AMZON residents and almost all West Berliners (98%) and residents of Bremen (94%) had heard of CARE packages. And almost all of these also knew that the packages originated in the United States. Fewer, however, were aware that such packages were sent by private individuals;

in fact, more than two in ten thought they were sent by the organization itself. In AMZON, only 9 per cent of the respondents said that they themselves had received a CARE package; in West Berlin the figure was somewhat higher (11%) and in Bremen it was the highest (15%) of any American-occupied area. In all areas, over half the population neither had received one nor knew anyone who had. Among people who had heard of CARE, 76 per cent in AMZON had a good impression of the organization, 22 per cent had no opinion, and only 2 per cent said they had a bad impression.

Report No. 8 (17 March 1950)

REACTIONS TOWARD THE WÜRTTEMBERG-BADEN DENAZIFICATION AFFAIR

Sample: a quota sample of 368 persons from the six major cities of Württemberg-Baden: Stuttgart, Karlsruhe, Mannheim, Heidelberg, Ludwigsburg, and Esslingen.
Interviewing dates: first week in March 1950. (6 pp.)

In mid-January two high-level officials concerned with denazification were arrested and charged with accepting bribes in connection with denazification cases. A large majority (74%) of those surveyed had heard of the scandal; and, of these, 68 per cent also knew the names of the persons involved. During the year and a half that the new denazification program had been in existence, it had become an extremely controversial and troublesome issue; this was heightened by the fact that fully 53 per cent of the respondents felt the entire process was nothing more than a fraud and a money-making scheme. Only 29 per cent thought it had any real value. Furthermore, 68 per cent believed there were many similar but undisclosed cases throughout AMZON. Nonetheless, 65 per cent of the Württemberg-Baden population felt the basic idea of denazification was a good one; in all of AMZON the figure was 66 per cent. The problem, according to 66 per cent of the respondents, was the way in which it was being carried out.

Report No. 9 (17 March 1950)

GERMAN ATTITUDE TOWARD AN ARMY AND MILITARY TRAINING

Sample: 1,500 persons in the American Zone, 250 in West Berlin, and 150 in Bremen.
Interviewing dates: mid-December 1949. (11 pp.)

As indicated in a previous flash survey taken on 9 December 1949 in AMZON, West Berlin, and Bremen, a definite majority of the German population was opposed to the establishment of an army for West Germany. The full-scale survey conducted in mid-December showed that 62 per cent of the respondents opposed such an army, 26 per cent favored it, and 12 per cent had no opinion. Opposition cut across all population segments. Among those who did favor an army, the most frequently cited reason in AMZON was that military training instills discipline in the young and prevents loafing; in West Berlin, by contrast, almost half of those in favor of establishing an army mentioned the threat of communism and the Soviet Union. Not surprisingly, those opposed to an army said they were fed up with war and all things military.

In January 1950, asked whether or not they saw any desirable influences on the young through military training, 43 per cent of AMZON residents responded positively, 48 per cent negatively. In West Berlin, 52 per cent thought the influences were good, while only 41 per cent felt they were bad. Support for military training ran through all population groups.

Report No. 10 (30 March 1950)

GERMANS VIEW THE U.S. REORIENTATION PROGRAM

I. Extent of Receptivity to American Ideas

Sample: 1,500 persons in the American Zone, 250 in West Berlin, and 160 in Bremen.
Interviewing dates: January 1950. (15 pp.)

This report is the first in a series of three stemming from a single survey designed to assess German views on the American reorientation program.

In AMZON as a whole, only 57 per cent of the population felt the Germans might learn something from the Americans; the lowest percentage was in Hesse (54%), while the highest was in Württemberg-Baden (63%). In West Berlin, however, the figure was far higher (80%); at the same time only 6 per cent in West Berlin were undecided on this question, whereas fully 14 per cent thought there was only little to learn from the Americans. Conversely, 65 per cent of AMZON Germans thought there were some things that the Americans could learn from the Germans, 8 per cent felt there was little they could learn, and over a quarter (27%) were undecided. In West Berlin the percentages were again higher and the people less uncertain about their feelings: 79 per cent felt the Americans could learn something from the Germans, 13 per cent thought there was little to be learned, and only 8 per cent were undecided. Population breakdowns revealed that the amount of education was the most important factor in the level of responsiveness to American reorientation efforts.

The field in which the greatest percentage of Germans (29%)

felt they could learn a great deal from the Americans was that
of industry and technology; another 29 per cent felt they could
learn something, and 20 per cent nothing. The figures for the
field of agriculture were almost as high; and those for poli-
tics--so crucial from the Americans' point of view at that time--
was third: 28 per cent felt there was much to be learned, 24
per cent something, 15 per cent nothing, and fully one-third had
no opinion on the subject. At the other end of the scale, 50
per cent of the AMZON respondents said there was nothing to be
learned from America in the field of fine arts; 38 per cent, by
way of contrast, felt the Americans might learn a great deal
from the Germans in this field.

Report No. 11 (30 March 1950)

GERMANS VIEW THE U.S. REORIENTATION PROGRAM
II. Reactions to American Democratization Efforts

> *Sample:* 1,500 persons in the American Zone, 250 in West Berlin, and 160 in Bremen.
> *Interviewing dates:* January 1950. (13 pp.)

Awareness of a specific American program to democratize
the German people was not widespread in AMZON: Only 34 per cent
had heard of it (in West Berlin, 50 per cent). Six out of ten
AMZON Germans, but fully 74 per cent of the West Berlin respondents, welcomed American efforts in this direction. The population breakdown on the question revealed an interesting problem
for the American authorities. Among 15- to 19-year olds, a crucial age group from the American point of view, a greater percentage opposed (47%) than welcomed (38%) the democratization
efforts on the part of the Americans; those most in favor were
in the age category of 50 to 59 (64%).
   Almost half (45%) of the AMZON respondents and 74 per cent
of the West Berliners felt that American efforts to familiar-
ize Germans with democratic ideas would have a favorable effect
on the German way of life. Of the 16 per cent who did not expect to see much difference in Germany as a result of the democratization efforts, 7 per cent said that Germans do not want
to accept any advice, they are proud, and like to go their own
way. Unfortunately, from a pedagogical point of view, a definite majority (55%) in AMZON and even more in West Berlin (77%)
felt that the American authorities themselves did not follow
democratic principles; especially noteworthy is the fact that,
according to the population breakdowns on this question, both
the pro and the con opinions were higher among the more informed
groups. The program and the Americans trying to carry it out
were not, however, seen only in a negative light. In answer to
the question of whether the goal was truly the democratization
of Germany or merely its Americanization--bubble gum and jazz--

59 per cent of the AMZON respondents said they thought it was really an effort to teach democratic ideals, 10 per cent felt it amounted to Americanization, 9 per cent thought it was half and half, and 22 per cent had no opinion.

Report No. 12 (30 March 1950)

GERMANS VIEW THE U.S. REORIENTATION PROGRAM

III. Opinions on the Cultural Exchange Program

Sample: 1,500 persons in the American Zone, 250 in West Berlin, and 160 in Bremen.
Interviewing dates: January 1950. (6 pp.)

Four out of ten people in AMZON were aware of the German-American exchange program, with the greatest percentage of knowledgeable persons residing in Hesse (51%) and the smallest in Bavaria (35%). Those with twelve or more years of education were far more aware of it (89%) than were those with eight years or less (34%); the population group with the very least awareness was the age group from 15 to 19. Among all areas and all population groups, West Berliners displayed the greatest awareness of the exchange program (59%).

Reactions to the program were extremely favorable. Asked whether the experiences in America were useful to the exchangee only or also to Germany in general, 78 per cent of the AMZON residents and 92 per cent of the West Berliners said they thought they were beneficial to the nation. Similarly, only 10 per cent felt those who participated became too influenced by America; 55 per cent in AMZON and 74 per cent in West Berlin did not believe this to be the case.

Report No. 13 (1 April 1950)

IMPLICATIONS OF THE H-BOMB IN THE EAST-WEST STRUGGLE

Sample: 1,500 respondents in the American Zone, 250 in West Berlin, and 160 in Bremen.
Interviewing dates: last weeks in February 1950. (10 pp.)

The survey was conducted shortly after President Truman's announcement that the United States was about to embark on the construction of a hydrogen bomb. At this time the Germans were fairly pessimistic about the cold war. In fact, during the preceding year there had been a steady increase in the percentage of persons who said they anticipated another war within the next ten years. In April 1949, 42 per cent of the AMZON population thought there would be war and 46 per cent thought not; by July there were more pessimists (44%) than optimists (43%) on this question; and the trend continued until February 1950, when as many as 57 per cent thought there would be war and only 34 per cent thought not. Of those who expected war within ten years, 34 per cent believed Russia to be stronger than the United States and 45 per cent thought the United States to be stronger; among those who did not expect war, 18 per cent felt the Soviet Union was stronger, and 57 per cent felt the United States to be the stronger of the two.

Of the 76 per cent of AMZON residents who had heard of President Truman's announcement, 15 per cent believed the Soviet Union to be making such bombs already, 32 per cent felt they were in the process of developing one, 3 per cent did not feel they were working on it at all, and 26 per cent had no opinion. In the event that the United States should get ahead of the Soviet Union in the production of atomic weapons, only 11 per cent of AMZON residents thought the USSR would call off the arms race, while fully 80 per cent felt the USSR would double its efforts. West Berliners were of a somewhat different opinion: 28 per cent thought Russia would stop the arms race, whereas 68 per cent felt it would double its efforts.

Majorities in all areas felt that the United States was correct in deciding to go ahead with the H-bomb. In AMZON, 63 per cent thought it was right, a fourth thought it was not right, 19 per cent wrong, and only three per cent had no opinion on the subject. Even greater percentages felt the Americans were making the bomb for defensive rather than offensive purposes.

Opinion was almost evenly divided on the question of whether the West should use the H-bomb in the event of an ordinary attack or should wait until attacked with a weapon of similar power: 38 per cent felt it should be used immediately, 37 per cent felt the West ought to wait, 17 per cent thought it ought not to be used at all, and 8 per cent had no opinion.

Report No. 14 (4 April 1950)

READERSHIP OF *HEUTE* AND OTHER ILLUSTRATED PERIODICALS

Sample: 1,500 adults in the American Zone, 250 in West Berlin, and 160 in Bremen.
Interviewing dates: January 1950. (9 pp.)

About four in ten AMZON residents (41%) reported reading magazines; in West Berlin the percentage was a good deal higher (58%) and in Bremen even higher (59%). Among these magazine readers, majorities in all population groups were also readers of illustrated periodicals. Of the 170 different illustrated magazines mentioned by respondents, the most frequently mentioned was *Quick*, second was *Heute*.

Report No. 15 (24 April 1950)

THE GERMAN PUBLIC ASSAYS POLITICAL DEMOCRACY

Sample: 3,000 residents of the American Zone, 500 in West Berlin, and 250 in Bremen, using split ballots.
Interviewing dates: February 1950. (11 pp.)

A fairly large minority (33%) of AMZON Germans did not venture a definition of democracy. Of those who did give a definition, the statements tended to fall into two categories: those describing democracy in terms of "freedom, equality, justice," and those describing it as a people's government or popular representation. Although quite a few respondents (33%) had no opinion on the subject, 45 per cent of the population thought that a democracy would be the best form of government for a united Germany. Interestingly, even among those who could not define the term, 19 per cent preferred this form of government for their country; 68 per cent had no opinion on the matter.

Only in West Berlin did a majority (61%) consider the Bonn government a true democracy; in AMZON only 36 per cent held this belief. In AMZON there was also a rather large percentage (35%) with no opinion; the population breakdown revealed that this was due mainly to the fact that women had not made up their minds on this question.

A majority in all regions advocated a multi-party system for West Germany, although a minority (18%) in AMZON hoped for a single-party system. There was little inclination to return to the pre-1933 days when splinter parties were numerous.

Residents of all areas seemed certain that they did not wish to call the East German government a democracy. Most of them referred to it as despotism, a dictatorship, a tyranny, or merely communist.

Report No. 16 (28 April 1950)

REACTIONS AND RECOMMENDATIONS OF WEST BERLINERS IN FACE OF PROSPECTIVE WHITSUNTIDE MARCH

Sample: 500 West Berliners.
Interviewing dates: 5 to 15 April 1950. (26 pp.)

This survey was conducted just prior to the large-scale meeting of the Free German Youth (Freie Deutsche Jugend or FDJ), the East German national youth organization.

West Berliners expressed considerably more confidence in their city's economic prospects than in its political future. Seven in ten predicted that, in the next six months, economic conditions would improve, while less than four in ten expected the next six months to bring an improved political situation. Furthermore, only 30 per cent thought that Berlin would have a united city government in the near future; this was 20 per cent fewer than had held such an opinion one year earlier. Nonetheless, few West Berliners were inclined to leave the city: only 27 per cent said they would leave if given the chance to do so; in the previous winter the figure had been 20 per cent.

Over half (54%) of those interviewed thought there would be another world war within the next ten years. This is somewhat more than the 47 per cent who held such an opinion in November 1949 but is far lower than the 80 per cent who thought so during the third month of the Berlin blockade in September 1948. Starting in July 1948, West Berliners expressed the unwavering belief that the United States would remain in Berlin as long as they stayed in Germany: 70 per cent said they thought the United States would do so and expressed their belief with great conviction; an additional 22 per cent held the same view but seemed less sure.

One month before the announced FDJ Whitsuntide march, only three in ten knew that 500,000 young people were supposed to take part. Less than a quarter of the population (23%) said that their friends and acquaintances were very much concerned about the planned meeting; 41 per cent were not at all concerned.

Report No. 17 (30 April 1950)

ATTITUDES OF STUDENTS AT ERLANGEN AND MUNICH UNIVERSITIES

Sample: 300 students at Munich and 260 at Erlangen, interviewed in their homes.
Interviewing dates: February 1950. (24 pp.)

Interest in politics was higher among university students than among AMZON adults: 80 per cent in Munich and 82 per cent in Erlangen, as compared with only 35 per cent of AMZON adults, said they were interested in politics. There was also a marked generational difference on the question of which is more important, a government that guarantees civil liberties or one that offers economic security: 61 per cent of AMZON adults chose the latter, while 71 per cent of the Munich students and 65 per cent of the Erlangen students chose the former. Just under half the students, as well as AMZON adults, thought the Germans could govern themselves democratically; somewhat over half the students and only a third of the adults said they could not, however, and very few students but as many as 18 per cent of the adults expressed no opinion.

Opinion was almost evenly divided among students on the question of whether or not the Germans tend to be more militaristic than others. In personal terms, very few showed any military interest. Only four per cent in Munich and nine per cent in Erlangen said they would want to be soldiers if Germany ever had an army again.

A majority of students (51 per cent in Munich and 59 per cent in Erlangen) agreed with AMZON adults that National Socialism was a good idea badly carried out. It is worth noting that there was not much difference between the arguments given by those who thought it bad or merely badly carried out.

Unlike their elders in AMZON, a solid majority of the students expressed satisfaction with the accomplishments of the West German government. They were less satisfied with the Bavarian government: 49 per cent in Munich and as many as 65 per cent in Erlangen said they were dissatisfied.

A solid majority of the students (74 per cent in Munich and 76 per cent in Erlangen) as well as 73 per cent of the AMZON adults felt that Germany would be reunited some day; but most thought it would not be until after the occupation forces had left. Almost seven in eight viewed the East German government as a puppet of Soviet occupation authorities.

A somewhat cynical attitude on the part of students became apparent in the responses given to questions concerning the Marshall Plan. While two-thirds felt the purpose of the plan was to prevent the spread of communism, one-third cited America's need to dump surplus goods, and another third mentioned that the United States would need friends in case of war with the Soviet Union.

Students were more inclined than were AMZON adults to prefer German participation in a European federation to a strong independent Germany--88 per cent of the students at Munich and 80 per cent of those at Erlangen--while only 56 per cent of the adults in AMZON thought it would be better for Germany to join a federation of European states; at the same time 12 per cent of the students at Munich, 19 per cent of those at Erlangen, and 30 per cent of the AMZON respondents favored a strong, independent state.

Although approximately half of the students at Munich and Erlangen did not ever visit an Amerika Haus, a quarter at each went occasionally and 11 per cent at Munich and 14 per cent at Erlangen went frequently.

An overwhelming majority at both universities favored the work of their student governments, and about three-quarters opposed student fraternities.

Special Report No. 17-S (May 1950)

TRENDS IN GERMAN PUBLIC OPINION
1946 through 1949

Sample: up to 3,000 individuals in the American Zone between the ages of 15 and 79, as well as 500 cases in West Berlin and 300 in Bremen.

Interviewing dates: from October 1945 to December 1949, during which time 80 full-scale surveys were conducted and 206 reports based on these surveys were issued. (65 pp.)

This is the fourth annual report summarizing in graphic form some major trends of German opinion in the American occupied areas. It covers eight major issues: background attitudes, economic affairs, American aid, government, German unity, international affairs, expellees, and media. An appendix details sampling procedures.

The section on background attitudes indicates that the Germans consistently wished to "leave politics to others" and only somewhat less than half the population even thought they were capable of governing themselves democratically. The question of whether "National Socialism was a bad idea or good idea badly carried out" was one of the most frequently posed; the trends show an increase in the number of persons who felt it had been basically a good idea. However, it is important to note that both groups cited as Nazism's negative features the persecution of Jews and other minorities, aggressive war, genocide, etc. The view that some races are inferior decreased. Consistently, six in ten AMZON residents indicated that, if they had to make a choice, they would prefer a government offering economic security to one guaranteeing civil liberties.

Concerning economic matters, the optimism following the currency reform in June 1948 continued to characterize AMZON thinking. In contrast with the pre-currency reform period, prices--rather than shortages--had become the major source of concern. In 1948, 54 per cent claimed that their living conditions were worse than they had been one year earlier; by January 1949, 52 per cent said they were better off than during the previous year. The latter picture remained almost the same throughout the year.

Knowledge of the Marshall Plan, as well as approval of it, was always fairly high. By November 1949 the figure had risen to six in ten. In addition, an increasing number of persons felt that the United States was giving sufficient aid to Europe; while an even greater number knew that aid was being given but felt it was not enough, the percentage of those holding this belief had decreased. As to whether the United States had furthered or hindered the reconstruction of Germany, the trend was toward the former and away from the latter. The low point occurred in November 1947, when only 39 per cent said that such aid had furthered reconstruction; by November 1949, 68 per cent felt this way.

Satisfaction with the government in Bonn declined somewhat between October and November 1949; it is important to note, however, that it was not the percentage of those dissatisfied that rose during this period but rather the percentage of those withholding their opinion. Although a fairly large minority felt that the Western Powers exercised too much influence on the West German government, only about one-seventh of the population would go so far as to call it a mere puppet of the Western Powers; in contrast, three-quarters of the AMZON respondents felt that the East German government was a puppet state. On the local government level, increasing numbers of people believed that local officials were doing their jobs for the common good rather than for selfish reasons. Increasing percentages also felt they were doing their work either well or very well.

While a large majority consistently believed that Germany would someday be reunified, increasing percentages of respondents felt that it was more important to check the spread of communism than to reunify the country; by September 1949 seven in ten persons held this view.

Majorities approved the idea of a Western European Union whenever this issue was raised, but the trend was neither consistent nor upward. Opinion also fluctuated on whether or not such a union would decrease the chances of war. The Atlantic Pact, however, was accorded far greater approval. Two-thirds who knew of it thought it would decrease the chances of war, and about three-fourths felt that Germany should be a part of it. A large majority consistently felt that the United States would have the greatest influence on world affairs during the next ten years, but increasing percentages of respondents thought the United States and the Soviet Union would both exert such influence.

Overwhelming majorities consistently felt that the expellees had been unjustly driven from their homelands in the East. While increasing numbers of native Germans felt that the expellees would get along well in AMZON, the trend among expellees themselves was toward less satisfaction.

Between April 1947 and November 1949, about 75 per cent of the AMZON population consistently claimed to read newspapers regularly or occasionally. The proportion of radio listeners among AMZON respondents increased slightly and stood at 63 per cent in November 1949. The magazine audience grew steadily, rising more sharply in 1949. Finally, the percentage of persons saying that the press was more trustworthy than it had been prior to 1945 rose from below 50 per cent to somewhat above half in the period between January 1948 and November 1949.

Report No. 18 (19 May 1950)

WEST GERMANS VIEW THE EAST-WEST STRUGGLE
I. General Evaluations and Extent of Allegiance to the West

Sample: 1,500 persons in the American Zone, 250 in West Berlin, and 160 in Bremen.
Interviewing dates: April 1950. (26 pp.)

This report is the first of three dealing with German

attitudes toward problems existing between the Eastern and Western worlds. Although the majority of AMZON residents (54%) said they preferred to side with the West in the cold war at that particular time, as many as four out of ten preferred neutrality. If there should be a war between the two major powers, however, only 14 per cent felt it would be possible for Germany to remain neutral. In fact, 86 per cent thought that most Germans would side with the West against the Soviet Union. Interestingly enough, the percentage of persons feeling that such a war might indeed break out within the next ten years had increased sharply during the preceding several months. In November 1949, 47 per cent foresaw war, by February 1950 the proportion had risen to 57 per cent, and in April 65 per cent held this opinion.

Asked which had had more success during the previous six months, the communists or the Western Powers, not quite a third (31%) said the communists, and 43 per cent said the West. Those mentioning the former cited the communist takeover in China; those mentioning the West most frequently cited economic gains. A solid majority (57%) nonetheless felt that, all things considered, the Western Powers appeared stronger than the communists. An even greater majority (69%) thought the West would ultimately win the East-West struggle; in West Berlin the figure was as high as 81 per cent.

As for communist strength within West Germany itself, only one per cent felt it was very great, a quarter thought it was moderately strong, 47 per cent said it had little strength, and 14 per cent very little. Majorities ranging from 62 per cent in AMZON to 72 per cent in Bremen and 88 per cent in West Berlin said that the Communist party in Germany was strongly under the influence of the Soviet Union; almost as many also felt that the party worked for the good of the Soviet Union rather than for Germany.

Report No. 19 (22 May 1950)

WEST GERMANS VIEW THE EAST-WEST STRUGGLE
II. Trends and Current Attitudes on Withdrawal of the Occupying Powers

Sample: 1,500 persons in the American Zone, 250 in West Berlin, and 160 in Bremen.
Interviewing dates: April 1950. (10 pp.)

Somewhat over three-quarters (76%) of the AMZON population and as many as 86 per cent of the West Berliners felt it would be unwise for the Western Powers to agree to the Soviet proposal calling for the withdrawal of all occupying forces from Germany. These results fit into the trend established by responses to a similar question posed between 1948 and 1949. Asked whether or not they would like to see the Soviet proposal carried out, 57 per cent said no in November 1948; by June of 1949 the percentage of those opposed to the Soviet suggestion had dropped sharply, to 46 per cent; but by September it had risen again to 50 per cent; and by November 1949 the figure had surpassed the original point, standing at 58 per cent. Population breakdowns revealed that those between the ages of 15 and 24 were more likely than their elders to consider withdrawal wise.

Confidence that the Americans would in fact remain as long as necessary for the security of West Germany was widespread. In AMZON 75 per cent were of this opinion, while in West Berlin an overwhelming 94 per cent thought so.

Report No. 20 (25 May 1950)

WEST GERMANS VIEW THE EAST-WEST STRUGGLE
III. Defense of Western Germany

Sample: 1,500 persons in the American Zone, 250 in West Berlin, and 160 in Bremen.
Interviewing dates: April 1950. (21 pp.)

A solid majority (69%) of AMZON residents believed that the Western Powers would try to defend Germany in case there were a war. Only about a quarter (27%), however, thought they would be able to do so without German help. The sort of German help needed was a subject of greater dispute. Of the 39 per cent of AMZON residents favoring the establishment of a West German army, 15 per cent felt it ought to be independent, while 21 per cent thought it should be part of the forces of the Western Powers. Among those opposed to the army, 36 per cent were unequivocally opposed and could conceive of no situation in which they would change their minds.

Awareness of the Atlantic Pact grew very slightly between April 1949 and April 1950, standing at the 63 per cent level at the latter date. Among those who had heard of NATO, almost three-quarters (72%) indicated that they thought Germany should join, while somewhat fewer (66%) felt that Germany ought to participate in a general army for the defense of Western Europe. Population breakdowns revealed the interesting fact that a solid majority (58%) of AMZON men--and they were the ones most concerned with this matter--favored participation in an Atlantic Pact army.

Concerning military forces in the Eastern portion of Germany, 60 per cent of those questioned felt that such forces were being established. Of these, 12 per cent felt that the forces would represent a very great danger for West Germany; 13 per cent termed them a great danger; and another 11 per cent thought they meant some danger.

Report No. 21 (31 May 1950)

VIEWS OF THE GERMAN PUBLIC IN THE U.S. ZONE ON CHANCELLOR ADENAUER'S PROPOSAL OF A FRANCO-GERMAN UNION

Sample: 1,500 persons in the American Zone, 250 in West Berlin, and 160 in Bremen.
Interviewing dates: during last two weeks of April 1950. (6 pp.)

More than a month after Chancellor Konrad Adenauer's 7 March proposal for a union between West Germany and France, slightly over half (51%) of the AMZON residents questioned on this matter had not heard of the suggestion. Of the 8 per cent who had heard of the proposal but were not in favor of it, 2 per cent based their opposition on the traditional enmity between France and Germany; another 2 per cent preferred a union of all European states, not just these two. Throughout the areas covered by the survey, a solid majority (62 per cent in AMZON) favored the idea of a Western European Union. Almost no one opposed it, but large minorities (34 per cent in AMZON) had not made up their minds on the subject or had no opinion. Large majorities (75 per cent in AMZON and as many as 88 per cent in West Berlin) would also have welcomed West German participation in such a West European federation.

Report No. 22 (5 June 1950)

THE PROBLEM OF UNEMPLOYMENT IN WESTERN GERMANY
I. German Appraisal of its Causes and Consequences

Sample: 3,000 persons in the American Zone, 500 in West Berlin, and 320 in Bremen.
Interviewing dates: February and April 1950. (18 pp.)

Over half of the residents of AMZON (52%), West Berlin (62%), and Bremen (56%) mentioned unemployment as the greatest problem facing the West German government. In AMZON the most frequently mentioned reasons for this unemployment were overpopulation and the loss of territories; in West Berlin more people placed first the lack of money and the government's financial policy. Asked who was mainly responsible for the situation, 29 per cent in AMZON blamed the Western Powers. Most people, however, felt that the solution to the problem rested with the German government: in AMZON, 54 per cent felt that Bonn could do more than it had theretofore done to alleviate unemployment. Those who said the government could do more tended to come from higher rather than lower income groups, to be university trained, men, and SPD adherents. The Social Democratic party was generally regarded as the political party doing most to solve the unemployment problem, although large proportions had no opinion on the subject.

Large numbers of AMZON Germans (47%) felt that, if the country remained split, the unemployment problem could not be solved. An even greater bar to a solution of the problem was seen in the presence of the expellees. In West Berlin just over half (54%) said that unemployment would remain a problem as long as the expellees were in West Germany; in AMZON as a whole, 64 per cent were of this opinion.

A large proportion of the population was aware of the measures undertaken by Hitler to get rid of unemployment. Two-thirds (66%) of the AMZON respondents and as many as 78 per cent of those in West Berlin said that he had done it by building a war machine. A solid majority (54%) in AMZON and even more (71%) in West Berlin were opposed to taking similar steps to solve the current situation. It should be mentioned that those who did favor adopting some of the measures undertaken by the National Socialists did not have the more reprehensible Nazi policies in mind. The measures most frequently mentioned were labor service for young men and the improvement and extension of traffic facilities.

In AMZON just over half (51%) felt the population would move toward communism if the unemployment problem were not solved, and another 20 per cent felt the population would tend toward National Socialism; 16 per cent thought the problem would have no such influence; and 13 per cent had no opinion.

Report No. 23 (5 June 1950)

THE PROBLEM OF UNEMPLOYMENT IN WESTERN GERMANY

II. Comparative Views of the Bavarian Unemployed and the Bavarian and U.S. Zone Public

Sample: in Bavaria the sample consisted of 544 persons whose names had been drawn from the unemployment lists in the Bavarian Labor Office; the comparison sample was based on 1,500 persons from Bavaria and 3,000 in the American Zone.

Interviewing dates: the survey in Bavaria was conducted in April 1950; the comparison study had been done in February 1950. (20 pp.)

Unemployment was clearly the most pressing problem facing the Bonn government according to the German population. Among the unemployed in Bavaria, 81 per cent held this opinion, while 52 per cent of the AMZON population in general did so. Most of the unemployed (73%) saw the major cause of the unemployment in the overpopulation of West Germany due to the influx of refugees. Also, more people blamed the Western Powers for the situation than the German authorities; among the unemployed of Bavaria, 50 per cent cited the former, whereas only 23 per cent mentioned their own government.

Asked who bore the main responsibility for solving the unemployment problem, a plurality of both employed and unemployed felt it was up to the German federal government.

Special Report No. 23-S (14 June 1950)

REACTIONS OF A MUNICH MOVIE AUDIENCE TO AN ANIMATED FILM BASED ON THE *RACES OF MANKIND*

Sample: respondents consisted of 278 persons who filled out a questionnaire (500 copies had been handed out) during a regular performance of the film.
Interviewing dates: 20 May 1950. (7 pp.)

The animated film *Races of Mankind* was based on a book of the same title by Ruth Benedict and Gene Weltfish. In the spring of 1950 a survey was conducted during a regular evening performance of the film to ascertain the public's reaction to it.

Almost all (93%) of the respondents said they liked the film, and a large majority (88%) said they had seen other such films. Of the 16 per cent who said they did not like it, the largest number (3%) found it artistically inferior or felt that the theme did not lend itself to animation. One-fourth of the respondents explained the theme as understanding among people; another 16 per cent mentioned unity and brotherhood. A solid majority (81%) felt the basic idea was well expressed, and 71 per cent claimed to be in complete agreement with the film's interpretation of the idea.

Report No. 24 (30 June 1950)

GERMAN YOUTH IN FIVE CITIES GIVE THEIR IMPRESSION OF THE SUPPLEMENT *JUGEND IN DER FREIEN WELT*

Sample: 357 young people, ranging in age from 15 to 25 years, in the four major U.S. Zone cities of Frankfurt, Nuremberg, Munich, and Stuttgart, as well as 142 young people in West Berlin.
Interviewing dates: first week in June 1950. (30 pp.)

The survey concerned a magazine entitled *Jugend in der*

Freien Welt (Youth in the Free World), published by the Information Services Division, Office of Public Affairs, HICOG. A few days after having received the magazine from the interviewer, nine in ten respondents had read all or part of it. About a quarter of those in West Berlin, but only five per cent of those in AMZON, had seen it previously.

A solid majority liked the cover, which showed a handsome young worker at a lathe. The cover story, about the refugee Fritz Scholz, was the best liked both in West Berlin (44%) and in the AMZON cities (32%). Among the 81 per cent who had read the story, however, predominant opinion was that Scholz had been extremely lucky to get the job he wanted, with a chance for advancement and an education. Far fewer felt that most Germans could do the same. The story entitled "Worauf es ankommt" ("What's Important") was second most well liked, primarily because it showed the problems and opportunities of other young people throughout the world.

Report No. 25 (6 July 1950)

POST MORTEM ON THE WHITSUNTIDE MARCH
A Survey of West Berliners' Evaluations

Sample: 300 West Berliners.
Interviewing dates: 8 to 12 June 1950. (22 pp.)

The survey dealt with West Berlin reactions to the rally held in East Berlin by the Free German Youth (Freie Deutsche Jugend, or FDJ), the East German national youth organization, during the last week of May 1950 (see Report No. II/16).

Very few West Berliners were either curious, interested, or concerned enough to attend any part of the march. Most (59%) stayed at home. Even more (83%) felt that the FDJ members themselves had not attended out of personal conviction but rather as a result of coercion or for adventure. Of the 68 per cent who said they had spoken to or seen some of the FDJ members, 19 per cent said they made a good impression, 16 per cent mentioned how pleased and surprised the young men had seemed at the living conditions in the West, and 10 per cent felt they looked scared and intimidated. A solid majority (80%) expressed opposition to a centralized state youth organization for the West.

Report No. 26 (26 July 1950)

TRENDS AND CURRENT ATTITUDES REGARDING THE "VOICE OF AMERICA" BROADCASTS

Sample: 3,000 persons in the American Zone, 500 in West Berlin, and 300 in Bremen.

Interviewing dates: May 1950. (12 pp.)

At the time of the survey, 36 per cent of the total AMZON population regarded themselves as "Voice of America" listeners. In Berlin, however, over half (55%) of the population claimed to be regular or occasional listeners, a jump of 17 per cent since the previous survey one year earlier, in June 1949. VOA listeners, among the more informed groups in the population, by and large rated the programs as good.

Report No. 27 (27 July 1950)

TREND IN GERMAN OPINIONS ON SOCIALIZATION OF INDUSTRY

Sample: in the earlier survey the sample comprised approximately 3,000 persons in the American Zone and 500 in West Berlin; the latter survey contained 1,500 respondents in the American Zone, 250 in West Berlin, and 160 in Bremen.
Interviewing dates: November 1947 and May 1950. (8 pp.)

In November 1947, 30 per cent of AMZON residents felt that the workers would be better off if industry were socialized, while 41 per cent thought they would not be. Two and a half years later, in May 1950, only 23 per cent still felt the workers would be better off, while over a majority (54%) had come to the conclusion that they would not. Among the workers themselves, the shift in opinion was even more pronounced. Whereas, in November 1947, 41 per cent thought they would be better off and the same percentage thought they would not, by May 1950 only 29 per cent felt they would be better off and fully 58 per cent thought not. In West Berlin the figures were still more striking. While 36 per cent of the workers felt, in November 1947, that they would be better off with the socialization of industry, by May 1950 almost three-quarters (72%) disagreed.

Since the Social Democratic party (SPD) at that time formally espoused the socialization of industry, it is interesting to note that even among SPD party members the percentage of those favoring socialization decreased between November 1947 and May 1950. At the earlier date, 17 per cent approved the socialization of all industry; by the later date, only 14 per cent still approved this move. The percentage of those approving socialization of heavy industry alone dropped even more sharply, from 50 per cent to 38 per cent. At the same time, the percentage of those saying that neither move should be undertaken rose from 18 per cent to almost a third (32%) of the party membership.

Report No. 28 (31 July 1950)

TRENDS IN OPINIONS ON THE WEST GERMAN FEDERAL REPUBLIC

Sample: for the two questionnaires used in the last survey discussed in this trend report, there were 3,000 respondents in the American Zone, 500 in West Berlin, and 300 in Bremen.
Interviewing dates: May 1950; comparisons are made with two earlier surveys conducted in November and December 1949. (14 pp.)

The percentage of persons satisfied with the activities of the West German government increased between November 1949 and May 1950, although neither steadily nor equally in all areas.

Majorities of 52 per cent in AMZON and 71 per cent in West Berlin felt that the Bonn government was keeping the public welfare uppermost in mind rather than merely following its party line. However, as many as a third (32%) in AMZON felt that party considerations did indeed come first; those most likely to have this opinion were men, those with middle-level education, and those with no party affiliation.

Increasing percentages of people had become aware of the fact that Konrad Adenauer was chancellor of the Federal Republic. In AMZON in November 1949, 44 per cent knew this to be true; but by May of the following year 62 per cent knew it. A majority of respondents said they were satisfied with the way Chancellor Adenauer had conducted the affairs of state up to that point. According to this survey, satisfaction with Adenauer's accomplishments was the predominant opinion among all population groups, including SPD members (59%), Protestants (60%), the well-educated (80%) as well as the little-educated (60%), and those who thought that the establishment of a West German government had widened the split between the East and West (63%). On this question of the split between East and West, West Germans had been fairly pessimistic before the establishment of the Bonn government. In September 1948, as many as 51 per cent thought it would widen the split. Shortly after its establishment, however, less than a fourth (23%) thought the split had in fact widened, 51 per cent felt the new government had not affected the situation, and 25 per cent had no opinion on the subject.

Although predominant opinion between November 1949 and May 1950 was that the Western Powers exerted too great an influence on the Bonn government, increasing percentages (28 per cent in November, 34 per cent in May) felt that their government was independent enough. Even among those who thought the influence too great, only 12 per cent termed the West German government a puppet government, 30 per cent said it was not, and

2 per cent had no opinion. In contrast, large majorities consistently thought the East German government a puppet state.

Special Report No. 28-S (31 July 1950)

RUMORS IN WEST GERMANY FOLLOWING THE KOREAN OUTBREAK

Sample: 300 urban dwellers in the American Zone, 100 in West Berlin, and 100 in Bremen.
Interviewing dates: 21 July 1950. (8 pp., plus a 4-page appendix.)

The report consists of two lists of topics, and their variations, in order of the frequency with which each type of rumor was mentioned. The first list is for AMZON, the second for West Berlin.

The largest single topic of rumor dealt with food: shortages, hoarding, and renewal of rationing. It is important to note, however, that rumors concerning food constituted only a small fraction of the total number of rumors circulating at that time. Rumors dealing with political and military matters made up the great bulk of all rumors.

An appendix (dated 3 August 1950) presents a further breakdown of rumors about Americans and employees of Americans, general war rumors and prophecies, rumors about German volunteers for Korea, food rumors, and miscellaneous rumors.

Report No. 29 (4 August 1950)

GERMAN REACTIONS TO THE AMERICAN-SPONSORED NEWSREEL *WELT IM FILM*

Sample: 3,000 residents of the American Zone, 500 from West Berlin, and 300 from Bremen.
Interviewing dates: May 1950. (5 pp.)

The survey was conducted among persons who said they went to the movies more or less frequently. *Welt im Film* (*World in Film*) was produced by the Motion Picture Branch, ISD, Office of Public Affairs, HICOG. At one time its showing was compulsory. A large majority of AMZON filmgoers (77%) reported seeing the newsreel every time they went to the movies; an additional 17 per cent said they saw it sometimes. Of those who had seen it, almost all thought it was good or fair.

Report No. 30 (8 August 1950)

HAVE THE WESTERN OCCUPYING POWERS FURTHERED OR HINDERED GERMAN RECONSTRUCTION?

Sample: 1,500 persons in the American Zone, 250 in West Berlin, and 160 in Bremen.
Interviewing dates: May 1950. (12 pp.)

Starting out from a low point of 39 per cent in November 1947, increasing percentages of AMZON Germans indicated their belief that the United States had furthered the reconstruction of Germany. By May 1950 the figure had risen to 68 per cent. The percentage of those thinking that the Americans had hindered such reconstruction remained a constant 9 per cent from September 1949 to May 1950. In contrast, between September 1949 and May 1950, the percentage of persons who said that the British had furthered reconstruction rose only from 6 to 10 per cent, while those feeling that they had hindered it also rose, from 32 to 37 per cent. The French fared even worse. The percentage of respondents saying that the French had furthered reconstruction rose from 3 to only 4 per cent, while those saying they had hindered it rose from 31 to 37 per cent. Group breakdowns of attitudes toward American reconstruction efforts showed that the increase in favorable attitudes was prevalent in all the groups examined rather than being confined to any particular segments of the population.

In all areas, the most frequently cited reason for saying that the Americans had furthered reconstruction was that they had provided economic assistance; the most frequently mentioned reason for the opposite view was that the Americans had dismantled industries. Similar reasons were given for either approving or disapproving the British and French actions. Some respondents were extremely harsh in their judgment of France: "They have been robbing and stealing here all the time;" "By taking the Saar territory from us which is an essential part of our economy;" "They have sucked out of Germany everything they could strip us of."

Report No. 31 (8 August 1950)

TRENDS IN AWARENESS AND PATRONAGE OF THE U.S. INFORMATION CENTERS IN THE U.S. ZONE, WEST BERLIN, AND BREMEN

Sample: 3,000 persons in the American Zone, 500 in West Berlin, 316 in Bremen.
Interviewing dates: May 1950. (8 pp.)

Majorities ranging from 62 per cent in AMZON as a whole to 63 per cent in West Berlin and 74 per cent in Bremen were aware of the existence of Amerika Häuser (United States Information Centers) in the larger German cities. Among the respondents in this knowledgeable group, almost half (45%) knew they had libraries, 34 per cent knew that lectures and discussion sessions were held there, and almost one-fourth (24%) had heard that they showed films and plays. Despite this awareness, however, only 7 per cent claimed to have been inside an Amerika Haus.

Report No. 32 (14 August 1950)

GERMANS VIEW THE KOREAN OUTBREAK
I. Urban Trends in U.S. Occupied Areas

Sample: in each of four flash surveys there were 300 respondents in American Zone cities of 25,000 population or more and 100 persons in West Berlin and Bremen.
Interviewing dates: 7 July, 21 July, 28 July, and 7 August 1950. (15 pp.)

During the period under consideration in these surveys, German newspaper reports of the Korean situation reflected fluctuations between optimism and pessimism as the Americans continued to send reinforcements and the North Koreans steadily advanced southward.

The overwhelming majority of urban AMZON Germans felt that the North Koreans were definitely the aggressors in this conflict. Less than 5 per cent thought the aggression justified. However, well over half believed that the attack had actually been instigated by the Soviets.

Twelve days after the attack, practically everyone (93 per cent in AMZON and 97 per cent in Bremen) knew that America had intervened. Over half of the AMZON respondents (56%) said they had expected America's reaction; in AMZON 72 per cent and in West Berlin as many as 90 per cent also said they approved of the measures taken. In addition, solid majorities were aware that the United Nations supported the American move. By the end of the first week in August, however, only 48 per cent in AMZON and 58 per cent in West Berlin knew that other countries were helping the United States militarily. Throughout the last three surveys, majority opinion in AMZON and West Berlin held firm that no offers to negotiate should be made before the North Koreans had withdrawn from the South.

80/Public Opinion in Semisovereign Germany

In addition to the fact that the number of persons anticipating another world war within the next decade had increased from 55 per cent in September 1949 to 69 per cent in early July 1950, the Korean situation seems to have made many people a little less certain that the United States was doing all it could to prepare for all future international developments. Only in Berlin was confidence consistently high; on 28 July in AMZON, only 68 per cent and in Bremen as few as 36 per cent felt that America was doing all it could. On 7 August, of the 59 per cent who said that the Western Powers were doing everything they should for the security of Germany, 23 per cent thought they should send more occupation troops, and as many as 15 per cent urged the establishment of a West German army.

Report No. 33 (23 August 1950)

GERMANS VIEW THE KOREAN OUTBREAK
II. Urban Opinions in Western Germany

Sample: 640 persons in West German cities with populations of 50,000 or more, as well as 200 persons from West Berlin.
Interviewing dates: 15 to 17 August 1950 in West Germany; 15 to 18 August 1950 in West Berlin. (13 pp.)

This is the first survey based on an urban sample from West Germany as a whole, that is, including the French and British zones as well as the American.

By the middle of August the number of AMZON Germans who thought the West ought to accept any offer to negotiate even before the North Koreans withdrew had risen to 35 per cent from 30 per cent on 21 July. For all of West Germany the figure was only slightly higher (36%). Hopes for negotiations did not, however, indicate pessimism regarding the American effort in Korea: only 18 per cent of the respondents in all of West Germany had no confidence whatever that the Americans would succeed in driving the North Koreans out of South Korea.

The effect of the events in Korea on West German opinion toward the German situation was not entirely clear by mid-August. Solid majorities continued to be certain that the United States would take a firm stand in case of communist aggression in Western Europe. But on the question of whether or not the Western Powers were doing all they could for the security of Germany, there were great variations over time and from one region to another. In one area of concern the Korean conflict did seem to have a definite effect: Should there be a West German army? In mid-August, 39 per cent of all West Germans favored the establishment of an army; in AMZON the percentage had risen from 25 per cent in December 1949 to 48 per cent in August 1950, while in Berlin the rise was even more remarkable, from 48 to 69 per cent. Still more people approved an army if it were part of a general European force: the lowest percentage (59%) in favor was in the British Zone, the highest (86%) in West Berlin. Nonetheless, West German urban dwellers were divided on the question of what their country should do in case of war. In West Germany as a whole, 48 per cent favored siding with the West, 47 per cent preferred neutrality; in AMZON the figures were the same. But in West Berlin as many as 71 per cent would have sided with the West, while only 28 per cent favored keeping out. Even among those who wished to remain neutral, however, very few saw this as a real possibility.

Report No. 34 (28 August 1950)

A SUMMARY OF TRENDS IN RADIO LISTENING IN WEST BERLIN

Sample: most of the surveys included here used 500 people, but in some instances 250 persons were interviewed.
Interviewing dates: January 1948 through May 1950. (5 pp.)

The number of radio listeners in West Berlin rose, although not steadily, from 69 per cent in January 1948 to 75 per cent in May 1950. Throughout this period, RIAS (Radio in the American Sector) was the most popular station; in fact, of the radio listening audience, 98 per cent said they listened to this station. During the same period, Radio Berlin, the Soviet-controlled station, lost about two-thirds of its audience, so that in May 1950 only about 15 per cent of the total West Berlin population (or 20 per cent of the radio audience) said they were listeners.

Special Report No. 34-S (29 August 1950)

FURTHER STUDY OF POST-KOREAN RUMORS IN GERMANY

Sample: 184 East Berliners and East Zone residents interviewed at currency exchange offices in West Berlin, 416 British Zone residents, 182 AMZON residents, 200 West Berliners.
Interviewing dates: East German interviews were conducted on 16 to 21 August 1950, while those in West Germany and West Berlin took place as part of a flash survey on 15 to 17 August 1950. (8 pp.)

Like Report No. 28-S, this report consists of lists of rumors. In East Germany the most frequently heard rumors concerned Russian troop concentrations in the GDR and other preparations for war. Rumors about food were in fifth place. In the British Zone the most frequently heard rumors dealt with remilitarization in West Germany. Food rumors were in third place. In AMZON, war between East and West was in first place, followed by food rationing. In West Berlin, war between East and West was followed by concern over the possibility of a Soviet attack; rumors about food were in third place.

Report No. 35 (8 September 1950)

OBSERVERS EVALUATE EFFECTIVENESS OF COMMUNIST PRESS IN WEST GERMANY

Sample: unspecified number of American Kreis Resident Officers and German interviewers employed by the Reactions Analysis Staff.
Interviewing dates: July 1950. (21 pp.)

Asked how many Germans in their area read communist newspapers, 88 per cent of the Resident Officers and 89 per cent of the German interviewers estimated that few or very few did so. However, 14 per cent of the former and 9 per cent of the latter felt that the communist press had a considerable effect in shaking West German confidence in Western policies and actions. Large majorities (83%) in both groups felt that the communist newspapers should not be suppressed in West Germany. The two most frequently given reasons for this opinion were that the newspapers would be published underground anyway and that such a ban would be against democratic principles.

Report No. 36 (15 September 1950)

THE QUESTION OF REMILITARIZATION IN WESTERN GERMANY

Sample: 1,500 persons in the American Zone, 300 in West Berlin, and 200 in Bremen.
Interviewing dates: 8 August to 8 September 1950. (12 pp.)

Majority opinion in the American-occupied areas of Germany was in favor of the idea of West German remilitarization, but only within the context of a West European force.
A solid majority (63%) of AMZON Germans and 58 per cent of the West Berlin population expressed the opinion that West Germany could not be defended without German help. Approval of the formation of a West German army--without specifying it as either an independent army or one integrated into a general European force--rose markedly between November 1949 and August 1950. In AMZON, in November 1949, 26 per cent approved the creation of an army; by April 1950 the figure had risen to 39 per cent, and by August it had reached 43 per cent. In West Berlin, the earliest figure was 48 per cent, and by August 1950 it had risen as high as 73 per cent. Population breakdowns on this question revealed that the only group in which approval of an army decreased

between May and August 1950 was among the 15- to 24-year olds; the group displaying the largest increase in approval comprised SPD adherents. Among the 43 per cent in AMZON in August 1950 who approved the formation of a German army, 24 per cent felt it should be part of the forces of the Western Powers, while 13 per cent were in favor of an independent army. When asked a more specific question about German participation in a general European army within the framework of the Atlantic Pact, a clear majority (63%) in AMZON and an overwhelming 90 per cent in West Berlin voiced approval. Population breakdowns revealed that, in all subgroups, approval of an Atlantic Pact army far outweighed disapproval.

Report No. 37 (28 September 1950)

GERMANS VIEW THE KOREAN OUTBREAK
III. Overall Opinions and Group Differences in the U.S. Occupied Areas

Sample: 1,500 persons in the American Zone, 300 in West Berlin, and 200 in Bremen.
Interviewing dates: 8 August to 8 September 1950. (28 pp.)

Despite heavy communist propaganda to the contrary, the majority (63%) of AMZON Germans had little doubt that the North Koreans had attacked first. Almost all of these (57%) also thought that the North Koreans had not acted on their own, but that the attack had been instigated by the Soviet Union. Preponderant opinion in all American occupied areas (42 per cent in AMZON) was that the communists were more interested in testing the power of the West than in starting another world war. In AMZON 28 per cent felt that the communists did want to start another war, 7 per cent thought the reason was neither one nor the other, and fully 23 per cent had no opinion. In West Berlin far fewer (3 per cent) were without an opinion on this subject, 34 per cent thought the communists wanted to start another world war, over half (55%) thought it was only a test of Western strength, while only 8 per cent felt it was neither one nor the other. Population breakdowns revealed that those who said the communists were not intent upon starting another world war were likely to come from the usually more critical and educated groups.

With regard to the more general question of another world war within the next decade, majorities in AMZON (57%) and West Berlin (68%) were pessimistic. The population breakdowns also revealed that this pessimism was the majority view in all groups examined. Opinions were nonetheless split as to whether the danger of a conflict such as the one in Korea occurring in Germany was relatively great or relatively small.

In AMZON as a whole, 51 per cent of the population was confident that within a reasonable length of time the Americans and the United Nations would succeed in driving the North Koreans out of South Korea; 22 per cent were less confident, 9 per cent were not confident at all, and 18 per cent had no opinion. The main reason given by confident respondents centered on American material and military superiority.

West German confidence in America in the event of communist aggression in Europe was fairly high (74%); in West Berlin it was even higher (92%). A solid majority (62%) in AMZON felt that the Western Powers were doing everything they should to insure the security of West Germany. It should be pointed out, however, that a sizable minority (25%) felt this was not the case; moreover, the population breakdowns revealed that this minority tended to come from the more critical and informed elements of society. While increasing numbers of AMZON Germans expressed a preference for remaining neutral in the East-West struggle, a substantial proportion of these respondents did not think it was a real alternative.

Report No. 38 (9 October 1950)

GERMAN YOUTH VIEW THE AMERICAN PROGRAM
I. Some General Evaluations

Sample: 1,750 young people (ranging in age from 15 to 25) and 1,250 adults from the American Zone, 275 young people and 225 adults from West Berlin, and 200 young people and 175 adults from Bremen.
Interviewing dates: July 1950. (22 pp.)

Majorities of young people (64%) as well as adults (57%) in AMZON felt that unemployment and the lack of vocational training opportunities were the greatest problems facing West German youth. Opinions were fairly evenly divided among young people and adults on the question of whether or not everything possible was being done for West German youth. Population breakdowns revealed, however, that teenagers between 15 and 19 years of age were more satisfied (46%) than were those ranging in age from 20 to 25 (37%). In addition, the breakdowns showed that the typically more critical and informed elements among the young tended to be less satisfied. Among those who felt that more ought to be done and also had specific suggestions on the subject, the more frequently mentioned suggestions dealt with provisions for work and vocational training opportunities.

While only 4 per cent of the AMZON youth questioned could name any measures or institutions in East Germany that they felt the West should adopt, 32 per cent could name some from the Third Reich. The Nazi youth measures most frequently mentioned were the various labor service plans; the Hitler Youth was also mentioned fairly frequently.

Fully 60 per cent of the young people questioned in AMZON and 62 per cent of those in West Berlin said they would be in favor of the establishment of a single youth organization in West Germany.

Report No. 39 (12 October 1950)

THE EFFECTIVENESS OF THE ERP INFORMATION PROGRAM IN WESTERN GERMANY

Sample: 1,500 persons in the American Zone, 287 in West Berlin, and 206 in Bremen.
Interviewing dates: August 1950. (25 pp.)

In August 1950, three-fourths of the residents of AMZON and almost everyone in West Berlin (95%) and Bremen (97%) claimed that they had heard or read something about the European Recovery Program (ERP) or, as it is more frequently called, Marshall Plan. While this did represent an increase from the earliest figure of 68 per cent found in February 1948, there had been no real increase--only strong fluctuations--since September 1948. In addition, when the more difficult question was posed of whether the respondent knew anything about an American aid plan and its name, only 57 per cent in AMZON could name ERP.

The most frequently mentioned sources of information about the Marshall Plan were newspapers (63%), with radio following in second place (44%). Relatively few people mentioned posters (7%) or magazines (3%). Among AMZON residents who were aware of the Marshall Plan, fewer than half (40%) said that it was occasionally mentioned in conversations with friends. Almost half (49%) of the AMZON respondents felt that the public ought to receive more information about the plan, 29 per cent thought the public had been sufficiently informed, 3 per cent went so far as to claim it had already been discussed too much, and 20 per cent had no opinion.

Among those who had heard of the Marshall Plan, almost two-thirds (65%) felt that it benefited all Germans, not just certain groups. The better educated, those with higher incomes, and urban residents were more likely to hold this view than were other population groups. In AMZON more than seven in ten, and in West Berlin as many as 91 per cent of the population, said they thought ERP had made a real contribution to German reconstruction. Among the 11 per cent who felt that ERP had brought about only a sham recovery, most respondents suggested that it had caused an unnatural stimulation of the economy.

Report No. 40 (23 October 1950)

GERMAN YOUTH VIEW THE AMERICAN PROGRAM
II. American Reorientation Efforts

Sample: 1,750 young people (from 15 to 25 years old) and 1,250 adults from the American Zone, 275 young people and 225 adults from West Berlin, and 200 young people and 175 adults from Bremen.
Interviewing dates: July 1950. (37 pp.)

The questions in the survey were divided into four main categories: Were American democratization efforts welcomed? Had the democratization efforts had much success? Were young people or adults more receptive to democratization? In what fields might the Germans learn from the Americans?

Although more AMZON Germans welcomed American democratization efforts than opposed them, fewer young people (47%) than adults (56%) did so. In fact, when the youth group was broken down into young people between the ages of 15 and 19 and those from 20 to 25, the younger group was even less favorably disposed (42%) than was the older one (51%).

Still fewer Germans felt that the democratization efforts had met with much success. In AMZON only 33 per cent of the adults and 24 per cent of the young people thought these efforts had achieved much success, 32 and 39 per cent respectively felt they had had little success, while 7 and 6 per cent respectively said they had been completely unsuccessful.

The field in which the smallest proportion of AMZON residents felt that Germans had anything to gain from American teachings was that of social welfare. Over one-third (34%) of the young people questioned and fully 45 per cent of the adults said there was nothing to be learned from the Americans in this field. The situation was quite similar with regard to the fine arts. Only 28 per cent of the young and 23 per cent of the adult respondents thought there was much or something to be learned in this field, while as many as 44 and 43 per cent respectively felt there was nothing to be learned. American education cut the third worst figure as far as Germans were concerned, although it should be mentioned that this field also received more no-opinion answers than the first two. As far as politics was concerned, the no-opinion group was also fairly large (40 per cent of the young and 41 per cent of the adults), but only 17 per cent of those under 25 and 15 per cent of the adults thought there was nothing to be learned from the Americans. In the remaining fields, industry and technology scored particularly high, with at least two out of three respondents-- young people as well as adults--saying that Germans could learn from Americans. Agriculture scored just as high, except in the cities of Berlin and Bremen. Science and radio came next, followed by the press and sports with appreciably less support.

Report No. 41 (23 October 1950)

GERMAN YOUTH VIEW THE AMERICAN PROGRAM
III. The "Voice of America" and General Radio

Sample: 1,750 young people (from 15 to 25 years old) and 1,250 adults from the American Zone, 275 young people and 225 adults from West Berlin, and 200 young people and 175 adults from Bremen.
Interviewing dates: July 1950. (13 pp.)

Although a greater percentage of young people (64%) claimed to be fairly regular radio listeners than was true among adult respondents (57%), a smaller percentage of the youth audience (73%) than of the adult audience (81%) listened to the "Voice of America." Extremely few people never listened to VOA and almost none of these said it was because they disliked the programs.

Report No. 42 (25 October 1950)

GERMAN YOUTH VIEW THE AMERICAN PROGRAM
IV. Awareness and Patronage of Amerika Häuser among Youth

Sample: 1,750 young people (from 15 to 25 years old) and 1,250 adults from the American Zone, 275 young people and 225 adults from West Berlin, and 200 young people and 175 adults from Bremen.
Interviewing dates: July 1950. (7 pp.)

While solid majorities of adults throughout the American-occupied areas were aware of the Amerika Häuser and their reading rooms, even higher percentages of young people knew of them. For the total AMZON region, the figure was 73 per cent; Hesse was well above this average with 80 per cent; and in Berlin and Bremen the figure was as high as 86 per cent. The extent of differences in awareness was greater within the younger age group than between the young and the adults. Whereas, for example, the range of difference between AMZON rural and urban youth or between the less and the better educated averaged about 30 per cent, the difference in awareness between youths and adults was only about 9 per cent.

Report No. 43 (25 October 1950)

GERMAN YOUTH VIEW THE AMERICAN PROGRAM
V. Audience of U.S. Overt Magazines and U.S. Documentary Film Program

> *Sample:* 1,750 young people (from 15 to 25 years old) and 1,250 adults from the American Zone, 275 young people and 225 adults from West Berlin, and 200 young people and 175 adults from Bremen.
> *Interviewing dates:* July 1950. (9 pp.)

In AMZON somewhat over half (53%) and in West Berlin as many as 79 per cent of the young people interviewed said they read magazines; among the adult respondents the figures were only 42 and 56 per cent respectively. Among the overt United States publications--*Heute, Neue Auslese, Amerikanische Rundschau,* and *Der Monat--Heute* was clearly the most popular with both young (11%) and adult (9%) magazine readers. The German publication *Quick,* however, was almost twice as popular.

About three times as many young people (17%) as adults (6%) claimed to have seen at least one American-sponsored documentary film. Slightly less than a third of both groups said they had not attended one but had heard of them, and over half of the respondents in both groups had neither attended nor even heard of these films.

Report No. 44 (30 October 1950)

GERMAN YOUTH VIEW THE AMERICAN PROGRAM
VI. The German-American Exchange Program

> *Sample:* 1,750 young people (from 15 to 25 years old) and 1,250 adults from the American Zone, 275 young people and 225 adults from West Berlin, and 200 young people and 175 adults from Bremen.
> *Interviewing dates:* July 1950. (9 pp.)

A majority of both young and adult respondents in AMZON said they had heard about a German-American exchange program. In West Berlin and Bremen almost three-quarters of the young people and as many as 81 per cent of the adults in West Berlin had heard of it. Very few Germans seemed to feel that those who took part in such an exchange program were unduly influenced by their American experiences. Among those under 25 only 8 per cent thought the influence too great, 67 per cent said it was not too great, and one-fourth had no opinion. Those least likely to feel that the exchangees were too strongly influenced tended to come from the most critical and informed population groups.

Report No. 45 (31 October 1950)

TREND IN OPINION ON WEST GERMAN REMILITARIZATION

Sample: 1,500 persons in the American Zone, 300 in West Berlin, and 200 in Bremen.
Interviewing dates: 5 September to 4 October 1950. (9 pp.)

Approval of German participation in an Atlantic Pact army dropped somewhat in AMZON during the one-month period from August 1950 (63%) to September 1950 (58%); in West Berlin the drop was negligible, with the September figure at an astonishing 86 per cent. As in August, there was no population group in which there were fewer who approved German participation than disapproved, although the differences were less strongly pronounced. Population breakdowns also revealed that almost all of the drop in support for German participation took place among women. Interestingly enough, somewhat less than half (46%) of the AMZON respondents felt that German public opinion was in favor of participation, almost a third (30%) thought most people were opposed, and a fourth (24%) had no opinion on the subject. Whereas in August 1950, 43 per cent of the AMZON population favored the creation of a German army--where the type of army was purposely left unspecified--by September 1950 this figure had dropped to 40 per cent. Both figures, however, were considerably higher than the original one of 26 per cent obtained in a survey of November 1949. Population breakdowns on this question revealed that there were increases in opposition to an unspecified type of army among Protestants, SPD adherents, and refugees.

Report No. 46 (10 November 1950)

GERMANS VIEW THE REMILITARIZATION ISSUE
Urban Opinion in Western Germany

Sample: 640 respondents from cities with populations of 50,000 or more throughout West Germany (that is, in the British, French, and American zones of occupation), as well as 200 persons from all three sectors of West Berlin.
Interviewing dates: flash survey on 31 October to 1 November 1950. (19 pp.)

Solid majorities of West German urban respondents continued to favor German participation in an Atlantic Pact army. Increasing numbers of West Germans were convinced that the Western Powers were doing everything to insure the security of West Germany. Only 23 per cent in West Berlin and as few as 6 per cent in AMZON, however, were satisfied that the French specifically were doing enough. Strong majorities throughout the urban centers were aware that the Washington Foreign Ministers' Conference had resulted in an agreement to defend Germany against attack. In line with this, it is interesting to note that about half (47 per cent in AMZON and 52 per cent in the British Zone) felt that West Germany had the right to expect to be defended by the Western Powers, even if the Federal Republic refused to participate in a West European army. Furthermore, 53 per cent in AMZON and the British Zone, and as many as 79 per cent in West Berlin, were convinced that West Germany would, in fact, be defended in such circumstances.

Despite intense propaganda efforts against German militarism, 45 per cent of AMZON Germans and 58 per cent of those in the British Zone felt that, in general, the German military during the previous fifty years had had a good effect on the German people. As far as the effects of German participation in a European army were concerned, only 16 per cent in AMZON, 13 per cent in the British Zone, and 8 per cent in West Berlin felt that it would have a bad effect on democracy in West Germany. A solid majority of West Germans felt that former Wehrmacht generals rather than newly trained men ought to be used for the German army. This opinion was expressed most frequently by the more educated and better informed respondents.

On the question of how the decision should be made concerning whether or not Germany should participate in a European army, a solid majority throughout the surveyed urban areas thought it ought to be through a vote among all West Germans. Less than 20 per cent thought it should be voted on by elected representatives in the Bundestag.

Report No. 47 (18 November 1950)

GERMANS VIEW THE REMILITARIZATION ISSUE
Further Findings and Some Limitations on Majority Approval

Sample: 640 respondents from cities with populations of 50,000 or more throughout West Germany (that is, in the British, French, and American zones of occupation), as well as 200 persons from all three sectors of West Berlin.
Interviewing dates: flash survey on 9 to 10 November 1950. (24 pp.)

Opposition in urban AMZON to West Germany's participation in a European army under the Atlantic Pact rose steadily from 21 per cent in August to 32 per cent in the October and November 1950 surveys. At the same time the percentage of those in favor declined from 67 to 57 per cent.

A solid majority throughout West Germany held that the Chinese intervention in Korea had considerably or somewhat increased the danger of a new world war. A somewhat smaller majority also felt that there was a great or fairly great chance that a similar conflict might erupt in Germany.

Over half the respondents (60 per cent in the French Zone and Bremen, 59 per cent in AMZON, and 58 per cent in the British Zone) did not think the federal government should have the right to draft men for military service. This disapproval outranked approval in all population groups examined. Less than one in ten, however, said they would volunteer for military service. Among those eligible for military service, most said they would serve only if drafted, and almost four out of ten indicated they would refuse to serve in any case.

Over 80 per cent of the respondents in all urban areas covered in the survey felt that Germany should have as much to say as the other countries about the command of the projected West European army. Only about one in five expected that German military leaders would in fact have equal say.

In West Berlin 81 per cent of the population, and in all other urban areas surveyed 59 per cent, said that the question of German participation in a European army should be settled soon. Although there was a slight decrease from a survey in October 1950, a solid majority still favored a plebiscite to determine whether or not Germany should participate in such an army.

The final section of the report contains a short statement on "the possible danger of a plebiscite to attainment of American policy objectives." Strong support for such a plebiscite, together with expressions of low support for German participation in a European army, made it possible to obtain majority opposition in any plebiscite--particularly if the question or its general context were posed in such a way as to draw upon emotions and inclinations rather than sober judgments. Elements opposed to participation had capitalized on this situation in their publicity and in conducting methodologically shoddy polls that phrased questions in emotionally biased ways.

Report No. 48 (22 November 1950)

AN ANALYSIS OF POSSIBLE DETERMINANTS OF OPPOSITION TO GERMAN PARTICIPATION IN THE DEFENSE OF EUROPE

Sample: 640 respondents from cities with populations of 50,000 or more throughout Western Germany (i.e., in the British, French, and American zones of occupation), as well as 200 persons from all three sectors of West Berlin.

Interviewing dates: flash surveys on 31 October to 1 November 1950 and 9 to 10 November 1950. (13 pp.)

The report is preceded by a number of fairly clear-cut suggestions for future policy based on the survey results, entitled "Some Implications for American Policy Projection." The report itself consists of seven questions related to German rearmament, with answers to them based on the survey data collected up to November 1950.

(1) To what extent was opposition related to fear of war? The question related specifically to the possibility of a Korea-like conflict arising in Germany. The data revealed that fear of such a possibility was not a major factor in accounting for either support for or opposition to German rearmament.

(2) To what extent was opposition related to concern over a possible renascence of German militarism? The fact that 35 per cent of those opposed to participation by Germany in a European army also felt that during the previous fifty years of German history the military had in general had a bad effect on the German people but that only 14 per cent of those favoring participation thought the previous military influence bad suggested that distrust of German militarism may indeed have played some part in determining the opposition's views. Again, while 24 per cent of those against participation thought the military would exert too great an influence on West German politics, only 8 per cent in favor of participation feared such influence. It should also be noted that, in all questions considered on this point, the no-opinion group for those opposed to participation was greater than for those in favor.

(3) To what extent was opposition related to an inclination to let the Western Powers carry the burden of German defense? The data revealed that fewer rather than more opponents of rearmament thought the Western Powers would defend West Germany even if the country did not participate in the European army. Opponents were also overwhelmingly opposed (61%) to more troops from the Western Powers being brought to Germany.

(4) To what extent was opposition related to an inclination to remain neutral in the East-West conflict? The data showed that opponents of German rearmament tended much more than supporters to feel that countries other than Germany would gain most from German participation in a European army. Moreover, twice as many people (54%) were against participation and preferred German neutrality in the East-West struggle as favored participation and preferred neutrality (27%).

(5) To what extent was opposition related to lack of confidence in Western resolve to defend West Germany? Majorities of both those opposing and those favoring participation in a European army indicated confidence in Western resolve to defend Germany.

(6) To what extent was opposition related to a feeling that the Western Powers are not doing enough for German defense? Whereas 32 per cent of those favoring participation felt that

the Western Powers were not doing all they could to insure German security, 46 per cent of those against participation felt the West was not doing enough. The data thus suggest that this factor played some role, although clearly not a major one, in influencing German opposition.

(7) To what extent was opposition related to apprehension of provoking Soviet aggression through German rearming? Fear of Soviet reaction seemed to have some bearing on German opponents' feelings but not to a very great extent. Less than a majority (49%) of anti-rearmament respondents felt that rearmament would increase the danger of Soviet aggression. In addition, 31 per cent of those who supported rearmament did so despite their feeling that it might provoke the Soviet Union.

Report No. 49 (27 November 1950)

A TEST OF READER REACTION TO THIRD REICH AND DEFEATIST ARTICLES

Sample: 300 Urban residents of American Zone cities with populations of 50,000 or more.
Interviewing dates: not specified. (28 pp.)

In the months preceding the survey, a number of German magazines had published articles recounting the careers of Nazi leaders during the Third Reich, as well as articles directed against German involvement in the East-West struggle. To assess the interpretation and impact of such articles, two typical ones were chosen for study. The first appeared in *Weltbild* (*Worldview*) and dealt with the Nuremberg trial; the other was published in *Revue* and was entitled "Verraten and Verkauft" ("Betrayed and Sold Out").

"Das wussten Sie nicht von Nürnberg" ("What you did not know about Nuremberg") concerned the final moments of the condemned Nazi leaders, their farewell statements, and speculations about the source of the poison used by Göring. A solid majority of the respondents had read all (70%) or part (14%) of the article. Six in ten said they were impressed--most of them sympathetically--with the farewell statements. Approximately the same percentage (57%) felt that the article gave a factual account. Since the purpose of the survey was to determine whether or not this article and others like it ought to be banned as detrimental to the American occupation efforts, it is interesting to note the report's final comment: "The fact that the persons who consider the verdicts just are more frequently inclined to think the article factual [74%] than do the groups who are critical of the verdicts [53 per cent of those who thought them unjust and 57 per cent of those thinking the verdicts only partially just] would support the judgment that the presentation is objective."

Questions concerning the publication *Weltbild* in general revealed that less than half the respondents (46%) had a good impression of it, 43 per cent rated it fairly good, and 8 per cent thought it poor.

"Betrayed and Sold Out," a three-page picture story with captions, was directed against German involvement in any future war with the Russians. About half (53%) of the respondents had read the article in its entirety, 24 per cent had read none of it, and a quarter had read parts of it. Slightly more than a fourth (26%) said they thought most Germans felt betrayed and sold out, 30 per cent felt that many held this view, 17 per cent attributed it to fairly many, and 20 per cent to few.

Report No. 50 (30 November 1950)

GERMAN YOUTH VIEW THE AMERICAN PROGRAM
VII. Acceptance of Democratic Responsibility and Related Political Issues

Sample: 1,750 young people (from 15 to 25 years old) and 1,250 adults from the American Zone, 275 young people and 225 adults from West Berlin, and 200 young people and 175 adults from Bremen.
Interviewing dates: July 1950. (21 pp.)

Seven in ten AMZON youths said they preferred to leave politics to others. This attitude made them even less politically inclined than their elders, of whom 62 per cent expressed such a view. It should be pointed out, however, that the better educated and those from urban centers and the higher income groups--that is, those most likely to enter the political arena-- showed a greater interest in politics than others. Lack of interest and lack of information seemed to go hand in hand. In AMZON, only 59 per cent of the young people questioned knew that Konrad Adenauer was the chancellor of West Germany; among adults the figure was 58 per cent. Bavaria had the least informed population on this question; residents of Hesse and Bremen were the best informed.

In answer to the question "Would you be interested in taking a responsible position in the political life of your community if you were asked?" less than 20 per cent of the young people in all areas except Berlin said they would; over 80 per cent, again with the exception of West Berlin, responded negatively. Furthermore, less than half of the young people (except in Berlin, where the figure was 53 per cent) felt that the Germans could really govern themselves democratically. The most frequently cited reason for this opinion was that the Germans were still too divided, that there were too many different opinions.

A majority of AMZON youth (58%) and just over half of their elders (52%) were satisfied with the work done up to that point by the Bonn government. Most of those expressing dissatisfaction cited economic complaints. In view of these responses and the fact that in the early postwar years there was still a great deal of real hardship, it is not surprising that the adult as well as the younger respondents, when given a choice between a government guaranteeing economic security or one offering the basic freedoms, preferred the government which offered security. In communist-surrounded West Berlin, by contrast, over half (52%) of the young chose civil liberties.

A majority of both adults (55%) and young people (51%) in AMZON said they thought it would be better for the future of Germany if it were to join an alliance of European states rather than becoming a strong independent nation; in West Berlin the figures were as high as 72 and 71 per cent respectively. Everywhere, except in West Berlin, between a quarter and a third favored an independent state, and up to 20 per cent had no opinion.

Report No. 51 (1 December 1950)

GERMANS VIEW THE REMILITARIZATION ISSUE
Pre-Election Trend and Further Findings

> *Sample:* 640 persons in cities with populations of 50,000 or more and 200 West Berliners.
> *Interviewing dates:* 15 to 16 November 1950. (24 pp.)

The report is based on a 48-hour flash survey conducted less than a week before the Hesse and Württemberg-Baden parliamentary (*Landtag*) elections of 19 November 1950.

While in West Germany as a whole on 1 November 1950 30 per cent of the population opposed West German participation in European defense through the Atlantic Pact, only two weeks later fully 41 per cent held this view. Approval, however, continued to outweigh this opposition: 63 per cent approved on 1 November, 51 per cent still did so two weeks later. West Berliners, meanwhile, continued to give overwhelming support to the prospect of West German participation in the Atlantic Pact (86 and 85 per cent respectively).

Further questioning showed that the majority of those opposed to German defense participation were not unconditionally opposed. The most frequently mentioned condition for approval was that Germany be given equal rights in the military and political realms. Assuming that such equality were given, this left only about 15 per cent of the West German population adamantly opposed to German participation in the Atlantic Pact. In West Berlin the final figure for opposition was only 3 per cent.

Most West German urban residents felt that German-French political relations were either not so good (44%) or bad (20%).

Cross-tabulations indicated that this attitude was not an important factor in determining levels of support for German participation in a European army. Furthermore, there was widespread awareness and considerable approval of one specific French proposal, the Schuman Plan, calling for the consolidation of heavy industries in France, West Germany, the Netherlands, Belgium, and England.

A very large majority of West German urban residents had heard of the Soviet Union's proposal to convene a four-power conference to deal with the West German question, but very few felt there was much or any value in such a meeting.

Large majorities throughout West Germany and West Berlin favored the idea of a plebiscite to determine whether or not Germany should participate in the Atlantic Pact.

Report No. 52 (7 December 1950)

GERMANS VIEW THE REMILITARIZATION ISSUE
New Korean Trend and Further Analysis of Opposition

Sample: 640 residents of cities with populations of 50,000 or more and 200 West Berliners.
Interviewing dates: 27 to 28 November 1950. (17 pp.)

Support for West German participation in the Atlantic Pact rose sharply just two weeks after it had hit an all-time low in mid-November. The flash survey conducted in late November showed that fully 64 per cent of the West German population approved German participation in European defense, an increase of 13 percentage points in the course of twelve days. Population breakdowns indicated that the upward trend occurred among all groups and that the opinion leaders in German society continued to favor participation more frequently than others. Among the one-in-four minority opposed to German participation in a West European army, the largest number felt that Germany ought to remain neutral; almost as many could suggest no alternative course; and quite a few expressed a resigned attitude: "We can't do anything, we'll just have to wait and see."

Over half of those who favored participation said their support rested on certain conditions; and about a third of those opposed said their opposition would give way if certain conditions were met. The condition most frequently mentioned by both groups of respondents centered on the question of equal rights for West Germany.

What accounted for opposition to German participation in a European army? Opposition rested largely on a neutralist, even defeatist, attitude. Whereas nine out of ten of those favoring participation recommended an all-out fight in the event of attack from the East, less than half of those opposed to participation suggested such a course. Moreover, opponents did not display great confidence in the West's ability to halt an attack from the East: while 33 per cent of those favoring participation thought a West European army had a good chance of stopping an attack from the East, only 13 per cent of those opposed thought it did.

Report No. 53 (14 December 1950)

GERMANS VIEW THE REMILITARIZATION ISSUE
Reactions to Korean Reverses and Associated Issues

Sample: 640 residents of cities with populations of 50,000 or more and 200 West Berliners.
Interviewing dates: 4 to 5 December 1950. (30 pp.)

In West Germany, support for German participation in European defense decreased markedly between 28 November, when the last flash survey on this question was conducted, and 5 December. Approval (55%), however, continued to outweigh disapproval (36%). It should be noted that West Berliners, in contrast to West Germans, showed continuously high support (85 per cent in mid-November, 88 per cent on 5 December), regardless of the course of events in Korea or propaganda on the remilitarization issue within Germany itself.

Together with the drop in support for German defense participation, there was an increase from 11 to 15 per cent in the number of persons who were willing to let West Germany fall without a fight under the East Zone government in the event of an attack from the East.

A large minority (34%) in West Germany felt that the Communist Chinese intervention in Korea would touch off World War III. In addition, a substantial number of respondents thought there was a great (37%) or fairly great (29%) chance that a conflict such as the one in Korea would break out in Germany. At the same time, decreasing percentages of West Germans were convinced that the United States would take a firm stand in case of communist aggression in Western Europe. Between mid-August and early December the figure dropped from 70 per cent to 55 per cent. Not surprisingly, fewer opponents than proponents of West German rearmament were convinced that America would deal resolutely with any communist aggression.

In late 1950 the German press carried a number of stories citing alleged evidence of growing disunity among the Western Powers in the face of events in Korea. Although a larger proportion of West Germans (46%) did not see any such disunity, a sizable minority (34%) said they did. In any case, very few West Germans (6%) perceived any real danger of a split among the Western Powers.

Except in West Berlin, somewhat larger percentages of West Germans thought the Korean conflict could be solved more satisfactorily through negotiation than by other means. Negotiations on the German question among the four major powers as proposed by the Soviet Union, however, continued to be viewed as having little or no potential advantage to Germany.

In the event that negotiations on the Korean conflict should fail, more West Germans felt the United Nations ought to carry on the battle (45%) than felt the U.N. ought to withdraw its troops (34%). In West Berlin fully 87 per cent of the population said the U.N. ought to carry on the battle. Solid majorities throughout West Germany were opposed to use of the atomic bomb in Korea; in West Berlin, however, opinion split almost evenly on this question.

Report No. 54 (21 December 1950)

GERMAN YOUTH VIEW THE ADULT EDUCATION SYSTEM

Sample: 1,750 young people (between 15 and 25 years old) and 1,250 adults from the American Zone, 275 young people and 225 adults from West Berlin, as well as 200 young people and 175 adults from Bremen.
Interviewing dates: July 1950. (7 pp.)

At the time of the survey, approximately one in ten adults and young people in AMZON was attending adult education classes. Fifty per cent had no idea there were such classes. In the urban center of West Berlin, by contrast, only 7 per cent were unaware of adult education facilities, and fully 27 per cent actually took part in classes.

Report No. 55 (28 December 1950)

GERMANS VIEW THE REMILITARIZATION ISSUE
Year-End Developments and the Present Status of Neutralism

Sample: 640 residents of West German cities with populations of 50,000 or more and 200 West Berliners.
Interviewing dates: flash survey on 19 to 20 December 1950. (47 pp.)

In late 1950 less than half (44%) of all West Germans favored German integration with the West. Almost as many (41%) preferred unification with East Germany, with the reunified Germany to assume a neutral position between East and West. The more educated and informed groups in the population tended to prefer integration with the West rather than the neutralist position. Deeper probing revealed that very few West Germans (21%) felt that neutralism was a real alternative given the world situation; as many as 66 per cent did not think Germany could remain uninvolved in the East-West conflict.

Despite almost unanimous opposition to communism, increasing numbers of West Germans--but still less than 20 per cent--felt that, in case of attack from the East, West Germany should not fight and should agree to East German rule.

At the same time, decreasing percentages of West Germans were convinced that the United States would take a firm stand in Western Europe in case of attack from the East.

The percentage of respondents favoring West German participation in the Atlantic Pact continued its fluctuations of previous months, reaching a near low of 53 per cent in late December in all areas (except West Berlin, where it continued to remain at a high 84 per cent). Group breakdowns revealed that the greatest drop in support occurred among men. A large minority (41%) felt that the establishment of a German army would, in fact, increase the danger of Soviet aggression. Only 22 per cent thought it would decrease that danger, 20 per cent did not feel it would have any influence, and 17 per cent had no opinion.

Over half (56%) of the West German respondents and as many as 69 per cent of the West Berliners had heard of East German Prime Minister Otto Grotewohl's letter to Chancellor Adenauer suggesting negotiations on the question of reunification. Except in West Berlin, where just over half of the respondents felt that Adenauer ought to refuse the invitation, more people thought he ought to accept (67%) than refuse (23%). Fewer respondents (53%) were confident that such a conference could in fact promote reunification. However, over three-quarters of the population preferred a continuation of the status quo if the alternative were unification under communism.

Furthermore, a large majority (73%) of West Germans and 88 per cent of the West Berliners felt it would not be wise for the Western Powers to agree to the withdrawal of all occupying forces at that time.

On the specific issue of Korea, opinion was almost evenly divided in West Germany regarding measures undertaken by the United Nations. Only in West Berlin did an appreciably greater percentage agree (48%) than disagree (36%) with what the U.N. was doing.

Report No. 56 (29 December 1950)

WEST GERMAN OPINIONS ON POLITICAL PARTIES AND ELECTION ISSUES

Sample: 640 residents of West German cities with populations of 50,000 or more and 200 West Berliners.
Interviewing dates: flash survey on 11 to 12 December 1950.
(34 pp.)

The survey on which this report was based was conducted some time after local elections were held throughout AMZON in fall 1950. West German participation in a West European defense army had been one of the most vehemently discussed issues of the campaign, with the Social Democratic party (SPD) strongly opposed.

Among the respondents who had voted for the SPD, four in ten said they did so for various personal and political reasons, most of which boiled down to a matter of family habit and the feeling that the SPD is the working man's party. Another four in ten mentioned economic reasons that also rested on the latter consideration. Three in ten Christian Democratic Union (CDU) voters had strong religious motivations; two in ten simply liked the party for general reasons. One in four of those who voted for the Free Democratic party (FDP) did so for professional and business reasons; another one in four was protesting against both the SPD and the CDU.

The European army was not, therefore, the primary issue in the voters' minds at the time they cast their ballots. In fact, almost half of all AMZON voters were not even aware that the SPD had stressed this issue in its campaign.

Asked how they would vote if a national election were to be held at that time, 50 per cent of the urban AMZON sample chose the SPD; 18 per cent said they would vote for the CDU and 20 per cent for the FDP.

Given American concern over the West European defense issue, it is interesting to note that only 27 per cent of West Germany's city dwellers felt that the SPD was unalterably opposed to West German participation in the Atlantic Pact. Another 38 per cent thought the SPD would agree if certain conditions were met, the most important of which seemed to be equal political, military, and economic rights. Among CDU voters, 59 per cent felt their party to be unconditionally in favor of defense participation. Of the 12 per cent who felt that CDU support depended on certain conditions, most again mentioned equal rights as the primary issue at stake.

In urban AMZON, as many as 56 per cent of the respondents said they were dissatisfied with the CDU government. The percentage for all of West Germany was somewhat lower (48%), and in West Berlin only 28 per cent expressed such dissatisfaction. Although Chancellor Adenauer was certainly more popular than any other CDU leader, he did not have majority popularity (40%); fully 34 per cent of the respondents, however, had no opinion on this question.

Asked to weigh the relative competence of the SPD and CDU regarding three specific problems, more West German urban dwellers indicated confidence in the SPD on economic (32%) and defense (30%) issues, while a greater percentage (34%) chose the CDU on the question of who would negotiate more satisfactorily with the Western Powers. Respondents' attitudes on all these measures of confidence were closely related to party preferences, certainly far more so than to their attitude toward defense participation.

Report No. 57 (12 January 1951)

GERMANS VIEW THE REMILITARIZATION ISSUE
Has Western Policy Changed on German Militarism?
—and Present-Day Attitudes on Nuremberg

> *Sample:* 1,500 persons in the American Zone, 300 in West Berlin, and 200 in Bremen.
> *Interviewing dates:* 9 October to 17 November 1950. (27 pp.)

Very few AMZON Germans (9%) held the out-and-out pacifist view that anything military is automatically evil. The vast majority in all surveyed areas felt that the value of military forces depended on the uses to which they were put. Pacifist trends were weakest among the most informed and educated class.

Throughout West Germany--except in Bremen and Hesse where the figures were somewhat lower--about one-fourth of the population felt that Western approval of German participation in European defense would indicate a shift in policy on German rearmament. Almost twice as many felt it would not indicate such a shift. It should also be noted that in almost all areas a large majority had no opinion on the subject. The suggestion that the Germans did not, in fact, feel that the West had condemned the German military as such is borne out by the fact that a solid majority (ranging from 63 per cent in Hesse to as many as 88 per cent in Berlin) felt the German generals had been indicted for crimes committed during the war and not simply because they were soldiers.

About half the German population thought that leading personalities of the Third Reich would gain considerable influence if West Germany were to rearm. Somewhat fewer--except in Bremen, where this second figure was higher than the first--did not think rearmament would have this effect. Going one step further, opinion split on the question of whether or not increased influence by former Nazis would constitute a threat to West Germany. Even among opponents to participation in European defense, fully a third of the respondents did not think they would pose a threat.

That portion of the survey in October 1950 dealing with the fairness of the Nuremberg trials revealed the largest shift in viewpoints ever recorded up to that time by the Reactions Analysis Staff. Whereas 78 per cent of the AMZON Germans expressed the feeling in October 1946 that the trials had been conducted fairly, only 38 per cent expressed this opinion in late 1950. Population breakdowns showed that the drop in favorable evaluations of the trials occurred among all elements of the population, and that the rise in adverse opinion was considerably greater among the more educated than among the less educated.

Report No. 58 (18 January 1951)

GERMANS VIEW THE REMILITARIZATION ISSUE
Further Trends on Neutralism, Defense Participation, and Associated Issues

Sample: 640 residents of cities with populations of 50,000 or more and 200 West Berliners.
Interviewing dates: flash survey on 3 to 4 January 1951. (50 pp.)

As the year 1951 began, support for German defense participation reached the lowest point recorded up to that time. Opinion in AMZON split about evenly, with 48 per cent opposed and only 45 per cent in favor. Population breakdowns showed that there was decreased support in all groups.

Although General Dwight D. Eisenhower's appointment as supreme commander of the Atlantic Pact defense forces had been announced some two weeks earlier, about a third of the German population did not know of the appointment.

The January 1951 survey also revealed that support for a neutral Germany had grown to the point where this view was the predominant one. Well over half the population nonetheless thought the chances of actually maintaining a neutral position were slim. In fact, 63 per cent of all West Germans felt that the West would need German help in order to defend West Germany in case of attack. Decreasing percentages of respondents felt that Germany had the right to ask to be defended, even if the country refused to participate in European defense arrangements; but 46 per cent thought the Western Powers would in fact defend West Germany despite such refusal.

Opinion was almost split on the question of whether or not the West could stop at the zonal border an attack from the East. Such pessimism was appreciably greater among opponents of German participation in European defense and those who favored a neutral position for Germany. Looking at the world situation as a whole, 64 per cent of urban AMZON residents felt that the communists had scored greater successes during the previous six months than had the Western Powers; in mid-April 1950 this figure had stood at 31 per cent. Furthermore, 51 per cent of urban AMZON residents felt that the communists were stronger at that moment than the West; in mid-April 1950 this figure had been as low as 14 per cent. Most Germans continued to feel, however, that the West would win out in the long run.

The number of persons who had heard about the letter from East Germany's Prime Minister Otto Grotewohl suggesting discussions on reunification had increased markedly over earlier surveys. Except in West Berlin, where 54 per cent of the population thought Adenauer ought to refuse the invitation, over half the West German respondents felt the invitation should be accepted.

The Soviet proposal for a four-power conference on the German question was regarded with considerable skepticism: in AMZON 62 per cent felt it would be of little or no advantage.

Report No. 59 (25 January 1951)

PUBLIC APPRAISAL OF EFFECTIVENESS OF COMMUNIST ACTIVITY IN WEST GERMANY

Sample: 1,500 respondents from the American Zone, 250 West Berliners, and 250 residents of Bremen.
Interviewing dates: October 1950. (36 pp.)

The survey was conducted during the same period as an electoral campaign in East Germany. The general finding was that, despite heavy propaganda on the part of the Communist party in West Germany (KPD) and the communist Socialist Unity party (SED) in East Germany, West Germans were neither sympathetic to nor impressed by communism.

Almost half (48%) of the AMZON public did not even venture to guess what ideas the communists were primarily interested in publicizing in West Germany. Whether or not they knew what communist propaganda was really all about, opinion was fairly evenly divided on its influence. In West Berlin 49 per cent said it had no influence, while the same percentage said they thought it had some.

Despite the general feeling that communist propaganda was ineffectual, the public favored taking strong action against communist elements in West Germany. Of the 58 per cent in AMZON who took this position, 13 per cent felt the Bonn government ought to ban the KPD, and 8 per cent said the government should stop communist agitation. And, when all respondents were specifically asked whether or not the KPD ought to be banned, 59 per cent in AMZON said yes; in West Berlin as many as 69 per cent replied in the affirmative. If it were outlawed, about a third of the AMZON respondents felt the party would grow stronger, about one-fourth thought it would be weakened, and another fourth thought it would have no effect. Far larger proportions felt that all communist newspapers ought to be prohibited; only about a quarter unqualifiedly opposed such a ban. A majority (ranging from just 51 per cent in Hesse to as high as 89 per cent in West Berlin) also approved the federal government's decision to remove all KPD members from the civil service.

Report No. 60 (31 January 1951)

NEW LIGHT ON GERMAN NEUTRALITY SENTIMENTS

Sample: 640 West Germans from cities with populations of 50,000 or more and 200 West Berliners.
Interviewing dates: flash survey conducted 18 to 19 January 1951. (33 pp.)

Whereas in the first week of January 1951 only 35 per cent

of the urban population preferred joining the West politically and militarily--in contrast to 46 per cent who preferred a unified but neutral Germany--a mere two weeks later the figure had once again risen to its pre-Christmas level of 44 per cent. When the question was posed somewhat differently and respondents were asked whether they would prefer (a) a Western offer of union with the West as an independent but politically and militarily equal nation or (b) a Soviet offer of unification with neutrality, 61 per cent chose the former, while only 24 per cent preferred the latter.

As for the issue of participation in an Atlantic Pact army, the percentage of those favoring such participation had reached an all-time low of 48 per cent in the first week of January 1951. Two weeks later it was again climbing and reached the 52 per cent level, still well below the high point of 64 per cent in late November 1950.

Asked what they personally felt should be done if Germany were attacked from the East, between two-thirds and three-fourths of the urban population said they would want to fight the aggressors.

Some two weeks prior to General Eisenhower's arrival in Europe to take over as supreme commander of the Atlantic Pact's armed forces, 31 per cent of the urban population was unaware of his appointment to that post.

With the Korean conflict about seven months old, decreasing percentages of West Germans were convinced that the United States would take a firm stand against communist aggression in Western Europe. Between mid-August 1950 and mid-January 1951 the figure had dropped from 70 per cent to a bare majority of 51 per cent.

Between mid-December and mid-January increasing percentages of West Germans had become aware that East German Prime Minister Otto Grotewohl had sent a letter to Chancellor Adenauer proposing a conference to discuss reunification; by the latter date the figure had reached 76 per cent. Respondents were also asked whether they thought the Western Powers would be indicating a fundamental opposition to reunification if they were to ask West Germany to join them. Almost three-quarters (71%) in West Germany and 88 per cent in West Berlin said they did not think so.

Between November 1950 and January 1951 consistently small percentages of West Germans felt that a four-power conference would be of great advantage to their country, but over half thought it would be of little or no advantage at all.

Report No. 61 (22 February 1951)

DEFENSE PARTICIPATION SENTIMENTS AND THE EXTENT OF "OHNE MICH"

With Other Current Developments on Issues Related to German Defense Participation

Sample: 6,500 residents of West German urban areas, as well as 2,000 West Berliners.

Interviewing dates: 1 November 1950 to 1 February 1951.

(37 pp.)

In the closing months of 1950 and early 1951, a majority of West Germans (55%) favored participation in the Atlantic Pact, 34 per cent opposed such a move, and 10 per cent were undecided. In West Berlin the overwhelming majority (84%) favored it. Population breakdowns on this question revealed that those who were usually better informed were also much more likely to be in favor than were the less informed.

Many of those in favor nonetheless rested their decision upon the assumption that West German membership in an Atlantic defense arrangement would imply no need for a tax increase, rationing, or a draft system. In fact, when West German respondents were asked how they would feel on this issue if all three measures had to follow, half of those previously favoring participation withdrew their support; only 27 per cent continued to express their approval of the move. Furthermore, 30 per cent of the men said they would refuse to serve in the army, 38 per cent said they would serve if drafted, 21 per cent claimed to be ineligible, and only 7 per cent said they would volunteer.

On the related issue of whether or not West Germany ought to accept reunification if the price were to be neutrality, decreasing percentages thought it would be a good idea. By February 1951 only 22 per cent in West Germany favored it.

Shortly after Eisenhower's visit to West Germany, almost three-quarters (72%) of the population knew that he had been appointed supreme commander of the Atlantic Pact's armed forces. Well over a third (38%) felt he was the right man for the job, but almost half (47%) had no opinion on the subject.

There was no clear-cut opinion on the question of whether or not a four-power conference would be to Germany's advantage. Twenty per cent felt it would be, 19 per cent felt it would not, 39 per cent thought it would make no difference, and 22 per cent had no opinion.

Increasing percentages of urban West Germans felt that the United Nations forces should withdraw from Korea if negotiations were to fail. By February, 39 per cent held this position. The better educated and better informed tended to favor a continuation of the fighting. Most Germans (54 per cent in West Germany, 62 per cent in West Berlin) felt that the United States was strong enough to carry on the war in the Far East and at the same time send troop reinforcements to West Germany.

Report No. 62 (28 February 1951)

FRANCO-GERMAN RELATIONS AS VIEWED BY RESIDENTS OF THE U.S. ZONE, BERLIN, AND BREMEN

Sample: not indicated.
Interviewing dates: November 1950. (15 pp.)

The issue of Franco-German relations was apparently not terribly important to the bulk of the public surveyed. In AMZON fully 36 per cent had no opinion to offer on the question. Of the 47 per cent who thought they were not so good or even bad, 12 per cent ascribed the problem to French hatred and prejudice toward Germany; only 5 per cent mentioned ancient rivalries on both sides. Among the 17 per cent who thought relations between the two countries were good or very good, there was a recognition of mutual interests and a readiness to let bygones be bygones.

Half of the AMZON respondents were unable to judge the adequacy of the French contribution to West German defense. At the same time, as many as 61 per cent said they were satisfied with the American contribution.

Population breakdowns on all the questions revealed that those with definite opinions were more likely than others to have negative attitudes.

Report No. 63 (6 March 1951)

WEST GERMAN REACTIONS TO THE LANDSBERG DECISIONS

Sample: 640 respondents from West German cities with populations of 50,000 or more, as well as 200 West Berliners.
Interviewing dates: flash survey on 26 to 27 February 1951.
(22 pp.)

The introductory remarks in the report state: "Whatever the press or other sources of information may have implied, public reaction to the Landsberg decisions . . . cannot be considered encouraging to American policy makers." A very large majority (80%) of all urban West Germans had heard of the decisions made by the Americans concerning the prisoners at Landsberg who had been convicted of war crimes. What evidently disturbed the writer of the report was the fact that almost as many people agreed (31%) with the decisions as disagreed (32%). Among the latter, the most frequently mentioned reason was the long delay in carrying out the punishment. The most frequently mentioned reason for agreeing with the decisions centered on the reduction or modification of several of the sentences.

Asked specifically about the seven death sentences which had been upheld, only three in ten urban residents could name one or more of the condemned men. One-fourth of the respondents felt these death sentences were justified, but a further 34 per cent had no opinion on the matter. Among those who opposed the death sentences, almost all knew the nature of the crime for which the penalty had been imposed.

As for Alfried Krupp, 62 per cent of the respondents knew that he had been released from prison as a result of the Landsberg decisions. Of these, 48 per cent thought the decision was the right one. Supporters of the decision pointed out that Krupp had merely been a businessman in the Third Reich; those opposed emphasized the general guilt of the munitions maker.

Most respondents mentioned opportunism or the desire to undo past errors as the reason for American modification of the sentences, rather than the process of legal review.

Special Report 63-S (9 March 1951)

ATTITUDES BEHIND THE IRON CURTAIN
A Survey Approach to East German Thinking
I. General Mood and Resistance Sentiments

Sample: 429 East Berliners and East Zone residents interviewed near currency exchange offices in West Berlin; quota sampling based on sex, education, and age parameters of the AMZON population.
Interviewing dates: 14 to 21 December 1950. (23 pp.)

The survey was conducted in an attempt to "help meet the needs of the psychological warfare program." Since the respondents were probably not representative of the general East German population, it is questionable whether the survey results could serve this purpose or even a more general informational one. As the Reactions Analysis Staff itself was aware, the data should, therefore, be studied with utmost care and with a certain measure of skepticism.

More East Germans (36%) said they were better off at the time of the interview as compared to six months earlier than said they were worse off (25%); however, even more (39%) said their economic situation was the same. Geographic breakdowns revealed that those respondents in or near East Berlin were more likely than persons from outlying regions to say they were better off. This finding supported West German suspicions that the East was trying to upgrade life in East Berlin to lessen the enormous differences between it and West Berlin. Other population breakdowns revealed that an astonishing 74 per cent of those between the ages of 15 and 24 said they were better off, with only 4 per cent saying things were worse. Interviews with Free German Youth (FDJ) participants in the Whitsuntide rally had produced similar data, suggesting that Soviet authorities were devoting considerable attention to this age group.

Asked what they thought was the general mood of the East German population following the elections of 15 October 1950, 51 per cent described it as bad, 21 per cent termed it very bad, 12 per cent said not so good, and 11 per cent gave no answer; only 5 per cent called the mood good. The most frequently cited reason for this low morale was the feeling that the situation had not improved. Others mentioned controlled elections, increasing restrictions on the freedom of speech, and the poor economic situation.

At the time of the GDR elections, Mayor Ernst Reuter of West Berlin had invited all East Germans to send the stub of their ration cards to the West Berlin City Council's office, to signify their "vote" for the West. The office received 400,000 such cards. Asked to comment on this move, 53 per cent of the East German respondents said they thought it had been useful, 20 per cent felt it had been of no use, and 26 per cent said they did not know. Those who argued that it had been of no use pointed out that nothing had changed, that such things did not disturb the Russians.

When asked what they thought the West could do to improve the political situation in the East, most of those respondents who had an opinion on the subject (28 per cent gave no answer) clearly indicated that they were hoping for some sort of direct action against the Russians. Quite a few also hoped for eventual negotiations.

A major finding of the survey was the fact that almost three out of four East German and East Berlin respondents (73%) said they did not think the East German people could do anything to improve their political situation.

On the question of which side was stronger, the East or the West, 46 per cent of urban West Germans felt at the outset of 1951 that the West held this position, and in West Berlin the figure was 36 per cent. In East Germany, by contrast, only 25 per cent felt that their own side was stronger. The single most frequently cited reason for Western strength was economic and military superiority. Those choosing the East as the stronger tended to point to the greater number of countries and people in the Soviet bloc.

Report No. 64 (14 March 1951)

GERMAN ATTITUDES ON EVE OF PARIS DEPUTIES CONFERENCE

Sample: 640 residents of West German cities with populations of 50,000 or more, as well as 200 West Berliners.
Interviewing dates: flash survey on 26 to 27 February 1951.
(31 pp.)

Urban support for West German participation in European defense had dropped to a low of 48 per cent on 3 to 4 January 1951. During the following eight weeks it rose somewhat but never reached the high of 64 per cent recorded in late November 1950.

To find out what sort of results the communists might obtain in case they were indeed able to circulate a petition in the West on the remilitarization issue, the survey included the question, "Supposing a plebiscite were held in the near future on the issue of whether West Germany should participate with a contingent of German soldiers in a West European defense army. Would you then vote for or against such a rearmament of West Germany?" In AMZON 48 per cent said they were against this military participation, and 42 per cent were for it; in West Berlin only 23 per cent opposed it, while fully 69 per cent were in favor.

Throughout January and February 1951, increasing numbers of West Germans said they would prefer that their country join the

West as an independent, politically and militarily equal nation, rather than being reunified with East Germany and remaining neutral between East and West. In late February the percentage favoring the former was as high as 72 per cent, while only 17 per cent chose the latter alternative. At the same time, as many as 40 per cent of AMZON Germans said they would accept a Soviet offer of neutrality if the Soviet Union would support free elections in a united Germany.

Although increasing numbers of Germans thought that a four-power conference would result in advantages for West Germany, by the end of February there were still only 27 per cent in AMZON voicing this opinion.

About the same percentage of AMZON Germans agreed (41%) as disagreed (46%) with Chancellor Adenauer's rejection of the suggestion by East Germany's Prime Minister Grotewohl that they discuss reunification. Over two-thirds (70%) of the West German population said that, if negotiations were in fact held, the GDR representatives would pursue the interests of the Soviet Union rather than those of Germany.

Report No. 65 (14 March 1951)

FRANKFURT SCHOOL-CHILDREN REACT TO THE BOOKLET *EIGHT GREAT AMERICANS*

Sample: 465 schoolchildren between the ages of 10 and 15 in ten selected schools in Frankfurt.
Interviewing dates: 28 February to 1 March 1951. (24 pp.)

Acht Grosse Amerikaner (Eight Great Americans) was a booklet utilizing the comic-book technique. The Americans discussed were: Jane Addams, Andrew Carnegie, George Washington Carver, Thomas Edison, Thomas Jefferson, Abraham Lincoln, George Washington, and Walt Whitman. Several days after receiving the booklet, 70 per cent of the children had read all of it, 29 per cent parts of it, and only one per cent had not looked at it. When asked what they thought of it, 30 per cent of the boys and 28 per cent of the girls said they liked it very much, 56 per cent of both the boys and the girls liked it, and 13 per cent said they did not particularly like it.

Report No. 66 (20 March 1951)

RUHR MINERS SPECIFY THEIR HOUSING WANTS

Sample: 269 interviews conducted with men from eight different mines.
Interviewing dates: 1 to 3 March 1951. (14 pp.)

Among the miners' families needing better housing and listed for the proposed Marshall Plan housing project, 63 per cent said they were sufficiently dissatisfied with their situation that they would prefer to move within half a year even if it meant a small apartment; 35 per cent said they would be willing to wait a year if it meant getting larger accommodations.

Report No. 67 (21 March 1951)

SURVEY STUDIES AMONG GERMAN OPINION LEADERS

I. German *Bürgermeisters* Evaluate the Landsberg Decisions

Sample: a total of 110 West German *Bürgermeisters* or mayors:
33 from cities with populations of more than 50,000;
30 from cities with 5,000 to 49,999 inhabitants; and
47 from towns with less than 5,000.
Interviewing dates: flash survey on 26 to 27 February 1951.
(21 pp.)

Whereas some 30 per cent of the urban West German public had heard of the Landsberg decision (see Report No. II/63), all the Bürgermeisters (or mayors) interviewed had heard of it. Like the general public, a fairly large proportion of these men (39%) disagreed with the decisions to varying degrees; however, the majority (56%) agreed with them. The most frequently given reasons for disagreement had to do with the length of time the prisoners had been held.

In contrast to the general public, almost all the mayors (90%) had heard that Alfried Krupp had been released from prison. Of these, 71 per cent agreed with that decision, with most (21%) explaining that Krupp had done no more than war industrialists in other countries.

On the seven death sentences that had not been commuted in the Landsberg decision, the mayors were also better informed than the general public. While only 29 per cent of the public knew something about these cases, 43 per cent of the mayors did. In addition, whereas only 25 per cent of the general public approved of all these sentences, 59 per cent of the mayors did. Those who disapproved brought up a variety of reasons: that the men were acting according to orders, that there was not enough proof, that capital punishment had been abolished, and that the Allies had committed similar crimes.

Asked why they thought some of the sentences handed down at Nuremberg had been modified, 37 per cent of the mayors interviewed said they thought the Americans had realized the injustice of the trials. Another 26 per cent said it was done to promote the growing understanding between the United States and Germany.

Report No. 68 (22 March 1951)

SURVEY STUDIES AMONG GERMAN OPINION LEADERS

II. A Note on *Bürgermeisters'* Reactions to a Four-Power Conference

Sample: 110 West German *Bürgermeisters*: 33 from cities with populations of 50,000 or more; 30 from cities with 5,000 to 49,999 inhabitants; and 47 from towns with less than 5,000.
Interviewing dates: flash survey on 26 to 27 February 1951.
(8 pp.)

Asked what they thought was the most important problem facing West Germany at that time, 35 per cent mentioned domestic issues such as unemployment, housing, the refugees, or the economy, but 33 per cent also cited the danger of war. While a rather large minority of both the general urban population (36%) and the mayors (33%) felt that a four-power conference would result in neither advantages nor disadvantages for Germany, almost twice as many mayors (43%) thought it would bring advantages than was true among the general public (23%). A further contrast was shown in the no-opinion groups, where the mayors had 3 per cent, while the urban population had 27 per cent. The most frequently cited reason for regarding the conference as advantageous was the possibility of discussing problems and eventually reaching an agreement. It was worth the risk.

Report No. 69 (29 March 1951)

THE WEST GERMAN PEOPLE VIEW DEFENSE PARTICIPATION, NEUTRALITY, AND RELATED ISSUES

Sample: 800 West German residents 18 years and older.
Interviewing dates: 7 to 15 March 1951. (25 pp.)

This was the first survey utilizing the new "intermediate" size sample of 800 adults throughout West Germany. On the question of German attitudes toward participation in European defense, the new larger sample was only slightly less in favor of such participation (48%) than had been respondents to an earlier flash survey (51%).

Opinion split in West Germany as a whole on whether it would be better for West Germany to join with the West or to unite with East Germany and remain neutral. Only in West Berlin did a large majority (74%) favor joining the West. About two-thirds of the West Germans nonetheless said that the federal government should turn down a Soviet-proposed neutrality in favor of a Western bid to unite with the West on a basis of political and military equality. When asked how they would respond if the Soviet Union were to agree to a four-power conference to support really free elections for a united and independent Germany, however, only 45 per cent said that the proposal should be rejected. Of these, 24 per cent would still reject the plan if the Western Powers accepted it and guaranteed Germany's neutrality. This left a quarter of the population opposed to neutrality even under the most favorable conditions.

About a fifth (21%) of the West German population expected Germany to benefit from a four-power conference, while a sixth (16%) saw only disadvantages to such a meeting, and a third (33%) felt it would be neither one nor the other. Another 30 per cent had no opinion.

On the question of negotiating directly with East German representatives, 49 per cent of the population thought this would be a good idea, primarily (15%) because no opportunity should be passed up to discuss this important issue.

Report No. 70 (30 March 1951)

SOME FURTHER FINDINGS ON WEST GERMAN REACTIONS TO THE LANDSBERG DECISIONS

Sample: 800 residents of West Germany, as well as 200 West Berliners.
Interviewing dates: 7 to 15 March and 15 to 22 March 1951.
(11 pp.)

Whereas a very large majority (80%) of the urban West German sample had heard of the decisions made somewhat earlier by the Americans concerning the prisoners at the Landsberg prison (see Reports No. 63 and 67), only 64 per cent of the general West German public had heard of them. Furthermore, of this 64 per cent a far smaller percentage (18%) agreed with the decisions than had been true of the urban sample (31%). The reasons given by both groups for their disapproval were very similar: most cited the length of time it had taken to make the decisions following the Nuremberg Trials.

In a survey made following the announcement that the executions of the seven condemned men were to be postponed pending an appeal to the United States Supreme Court, the West German respondents were asked what they thought were the reasons for the postponement. About four in ten could give no answer. Of those who could, most of the responses centered on American uncertainty, weakness, or some ulterior motive such as winning German sympathies.

Special Report 70-S (2 April 1951)

A NOTE ON THE COMMUNIST PROJECTED PLEBISCITE ON WEST GERMAN DEFENSE PARTICIPATION

Sample: 800 West German residents.
Interviewing dates: 7 to 15 March and 15 to 22 March 1951.
(4 pp.)

This special report was drafted because there were "indications that the Communists are planning to throw into high gear their long projected campaign in West Germany for a plebiscite on the remilitarization issue. . . . Any such plebiscite could pose serious difficulties for the attainment of American policy objectives in this area." In response to a question on West German participation in a European defense army, using the words *rearmament* and *contingent of German soldiers*, as many as 59 per cent of the respondents said they would oppose such participation. Of these, 31 per cent would still be opposed even if this participation were on a completely equal basis. When the entire question was asked in more general terms, only 40 per cent were opposed, 48 per cent approved, and 12 per cent had no opinion.

Report No. 71 (5 April 1951)

WEST GERMAN REACTION TO THE SCHUMAN PLAN

Sample: 800 West German residents and 200 West Berliners.
Interviewing dates: 7 to 15 March 1951. (18 pp.)

Approximately one week prior to the initialing of the Schuman Plan, which called for the pooling of heavy industry in Western Europe, 68 per cent of the West Germans interviewed and 72 per cent of the West Berliners had read or heard of it. However, only 26 per cent in West Germany and 34 per cent in West Berlin could describe the plan with any degree of accuracy. Among those who were able to give a reasonable description of it, 58 per cent thought it a good idea and 29 per cent disagreed with it.

Asked why they thought the French had sponsored the plan, most (64%) of those with opinions said that France hoped to gain at the expense of other participants. Only 31 per cent felt that France supported it in the hope of promoting general economic cooperation.

The West German public had mixed feelings on the question of whether or not the Schuman Plan would contribute to West European unity. Whereas 37 per cent regarded it as a major step toward this goal, 20 per cent felt it was only a small step, and 13 per cent did not think it represented any progress at all. However, among those who were able to describe the plan correctly, 54 per cent saw it as a major step toward unity, while only 35 per cent felt it represented a small or no step at all in this direction.

Using questions designed to ascertain whether respondents had "nationalist" or "internationalist" sentiments, the survey revealed that, although supporters of the Schuman Plan were predominantly internationalists, fully 40 per cent were nationalists. Conversely, although opponents of the plan were predominantly nationalists, 40 per cent could be considered internationalists.

Special Report 71-S (10 April 1951)

ATTITUDES BEHIND THE IRON CURTAIN
II. Current Views on Unity, Neutrality, and Related Issues

Sample: 400 East Zone and East Berlin residents during visits to West Berlin; see Special Report No. II/63-S on sampling problems and representativeness.
Interviewing dates: 13 to 16 March 1951. (35 pp.)

Approximately the same proportions of respondents in East and West Germany (ranging from 76 to 82 per cent) were aware of the suggestions by East German Prime Minister Grotewohl to Chancellor Adenauer that there be negotiations on reunification. Very few from the East, however, knew what the West's response had been. When informed that Adenauer had agreed, on the condition that free and secret elections be held first, 79 per cent of the Eastern respondents said they felt Adenauer had done the right thing.

Despite the West's repeated rejection of GDR proposals for unification and its policy of integrating West Germany into the Western world, 86 per cent of the East Germans said they thought the Western Powers were fundamentally in favor of German reunification. At the same time, more than half the East Germans supported the view that West Germany should integrate with the West rather than agree to any Soviet proposal for a unified neutral Germany.

On the question of whether or not the Western Powers ought to agree to a four-power withdrawal from Germany, twice as many (62%) East Germans thought it unwise to do so as thought it wise (31%).

Whereas less than a fourth of the urban West German population thought that a four-power conference would be advantageous for Germany, 38 per cent of the East German respondents thought it would be. There was also a large difference in the no-opinion category between the two groups: 30 per cent among the urban West Germans, as opposed to only 13 per cent among the total East German sample.

Report No. 72 (12 April 1951)

WEST GERMAN REACTIONS TO INCREASED OCCUPATION COSTS

Sample: 800 West German residents and 200 West Berliners.
Interviewing dates: 15 to 22 March 1951. (16 pp.)

The survey was conducted at the time of the announcement of an increase in occupation costs from $1.31 billion to $1.57

billion. Only 16 per cent of the population had any idea what the true costs borne by the German government were. The largest segment (40%) guessed a sum that was too small, and 34 per cent could not even hazard a guess. Most (69%) expected an announcement of higher costs.

Almost half of all West Germans (but only 33 per cent of West Berliners) felt that the occupation costs were used for something other than the security of West Germany. Most of these respondents said the costs went for the maintenance of an unnecessarily large and expensive occupation force and their dependents. The few who mentioned defense said it was for Europe's or America's defense, not that of Germany.

Report No. 73 (13 April 1951)

DO GERMANS WANT A SINGLE YOUTH ORGANIZATION IN WEST GERMANY?

Sample: 1,500 residents of the American Zone, 250 West Berliners, and 175 people in Bremen.
Interviewing dates: early 1951. (9 pp.)

Postwar American policy on German youth organizations had been to encourage decentralization and diversification rather than the unitary and monolithic type of the Hitler period. The East German government followed the latter pattern.

Opinion varied widely throughout West Germany on the question of unitary vs. diversified youth organizations. Whereas in West Berlin half (51%) favored the latter type (and only 6 per cent had no opinion on the subject), as few as 31 per cent held this view in Hesse (with 27 per cent in the no-opinion category). More than two in five AMZON Germans (44%) and West Berliners (43%) preferred a single, comprehensive youth organization. Among young people between the ages of 15 and 24, 55 per cent favored a single youth organization. A fifth (21%) of these youths would, in fact, have forbidden all other groups.

The most frequently cited reason for favoring a single organization was the concept of strength through unity. Those favoring diversification stressed the view that people have different interests and hence different needs.

Report No. 74 (16 April 1951)

WEST GERMAN VIEW ON TWO CURRENT ISSUES: THE PROPOSED FOUR-POWER CONFERENCE AND THE REVISED OCCUPATION STATUTE

Sample: 800 West Germans and 200 West Berliners.

Interviewing dates: 15 to 22 March 1951. (12 pp.)

Nearly two weeks after the negotiations on an agenda for the four-power conference at Paris had begun, about two-thirds (68%) of the West German population were aware that discussions were in progress. Over half (54%) of the West Berliners interviewed felt that such a conference would benefit Germany, but only 34 per cent of the West German population thought so. At the same time, 63 per cent of the West Germans thought the Western Powers would represent West German interests.

Roughly one week after a revision in the occupation statute for West Germany had been announced, only 37 per cent of the West German population and 44 per cent of the West Berliners had heard of it.

Report No. 75 (18 April 1951)

GERMAN REACTIONS TO THREE CURRENT ECONOMIC ISSUES: CODETERMINATION, DECARTELIZATION, AND FREEDOM OF ENTERPRISE

Sample: 800 West Germans and 200 West Berliners.
Interviewing dates: 7 to 15 March and 15 to 22 March 1951. (24 pp.)

Shortly before the law introducing codetermination in West Germany's coal and steel industries was passed by the Bundestag, 61 per cent of the West German population (and 69 per cent in the British Zone, where these industries were centered) had heard that this issue was under discussion. Of these, 46 per cent thought codetermination ought to be granted. When the respondents were informed that one major aspect of codetermination was an equal voice for labor in managerial matters, however, only 39 per cent of the population expressed approval of the move, with 50 per cent saying that many important issues could only be decided by the employer.

Regarding decartelization, only 16 per cent could name the law under which the big industrial concerns like I. G. Farben and Krupp had been split up into smaller, independent companies. Population breakdowns on this question revealed that there was no single group in which more than half knew about the law.

In an effort to eliminate traditional guildist restrictions on free enterprise, the Bundestag in early 1951 was considering passage of a bill establishing a council of tradesmen which would determine whether or not an individual could enter a trade. The Allied High Commission was critical of such legislation. When presented simply as a slogan, *"Gewerbefreiheit"* ("freedom of enterprise") made a favorable impression on 47 per cent of the West Germans and 59 per cent of the West Berliners. However, when the respondents were given a specific illustration of how the measure would work--Should a man who wishes to open a radio shop have to obtain prior approval from members of the trade?-- 47 per cent felt a person ought to be able to open a business without permission.

Report No. 76 (24 April 1951)

CONTINUING TRENDS IN AWARENESS AND PATRONAGE OF THE AMERIKA HÄUSER IN THE U.S. ZONE

Sample: 1,500 American Zone residents; supplementary table in the appendix is based on a sample of 465 Frankfurt school children between the ages of 10 and 15.
Interviewing dates: January 1951. (9 pp.)

Between May 1950 and January 1951 the percentage of AMZON residents who said they were aware of the existence of United States Information Centers, or Amerika Häuser, rose by a total of 12 percentage points, from 62 per cent to 74 per cent. Asked whether or not they had ever visited one of the centers, in January 1951 31 per cent of the residents of cities with populations of 100,000 to 249,999 claimed to have done so.

Report No. 77 (24 April 1951)

INITIAL REACTIONS OF URBAN WEST GERMANS TO THE RECALL OF GENERAL MacARTHUR

Sample: 640 West Germans from cities with populations of 50,000 or more.
Interviewing dates: flash survey on 16 to 17 April 1951. (13 pp.)

Less than one week after the event, 74 per cent of urban West Germans knew that President Harry S. Truman had relieved General Douglas MacArthur of his duties as supreme commander in the Far East. After those who were unaware of this dismissal were given the basic facts, all respondents were asked whether or not they thought the move justified: 34 per cent agreed with the dismissal, 24 per cent disagreed, and 42 per cent offered no opinion.
A strong majority (70%) of the urban population was also aware of the fact that MacArthur's dismissal occasioned strong differences of opinion in the United States itself. But only 25 per cent of these thought such differences would bring about a change in American foreign policy. As for influencing the East, 53 per cent felt that the dismissal would have no effect

on the communists' reaction to Western peace terms, a sixth (17%) thought the communists would be more inclined to accept them, and an eighth (12%) expected them to be less inclined to do so.

Report No. 78 (14 May 1951)

U.S. ZONE GERMANS VIEW THE KREIS RESIDENT OFFICERS

Sample: 1,500 residents of the American Zone.
Interviewing dates: late January and early February 1951. (25 pp.)

Although the Kreis Resident Officers (KROs) were the local representatives of the United States High Commission, the vast majority (66%) of AMZON Germans had never heard of them or the position. Of the 34 per cent who claimed they knew of the office, only 12 per cent could give the correct or at least an acceptable version of the title. Furthermore, only 9 per cent had ever seen their KRO and, of these, 2 per cent had talked with him. As for knowledge of the KRO's function, even among the respondents who were considered most aware of the office, almost all thought he was supposed to control the German authorities rather than act as a liaison between Americans and Germans.

Among those who knew of the KROs, more people thought they served a useful function than thought not.

Report No. 79 (17 May 1951)

ATTITUDES BEHIND THE IRON CURTAIN
III. A Preliminary Exploration of Attitudes Among East Zone Male Youth

Sample: 162 young East German men between the ages of 15 and 24 chosen from visitors to a sports exhibition held in West Berlin; see Special Report No. II/63-S on sampling problems and representativeness.
Interviewing dates: 7 to 15 April 1951. (61 pp.)

Asked how they would rate their general personal situation in East Germany at that time, 49 per cent of the young men questioned replied, "Fair." Group breakdowns on the question revealed that favorable responses were less frequent among the better educated than among the less well-educated and that there was no group in which more respondents were clearly dissatisfied than satisfied. As far as their futures were concerned, the largest percentage (46%) thought their personal situation would improve, almost a quarter (24%) thought it would get worse, and about the same percentage (26%) felt it would remain the same.

The overwhelming majority (91%) of the respondents said that the young people in the East were interested in learning something about the West; 68 per cent of the young people interviewed said they read Western newspapers, and fully 91 per cent said they listened to Western radio programs. As for the actual situation they found when they came to the West, the majority of respondents said they were impressed with life in West Germany, especially the economic situation. At the same time, 37 per cent of the respondents guessed that the East had won up to 40 per cent of the young over to its aims; only 19 per cent thought the figure was 10 per cent or less.

Asked whether they preferred a single national youth organization (as in fact existed in the East) or several, 63 per cent of the respondents from the East said they considered the latter better. (When this question was asked of young men and women in the West [cf. Report no. 73], only 32 per cent said they liked several organizations better.) Furthermore, 60 per cent of the young men from the East said they liked absolutely nothing about the central youth organization of East Germany, the Free German Youth (or FDJ). Even the national rally held by the FDJ at Whitsuntide 1950 in East Berlin was remembered by as many as 45 per cent of the respondents as having left a bad impression, primarily because of the contrast it offered with West Berlin. All but two respondents in the entire sample were aware that a World Youth Festival was scheduled for August 1951 in East Berlin, but only 31 per cent expressed any interest in participating in it.

An overwhelming majority (90%) of the young men interviewed said they did not think the East German government represented the will of the people. At the same time, however, almost a third (31%) felt that both the East and West were responsible for the prevailing world tension. About the same percentage (30%) said they thought most East Germans would prefer to stay out of the struggle between East and West. On the question of whether or not there would actually be armed conflict in Europe in the near future, about three-quarters as many said yes (41%) as said no (56%). Almost all (95%) respondents favored the idea of promoting a union of all the European nations.

Three-quarters of the young people interviewed expressed dissatisfaction with their school system, primarily because the "subject matter is saturated with politics." Over half (57%) felt that all students in the East did not have an equal chance to attend a college preparatory program or a university. Over half (59%) said the church did not have the freedom to teach what it considered to be right. Almost as many (54%) said that parents did not have this freedom either.

Report No. 80 (28 May 1951)

CURRENT TREND ON DEFENSE PARTICIPATION
With West German Reactions to the Communist Remilitarization "Plebiscite"

Sample: 800 West German residents.
Interviewing dates: 30 April to 11 May 1951. (12 pp.)

120/Public Opinion in Semisovereign Germany

Support for West German participation in the Atlantic Pact dropped--with extensive fluctuations--from 63 per cent in October and November 1950, when the question was posed for the first time, to just 43 per cent in spring 1951. Not only was this an all-time low, it was also the first time that opposition outweighed agreement in some areas. Population breakdowns revealed that the more educated and generally better informed elements in the society continued to tend toward support for participation in the defense of Europe.

For some months the communists had been speaking of conducting a plebiscite in West Germany on the remilitarization issue. As of mid-May only 37 per cent of the West German population had heard of this proposal. When asked whether they were generally in favor of a plebiscite--with the question of sponsorship set aside for the moment--three-quarters (76%) of the respondents replied affirmatively, 15 per cent were opposed, and 9 per cent had no opinion on the matter.

Report No. 81 (30 May 1951)

THE EFFECTIVENESS OF RECENT INFORMATIONAL EFFORTS ON THE SCHUMAN PLAN

Sample: 800 West German residents.
Interviewing dates: two separate surveys on 15 to 20 March and 2 to 9 May 1951. (20 pp.)

Despite efforts to publicize the Schuman Plan following its initialing in Paris on 19 March, the percentage of West Germans aware of the plan remained at 68 per cent. The number of persons displaying specific knowledge about it rose, however, from 26 per cent to 36 per cent. Outright rejection of the plan had decreased to the point where agreement (44%) outweighed disagreement (19%) by a wide margin. The most marked decrease in opposition was among trade union members, SPD adherents, and those under 40.

Although Kurt Schumacher, head of the SPD, had been an extremely active and articulate opponent of West German participation in the Schuman Plan, over half the population did not know what his views on the subject were; 40 per cent knew that he was opposed to it. Knowledge of Schumacher's opposition seemed to have little bearing on a respondent's attitude toward the Schuman Plan. Just as many who agreed as disagreed with it were aware of his opposition.

Report No. 82 (31 May 1951)

DOES EAST OR WEST REALLY WANT A FOUR-POWER CONFERENCE?

Sample: 800 West German residents.

Interviewing dates: 2 to 9 May 1951. (14 pp.)

Between late March and early May the percentage of persons aware of preliminary negotiations for a four-power meeting dropped from 68 per cent to 61 per cent. Asked whether they thought the United States really wanted such a meeting to be held, 64 per cent replied affirmatively. Only 13 per cent thought Russia did.

Report No. 83 (12 June 1951)

THE PRESENT STATE OF WEST GERMAN CONFIDENCE IN THE WEST
With Reactions to General MacArthur's Recall

Sample: 800 West German residents.
Interviewing dates: 2 to 9 May 1951. (31 pp.)

Some two weeks after President Truman had recalled General MacArthur from his post in the Far East, 66 per cent of the West German population had heard of the dismissal. Although over half had no opinion on the matter, 25 per cent felt the action was wrong, while only 19 per cent thought Truman had done the right thing. Among those who thought the dismissal justified, the most frequently cited reason was the fear that the General's course of action might have led to another world war. In fact, 59 per cent of the West German population was opposed to policies such as those advocated by MacArthur. Cross-tabulations revealed the interesting fact that by no means all those who deplored the General's dismissal recommended an extension of the Korean conflict: almost as many (11%) felt broader measures should be undertaken as felt such measures should not be undertaken (14%).

MacArthur's dismissal and the consequent debate within the United States about American foreign policy did not imply, according to almost a third (32%) of the Germans, any policy change at least with regard to the communists. Only 9 per cent expected a more conciliatory American policy and 30 per cent thought it would become firmer.

Increasing numbers of West Germans felt that the Western Powers were stronger than the communists. In January 1951, 24 per cent felt the Western Powers were stronger, as opposed to 46 per cent who ranked the communists in this first position. By May 1951, 45 per cent said the West was stronger, while only 19 per cent gave this position to the communists.

Asked which side they thought had had the greater political success during the preceding year, 37 per cent of the population replied the Western Powers, while 31 per cent chose the communists. The population breakdowns on this question showed that the better educated, those in the upper income brackets,

and those with higher socioeconomic status tended to give the
edge to the communists rather than the Western Powers. As for
the long-range outlook, 64 per cent of the population as a
whole felt that the Western Powers would emerge on top; this
represented an increase, from January 1951, of nine percentage
points.

Report No. 84 (14 June 1951)

GUNS OR BUTTER?
West German Opinion on the Use of Marshall Plan Funds

Sample: 800 West German residents.
Interviewing dates: 2 to 9 May 1951. (10 pp.)

With defense costs rising and most Western European nations
still paying for the last war, the use of Marshall Plan funds
was a critical problem. In West Germany, the majority (61%) of
the population thought that part of the funds would be diverted
for defense purposes. Almost a majority (45%), however, felt
that it would be better if the European Recovery Plan (ERP) funds
were used solely for economic purposes, as had been the case in
the past. Of the 36 per cent who thought that some of the money
should be used for defense purposes, 14 per cent felt that about
half should be thus used, and 12 per cent felt it ought to be
less than half.

Report No. 85 (15 June 1951)

THE IMPACT OF THE EUROPA TRAIN
A Preliminary Study on a Mainz Audience

Sample: 180 visitors to the Europa Train while it was at Mainz.
Interviewing dates: 17 to 19 May 1951. (14 pp.)

The Europa Train, viewed as an information medium, seemed
to be a success as far as the visitors to it in Mainz were concerned. Fully 74 per cent of them grasped the message it sought
to transmit: unified Europe will be strong. Although the majority of visitors (62%) said their views on European cooperation
were not changed by their visit, three in ten said the train had
influenced their thinking, either by confirming previously held
ideas or by teaching them something new. The vast majority (83%)
of respondents felt that close cooperation among European nations
would be advantageous to all, while 12 per cent thought it would
bring advantages only to a select few, with France being mentioned most frequently. Almost as large a majority (75%) held the
view that economic cooperation would strengthen Europe.

Report No. 86 (21 June 1951)

THE EAST-WEST TRADE ISSUE AS VIEWED BY THE WEST GERMAN PEOPLE

Sample: 800 West German residents.
Interviewing dates: 16 to 26 May 1951. (13 pp.)

Half the West German public was unable to say whether or not there was any trade between East and West Germany. Of the rest, 11 per cent said there was none, 28 per cent thought there was some but not very much, and 9 per cent thought there was considerable trade. (In fact, such trade--exports plus imports--amounted to $160 million in 1950, in contrast to the Federal Republic's total foreign trade, excluding interzonal trade, of $4.7 billion in 1950.) Asked whether they thought the East or the West would gain more by this trade, 22 per cent said East Germany, 15 per cent said West Germany, and 37 per cent felt both sides would have the same advantage. Very few West Germans (8%) felt that East-West trade ought to be banned altogether, but 47 per cent did think there ought to be a ban on potential war materials; 29 per cent thought there should be no limitations to trade between East and West Germany.

Cross-tabulations on a number of questions revealed that attitudes on the trade question did not appear to be related to a neutralist orientation in the East-West struggle.

Report No. 87 (29 June 1951)

WEST GERMANS VIEW THE SOCIALIST REICH PARTY
With a Preliminary Analysis of SRP Attitudes

Sample: 800 West Germans, as well as 100 SRP adherents from Lower Saxony.
Interviewing dates: 16 to 28 May 1951. (44 pp.)

Two to three weeks after the Lower Saxony state elections, the majority (63%) of West Germans and over a third (37%) of the population of Lower Saxony itself, had not heard of the new Socialist Reich party (SRP). That West Germans were generally unaware of political developments in Lower Saxony was also pointed up by the fact that 70 per cent were unaware that an election had even taken place. Only a quarter knew that the Social Democratic party (SPD) had emerged victorious.

Among West Germans who had heard of the party, the most frequently cited goal of the SRP was the reestablishment of National Socialism. Adherents of the SRP, however, dissented strongly from this characterization, with 52 per cent describing its goal as the betterment of economic and social conditions in Germany.

Opinions split rather evenly (27 to 26 per cent) in West Germany on the question of whether or not the party's achievements warranted close attention; 47 per cent, however, expressed no opinion on the matter.

Almost as many West Germans who expressed an opinion on the subject opposed (16%) a ban on the party as favored (22%) such a move.

A comparison of attitudes revealed that SRP adherents were considerably more widely dissatisfied with the achievements of the Bonn government (85%) than were their fellow Lower Saxony residents (52%), who in turn were more dissatisfied than West Germans outside Lower Saxony (42%). The most frequently cited reasons were "bad economic policy" (16%) and the feeling that "the government doesn't care for the little people" (15%). Almost nine in ten SRP sympathizers felt that the Western Powers exerted too much influence on the decisions of the West German government, and about half of these (44%) went so far as to say that the Bonn government was merely a puppet of the Western Powers.

Of considerable interest to American authorities were SRP sympathizers' attitudes toward National Socialism. Whereas 34 per cent of the West German population as a whole said they thought there had been more good than evil in the ideas of National Socialism, the figure for Lower Saxony residents, excluding SRP adherents, was 47 per cent, and for SRP adherents it was as high as 86 per cent. The most frequently cited reasons for this view were the good job opportunities and living standards under the Nazis. Not surprisingly, then, 79 per cent of the SRP adherents interviewed said they thought denazification was a bad idea. Regarding the specific issue of the Landsberg prisoners who had been condemned to death at the time of the survey, 68 per cent of the SRP sympathizers thought they should have been released. Half of the rest of the Lower Saxony population and as few as 35 per cent of the rest of the West Germans also felt this way.

Report No. 88 (6 July 1951)

CURRENT THINKING ON WEST GERMAN DEFENSE PARTICIPATION
With Projected Reactions to a Possible Bonn Agreement

Sample: 800 West Germans and 200 West Berliners.
Interviewing dates: 16 to 23 June 1951. (48 pp.)

Whereas in May and early June 1951 popular approval of West German participation in an Atlantic Pact army had dipped to an all-time low of 43 per cent, by mid-June 1951 the figure rose once again to 46 per cent, with 33 per cent opposed. In West Berlin, approval continued by far to outweigh disapproval, 75 per cent to 19 per cent.

Most of those who favored participation said they would approve only if certain conditions were met (31%), and at the same time an appreciable proportion of those opposed to participation said they would drop their opposition if certain conditions were met (9%). This left 21 per cent of the West German population unconditionally opposed to participation.

Asked whether they would accept a decision by the West German government to participate in a West European army, 22 per cent said they would welcome it; 45 per cent said they would accept it, even if they were not enthusiastic about it; 13 per cent they would oppose it but do nothing about it; and 2 per cent said they would be opposed and take some action against it.

Very few West Germans (2%) said they would volunteer for service in a European army. However, 48 per cent said they would serve if drafted. In West Berlin, 8 per cent said they would volunteer, and 49 per cent said they would serve if drafted. Despite the willingness to serve if drafted, almost half (48%) of the West German population felt that the Bonn government should not have the right to conscript its citizens.

To underscore Western interest in German security, American authorities publicized recent Western troop reinforcements. In addition, Kurt Schumacher, head of the SPD, stressed the necessity of such reinforcements as a prerequisite to German defense participation. In light of these two facts, it is interesting to note that 50 per cent of the West German population opposed these troop reinforcements; only in West Berlin did a majority (74%) favor the move. The most frequently mentioned reason for this opposition was the increased financial burden connected with it.

As in previous months, most West Germans said they would prefer to stay out of the East-West struggle. If, however, the consequence of such neutralism were the withdrawal of Western defense guarantees, a majority (63%) said they would then want to side with the West. Asked then whether, if the danger of war were steadily to increase, they would rather see West Germany side with the West, the East, or stay neutral, somewhat fewer (60%) said they would want to side with the West. Whatever the West Germans may have thought about the desirability of neutrality, in the event of an attack from the East fully 73 per cent said the West should fight with all means available. This sentiment was even maintained by a majority (62%) of those opposed to West German participation in a European army.

Responses to a question dealing with the dependability of Great Britain, the United States, France, Italy, and West Germany revealed a serious lack of confidence in some of the Western Allies. Two out of three thought that West Germany and the United States could be depended on. About half thought this was also true of Great Britain. But only four in ten felt France could be relied on to take action in defense of the West, and as few as 15 per cent felt this way about Italy.

Report No. 89 (13 July 1951)

URBAN WEST GERMAN REACTIONS TO THE KEMRITZ CASE

Sample: 640 West Germans in cities with populations of 50,000 or more, as well as 200 West Berliners.
Interviewing dates: flash survey on 27 to 29 June 1951. (22 pp.)

Hans Kemritz, a German attorney living in Berlin at the time of the alleged events, was accused of turning fellow Germans over to the Russians in the first years of the occupation. The United States High Commission intervened on his behalf, prompting a resolution in the Bundestag criticizing the American move.

Only about half (53%) the West German urban population was aware of the Kemritz case; in West Berlin the figure was somewhat higher (66%). Of the 53 per cent, only three-fifths (33%) knew that the American authorities had intervened. When asked whether American intervention on behalf of Kemritz had caused a change in attitudes toward the Americans, about three times as many replied in the negative (24%) as in the affirmative (7%).

Report No. 90 (25 July 1951)

ATTITUDES BEHIND THE IRON CURTAIN
IV. Radio Listening in the East Zone

Sample: 100 East Berliners and 390 other East Germans, interviewed both in West Berlin and at the East-West crossing point of Helmstedt; see Special Report No. II/63-S on sampling problems and representativeness.
Interviewing dates: 24 May to 9 June 1951. (59 pp.)

Radio listening was popular in East Germany, as indicated by the fact that 90 per cent of the respondents described themselves as listeners (in contrast to 78 per cent in West Germany). Again in contrast with the West, where the opinion-leading elements tended to do the most listening, the typically more inert and unresponsive population groups in East Germany recorded almost as widespread radio-listening habits as did the typically more alert groups. RIAS was by far the most popular station (81%); the Leipzig station was second, with 11 per cent. Those who liked RIAS best ventured the opinion that it was truthful, besides being versatile and up-to-date. Asked which of the RIAS programs they liked best, 42 per cent said the news, 28 per cent mentioned an audience participation program, and 22 per cent said the musical programs were their favorites. Musical programs were the most popular on Radio Leipzig.

Report No. 91 (6 August 1951)

WEST GERMAN ATTITUDES ON SOME CURRENT POLITICAL ISSUES

Sample: 800 West Germans.
Interviewing dates: 9 to 21 July 1951. (30 pp.)

This survey is the German portion of a seven-nation study conducted for the Department of State by International Opinion Research, Inc.

Well over half the West German public (60%) said they felt that America was more in the right than Russia in the East-West struggle. Only 3 per cent gave such credit to the Soviet Union, 18 per cent felt both were right, and 19 per cent ventured no opinion on the subject. Although 54 per cent thought the United States was doing all it could to prevent war, almost a quarter (24%) did not think this was the case. Of the latter group, 6 per cent felt that the United States should seek an understanding with the Soviet Union, while 4 per cent said America ought to stop rearming. As for the Soviet Union, while 8 per cent felt it was doing all it could to prevent war, 63 per cent held the opposite view.

More people (36%) said that, militarily speaking, America was stronger at that moment, but a fourth of the population put the Soviet Union in this first position, and 16 per cent said they thought both were equal. However, if war were to break out, 56 per cent thought America would have a better chance of winning.

Asked whether they thought the United States would use the atomic bomb at the outset of a new war or wait for the other side to use one first, 23 per cent thought the United States would use it immediately, while 49 per cent felt America would wait. Asked the same question with regard to the Soviet Union, 37 per cent said they thought Russia would use it immediately, while 33 per cent thought the Russians would wait. In the event that the Soviet Union invaded Western Europe, 35 per cent favored using the bomb immediately, and 36 per cent said it should be used only after the Soviet Union had done so.

Although West Germany was not a member, 68 per cent of its population had heard of the United Nations. Among these, 29 per cent thought the U.N. would help considerably in preventing a third world war, 19 per cent felt it could help but not considerably, and 7 per cent thought it could not help at all.

Over half the German population (51%) expressed dissatisfaction with the Bonn government's efforts to improve West German living conditions. At the same time, 39 per cent said they were satisfied with their government's efforts on this score. Asked what they thought were the most pressing problems facing West Germany at that time, almost a fourth mentioned high taxes and prices; 17 per cent mentioned the preservation of peace; another 16 per cent spoke of better economic conditions and a higher standard of living.

Report No. 92 (20 August 1951)

WEST GERMAN REACTIONS TO THE KOREAN ARMISTICE NEGOTIATIONS

Sample: 800 West Germans.
Interviewing dates: 27 July to 8 August 1951. (37 pp.)

This was the first survey conducted by the newly established German opinion research organization, Deutsches Institut für Volksumfragen (DIVO).

About four-fifths (79%) of the German public had heard of the Korean cease-fire negotiations which had opened barely a month earlier. The talks were regarded with some skepticism: 17 per cent felt the communists had decided to negotiate to win time and to prepare new attacks; another 9 per cent thought they were doing so to launch a new war elsewhere. Furthermore, 42 per cent did not think the talks would end in an armistice; only 31 per cent thought they would. Almost half (47%) saw a truce only as a temporary easing of East-West tension; 18 per cent thought it would have no significant influence on this tension. Asked what they thought would happen if the armistice talks failed, over half (52%) said the war would spread beyond Korea, 32 per cent had no opinion on the subject, and 16 per cent thought the war would remain limited to Korea.

Forty per cent of the West Germans said they did not think a division of Korea along the 38th parallel was a satisfactory solution; 37 per cent, however, ventured no opinion on this matter. Of those opposed to such a move, about one-third said that division breeds conflict, while half again as many stated that a divided Korea would be as unfortunate as a divided Germany.

Despite the skeptical eye with which many West Germans viewed the Korean truce parley, the prevailing view was one of optimism. The United Nations (30%) was seen as having a better chance than the communists (13%) to get its conditions for a truce accepted.

Special Report 92-S (23 August 1951)

A NOTE ON WEST GERMAN REACTIONS TO ENDING THE STATE OF WAR

Sample: 800 West Germans.
Interviewing dates: not given. (6 pp.)

A solid majority (68%) of the West German population was aware of the Allied decision to end the state of war with Germany.

In contrast to the views expressed at the time in various

publications and by various politicians, most respondents (59%) considered the Allied move a step forward on the road to equality for Germany. Of the 18 per cent who considered the move unimportant in this regard, almost half said that it was merely a formality, nothing had been changed, or that Germany was still an occupied country.

Report No. 93 (24 August 1951)

WEST GERMAN REACTIONS TO THE PROJECTED AMERICAN-SPANISH MILITARY AND ECONOMIC PACT

Sample: 800 West Germans.
Interviewing dates: 27 July to 8 August 1951. (15 pp.)

At the time of the survey almost half (44%) the West German population was aware of the American move to establish military and economic relations with Spain. Approximately the same percentage (49%) had not heard of the plan, and the remaining 7 per cent said there was no such plan under consideration. Asked whether they favored or opposed American relations with Spain, 49 per cent of the respondents said they welcomed the move; almost as many (46%), however, expressed no opinion on the matter. Those who favored the American intentions most frequently mentioned Spain's political and military importance to the West in the struggle against the East. Those opposed mentioned the Spanish dictatorship, the feeling that Spain was unreliable, or that the move would be to Spain's disadvantage.

Not only did a large percentage of West Germans approve a Spanish-American agreement, over half (57%) felt that Spain ought to be admitted to NATO; only 9 per cent opposed such a move. Asked the same question about Yugoslavia, slightly fewer (36%) said it should be admitted, 22 per cent were opposed, while the largest percentage (42%) had no opinion on the matter. Population breakdowns on the last two questions showed that among leadership groups about seven in ten felt Spain should be admitted to the Atlantic Pact, while slightly smaller percentages also felt that Yugoslavia should be admitted.

Report No. 94 (27 August 1951)

THE VIEWS OF WEST GERMANS ON THE DEFENSE OF WEST EUROPE

Sample: two surveys, each using a sample of 800 West German residents.
Interviewing dates: 10 to 20 July and 27 July to 8 August 1951. (29 pp.)

West German approval of participation in the defense of West Europe fluctuated somewhat in spring and summer 1951. The percentage of those in favor was lowest in the French Zone, highest in the British Zone, and in West Germany as a whole reached majority status only once--in mid-July 1951. Support for participation was highest among the better educated and informed elements of the population; in addition, a majority of men (almost two out of three in late July and early August) were in favor of participation.

Since it was increasingly clear that German entry into the Atlantic Pact would be decided by West German political leaders rather than by referendum, it became important to know how the public would respond to a decision by Bonn to participate in the pact. In West Germany 26 per cent said they would welcome the decision, 45 per cent said they would accept it even if they were not enthusiastic about it, 14 per cent said they would oppose the decision but do nothing about it, 2 per cent said they would be actively opposed, and 13 per cent offered no opinion. Almost three-quarters (73%), however, said that such participation was inevitable.

While a great many (49%) West Germans liked the idea of a former German general in command of the German troops, no single man was mentioned by an appreciable proportion of the public.

A majority (55%) of the respondents felt that a Korean armistice would not influence German thinking on the participation issue. A large proportion (41%) believed the end of that conflict would bring an increase in American defense aid, another 31 per cent thought such aid would remain the same, and 26 per cent gave no opinion. A quite sizable majority (80%) felt that Western Europe would not be able to turn back the Soviet army if the United States did not help; of these, almost all (51%) felt Russia could be prevented from overrunning Europe with American aid.

Dependence on United States help did not, however, mean that the West Germans hoped thereby to shirk the duty themselves. In late July almost three-quarters (75%) said they would favor an all-out fight in case of attack from the East. Attitudes toward the question of whether or not West Germany should once again have an armaments industry were less clearcut. Whereas 48 per cent favored such a move, almost a third (31%) was opposed, and 21 per cent gave no opinion. Cross-tabulations on a variety of related questions showed that advocates of West German participation in NATO tended to favor armaments production. In addition, the greater the confidence in the West's ability to withstand a Soviet attack, the greater was the inclination to advocate arms production.

Report No. 95 (28 August 1951)

GERMANS VIEW THE "VOICE OF AMERICA"
I. The Extent and Characteristics of the VOA Audience in West Germany and West Berlin

> *Sample:* 3,000 West Germans and 600 West Berlin residents.
> *Interviewing dates:* 27 March to 16 May 1951. (26 pp.)

Although the figures were not quite as high as in the United States, the number of West German radio listeners was fairly substantial (78%); in West Berlin the figure was even higher (91%). Among radio listeners, well over half (65 per cent, or 51 per cent of the total population) said they listened to the "Voice of America," while 10 per cent had never listened but knew what it was, and almost a quarter (24%) had never heard of it. In West Berlin, almost all radio listeners (98%) also listened to VOA.

Report No. 96 (30 August 1951)

HOW DO WEST GERMAN YOUTH REACT TO AMERICAN HISTORY?
A Preliminary Study of Stuttgart Pupils' Appraisal of *An Outline of American History*

> *Sample:* 200 pupils ranging in age from 13 to 20.
> *Interviewing dates:* 5 to 6 July 1951. (26 pp.)

During the last week of June 1951, 200 copies of the brochure *An Outline of American History*, published by the United States Information Service, was distributed in four different types of schools in the city of Stuttgart: elementary school *(Volksschule)*, middle school *(Mittelschule)*, upper secondary school *(Höhere Schule)*, and trade school *(Gewerbeschule)*. The respondents were given a week in which to read the pamphlet. Background information on the pupils and the names of the schools used in the survey are contained in two appendices at the end of the report.
  A solid majority (71%) of the Stuttgart pupils liked the brochure, while an additional 13 per cent even liked it very much. Pupils going to a high school (those most likely to attend a university later) were somewhat more reserved (66%) than the others.
  Although most pupils in all the schools thought the brochure gave a satisfactory general view of the history of the United States, a sizable minority felt it had not clarified certain things. The topic most frequently mentioned as needing further clarification was the racial problem.

132/Public Opinion in Semisovereign Germany

Among high school students, only 31 per cent described the brochure as objective, while 42 per cent thought it presented American history in too favorable a light. By contrast, 96 per cent of the trade school pupils described it as objective. Asked whether or not the brochure had influenced their opinion of the United States, a majority of all groups, except the trade school pupils (40%), said their opinions had remained unchanged; almost no one said it had changed their opinion for the worse; and percentages varying from 12 per cent of the high school pupils to 60 per cent of the trade school pupils said their opinions had changed for the better. Majorities ranging from 98 per cent of the pupils in elementary and middle schools to 58 per cent of the high school students felt that American history ought to be taught more thoroughly in German schools.

Report No. 97 (31 August 1951)

GERMANS VIEW THE "VOICE OF AMERICA"
II. Some Technical Factors in VOA Listenership

Sample: 3,000 West Germans and 600 West Berliners.
Interviewing dates: 27 March to 16 May 1951. (26 pp.)

Over 90 per cent of all West German radio listeners were able to receive stations carrying the "Voice of America" program. Among the respondents who could receive stations that carried VOA programs as well as stations that did not, approximately the same percentages said they listened to VOA as was true of those who could get nothing but VOA stations. Comparisons of figures for general listening with VOA listenership revealed that those more inclined to listen to VOA were generally more interested in listening to the radio in the first place.

Report No. 98 (13 September 1951)

REACTIONS OF THE BERLIN AUDIENCE TO THE TRAIN OF EUROPE

Sample: 141 East Germans and 114 West Germans.
Interviewing dates: 1 to 15 August 1951. (16 pp.)

The study was made during the Communist World Youth Meeting held in East Berlin. Most of the East German respondents were, therefore, participants in that meeting. The report also draws comparisons with results of an earlier study (Report No. 85) made in Mainz.
Most Germans--those from Mainz (78%), West Berlin (83%), and especially those from East Berlin (93%)--understood the basic theme expressed by the "Train of Europe": a rallying call

for economic and political unification as a basis of strength for Europe, as well as an expression of the need to unite in protection against the East. An even greater percentage of the East and West German visitors also agreed that this theme was a valid one.

As to the general question of West European economic integration, the vast majority of both East and West Germans (92 and 95 per cent respectively) said it would be better for West Germany to join the economic system of the West rather than that of the East. Almost all respondents (96%) also thought that some of the Eastern European countries would join the West, too, if they could. Half (51%) of the East Berliners and 86 per cent of the West Berliners felt that the GDR would join the West European economic system if it could.

Report No. 99 (21 September 1951)

WEST GERMAN REACTIONS TO A "PRESERVATION OF DEMOCRACY" CLAUSE IN THE PROJECTED CONTRACTUAL AGREEMENT

Sample: 800 West Germans.
Interviewing dates: 20 to 31 August 1951. (16 pp.)

In the course of the discussions on a contractual agreement between the Western Powers and the Federal Republic to replace the statute of occupation, the problem of what to do in case a domestic group should try to overthrow the government became a matter of some concern. Although a third of the population had no opinion on the matter, one fourth (24%) of all West Germans felt the Allies should have the right to intervene in such a situation, while almost twice as many (42%) thought the federal government should deal with it.

Report No. 100 (27 September 1951)

PROGRAM TASTES OF WEST GERMAN AND WEST BERLIN RADIO LISTENERS

And Tabular Summary

Sample: 3,000 West Germans and 600 West Berliners.
Interviewing dates: 27 March to 16 May 1951. (57 pp.)

News programs headed the list of programs that West Germans (71%), as well as West Berliners (87%), would not want to miss. Variety programs, folk music, and operettas followed. At the bottom of the list came American jazz. There was considerable agreement between men and women on favorite programs. Differences according to age, however, were rather marked.

Whereas those over 25 preferred news programs, those under 25 preferred variety programs and dance music. The remaining 44 tables present breakdowns on each of fifteen different types of program according to ten different sociological variables, as well as four psychological variables (a measure of political activity and interest, attitude toward democracy, attitude toward America, and degree of readiness to learn from America).

Report No. 101 (29 September 1951)

ATTITUDES OF EAST GERMAN YOUTH
I. Evaluations of the Berlin Youth Festival and Impressions of West Berlin

Sample: not given; see Special Report No. II/63-S on sampling problems and representativeness.
Interviewing dates: 5 to 19 August 1951. (34 pp.)

The survey was conducted in West Berlin youth centers among young people who had crossed the border during the East Berlin Youth Festival. The geographic distribution of the sample corresponded fairly closely to that of the population as a whole (except that there were almost no respondents from East Berlin). It contained only 25 per cent girls, however, which was definitely not representative of the percentage of girls in the East German population. There were almost no respondents under the age of 14.

Less than half (47%) of the respondents said they had gone to the Communist Youth Festival because of its political aims and purposes. Of these, 19 per cent said they had gone to get a chance to visit West Berlin; another 10 per cent said they had wanted to do something new and different. In fact, 85 per cent of those interviewed said they had planned on a visit to West Berlin right from the outset.

Asked whether or not West Berlin had lived up to their expectations, 35 per cent said it had, while 62 per cent claimed it was better than they had expected. Economic well-being and the free way of life were most frequently mentioned as aspects of West Berlin that had been better than expected. Three-quarters (75%) of the youngsters said they could think of nothing they didn't like in West Berlin.

Over half (56%) of those interviewed said they had learned something they had not known before their visit to the West. In this connection most mentioned freedom and democracy. About a fourth (27%) said they had no further questions since their visit; but 14 per cent wondered whether there was, in fact, rearmament going on in the West, and another 10 per cent wanted to learn more about economic and social problems in general. Eight per cent wondered whether it would be possible for them to stay and live in the West.

As for the youth festival that had brought them to East Berlin in the first place, 54 per cent said that those in their group did not like it. Four in five termed the festival a failure. Asked what they thought had been the East's aim in holding it, 27 per cent responded that its purpose had been to win the youth for communism, and another 22 per cent thought it was seen as a means to show off the East's strength and the solidarity of its youth with communism. Ten per cent saw it as a demonstration for peace.

Fifty per cent of the young respondents said the West should not have tried to prevent Western youth from attending the festival in the East.

Report No. 102 (29 September 1951)

ATTITUDES OF EAST GERMAN YOUTH
II. What Young Germans Would Like to Ask Mr. McCloy

Sample: number of East German youth surveyed was not given (see Special Report No. II/63-S on sampling problems and representativeness); 266 West German respondents were chosen from among participants at a European youth meeting held in West Germany.
Interviewing dates: 5 to 19 August 1951. (13 pp.)

The report focuses on questions that East German youth would pose to United States High Commissioner for Germany, John J. McCloy, if they could.

The most frequently asked questions centered on reunification of Germany. Some respondents revealed disillusionment with the intent or ability of the wartime Allies to bring about reunification. Others seemed to recognize the responsibility of the German people but to be uncertain about what they could do.

The second largest group of questions focused on the liberation of East Germany. Again, the hope seemed to be that the West could solve the problem; in fact, a number of rather desperate measures were proposed, such as asking McCloy to suggest to the American government that it wage war with the Soviet Union.

The third most frequently posed type of question concerned the future development of Germany in general. Many respondents mentioned the projected peace treaty.

In contrast with the questions from their Eastern peers, which seemed to call for reassurance and more information, the tenor of questions from the Western group was more specific and basically critical. Most dealt with particular aspects of the economic and political policies of the West (especially the United States) toward Germany. They wanted to know why the occupation costs were so high, why Germany had to sell its own coal and then import expensive American coal, whether Germany would have to repay all the Marshall Plan funds, or why the pay

of American GI's in Germany was so high compared with the pay
of other soldiers. They also asked about reunification; but,
in contrast with the 23 per cent of East German youth inquiring
about this issue, only 6 per cent of the Western youth asked
about it. The Western group also asked about two problems not
raised by the East Germans: the question of a united Europe
and that of equal rights for Germany among the nations of the
world.

Report No. 103 (12 October 1951)

THE CURRENT STATE OF GERMAN-AMERICAN RELATIONS

Sample: 800 West Germans.
Interviewing dates: mid-September 1951. (39 pp.)

An introductory statement to the report explains that
"The study was undertaken in order to ascertain whether the
picture presented by the West German press in early September
of deteriorating Allied-German relations, brought on it was
said by recent Allied High Commission decisions, was as black
as the newspapers said." The results of the survey indicated
that the newspapers did not reflect public opinion.

Only a 10 per cent minority of the German people felt that
relations between West Germany and the occupation powers had
grown worse. In fact, as many as 38 per cent expressed the
view that these relations had improved. There were nonetheless
certain areas of stress. For example, 53 per cent of the population said they thought the Western Powers were exerting too
much influence on the Bonn government. Less than half of these,
however, went so far as to claim that Bonn was merely a puppet
government. Over a third (36%) of the respondents said they
thought the Americans wanted to keep West Germany in a dependent position; 41 per cent felt the goal was an independent West
Germany. Opinion-leading groups tended to be more critical than
others of the occupied status of their country. At the same
time, however, these groups tended to express the view that the
United States wished to see an independent Germany as soon as
possible.

When asked about the effect of actions taken by each occupying power, 55 per cent said that American actions had been to
the advantage of Germany; only 13 per cent felt that Britain had
worked for the advantage of the Germans; and as few as 4 per
cent felt this positively toward the French.

Over half (55%) of the West German population knew the
name of the American High Commissioner for West Germany, John
J. McCloy. By way of contrast, only about a quarter knew the
names of the British and the French High Commissioners.

On the more general question of the reasons for the continuing occupation of Germany, 51 per cent cited the danger from
the East. Over a third (34%), however, criticized the West for

its prolonged presence, citing the West's fear of Germany, its desire to exploit Germany economically, and the soft life led by the occupying forces. Well over half (59%) said they preferred that the Western Powers remain in West Germany, given the then existing political situation. Most also regarded the individual soldiers in the occupation forces in a positive light: 59 per cent said the men generally behaved in the same way as German soldiers would in similar circumstances. Four per cent said they behaved better.

Report No. 104 (17 October 1951)

GERMANS VIEW THE "VOICE OF AMERICA"
III. Program Preferences and Evaluations of VOA Listeners

Sample: 3,000 West Germans and 600 West Berliners.
Interviewing dates: from 27 March to 16 May 1951. (83 pp.)

In an effort to ascertain general feelings toward VOA, respondents were given a list of adjectives from which they were to choose those they felt best described the program. The largest proportion (52%) chose favorable adjectives, 18 per cent chose unfavorable ones, 9 per cent chose some of both, and 21 per cent either could find none that was suitable or chose to give no response. Not unexpectedly, favorable evaluations were most frequently given by VOA's most frequent listeners.

To illuminate further the above findings, the figures were presented in tabular form: first, according to the usual demographic groupings (sex, education, income, etc.); and, second, according to psychological variables (political interest and activity, attitudes toward democracy, attitudes toward America, and readiness to learn from America.)

The third section of the report deals with comparative preferences for VOA over other political programs.

Report No. 105 (17 October 1951)

GERMANS VIEW THE "VOICE OF AMERICA"
IV. The Question of Effectiveness

Sample: 3,000 West Germans, as well as 600 West Berliners.
Interviewing dates: between 27 March and 16 May 1951. (30 pp.)

Almost a quarter (24%) of all West Germans, and as many as 33 per cent of the West Berlin respondents, said that there had been instances in which a VOA program had changed their impression of some aspect of America. The largest proportion of these were in the realm of agricultural conditions, although life in general and social conditions were also mentioned rather frequently.

A large number of West Germans indicated that VOA was an important source of information not readily available elsewhere. Almost half (45%) of West Germans who considered themselves very frequent listeners (more than once a week) said it was difficult to obtain from some other source the information presented by VOA. Even among the better educated and those who scored highest on political interest and activity, a large minority claimed it was difficult to get such information elsewhere.

VOA had astonishing success in attracting listeners who were basically unimpressed by the United States. Among those who had a negative score on their attitude toward America, 28 per cent were either very frequent or simply frequent listeners to VOA; in Berlin this figure was as high as 77 per cent. In fact, a far more important variable than negative attitudes toward America seemed to be a feeling that there was nothing to learn from America: fully 49 per cent of those who claimed there was nothing to be learned from the United States also said they never listened to VOA.

Report No. 106 (22 October 1951)

SOME EVALUATIONS OF THE BONN GOVERNMENT
With Current Thinking on the Issue of New Federal Elections

Sample: 800 West Germans.
Interviewing dates: 18 to 27 September 1951. (20 pp.)

In the late summer of 1951, a number of SPD successes in Länder elections prompted opposition spokesmen, including Kurt Schumacher, head of the SPD, to call for new parliamentary elections. The survey results indicated that the general public did not entirely agree with SPD contentions and demands.

Almost half the respondents said they were either very satisfied (5%) or fairly satisfied (44%) with the activities of the federal government in Bonn. Another 29 per cent expressed dissatisfaction, 8 per cent said they were very dissatisfied, and 14 per cent offered no opinion. Asked for the causes of their dissatisfaction, 13 per cent mentioned Adenauer's economic policy, and another 11 per cent spoke of a lack of economic help for certain groups. Only 3 per cent brought up the subject of remilitarization, and the same percentage pointed to what they termed Adenauer's subservience to the occupation powers. Close to half (44%) did not think new elections for the Bundestag were necessary; 23 per cent favored such elections; and a third of the population reserved judgment on the issue.

Eight in ten West Germans knew that Konrad Adenauer was chancellor of the Federal Republic. Residents of the French

Zone were the best informed on this subject (88%), those in AMZON were the least well informed (76%). At the same time, only 55 per cent knew that Adenauer's party, the CDU, was the leading party in the federal government. Asked their views about Adenauer's policies until then, 51 per cent said his actions had been to West Germany's advantage, 14 per cent felt they had been to its disadvantage, 13 per cent felt they had been neither one nor the other, and 22 per cent gave no opinion. Comparison of the relevant figures showed that, even among those who thought new elections ought to be held, 39 per cent felt that Adenauer's accomplishments had been to Germany's advantage.

A large minority (39%) did not think that the occupation powers were supporting the policy of any particular party in West Germany, as had been claimed by a number of people. Of the 23 per cent who thought such support was being offered, 18 per cent felt it was being given to the CDU. Population breakdowns on this question showed that in all groups this view outweighed the possibility that the SPD was being helped.

Report No. 107 (30 October 1951)

A BALANCE SHEET ON WESTERN INFORMATION EFFORTS
Extent of German Accord with Western Viewpoints on Some Major East-West Issues

Sample: 800 West Germans, as well as 200 West Berliners for comparative purposes.
Interviewing dates: West German survey in summer of 1951; West Berlin interviews on 6 to 16 June 1951. (61 pp.)

An introductory comment to the report notes that "an indirect approach was utilized" in the survey: "Respondents were simply asked a series of open questions bearing upon significant political issues each of which could be answered in terms espoused by the West or in ways that would indicate that the Western thesis on the issue had not been absorbed. . . . A certain amount of subjective judgment was required." The results of the study indicated that, on the basis of the twelve issues chosen, there was less than majority support among West Germans for the Western side. That is not to say that a majority opposed the West: only about 11 per cent expressed views in direct opposition to the American viewpoint, while 13 per cent could have been categorized in one way or the other.

On the issue of responsibility for the continued division of Germany, only a minority (24%) of the West German public ascribed it solely to Soviet or GDR insincerity and intransigence. Three out of ten were clearly not in accord with the American view, 15 per cent assessed responsibility in an ambiguous manner, and 31 per cent were unable to give a response. Far more West Berliners (45%) agreed with the American view, but over a quarter (28%) rejected it.

Although a relatively large minority (40%) took the American stand on reasons for rejecting East German offers to unite Germany, almost half (48%) of the population seemed to know so little about the issue that it could offer no opinion.

West Germans were overwhelmingly of the same opinion as the Americans (79%) in assessing reasons for the stream of refugees from East Germany; in this case only ten per cent had no opinion.

The Western view of the East German People's Police was that it was an instrument for potential military aggression and for the oppression of the East German people. Just over half (51%) of the West Germans agreed with this description, while 15 per cent disagreed, referring to them as simply another police force. Over a fourth (29%) had no opinion.

Only a quarter of the population in West Germany (but as many as 59 per cent of the West Berliners) held the same views as the official American one regarding reasons for the failure of the four-power conference in Paris. Once again, the largest percentage (43%) seemed to know too little about the issue to have formed an opinion.

The American case for Western rearmament was generally accepted by the West Germans (68%) and overwhelmingly so by the West Berliners (84%).

As for the Western views on Soviet rearmament, only 56 per cent agreed, 22 per cent thought the American assessment wrong, and 17 per cent offered no opinion.

Less than a third of the West German respondents were in accord with the American reasons for favoring West German participation in the European defense system. A far smaller percentage (12%) rejected the official view, advancing the more negative one that America merely wanted to use German soldiers as cannon fodder. Somewhat over a third (36%) gave reasons that could be categorized either way: in accord, as well as not in accord, with the American view. Finally, 21 per cent gave no opinion.

Over half (51%) of the population had no opinion on the purpose of the Atlantic Pact. By comparison, then, the 44 per cent who gave reasons in accord with the American view did not comprise a very impressive number.

A large minority (42%) indicated agreement with the reasons given for American involvement in the Korean conflict; 16 per cent clearly rejected these reasons, however, and another 28 per cent offered no opinion.

Only 37 per cent of the German public defined the Marshall Plan in accordance with official United States policy; 45 per cent offered no view on the matter.

As for the reasons why the East European nations were not included in the Marshall Plan, only 32 per cent shared the American view on the subject, while fully 45 per cent offered no opinion.

Report No. 108 (31 October 1951)

ATTITUDES OF EAST GERMAN YOUTH
III. Reactions to Eastern versus Western Propaganda

Sample: not given; see Special Report No. II/63-S on sampling problems and representativeness.
Interviewing dates: 5 to 19 August 1951. (41 pp.)

The basic question to be answered by this survey of East German youth attending the Communist Youth Festival in East Berlin was whether or not the West ought to limit the amount of propaganda it was sending to the East. On the basis of the findings, the Reactions Analysis Staff concluded that "East Zone youth, far from being satiated with propaganda, are remarkably anxious for information--if it comes from the West."

Asked whether or not they felt sufficiently well informed about conditions in the world, seven in eight (88%) of the young people said they would like to know more, while 12 per cent felt they were already sufficiently well informed. Substituting the word propaganda for information, the respondents were asked whether the West was employing propaganda methods. Just over half (52%) responded negatively; the rest said yes, to varying degrees. Of the latter group, somewhat more than half thought the West should make more propaganda. Among those who thought the West did not use these methods, opinion divided fairly evenly on whether or not the West should do so.

According to the young East German respondents, radio was the best medium for the West to use to reach the East.

Almost eight in ten (77%) felt that the good aspects of America outweighed the bad, with most mentioning, as the most positive aspects, political and economic freedom, as well as the high standard of living. The bad aspects listed included social conditions and the race problem.

A large majority (66%) of East German youth questioned in this survey felt that responsibility for tension in the world lay with the Soviet Union; 18 per cent blamed both Russia and America. Those blaming the United States (8%) most frequently cited its greater power and, therefore, its responsibility for leading in international affairs.

Three-quarters of the respondents thought that West Germany would be justified in rearming, primarily (36%) because it should be able to defend itself, but also (31%) as a countermeasure to Eastern rearmament.

Of the 69 per cent who knew of the Marshall Plan, well over half (44%) did not think it endangered West German economic and political freedom, as so often maintained by Eastern propaganda.

Asked what they thought was the main purpose of the East German People's Police, most respondents made negative comments, the majority of which suggested that it was a camouflaged army.

Although 70 per cent of the young people interviewed were

142/Public Opinion in Semisovereign Germany

members of the national communist youth group, the Free German Youth (FDJ), over half (38%) claimed they had joined because of professional necessity; most of the rest mentioned other sorts of pressures. A small percentage cited positive advantages to membership.

Special Report 108-S (7 November 1951)

A NOTE ON THE REPRESENTATIVENESS OF GERMAN LISTENER LETTERS TO VOA

Sample: 3,000 West Germans and 600 West Berliners.
Interviewing dates: 27 March to 16 May 1951. (4 pp.)

Among all persons interviewed who were radio listeners and had heard of the "Voice of America," only 1.3 per cent in West Germany and 3.9 per cent in West Berlin--or a total of 41 of the 3,600 persons interviewed--had ever written a letter to VOA. These letter writers tended to be better educated, Protestant, and older than the typical VOA listener.

Report No. 109 (19 November 1951)

ATTITUDES OF EAST GERMAN YOUTH
IV. Radio Evaluations and Recommendations of East Zone Youth

Sample: not given; see Special Report No. II/63-S on sampling problems and representativeness.
Interviewing dates: 5 to 19 August 1951. (33 pp.)

Whereas 26 per cent of the respondents--East German youth, attending the East Berlin Communist Youth Festival, who had crossed over for a visit in West Berlin--saw an Eastern newspaper every day, 18 per cent saw one several times a week, and 12 per cent saw one at least once a week; only 4 per cent saw a Western paper once a week, and another 4 per cent saw one up to three times a month. Only 17 per cent ever saw any magazines from the West. All in all, 64 per cent of the young people said they had no opportunity to read Western newspapers or magazines, in contrast to 28 per cent who said they never read Eastern publications.

Although newspaper readers were relatively few in number, 88 per cent of those interviewed said they listened to the radio. When asked to which stations they listened mainly, nearly three-fourths (72%) of the listeners named RIAS; another 11 per cent named other Western stations. RIAS's nearest competitor in first position was the Eastern station, Radio Leipzig (22%).

The reason cited most frequently for listening to Western stations was their reliability, especially in the case of news, which these young people seemed particularly anxious to get. Not only did the majority of respondents say they themselves listened to news broadcasts from the West, over half said almost everyone did so. Another 25 per cent thought that from one-third to two-thirds of East German youth listened to these broadcasts.

At least two-thirds of the respondents listened to two of five Western programs listed: "Berlin Speaks to the Zone" and "Voice of America."

Far fewer respondents (33%) said they listened to the Soviet-sponsored program "The Truth About America." Of these, 8 per cent said they listened in order "to hear their lies," while another 8 per cent said they did so as a basis for comparison.

As for changing the attitudes of convinced Free German Youth (FDJ) members, 54 per cent of the young people interviewed felt that many FDJ members also listened to Western broadcasts; an additional 30 per cent felt that a few did so.

Report No. 110 (26 November 1951)

ARE EAST ZONE YOUTH SPREADING THE MESSAGE OF WEST BERLIN?
A Study of the Effects of the Berlin Youth Festival on the East Zone Population

Sample: 201 East Zone residents visiting an automobile exhibit in West Berlin; see Special Report No. II/63-S on sampling problems and representativeness.
Interviewing dates: 13 to 19 September 1951. (13 pp.)

Three-quarters of the East German respondents said they knew someone who had participated in the East Berlin Youth Festival of August 1951; in addition, 11 per cent had participated in it themselves. Among the 86 per cent affected in one way or another by the festival, a fourth knew from one to five participants, another 32 per cent knew between six and fifteen participants, and 15 per cent knew sixteen to thirty participants; 7 per cent knew fifty or more. Just under half (42 out of 86 per cent) said that all the participants they knew had visited West Berlin; 26 per cent said that between 60 and 99 per cent had crossed the border. Almost all (63%) said that everyone who had made the visit had also reported on it upon returning.

A solid majority (70%) of all those interviewed felt that the youth festival had had an effect on GDR residents. Most thought it had had positive repercussions for the West, but a few mentioned improved morale resulting from enthusiasm engendered by the festival. Asked what the young people who had gone to West Berlin had said about their visit, 40 per cent commented on the friendly reception they had been given, a further 39 per cent spoke of the high living standard, and 24 per cent mentioned political freedom. Unfavorable perceptions were infrequent but centered on West Berlin's complacency and reemerging militarism. Over half (57%) the respondents felt that reports about West Berlin had influenced the GDR population greatly, primarily by increasing confidence in the West. Twenty per cent perceived no influence, but most of these explained that the East German population was already on the side of the West.

Over three-quarters (78%) of the respondents felt that life would be harder for the participants in the festival who had gone to West Berlin, mainly because it was felt they would realize the hopelessness of their situation.

Report No. 111 (28 November 1951)

WEST GERMAN THINKING ON A FEDERATION OF EUROPE

Sample: 800 West Germans.
Interviewing dates: late August 1951. (54 pp.)

When asked whether they were for or against a union of Europe, without any further elucidation, over two-thirds (68%) said they were for it. However, perceptions of what such a union might look like varied greatly: some saw it confined to economic cooperation, while others viewed it as following the pattern of the United States or Switzerland.

Enthusiasm for European union fell off somewhat when the issue was presented in terms of a United States of Europe: 48 per cent felt that West Germany should join in this case, while one-fourth opposed such a move. Even fewer favored it when, as an alternative, a loose confederation of states was suggested: opinion split evenly with 36 per cent favoring each.

Population breakdowns revealed that higher status groups tended to hold the internationalist position. Lower status groups did not, however, tend to take the nationalist point of view; rather, they tended frequently to have no views at all.

On the more specific issue of a European army, 39 per cent of all respondents had no opinion to offer, 33 per cent felt that each nation's army should have its own uniform and flag, while only 28 per cent felt there ought to be a single uniform and flag.

Among those generally in favor of a united Europe, most (45%) did not think Europe's statesmen were moving ahead fast enough. Nationalistic selfishness was seen as the primary reason for this slow movement.

If a United States of Europe were in fact established, a majority (37%) of those with opinions on the subject felt that Germany ought to wait for reunification before joining, while

33 per cent thought it ought to join immediately. Among the former group, almost half were of the opinion that West Germans had no right to make a decision without their fellow countrymen in the East, and still others feared that membership would only make reunification more difficult. Apart from personal opinion on the question, fully three-quarters of the population felt that Germany would join a United States of Europe. Furthermore, majorities also felt that England (52%) and France (63%) would join.

The third section of the report consists of a series of cross-tabulations of views on European unity with the question of whether National Socialism contained more good or evil. On the general idea of European union, there was approximately the same degree of approval from those respondents who saw more good (72%) as from those who saw more evil (76%). Greater differences did arise between the two groups, however, on some of the more refined questions. The greatest difference appeared on the question of the future of a united, unoccupied Germany: half again as many more of the group that saw more good than evil in National Socialism voted for full sovereignty under such conditions (43%) than was the case in the group that saw more evil than good in National Socialism (29%). Finally, comparisons were made between the nationalist-internationalist questions and an index of political interest and activity, as measured by questions about attendance at political meetings, discussion of politics, and so on. Those people who showed the most interest in politics were most inclined to favor internationalism.

Report No. 112 (30 November 1951)

WEST GERMAN VIEWS ON VETERANS' ORGANIZATIONS AND THEIR ROLE IN POLITICAL LIFE

Sample: 800 West Germans in the first survey and 1,200 West Germans in the second.
Interviewing dates: late August and mid-October 1951 respectively. (13 pp.)

West German opinion split on the general question of the desirability of veterans' organizations and reunions. On the crucial question of whether or not veterans' groups should play an active role in politics, however, opposition strongly outweighed agreement.

In late August 1951, shortly after various veterans' groups held a number of meetings throughout West Germany, 39 per cent of the population said they thought such meetings were desirable, primarily for the purpose of comradeship and recalling old times. A quarter of the population felt such meetings to be undesirable because of the danger of a military revival (and 36 per cent offered no opinion on the subject.)

In mid-October, after the formal organization of veterans' groups had been extensively publicized in the press and on radio, less than half (48%) of the West German public was aware of the fact. Eleven per cent denied that such groups had been organized, and the remaining 41 per cent did not venture an answer. Asked whether or not they thought the veterans' organizations should become politically active, only 8 per cent said yes, in contrast with 56 per cent who said they would be against such activity; 16 per cent said they didn't care and 20 per cent had no views to express on the matter.

Report No. 113 (5 December 1951)

GERMAN OPINIONS ON JEWISH RESTITUTION AND SOME ASSOCIATED ISSUES

Sample: 1,200 West Germans.
Interviewing dates: 11 to 27 October 1951. (28 pp.)

Well over half (63%) of all West Germans felt that only those who had actually committed a crime against the Jews during the Third Reich need feel guilty and be made to acknowledge their guilt. This was the majority view in all population groups under examination. When asked specifically whether Jews who had suffered should receive help, two-thirds (68%) of the respondents said yes. It should be noted, however, that when this question was asked about war widows and orphans, 96 per cent of the population responded in the affirmative; and even for the relatives of those involved in the July 20 assassination attempt on Hitler, 73 per cent thought there should be some form of help. Comments by those opposed to giving aid to the Jews revealed that most thought they were already getting enough help from various sources or that "they could help each other."

A fifth (21%) of the West German respondents said the Jews themselves were partly responsible for what happened to them during the Third Reich. Of these, 59 per cent nonetheless thought the Jews ought to receive help, while 36 per cent felt they should not.

West German opinion was fairly evenly split on the issue of whether or not the federal government ought to pass a proposed law prohibiting expressions of anti-Semitic sentiments: 38 per cent approved such a law, 33 per cent disapproved, and 29 per cent offered no opinion. Not quite one-fourth of those expressing disapproval said it would violate the democratic ideal of freedom of expression.

Report No. 114 (5 December 1951)

THE JULY 20 PLOT ON HITLER'S LIFE: DOES IT AFFORD A RALLYING POINT FOR RIGHTIST GROUPS?

Sample: 1,200 West Germans.
Interviewing dates: last two weeks of October 1951. (9 pp.)

During the 1951 state parliamentary campaigns, the SRP (Socialist Reich party) under General Otto Remer sought to rally support for its neo-Nazi program by decrying the attempt to assassinate Hitler on 20 July 1944, which Remer had had a hand in thwarting. The survey sought to measure West German sentiment toward Remer's political movement.

Seven years after the event, 38 per cent of the West German population approved of the attempt on Hitler's life, 24 per cent disapproved, and 38 per cent were uncertain of their feelings. Comments by those who disapproved suggested that only about 13 per cent could actually be considered supporters of Remer.

Not quite three-quarters (73%) of the population felt that the West German government ought to aid the relatives of the plotters. It should be noted, however, that fully 96 per cent of the population felt that such aid ought to be provided for war widows and orphans, 90 per cent thought it should be given to refugees and expellees, and 68 per cent to Jews who had suffered during the Third Reich.

Report No. 115 (19 December 1951)

SOME FURTHER SOUNDINGS OF WEST AND EAST GERMAN OPINIONS ON UNITY ISSUES

Sample: each of the first two surveys consisted of interviews with 800 West Germans; the third used a sample of 215 East German residents who had crossed the border to visit the Industrial Fair in West Berlin; see Special Report No. II/63-S on sampling problems and representativeness.
Interviewing dates: October 1951. (22 pp.)

A month after the East German invitation of 15 September 1951 to the West German government asking for discussion on reunification, more West Germans thought the chances for such reunification were bad or even very bad (44%) than thought the chances fair to very good (39%). The East Germans interviewed were even more pessimistic: 58 per cent felt the chances were bad or very bad, while 40 per cent thought they were fair to very good. The most frequently given reason for a pessimistic view by the East German respondents was the feeling that the Soviet Union did not want to give up its sphere of influence, did not want reunification.

Despite the frequency with which the Soviet-sponsored East German government invited West Germany to unite with it, only a small fraction (11%) of the West German population considered the Soviet Union more in favor of German unity than the Western Powers; 47 per cent thought the West was more in favor of reunification. (Nineteen per cent thought both sides were equally interested in reunification, and as many as 23 per cent had no opinion to offer on the subject.) A clear majority (60%) said they thought the Western Powers' ideas of reunification corresponded more closely with those of the German people than did the Soviet Union's; again, however, there was a large percentage with no opinion (27%).

In October 1951 about a quarter (27%) of the West German population felt that West German participation in NATO would impede unification, while almost as many (23%) did not think the move would have any effect on the issue. A minority of 16 per cent thought it would even increase the chances of unification, but more than twice as many (34%) withheld judgment altogether. Even among those who thought participation would impede unification (27%), only 6 per cent thought the move would make it totally impossible; 17 per cent said it would merely make reunification more difficult. The East German respondents were more inclined than their fellow Germans in the West to consider West German participation in European defense as improving the chances for unification (36%).

Report No. 116 (19 December 1951)

ARE EAST ZONE YOUTH RESISTING TOTALITARIAN EDUCATION?

Sample: 100 young people who attended elementary or secondary schools in the Soviet Zone of Germany; see Special Report No. II/63-S on sampling problems and representativeness.
Interviewing dates: 5 to 19 August 1951. (18 pp.)

This is the fifth in a series of reports based on a survey conducted among young people attending the East German Communist Youth Festival who had crossed over into West Berlin for a visit. There were relatively few youngsters under 14 in the sample and not very many girls as compared with boys.

When asked a general question about what caused them the greatest difficulty in school, four out of ten specifically mentioned political pressure constantly applied in the classroom. Most of the other complaints were also related to politics: three in ten disliked compulsory courses teaching the Russian language, and two in ten mentioned the current events courses with their emphasis on propaganda.

According to those interviewed (80 per cent of whom were themselves members), 82 per cent of their fellow classmates were members of the Free German Youth (FDJ). Although the estimated share of convinced members averaged 14 per cent of all members, they were felt by one out of three of the respondents to play an influential role in the schools; at the same time, five in ten denied that the FDJ members had any influence.

Seven in eight of the young people interviewed said they frequently (69%) or sometimes (18%) disagreed with their teachers; but only one in ten claimed to express this disagreement openly. One point of contention was the picture given by teachers of conditions in East Germany: fully 61 per cent said they did not present a true picture, and of these only 7 per cent said they thought the teachers believed what they were saying.

Asked about responsibility for East-West tensions, 55 per cent said the Soviet Union was responsible, while 26 per cent blamed both sides. Regarding the Marshall Plan, 28 per cent knew too little to respond to any question (in contrast with 45 per cent in the West who were unable to come up with a response). Almost all the rest gave a favorable interpretation to American motives for the plan.

Report No. 117 (21 December 1951)

CURRENT GERMAN VIEWS ON A NATIONAL VERSUS A EUROPEAN ARMY

With Sidelights on Defense Participation Trends and East German Opinion

Sample: 1,200 West Germans, as well as 215 East German visitors to the West Berlin Industrial Fair; see Special Report No. II/63-S on sampling problems and representativeness.

Interviewing dates: in West Germany, 29 October to 12 November 1951; interviews of East Germans on 12 to 20 October 1951. (18 pp.)

In October 1950, one year before the survey, preference for German participation in a European army outweighed, by a two to one margin, support for a West German national army. A year later the situation was reversed: 48 per cent of the West German respondents said they favored a West German national army, while only 20 per cent felt that German troop contingents should be integrated into a general West European army. Among the East German respondents interviewed in mid-October, 73 per cent were in favor of West Germany's participation, primarily because they thought it necessary as a defense against communism. Most of those opposed (20%) centered their arguments on a general disapproval of war. Asked whether West German remilitarization would increase or decrease the chances of Russian aggression, 70 per cent said they thought it would actually

decrease the danger. Compared to integrationists, supporters
of a national army were more likely to express nationalist and
neo-Nazi sentiments, neutralism, and the feeling that the Bonn
government was merely a puppet of the Western Powers.

Report No. 118 (10 January 1952)

THE PRESENT STATUS OF "NEO-NAZISM" IN WEST GERMANY

Sample: 1,200 West Germans.
Interviewing dates: 29 October to 10 November 1951. (39 pp.)

Between mid-May and early November 1951, the percentage of
West Germans expressing awareness of the newly formed SRP (Socialist Reich party) rose from 37 per cent to 41 per cent.
About a third of these described the SRP's main goal as the reestablishment of National Socialism. Asked why they thought
people voted for the party, 8 per cent said it had to do with
dissatisfaction with the economic and social situation, as well
as the appeal of the social welfare ideas of National Socialism. Although 17 per cent said they hoped the SRP would not
have any influence in West Germany, almost as many (13%) hoped
it would, while 11 per cent expressed no opinion on the matter.

SRP support was not, however, considered a valid measure
of neo-Nazi sentiment in West Germany. In an attempt to get at
this, a question that had been asked several times previously
was repeated: "When you consider everything, was there more
good in the ideas of National Socialism or more evil?" In May
1951, 34 per cent said they thought there had been more good,
while 40 per cent thought there had been more evil. By September the figures had changed dramatically: 46 per cent
thought there had been more good, 32 per cent more evil. In
early November, minor changes were apparent, but there were
still more who thought Nazism had contained more good (42%)
than evil ideas (37%). Population breakdowns showed that the
better educated tended to see more good than evil in National
Socialism; this was also true of those between the ages of 25
and 34, as well as among Protestants. The most frequently
given reason for saying that National Socialism had contained
good ideas dealt with job opportunities and the living standard. Quite a few respondents also mentioned social welfare.
Both among those who saw more good than evil in National Socialism and among those who saw more evil than good, about a
third mentioned racial policy and persecution of the Jews as
one of its evils. Another evil mentioned was the lack of free-
dom--dictatorship. Among those who saw more good in Nazism,
25 per cent pointed out these evils; among those who saw more
evil, there were 38 per cent who mentioned them.

Since it was clear that the above questions and responses
did not necessarily represent a true picture of neo-Nazi sen-

timent, a number of other questions were asked. The report termed the results of the first "disquieting": only 20 per cent of the population said they would do everything they could to prevent the rise of a party similar to the NSDAP; 30 per cent said they would not like it but would do nothing to prevent it. Disapproval was highest among the better educated, trade unionists, and Catholics. In a lengthy section entitled "A Hypothesis and its Implications," the report suggests: "Reorientation efforts might have done better to stress that there was nothing wrong *per se* with some of the elements of Nazism . . . but that there are good and bad ways to go about achieving those ends. . . ."

The fourth section of the report contains a number of cross-tabulations with responses to questions considered relevant to the larger issue of reorientation. Those showing anti-Nazi orientations were also the ones who tended to have attitudes considered desirable by the Western Powers. The figures also showed no clear-cut relationship between economic dissatisfaction and neo-Nazism.

Finally, respondents were asked whether they thought the Germans in general felt the same then about National Socialism as they had immediately after the war. About a third (35%) thought they had a higher regard for Nazism in 1951 than in 1945, while 16 per cent felt they thought worse of it, and 22 per cent said people had not changed their views. Those in the first group tended to be from among the usually better informed segments of the population, as well as among the young, trade union members, and veterans. The most frequently cited reason for this feeling was the recollection of better living conditions under National Socialism.

Report No. 119 (28 January 1952)

THE GERMAN APPRAISAL OF THE ALLIED FORCES IN WEST GERMANY
With Recommendations for Improved Citizen-Soldier Relations

Sample: 1,200 West Germans.
Interviewing dates: 21 November to 6 December 1951. (77 pp.)

A majority (58%) of the West German population felt that the armed forces of the Western Powers stationed in Germany were there to safeguard German security. However, in considering this security, a considerable minority (22%) were of the opinion that it would be better for Germany if all these troops were to leave. The two most frequently cited reasons for the latter judgment were the high monetary costs to the German population and the feeling that the Germans could defend themselves better. When the question of security was left aside, 51 per cent of the respondents said that the presence of Allied troops brought more disadvantages than advantages. In fact, when asked what the advantages were of the troops' presence, a third of the respondents said they could think of none at all; 16 per cent mentioned business and commercial benefits. As for disadvantages, 53 per cent commented on the high cost, increased taxes, and prices; still another 28 per cent bemoaned the homes requisitioned for the soldiers while the Germans were suffering from an acute housing shortage.

In case of Soviet aggression, 27 per cent of AMZON residents thought American soldiers would fight well, but even more (34%) said they would do poorly. French Zone residents thought even less highly of French soldiers: only 19 per cent thought they would do well, while 40 per cent said they would do poorly in case of an attack from the East. Most of the skepticism was based on the feeling that the troops were badly trained, led too soft an existence, and had no interest in defending a foreign country anyway.

Although a large percentage (38%) had no opinion to offer on the subject, 44 per cent of the AMZON respondents--where the question was most relevant--felt that the Negro soldier was as good a soldier as his white brother-in-arms; 16 per cent felt this to be true because of certain racial qualities, such as primitiveness and a fighting instinct.

Of all soldiers, the Germans (77%) rated their own as the best and the Soviets as second best (31%); 13 per cent felt the British belonged in second place, while 12 per cent put the Americans there.

While ranking low on their potential fighting qualities, the Allied troops scored fairly high on behavior. In AMZON, 55 per cent of the residents said the behavior of American troops was good, 20 per cent called it fair, and only 8 per cent termed it bad. The troops enjoyed a better reputation among those persons most likely to come in contact with them. It is also worth noting that 65 per cent of the respondents felt that troops of the three Allied nations were conducting themselves just about as they would have expected their own men to do in the same sort of situation.

Asked about civilian-soldier contacts, only about a quarter (24%) of the population felt there was much contact, while over a third (36%) termed it little. When asked then, how much contact there should be, 11 per cent said very much, 42 per cent said much, 15 per cent little, and another 15 per cent said it made no difference. Responses to a list of possible joint activities suggest that the Germans were happier at the thought of public rather than close personal contact. A majority of 58 per cent said they would welcome joint sports activities, and 48 per cent approved of mutual church activities. However, only 18 per cent liked the idea of dances for civilians and soldiers. Asked whether or not they would be willing to invite soldiers into their homes, a majority (55%) of the respondents said yes. But, of these, only 23 per cent would do so if the soldier were a Negro. Population breakdowns on this last question revealed that men, younger people, and professionals (rather than simply persons with higher socioeconomic status or income) showed a good deal more willingness than did their counterparts to accept Negroes into their homes.

Report No. 120 (29 January 1952)

GERMAN EVALUATIONS OF NATO
With Other Opinions on European Defense Issues

Sample: 800 West Germans.
Interviewing dates: 14 to 22 December 1951. (34 pp.)

The survey was undertaken to determine the impact of NATO on the German population just before specific decisions were to be made about Germany's role in that organization. Despite the great amount of publicity and importance attached to NATO by many groups in West Germany, only 46 per cent of the population could correctly describe the Atlantic Pact organization. Among those who knew of NATO's existence, 12 per cent thought it was functioning well, while 16 per cent thought it was not. The negative judgment rested primarily on the feeling that the members could not agree with each other and that the individual nations were too selfish to be able to renounce their national interests.

Of the 43 per cent who knew that Eisenhower was in charge of establishing a common West European defense army, 10 per cent said they had great confidence in him, and 15 per cent placed a fair amount of confidence in him; only 6 per cent had little confidence and 4 per cent had no confidence at all.

On the very sensitive question of whether or not Eisenhower would treat the Germans as equals if they were to participate in the European army, more people said yes (47%) than no (21%).

Although 37 per cent of the population said they thought defense preparations by the West increased the danger of another war, fully 61 per cent were in favor of such preparations.

With German participation in a European army rapidly becoming a real possibility, the question of how the Germans would provide the manpower took on some significance. In mid-June 1951, 35 per cent of the population said the government should have the right to draft men if not enough volunteered. Less than four months later, only 17 per cent said they would welcome the decision to draft men for the army, while 40 per cent said they would accept it but without enthusiasm; 35 per cent said they would oppose it outright. Breakdowns on these responses showed that the greatest opposition came from younger age groups. Regardless of what they may have hoped for, as many as 74 per cent of the German people said there would be conscription if Germany participated in the European army.

Three-quarters of the people also thought there would be an increase in taxes to cover the costs of the army. However, four in ten felt that the Germans should pay a smaller proportion of their taxes for defense costs than other Europeans; 32 per cent felt they should pay proportionately the same.

Report No. 121 (29 January 1952)

ANXIETIES AND ASPIRATIONS OF EAST ZONE YOUTH

A Study in Certain Morale Factors as Reported During the Communist Youth Rally

Sample: not given; see Special Report No. II/63-S on sampling problems and representativeness.
Interviewing dates: 5 to 19 August 1951. (18 pp.)

This is the sixth in a series of reports based on surveys conducted with young people from East Germany during the Communist Youth Festival in East Berlin.

Asked how they would rate their personal situation in general, only one per cent said very good, 11 per cent termed their situation simply good, 48 per cent fair, 22 per cent bad, and 18 per cent very bad. Optimism about the future was strong; 46 per cent were of the opinion that things would get better. Judging from their comments many of the young people were looking to the West as the source of a better future. Some spoke of going to live and/or work in the West, while others mentioned the possibility of a revolution and help from the West in driving out the Soviets.

Although their cares and worries might be great, the majority (64%) of the young people interviewed said they had someone (usually their parents) in whom they could confide. Furthermore, almost all (89%) had a goal in life toward which they were working. As for what they enjoyed most at that time, 41 per cent said they liked sports. Basic optimism was also revealed in the East German youths' (85%) expression of confidence in West German support; of those, 52 per cent said they had felt this way before, while 33 per cent claimed to have gained this impression from the visit to West Berlin.

Report No. 122 (31 January 1952)

PROGRESS TOWARD POLITICAL EQUALITY AND ECONOMIC WELL-BEING

Sample: 800 West Germans interviewed in each of two surveys.
Interviewing dates: early November 1951 and 14 to 22 December 1951. (12 pp.)

Only about a third of the German people thought their country had made either good (15%) or at least fairly good (17%) progress toward equality with other Western nations. Less than a third (30%) described it as little or none at all, a situation they blamed on Allied distrust and opposition.

A somewhat higher percentage of respondents regarded their own personal situations as improved (19%) or at least as good a year earlier (30%). About a third (34%) said they were worse off and 17 per cent described their situations as being just as bad as a year earlier. By personal situation almost all meant their economic situation. When asked then specifically about the development of their economic situation during the preceding year, only 4 per cent responded that they were very satisfied; 44 per cent said they were moderately satisfied; 39 per cent were dissatisfied; and 12 per cent were very dissatisfied. Most of the dissatisfaction (30%) lay with high prices and low incomes.

Report No. 123 (11 February 1952)

WEST GERMAN REACTIONS TO THE WEST'S DISARMAMENT PROPOSALS AT THE PARIS MEETING OF THE UNITED NATIONS

Sample: 800 West Germans.
Interviewing dates: 18 to 28 December 1951. (9 pp.)

Some five weeks after the West had first introduced the issue, less than half (48%) of the West German population had heard of the West's disarmament proposals and Soviet counter-proposals made before the United Nations assembly in Paris. Lack of awareness did not, however, mean disapproval: fully 69 per cent of all respondents, when apprised of the move, said they welcomed it. Only 12 per cent were opposed, while 19 per cent had no opinion on the subject. Among those who disapproved, most voiced skepticism in the sincerity of both East and West in proposing disarmament.

Report No. 124 (26 February 1952)

REPERCUSSIONS IN WEST GERMANY OF THE FRENCH AMBASSADORIAL APPOINTMENT TO THE SAAR

Sample: 400 West Germans.
Interviewing dates: 6 to 11 February 1952. (18 pp.)

Although the press and many political figures reacted vehemently when France appointed an ambassador to the Saar, most (60%) of the West German public were unaware of the event. Only

31 per cent knew of the appointment. Within this latter group, very few expressed anything but a distinctly negative reaction. In addition, over a third of the knowledgeable respondents (11%) felt that not enough attention was being paid to the Saar issue by the Bonn government; 16 per cent thought there was enough attention. Asked whether, in general, the relationship between West Germany and France had improved or deteriorated during the previous month, almost half (49%) said it had deteriorated, while 33 per cent had no opinion on the matter. Among the usually better informed elements of the society, this negative sentiment reached majority status.

Two-thirds of the population thought that the Saar was under French control at that time (66%); somewhat more (68%) felt it ought to be incorporated into West Germany. Only 14 per cent thought it should come under international control. Asked what they thought America hoped for, 35 per cent thought America would like the Saar to come under international control.

Report No. 125 (29 February 1952)

THE CURRENT STATE OF WEST BERLIN MORALE

Sample: 600 West Berliners.
Interviewing dates: December 1951. (65 pp.)

The survey was made at a time when the West Berlin situation was relatively quiet. The general finding was that West Berliners were able to maintain their high morale even when there was no immediate crisis requiring great courage on their part.

Most West Berliners (66%) felt that their city was a vital center in the world situation, a symbol of the East-West struggle. Asked how they accounted for the high morale in the city, 26 per cent mentioned the traditional Berlin spirit (humorous, tough sophistication), 24 per cent pointed to the Berliner's awareness and understanding of the Soviet threat, and 19 per cent mentioned a feeling of optimism inherent in Berliners and also fed by Western support. So high was morale that 77 per cent maintained they would not leave the city even if given the opportunity to do so; of these only 14 per cent changed their minds when work and housing in West Germany were mentioned. The former figure was down from the record high of 83 per cent in May 1949, just after the end of the blockade, but was up four percentage points from the April 1950 figure of 73 per cent.

West Berliners expressed confidence not only in themselves but also in their city government, the Senate. Nine per cent were very satisfied and 57 per cent were satisfied. In addition, 73 per cent felt the Senate was doing everything possible to ease the city's difficult situation. However, 61 per cent did not think that the economic situation would be improved unless the political situation changed. Over half (59%) thought there would be a decisive change for the better in the political realm during the next ten years. Of the 81 per cent who anticipated some sort of change in the coming decade, 24 per cent thought it would come in one to two years, while 26 per cent put it at three to five years. Quite a few (16%) thought the change would occur because the Russians would leave; 9 per cent thought that Western power would persuade the Soviet Union to leave but that there would be no war; and another 9 per cent felt there would be a war that would drive the Russians out.

The fact that the West Berliners expressed such loyalty to their city and optimism about its future did not mean that they also saw their own personal situations in a rosy light. Far from it: over a third (36%) said things were worse for them than a year earlier, while 22 per cent termed their situation just as good, and 34 per cent said they were better off. By way of contrast, in West Germany where the economic situation was clearly better, only 19 per cent of the population said they were better off than in the previous year, while 30 per cent said things were just as good, and 34 per cent said they were worse. Not only did a third of the West Berlin population see themselves as worse off, a large minority (42%) also saw the general mood of the city as worse than a year earlier; only 15 per cent said things were better on this score. Furthermore, there was a close relationship between what Berliners thought the mood of the city to be and their estimation of their own personal situations.

The end of 1951 marked the first time that more people said their income was sufficient to take care of necessary expenses (57%) than said it was not sufficient (43%). In August 1948, 34 per cent had said their income was sufficient, while 66 per cent had said it was not.

Despite the feeling that things were not going well for them as individuals, the large majority of West Berliners did think the Western world was paying sufficient attention to their city (70%) and doing everything possible to ease its difficult situation (62%). However, a large minority of West Berliners (45%) felt that West Germany was indifferent to their city's plight; another 10 per cent even felt they had been written off by their West German brothers. Nonetheless, 53 per cent expressed satisfaction with the activities of the Bonn government--a figure down from that of May 1950 (77%). As for the question of whether or not West Berlin would be permitted to join the Federal Republic as the twelfth state, there was considerable pessimism: 36 per cent did not think Berlin would become part of West Germany, and 41 per cent went so far as to say they did not think Bonn seriously wanted the city to join.

The final section of the report deals with unemployment in West Berlin. Sixteen per cent of those interviewed were in this category. Attitudes of the unemployed did not differ markedly from those of all other West Berliners regarding sentiments toward the city of Berlin, optimism about the future, or confidence in the Bonn government.

Report No. 126 (29 February 1952)

EAST ZONE YOUTH'S APPRAISAL OF WESTERN POLITICAL PAMPHLETS
With Sidelights on Penetration of Printed Matter into East Germany

Sample: 146 young East Germans; see Special Report No. II/63-S on sampling problems and representativeness.
Interviewing dates: 5 to 19 August 1951. (16 pp.)

This is the seventh in a series of reports based on a survey conducted among young East Germans attending the Communist Youth Festival in East Berlin.

When asked which they preferred of seven information media available to them in West Berlin, 34 per cent named films, 15 per cent television, 14 per cent discussions, and 12 per cent political pamphlets. While certainly less appealing to these young people, political pamphlets were nonetheless considered very valuable as a means of enlightenment by fully 62 per cent. Of the 79 per cent who said they had had an opportunity to look at such a pamphlet, 46 per cent claimed to have looked at some of them thoroughly, and 20 per cent said they had read some of them all the way through. Further questioning revealed that almost all could substantiate their claim by either naming a title or the contents of one or more of the pamphlets. Somewhat over a third (36%) said they would take some of the pamphlets home with them; 21 per cent felt it would be personally too dangerous to do so.

Although most respondents (59%) claimed never to have seen any printed matter from the West before, a solid minority (38%) said they had seen newspapers or magazines. Furthermore, even though months had passed since seeing them, most of those saying they had seen such material were also able to identify one or more publications specifically. Asked what they thought was the best way to get printed matter across the border, 48 per cent suggested carrying it across personally, 25 per cent mentioned using it as packing material in packages being sent to the East, and 21 per cent thought it should be dropped from airplanes.

As for what they would most like to see in future publications, 46 per cent said information about the West; 23 per cent hoped for information about the East; and 14 per cent wanted comparisons between East and West.

Report No. 127 (10 March 1952)

AN APPRAISAL OF THE IMPACT OF THE BERLIN CULTURAL FESTIVAL

Sample: 406 West Berlin residents.

Interviewing dates: November 1951. (12 pp.)

The survey dealt with the cultural festival held in West Berlin during September 1951, which offered a number of concerts, plays, operas, and guest appearances from the United States, Great Britain, and France.

When asked the very general question, "What was the most important recent cultural event in Berlin?" 38 per cent mentioned the cultural festival, and 5 per cent gave the name of one specific event in that festival. Of the 62 per cent who had not mentioned it in response to this general query, 41 per cent, when asked about it specifically, said they had heard of the cultural festival.

Despite the fact that many had not attended any of the events, the vast majority (86%) of West Berliners thought the festival had been a good thing for the city. If the hope had been to make the West Berliners aware of a high level of cultural competence among Americans, however, the festival failed badly. As was usually the case when this question was asked, almost four in ten (37%) stated that the Germans could learn nothing culturally from the United States. About half (49%) said they thought the two countries were approximately on the same level in the cultural field; 14 per cent thought America ranked higher; but 24 per cent ranked America lower than Germany.

Report No. 128 (29 March 1952)

CURRENT TRENDS IN WEST BERLIN OPINIONS ON ISSUES RELATED TO THE EAST-WEST STRUGGLE

Sample: 600 West Berliners.
Interviewing dates: December 1951. (18 pp.)

West Berliners continued in the winter of 1951 to express a strong allegiance to the West. Slightly more (41%) said they were satisfied than dissatisfied (39%) with American policy toward the Soviet Union. Fully 85 per cent said they thought the Americans would remain in Berlin as long as was necessary for the security of the city, and 45 per cent felt the Western Powers continued to be stronger than the communists. A solid majority of 74 per cent said they would want the West to use all means necessary to fend off an attack from the East. And, for the first time since 1947, a majority (55%) said they would prefer a government guaranteeing freedom over one offering economic security (39%).

On the issue of American policy toward West Germany, 71 per cent of the West Berlin population expressed satisfaction with it; by contrast, only 55 per cent of the West German population expressed satisfaction. A similar contrast may be noted

in the responses to the question of which side West Germany
should join in the East-West struggle. In West Berlin, 68 per
cent chose the West, while only 25 per cent said Germany should
try to remain neutral. In West Germany, only 33 per cent felt
they should side with the West, while over half (52%) felt they
should try to remain neutral. A solid majority (74%) of West
Berliners (37 per cent in West Germany) continued to favor West
German participation in the defense of Western Europe.

Report No. 129 (31 March 1952)

WEST GERMAN PUBLIC OPINION ON DEFENSE PARTICIPATION FOLLOWING THE FORMAL BUNDESTAG DEBATE

I. Impact of the Bundestag Debate

Sample: 800 West Germans and 200 West Berliners.
Interviewing dates: 18 to 26 February 1952. (24 pp.)

The Bundestag debate, from 7 to 9 February 1952, on the
issue of West German participation in a European defense army
was clearly of tremendous interest to the West German population: only 29 per cent had not heard of it at all. Over half
(58%) had heard about it on the radio, 28 per cent had read
about it in the newspaper, and 6 per cent knew of it from some
other source. A great many had listened to the speeches themselves on the radio. Although the Bundestag in fact only tentatively approved a German defense contribution, one-sixth of
those aware of the debate expressed the view that a final decision had been reached; 36 per cent (or about half of those
aware of the debate) said the decision had been tentative. Asked
whether the debate had engendered clarification or more confusion
on the issue of defense participation, 29 per cent said there was
greater confusion following the debate; only 18 per cent thought
the debate had clarified matters. Population breakdowns revealed
that the feeling that the debate had caused confusion rather than
clarification was just as prevalent among opinion-leading elements of the population as among the less educated and usually
less informed segments.

Over half (57%) of the population said their attitude toward defense participation had remained the same after the Bundestag debate, but 8 per cent reported increased approval and
another 4 per cent decreased approval.

Whereas in earlier studies respondents invariably pointed
to some economic matter when asked to name the greatest problem
facing West Germany, the Bundestag debate shifted interest to
political-military questions. In the summer of 1951, 43 per
cent of the population had mentioned political-military issues,
in contrast with mid-February 1952 when 67 per cent spoke of
them--25 per cent mentioning remilitarization specifically.

Report No. 130 (31 March 1952)

WEST GERMAN PUBLIC OPINION ON DEFENSE PARTICIPATION FOLLOWING THE FORMAL BUNDESTAG DEBATE

II. Current Support and Resistance—and Some of the Factors Related Thereto

Sample: 800 West Germans and 200 West Berliners.
Interviewing dates: 18 to 26 February 1952. (48 pp.)

Following the Bundestag debate of 7 to 9 February 1952 on the issue of German participation in the defense of Europe, almost half the population expressed opposition to such participation; 14 per cent were somewhat against it, and 34 per cent were very much against it. However, if certain conditions were to be met, opposition dropped considerably. Only about a quarter of the population said they would find it difficult to reconcile themselves to a Bonn decision to contribute divisions to a European army; 50 per cent said they would accept it even though not enthusiastic about it.

A major fear raised by Germans concerned fair and equal treatment as participants in a general European army. Twenty-seven per cent felt America was trying to take advantage of Germany's situation; and 29 per cent expressed no opinion, hardly a positive judgment. This negative attitude was most widespread among opinion-leading elements of the population. Attitudes toward the French on this issue were even less positive. Over half (53%) felt that France was trying to take advantage of Germany, while 36 per cent expressed no opinion, and only 10 per cent felt France was trying to do justice to the German point of view. Traditional German-French antagonism, as well as the Saar question, at that time the focus of hot dispute, figured prominently in respondents' comments.

Whatever reservations the Germans may have had about participating in the European defense pact, increasing percentages felt that West Germany would in fact join: by February 1952, fully 84 per cent said Germany would participate sooner or later. The most frequently cited reasons for this view were that the government had already decided to do so, Germany had to do so to protect itself against the East, and the Western Powers--especially the United States--would force West Germany to join.

Opposition to the European army may have lain in the fact that 62 per cent of the German population felt reconstruction was the most important problem facing the country at that time; only 25 per cent cited military defense. In fact, cross-tabulations showed that, of those saying reconstruction was more important, 62 per cent were opposed to the European army. Another factor in the opposition may have been the view of 35 per cent of the population that living conditions would grow worse if Germany participated in the European army. Indeed, among those who held this view, 60 per cent opposed participation.

162/Public Opinion in Semisovereign Germany

Increasing percentages of Germans saw little danger of attack from the East. Among those who regarded the possibility as very slight, 61 per cent opposed participation in the European army.

Increasing numbers of Germans opposed the draft. Whereas in June 1951 48 per cent opposed it, by February 1952 over half (55%) did so. Again, among those opposed to the draft, the vast majority (80%) were also opposed to German participation in the defense of Europe.

Report No. 131 (31 March 1952)

WEST GERMAN PUBLIC OPINION ON DEFENSE PARTICIPATION FOLLOWING THE FORMAL BUNDESTAG DEBATE
III. National versus Integrated Army

Sample: 800 West Germans and 200 West Berliners.
Interviewing dates: 18 to 26 February 1952. (18 pp.)

After October 1950, decreasing numbers of West Germans favored participation in a West European army. In fact, in early 1952, more people preferred a national army (43%) to an integrated one (25%) for the first time since the question had been posed. Opposition to a European army rested primarily on the feeling that it would expose German troops to exploitation and abuse.

If convinced that Germany would be granted equality in an integrated army, however, a fairly large number of those opposed to participation said they would drop their opposition. Of the 43 per cent who expressed a preference for a national army, 15 per cent said they would favor an integrated army if the condition of equality were met, while 27 per cent continued to support a national army, guarantees of equality notwithstanding, primarily because they thought that a national army would better safeguard German interests.

Regardless of what they hoped for, 74 per cent of the population felt Germany would in fact participate in the defense of Europe. Of these, 8 per cent felt Germany would contribute to a national army, and 44 per cent thought there would be an integrated army (primarily because the Western Powers were opposed to a German national army); 22 per cent had no opinion.

Report No. 132 (10 April 1952)

EAST ZONE FARMERS' REACTIONS TO RIAS FARM BROADCASTS
With Sidelights on the Extent of VOA Listenership

Sample: 267 farmers from East Germany; see Special Report No. II/63-S on sampling problems and representativeness.

The HICOG Surveys/163

Interviewing dates: February 1952. (9 pp.)

The report is based on a survey conducted in Berlin during the "Grüne Woche," an annual agricultural exhibit held in West Berlin. As was found in surveys among other population groups, RIAS was by far the most popular station--East or West--among East German farmers, particularly because its farm programs were seen as informative and objective. A large majority (85%) of the farmers said they listened to the "Voice of America" broadcasts. Moreover, 39 per cent said they listened six to seven times a week, in other words almost every time VOA was broadcast.

Report No. 133 (10 April 1952)

ARE EAST GERMAN FARMERS RESISTING COLLECTIVISM?
A Study of Farmers' Evaluation of East German Agriculture

Sample: 267 farmers from East Germany; see Special Report No. II/63-S on sampling problems and representativeness.
Interviewing dates: February 1952. (39 pp.)

Most of the farmers interviewed felt that their situation, as compared with a year earlier, was either somewhat (20%) or much worse (41%). Most of those expressing this view attributed the situation to the rise in state-imposed quotas; high taxes and high prices were also mentioned. Moreover, 75 per cent thought the situation would be much worse at the end of the Five-Year Plan then in operation; another 10 per cent felt it would be somewhat worse, and only 4 per cent thought things would get better. Asked whether they thought the farmers' economic interests were better safeguarded by the traditional cooperatives or the new state-controlled unitary cooperative system (BHG), fully 72 per cent chose the former. The three most frequently cited reasons for this assertion were that the cooperatives had not exerted any pressure, that they had provided what was needed, and that they had had the economic interests of the farmers at heart. If the BHG was considered bad, most expected worse to come: as many as 73 per cent anticipated full collectivization to be introduced at some future date.

Among the land-reform programs instituted by the GDR, one of the most ambitious was the resettlement of workers to small private farms. Asked about these new arrivals, 65 per cent of the respondents said there were many of them in their area, and 39 per cent said that almost all of them were dissatisfied. The majority (58%) estimated that at least half of the new settlers had already left their farms, primarily because the privileges accorded them at the outset had been withdrawn. Although 39 per cent of the respondents said the relationship between the

164/Public Opinion in Semisovereign Germany

new settlers and the old established farmers was good, 30 per cent felt it was only fair, and 13 per cent termed it bad.

In contrast with the attitude toward the new settlers, 59 per cent of the respondents said the relationship between the big farm owners and the small owners was good; only 5 per cent termed it bad.

A solid majority (88%) of the farmers reported a lack of farm workers in their community, and 79 per cent claimed the lack was greater then than it had been a year earlier. Most (77%) thought it due to higher pay and less work in other fields, but 13 per cent maintained it was a government plan to undermine the farmers' independence and ultimately force them into collectivization.

A majority (57%) felt that the GDR's land reforms should be abolished. Despite the general dissatisfaction with the farming situation at that time, a sizable minority (37%) felt that some sort of reform was necessary. Very few (4%) would retain the policies instituted by the GDR if Germany were reunified. When asked what they thought the West could do to improve the farmers' situation in East Germany, about half the responses dealt with some sort of reunification and expulsion of the Soviet Union.

Report No. 134 (29 April 1952)

HOW ARE WEST BERLINERS REACTING TO THE ECONOMIC BLANDISHMENTS OF EAST BERLIN?

Sample: 600 West Berliners.
Interviewing dates: December 1951. (17 pp.)

The survey represents part of a continuous effort on the part of the West to measure West Berlin's loyalty and resistance to pressures from the East. Despite full shopwindows and extensive rubble-clearing and building activity in East Berlin, four in five (81%) West Berlin respondents claimed that the West had made greater progress during the previous year. Furthermore, they saw conditions in East Berlin as atypical for the GDR: 89 per cent said the East Sector was better off than the rest of the GDR.

Regardless of their feelings about the East and the official request that West Berliners not shop there, many did so. They did this in spite of the fact that 90 per cent agreed that such purchases hurt the West more than the East. About a quarter of the population saw no justification for shopping in the East, but 40 per cent felt it was justified for the unemployed and those on pensions; another 20 per cent thought it justified if the economic need were great enough. In fact, 55 per cent said they themselves would buy in the East if economic conditions were bad enough; among those under 30, this was as high as 75 per cent. Asked directly whether or not they shopped in the East, about one-third said they did; among the unemployed the figure was 48 per cent; and among those under 30, it stood at 47 per cent. The items most frequently mentioned as purchased in the East were bread, flour, potatoes, and vegetables. In the opinion of almost half the respondents (45%) many more people were shopping in the East than had been doing so a year earlier.

Cross-tabulations revealed that by and large shoppers in the East were simply taking advantage of the cheap goods without their political ideology being seriously involved or affected.

Report No. 135 (30 April 1952)

CONTRACTUAL AGREEMENT VERSUS RUSSIAN UNITY PROPOSAL
A Preliminary Report on West German Views

Sample: 400 West Germans.
Interviewing dates: 18 to 21 April 1952. (24 pp.)

Slightly more than half (53%) of the West German population was aware of German-Allied negotiations in progress at the time of the survey on a contractual agreement that would grant greater independence to Germany. Among these, almost all (41%) were also aware that West Germany was expected to join the West European defense army as a condition of the agreement. About half of those aware of the negotiations, or 26 per cent of the total population, viewed them favorably, but it should be noted that a fairly large minority (14%) had no opinion on the matter. Only 21 per cent felt that the conclusion of the agreement would represent a great step toward German independence.

A 57 per cent majority of the West German population was aware of the Soviet proposal for German reunification. After those unaware of the proposal had been told what it was, all respondents were asked whether they considered it nothing but propaganda or if they thought the Soviet Union was prepared to make real concessions on this issue. Sixty-seven per cent considered it propaganda, 22 per cent gave no opinion, and only 11 per cent felt it represented a real desire for settlement.

Among the 55 per cent favoring Bundestag approval of the contractual agreement, 30 per cent felt it should be put into effect as soon as possible, 17 per cent thought the Soviet proposal ought to be discussed first, and 6 per cent had no opinion.

Report No. 136 (16 May 1952)

HARD CORE REFUGEES EVALUATE THEIR SITUATION
A Study of Camp Inmates in Western Germany

Sample: 700 refugees living in camps in West Germany.
Interviewing dates: 8 to 18 August 1951. (96 pp.)

More than half (53%) of the refugees said that housing was the greatest problem still facing them at the time of the interviews; 32 per cent mentioned unemployment. Despite such major complaints, however, 44 per cent of those interviewed did not think their situation would be any better if they could move out of the camp. Over two-thirds (68%) would nonetheless like to move out, and 41 per cent had in fact tried to do so. Of the latter, 14 per cent failed because of the housing shortage, and 13 per cent were waiting for their applications to be processed or had already been rejected.

A sense of rejection by the outside world was extensive. As many as 42 per cent had never been helped by any relief or welfare group, and some had never even heard of such organizations. Asked about the high rate of unemployment among the refugees, 29 per cent claimed it was due to discrimination against them; 48 per cent felt that employers preferred to hire natives. Of the 22 per cent unemployed, 15 per cent claimed they had never been offered a job by the employment office. Most thought the situation would be better in some other part of Germany, especially in the Ruhr, but moving was considered impossible. Despite their personal fear of moving, 21 per cent felt that those who had moved had adjusted well to life outside the camp; 29 per cent termed the adjustment satisfactory; and another 29 per cent had no opinion on the matter.

A large number of the respondents in this survey did not seem to want to be assimilated into German life. Asked whom they would prefer to have as a friend--an expellee or a native-- 18 per cent said a friend would have to be an expellee, and 10 per cent said they would prefer to work with expellees. As many as 64 per cent claimed to have no friends among native Germans. But 52 per cent said they thought the two groups generally got along well together.

Nearly half (45%) of the camp refugees said they took no part in any kind of political activity, even reading political articles in newspapers. This did not include meetings of expellees, which 48 per cent said they had attended at some time. Although the Refugee party (BHE or, literally, League of Expellees and Those Deprived of Their Rights) claimed to represent the refugees, only 26 per cent mentioned it when asked which political party was doing the most to solve the refugee problem; 16 per cent mentioned the SPD. Over half (52%) felt that the Bonn government was making an honest effort to solve the refugee problem. A large majority (73%) felt the problem required the help of other nations, but less than a third of these thought there would be much of this sort of help.

A plan under discussion at the time of the survey was the Law for the Equalization of Burdens. It would require those who had not suffered economically or financially from the war to be taxed and the revenue distributed among those who had been bombed out, expelled from their homelands, or had otherwise suffered because of the war. Well over half (65%) did not think this plan would ever be put into effect.

A solid majority (72%) said they would like to return to their homeland; 23 per cent wanted to stay in West Germany, and only 3 per cent were interested in emigrating. Most felt that the Eastern nations and their communist governments, as well as the Great Powers, were responsible for their expulsion; about a quarter mentioned Hitler and the war. Over half (43%) of those who said they wanted to return felt they would in fact be able to do so at some future date, even though many (39%) said it would not be possible until after a war. Evidently, however, for most war was too high a price to pay for this chance to go home. Only 13 per cent of the 72 per cent wishing to return said they would approve a war if that were the only way to get rid of the communist governments and let them go home.

Two appendices describe the sample and method of selection, and present population breakdowns on each question.

Report No. 137 (21 May 1952)

FOLLOW-UP STUDY OF GERMAN VIEWS ON THE CONTRACTUAL AGREEMENT VERSUS THE RUSSIAN UNITY PROPOSAL

Sample: 800 West Germans.
Interviewing dates: 28 April to 10 May 1952. (24 pp.)

Confirming a study made about a week earlier, this survey showed that very few West Germans thought the Soviet proposal for reunifying Germany represented any real concessions. Two-thirds (67%) felt it was nothing but propaganda. Almost as many (62%) preferred to see the plan rejected, while only 17 per cent hoped it would be accepted. The most frequently cited reason for rejection was the feeling that the Eastern territories ought not to be relinquished. In fact, of those who hoped the plan would not be accepted, quite a few (22%) changed their minds if they were asked to suppose that the Russians dropped the demand for recognition of the Oder-Neisse boundary between Poland and Germany. Population breakdowns on the Soviet proposal as presented showed that the more influential population groups tended to be most opposed.

Respondents in the earlier study were told that the contractual agreement under discussion between the Western Powers and the Bonn government provided for almost complete independence

168/Public Opinion in Semisovereign Germany

and partnership in West European defense on a basis of equality. Given this description, 55 per cent expressed approval of the plan, 14 per cent opposed it, and 31 per cent expressed no opinion on it. In the survey under discussion here, respondents were told that the agreement would grant considerable independence and that Germany would accept responsibility for participation with divisions in a West European army. Far fewer were willing to accept this wording (39%), while more than twice as many rejected it (31%), and about the same percentage expressed no opinion (30%).

Given a choice between the Soviet proposal and the projected contractual agreement, over half (56%) preferred the latter, only 16 per cent favored the former, and 28 per cent gave no opinion.

Of those not in outright opposition to the contractual agreement, 26 per cent thought it ought to be put into effect as soon as possible, while 17 per cent felt it should be delayed until the Soviet proposal had been discussed. Regardless of their preference, however, 43 per cent thought the agreement would in fact be speeded up.

Report No. 138 (23 May 1952)

EAST ZONE THINKING ON THE RUSSIAN UNITY PROPOSAL VERSUS THE CONTRACTUAL AGREEMENT
With Comparisons to West Berlin and West German Reactions

Sample: 189 East Germans, 800 West Germans, and 178 West Berliners; see Special Report No. II/63-S on sampling problems and representativeness of East Germans.

Interviewing dates: East German survey on 2 to 5 May 1952; West German survey on 28 April to 10 May 1952; West Berlin survey on 30 April to 12 May 1952. (22 pp.)

Awareness of the Soviet unity proposal was quite high among West Berliners (73%), somewhat lower among East Germans (62%), and even lower among West Germans (49%). The majority of East German respondents (69%), West Berliners (83%), and West Germans (67%) felt the proposal to be nothing but propaganda. Upon presentation of a brief outline of its salient points, 72 per cent of the East Germans, 86 per cent of the West Berliners, and 62 per cent of the West Germans advocated rejection of the unity proposal.

Forty-three per cent of the East Germans, 62 per cent of the West Berliners and 37 per cent of the West Germans opposed the stipulation that Germany relinquish all claims to territories east of the Oder and Neisse rivers. Even without this stipulation, rejection continued to outweigh approval among East German (48%) and West Berlin (59%) respondents. In West Germany, however, the removal of this provision caused the Russian proposal to be acceptable to more people (39%) than would reject it (33%).

A majority of East German respondents (61%) had heard of the negotiations on the contractual agreement between the Western Powers and the federal government. Although they expressed considerable skepticism, 65 per cent of those from the GDR indicated they would favor Bundestag acceptance of the contractual agreement. Sixty-eight per cent of the West Berliners also favored acceptance, but nearly as many West Germans (31%) voted to reject the agreement as voted to accept it (39%). When the contractual agreement and the Russian proposal were presented simultaneously, almost six times as many East German respondents chose the former (72%) as the latter (13%). Of the West Berliners, 79 per cent preferred the contractual agreement to the Russian proposal (13%). In West Germany, approval of the Soviet proposition rose to 16 per cent, while preference for the contract fell to 56 per cent.

The most frequent argument of all Germans (18 per cent of the East Germans, 32 per cent of the West Berliners, 13 per cent of the West Germans) for recommending acceptance of the contractual agreement was that it meant greater security for both West Germany and the West against an Eastern threat. Almost as many of the East Germans (15%) counted on an improvement in the economic and political situation in West Germany--and, as a result, in East Germany--by joining firmly with the West.

Of those respondents who had not previously expressed opposition to the projected contract, the majority of East German respondents (53%) and West Berliners (58%) urged prompt execution of the agreement. These findings contrasted directly with the situation in West Germany, where only 26 per cent favored speed, against 48 per cent who favored delay.

Report No. 139 (27 May 1952)

DO THE WEST GERMAN PEOPLE BELIEVE THE U.S. IS FOR GERMAN UNITY?

With Comparative Judgments about the British and French

Sample: 800 West Germans and 189 East Germans; see Special Report No. II/63-S on sampling problems and representativeness of East Germans.

Interviewing dates: West German survey on 28 April to 10 May 1952; East Germans interviewed on 2 to 8 May 1952. (29 pp.)

When presented with a list of tasks facing West Germany, unity was selected as having the highest priority by more people (39%) than any other issue. An additional 18 per cent selected it as the second most pressing problem. Although 47 per cent believed that the United States favored reunification and only 3 per cent felt that it definitely opposed such unity, 25 per cent were doubtful, and another 25 per cent did not know what the American position was. Those expressing most doubt were residents of the American Zone.

Those respondents who were certain that the United States favored German unity offered various reasons for their belief: America desired a bulwark against the Russians (13%); America wanted the economic advantages of a reunited Germany (11%); America had proved itself friendly to Germany (10%). Among those who doubted American intentions, 6 per cent felt that the Americans feared trade and business competition from a united Germany; 5 per cent that the United States was interested only in its own advantages; 5 per cent that America had not tried to achieve German unity; and 4 per cent that the United States feared growing German strength.

Although opinions on the British position regarding German unity followed a pattern similar to those vis-à-vis the American stand, fewer West Germans (33%) were firmly convinced that Britain was for reunification, and more (39%) had no opinion at all.

Many West Germans (59%) were unconvinced that France favored German reunification. Twenty-one per cent were sure the French definitely opposed such unity. Only one in nine (11%) believed France supported the unification, and 30 per cent expressed no opinion.

The crux of the unity issue in German thinking was not so much whether or not the Western Powers were for German unity as what they were doing to further it. More than a third of the respondents (36%) said the United States was doing everything it could to reunite Germany. But nearly as many (33%) thought America could do more, and 29 per cent were unprepared to express any opinion. The critics of American efforts were largely concentrated (70%) among those who were doubtful of American intentions. Within almost all population groups, about as many said the United States could do more as said it was doing everything possible.

Findings obtained in a concurrent survey suggested that East Germans were more appreciative of American efforts on behalf of German unity. Although 37 per cent felt more could be done, 55 per cent believed the United States was doing all that it could. Of those who felt more could be done, more than half offered reasons that tended to extenuate the Americans rather than accuse them.

In a previous West German study, adverse judgments on the adequacy of efforts by the Western Powers had outweighed satisfaction 41 per cent to 35 per cent, with 29 per cent having no opinion. The respondents felt the West wanted to take advantage of Germany (9%); feared a united, strengthened Germany (9%); and was not interested in reunification (6%). The opinion that the Western Powers could do more for German unity was strongest among the more influential population elements.

The West German people were far more assured that Bonn was working toward German reunification (53%). The quarter (26%) that felt more could be done attributed Bonn's failure more to excessive control by the Western Powers (11%) than to anything else. Although opinion leaders believed Bonn was doing its utmost for Germany's unity, a third of this group was critical of the government's effort.

Report No. 140 (30 May 1952)

HOW DO GERMANS REACT TO EAST-WEST TRADE RESTRICTIONS?

Sample: 800 West Germans and 178 West Berliners.
Interviewing dates: 29 April to 13 May 1952. (13 pp.)

Although few West Germans supported complete abolition of trade between East and West Germany, nearly half (47%) felt trade to the East should restrict potential war materials. A sizable minority (30%) nonetheless approved unlimited trade as being essential to the German economy. West Berliners were more prepared to impose a limitation on interzonal trade, with 60 per cent favoring some restriction and 16 per cent favoring abolition of all trade. Restriction of Eastern trade received its widest support from the more influential elements of the population--men, the better educated, and the more affluent. Half or more in these groups advocated limited restrictions.

A fairly large minority (19%) of West Germans claimed that the United States, in limiting West Germany's trade with the East, was unjustly taking advantage of its own position. The fact that the United States restricted East-West trade at all was, to some (4%), all that was needed to inspire lack of confidence in American amity toward West Germany. In the case of France, more than half of the West Germans (54%) took no stand; but among those who did, twice as many distrusted French motives (30%) as believed France was seriously interested in West Germany's welfare (16%) regarding East-West trade. Regarding Britain, 50 per cent of the West Germans had no opinion. The half who voiced an opinion divided almost evenly in ascribing just (26%) and unjust (24%) motives to the trade regulations imposed by the British.

Report No. 141 (May 1952)

INITIAL WEST GERMAN REACTIONS TO THE SOVIET WAR OF NERVES

Sample: 800 West Germans.
Interviewing dates: 16 to 21 May 1952. (29 pp.)

During the concluding phase of negotiations between the Western Powers and West Germany on a contractual agreement replacing the Occupation Statute of 1949, the communists attempted to increase public opposition to the treaty. Following the Russian attack upon a French passenger plane en route to Berlin and the Essen riot, only a third of the respondents indicated having been disturbed by these occurrences. Sixty-two per cent were aware of the Essen riot, and among these, a majority (44%) believed the incident was communist inspired and was likely to be followed up by similar demonstrations (36%). Almost three-quarters of the people (72%) knew of the plane attack, and 42 per cent of these believed the incident was planned by the Russians. The major expectation among all respondents (58%) was that communist measures could be expected against the contractual agreement and West Germany's defense participation. Anticipation of trouble was most widespread among the more alert and informed population segments.

Various kinds of communist measures were expected: disturbances and demonstrations (20%), another Berlin blockade (11%), intensified rearmament in the East (11%), and all-out war (4%). Most (69%) felt a firm attitude was the best resistance against the Russians. The largest proportion (51%) recommended severe countermeasures should such disturbances continue. Only one in twelve (8%) expressed the opinion that no countermeasures should be taken. The most frequently recommended courses of action were quelling demonstrations (20%), arresting and punishing the ringleaders (19%), and banning the Communist party (KPD) and its affiliates (9%).

The Soviet campaign also failed to alter public attitudes toward the agreement. In fact, acceptance of the treaty rose slightly from 39 per cent before the incidents to 41 per cent following them. Because of the communist pressure, 49 per cent favored immediate acceptance and implementation of the treaty. The communist pressure also failed to increase the extent of war apprehension, neutralism, defeatism, and opposition to German defense participation.

Among West Germans in general (36%), and in most population subgroups, satisfaction outweighed dissatisfaction with American policy toward Russia. However, in no population group did approval achieve majority status. The dissatisfied minority (17%) recommended a firmer attitude in dealing with the Russians.

Report No. 142 (11 June 1952)

FIRST REACTIONS OF WEST BERLINERS TO THE CURRENT SOVIET PRESSURE CAMPAIGN

Sample: 160 West Berliners.
Interviewing dates: last two weeks of May 1952. (20 pp.)

West Berliners (from 82 to 97 per cent) were aware of

Soviet-inspired maneuvers to thwart the integration of Germany with the West, and 73 per cent anticipated more incidents. Most (59%), however, did not find them disturbing. According to the West Berliners, the communists were trying to undermine West Germany (44%), promote communism especially among the young (23%), and prevent acceptance of the contractual agreement with the Western Powers (18%).

Although many expected a continuation of trouble, the majority (63%) did not anticipate another Berlin blockade. In the event of another blockade (and 35 per cent believed this would occur), sterner countermeasures were advocated by more than half (58%) of the West Berlin public. Ninety-two per cent of the West Berliners felt a firm, uncompromising attitude was the only way to deal with the Russians. About four in ten (43%) considered the American handling of Russian affairs satisfactory; nearly as many (37%) found it unsatisfactory or only partially acceptable (13%), primarily because it lacked firmness (49%).

Despite the Russian actions, 72 per cent of the residents of West Berlin recommended Bundestag ratification of the contractual agreement, and almost as many (66%) believed both the contract and German defense participation should take effect as soon as possible.

Seventy-eight per cent felt that West Germany should go ahead with the treaties, while only 7 per cent recommended delay. Eighty-one per cent further believed that Russian efforts to block acceptance of the peace contract should be met with strong countermeasures, such as the arrest and punishment of ringleaders (34%), a police-enforced ban on demonstrations (29%), a ban of the Communist party of Germany (13%), and the expulsion of communists from West Germany (12%).

A considerable proportion of West Berliners (56%) was unaware of the Western proposal to Russia on German unity. The four in ten (42%) who were informed tended to approve of the proposal. Eighty-two per cent of the respondents were sure the Americans wanted to see Germany reunited.

The communist war of nerves had little influence on the way West Berliners voted on West German military participation (72 per cent for it), on neutrality (66 per cent opposed to it), and on the relative successes of the Communist and Western Powers (72 per cent believed the West to be stronger; 62 per cent felt the West had more success politically).

Over half (56%) perceived little likelihood of an immediate communist attack on West Germany, but nine out of ten advocated unreserved resistance should it occur. Nearly a third (32%) held that the West European and American forces would not let the Russians invade West Germany, while a little more than a third (36%) felt the Russians would overrun West Germany. Only 14 per cent felt that the Russians would overrun the whole of Europe.

Report No. 143 (30 June 1952)

SOME BASIC GUIDES TO PREDICTING THE FUTURE BEHAVIOR OF WEST GERMANY

Sample: 1,200 West Germans and 200 West Berliners.
Interviewing dates: 17 March to 1 April 1952. (66 pp.)

The majority (57 per cent of the West Germans and 65 per cent of the West Berliners) asserted that they would like Germany to be the strongest country in Europe. Patriotic considerations, some with a distinctly nationalistic flavor, ranked highest (20%) among those with ambitions for a powerful Germany, but nearly as many (17%) argued in political terms or cited economic considerations (13%). Of those respondents who wanted Germany to be the strongest state in Europe, 35 per cent (42 per cent in West Berlin) wished Germany to be the most powerful member of a West European union. Although 49 per cent of the West Germans and 74 per cent of the West Berliners felt that West Germany was likely to become a strong nation in Western Europe, not quite half as many expected it to have a very powerful role (23 per cent in West Germany and 36 per cent in West Berlin). The main contention of those who believed Germany would not again become a strong nation was that the Western Powers, individually or collectively, would prevent this development (13 per cent in West Germany and 8 per cent in West Berlin). Seven per cent of the West Germans and 5 per cent of the West Berliners believed the separation of East from West Germany made a strong Germany impossible. In all population groups, the majority favored a powerful Germany.

Recommended ways of achieving a position of strength were modest and generally unaggressive. Most West Germans suggested hard work and unity of purpose: a strengthened economy (10%); an end to internal dissension (8%); an end to unemployment (5%); and increased efforts at reconstruction (4%).

Almost all West Germans (90%) felt that the addition of millions of refugees and expellees had resulted in a population problem. More than half of these also said that a decent living standard was impossible as long as the country was overcrowded. The only solution that had any great popular appeal was the reunification of Germany and the recovery of lost territories in the East. And although three in ten (30%) thought economic integration within the framework of a West European union would be of some help, almost as many (26%) believed such cooperation would ease the situation hardly at all.

A large number of West Germans expressly or implicitly assumed that the reunion of East and West Germany was not only desirable but essential to the future well-being of the German people. Most (73 per cent in West Germany and 60 per cent in West Berlin) opposed the use of force to gain reunification. More than half (56 per cent in West Germany and 65 per cent in

West Berlin), however, did not see anything wrong with using aggressive means should other measures fail. Few West Germans (14%) were prepared to compromise with communist forces to achieve reunification. If it were to result in more widespread communist influence, three in four West Germans (76%) would oppose reunification. The men and the better educated were somewhat more inclined to favor reunification, even with increased communist influence. While the preponderance in all groups opposed the use of force, the majority in all groups claimed that Germany had the right to use it.

The vast majority of West Germans (85%) and West Berliners (96%) asserted that Germany had a rightful claim to East and West Prussia, Pomerania, and Silesia. A legal claim was also staked out for the Sudetenland by 54 per cent of the West Germans and 40 per cent of West Berliners. Eight out of ten West Germans (79%) and almost all West Berliners (96%) urged that everything possible be done to regain the former possessions. Almost half the West Germans (46%) and eight in ten West Berliners (79%) thought the West would agree to Germany's recovering her lost territories. A firm majority (62%) said they would go ahead even if the West were to oppose it. Most (54%) advocated recovery through negotiations with the Russians, with or without participation of the Western Powers, rather than the use of force (20%). An even larger majority (67%), however, reserved the right to use aggressive measures if other means failed.
Six in ten West Germans and eight in ten West Berliners (78%) were confident that the Eastern territories would eventually be recovered.

Eight in ten West Berliners (55 per cent in West Germany) chose to cooperate with the West for the duration of the cold war, even though joining with the East appeared to have greater economic and political advantages. Allegiance to the West was based more frequently on the rejection of communism (23%) than on any positive virtue attributed to the West. Although seven in ten Germans (69%) recommended future trade with the Eastern countries, only two in ten (19%) recommended such trade against the wishes of the West, and nearly half (40%) opposed it if it should jeopardize Western relations. Opinion-leading elements were particularly inclined toward cooperation with the West.

Regarding the Schuman Plan, three in ten West Germans said they agreed with it, but more than a third (45 per cent in West Berlin) said West Germany should abandon the organization if it should prove disadvantageous to Germany.

Report No. 144 (8 July 1952)

GERMAN VIEWS ON THE CONTRACTUAL AGREEMENT FOLLOWING INITIALING AND PUBLICATION

Sample: 800 West Germans.
Interviewing dates: 4 to 11 June 1952. (29 pp.)

Following publication on 26 May 1952 of the German Treaty, awareness of the contractual agreement increased to 73 per cent. Many people, however, were still vague about the details. A majority (58%) indicated they knew that the agreement had already been signed by Chancellor Adenauer, but only a third (31%) knew that a Bundestag ratification was still necessary before the contract went into effect.

More West Germans approved of the treaty (33%) than disapproved (19%). Most were aware that the contract obliged West Germany to participate in European affairs. Disapproval of the military corollary, rather than dissatisfaction with the contract per se, was the most frequently cited reason for opposing ratification. Respondents opposed to the treaty suggested neutrality and negotiations with the East as alternative courses of action. Whatever their attitude toward the contractual agreement, a solid majority (67%) believed that the contract would be ratified by the Bundestag.

The trend of West German approval of defense participation edged upward to the point where it exceeded the opposition (47 to 42 per cent). Support was most widespread among the opinion-leading elements of the public. Among the crucial 18- to 24-year olds, however, the extent of support fell off to 32 per cent, while opposition rose to 54 per cent.

Many West Germans (40%) felt the contract reduced chances for German reunification, but half of these said the difficulty was only temporary. More important, a third (15%) of those who saw unity delayed by the agreement indicated that Adenauer was right in concluding the treaty.

Most West Germans (49%) were fairly satisfied with the activities of the federal government. The dissatisfied minority (25%) cited economic difficulties (19%), the new German military (5%), and the contractual agreement (2%) as reasons for their disapproval.

Whatever the pattern of German attitudes on the contractual agreement, a large majority (75%) favored an East-West four-power conference on German problems. This held true in all population groups, even among those from whom Adenauer characteristically drew his greatest support. Still, only a third of the respondents (33%) considered it at all likely to result in advantages for West Germany.

Report No. 145 (10 July 1952)

A FURTHER ASSESSMENT OF GERMAN REACTIONS TO THE SOVIET WAR OF NERVES

Sample: 800 West Germans.
Interviewing dates: 3 to 12 June 1952. (16 pp.)

Among the 57 per cent who could, with assistance, think of disturbing manifestations of Russian activities, only 20 per cent termed them "quite disturbing." Half (50%) advocated severe countermeasures if the Russians continued to threaten German efforts to integrate with the West, while another quarter (25%) recommended some kind of retaliation. Only one in fourteen (7%) opposed retaliation.

The likelihood of an imminent Russian attack on West Germany was largely discounted by many (50%), although 30 per cent believed the communists might take such action. Three in ten (29%) anticipated a second Berlin blockade, while another 17 per cent foresaw other serious difficulties for Berlin. The majority (54%), however, expected no great problems.

In the event of a second blockade, only 22 per cent recommended repetition of the measures used in the 1948-49 blockade, while nearly half (47%) thought the West should adopt a firmer course of action. Most (35%) urged a policy of firmness as the only answer to Russian threats, stating that Russians understand the use of power. If another airlift proved unfeasible, some 18 per cent proposed the use of force to break the blockade even at the risk of war. Half the respondents, however, offered no suggestions at all.

While the weight of opinion in all population groups was toward firmness in the face of Russian threats, this view was particularly prevalent among the upper status segments.

Report No. 146 (28 July 1952)

HOW STRONG IS RESISTANCE MORALE IN WEST BERLIN TODAY?

Sample: 300 West Berliners.
Interviewing dates: last two weeks of June 1952. (35 pp.)

As communist pressures on West Berlin again reached critical proportions in mid-summer 1952, the vast majority of West Berliners (78%) wanted the Western Powers to remain in Berlin even though war could be avoided by their withdrawal. In the case of a Soviet attack on West Berlin, 66 per cent felt that the West would declare war. An even larger percentage (81%) believed that the West would defend Berlin, with nearly half (48%) asserting that the Western defense would be successful. Two-thirds of the respondents (65%) declared that an armed Berlin citizenry would stand side by side with the West--to the death if necessary--in any future battle for Berlin. Defeatism arising from the memory of the Russian conquest of Berlin in 1945 and from awareness of the city's exposed position largely characterized the thinking of the 26 per cent who opposed defending Berlin. Few, however, thought they would actually have to take up arms. Many West Berliners (37%) did not believe there would be another world war within the next ten years, with most (65%) saying that the Russians would yield to strong countermeasures from the West.

On the issue of West German participation in the European Defense Community, West Berliners indicated more extensive approval (72%) than West Germans (44%). A majority of West Berliners (53%) believed that West Berlin should also join the Western European defense organization.

Though generally cognizant of the Russian scare tactics, less than half (45%) said they were disturbed; and of these only a third (15%) were quite disturbed by the incidents. Despite the fact that more West Berliners were giving attention to East-West pressures in June 1952 (38%) than in November 1951 (28%), economic problems--unemployment, high prices, taxes--were still considered to be more pressing issues (59%).

West Berliners (55%) ascribed the increased tension to signing of the contractual agreement with the Western Powers, and many (41%) believed the tensions would increase. According to a quarter (26%) of the West Berlin populace, the ratification of the contract with the West would produce another Berlin blockade. Almost as many (21%) predicted other pressures, ranging from increased harassment of Berlin to war.

In the event of another blockade, West Berliners advised stricter measures than in the previous blockade (68%), dividing between two recommendations: to impose a counterblockade on the East (26%) or to keep routes to Berlin open by force (20%). More than four in ten (44%) urged force even at the risk of war.

Although many West Berliners were aware of the contractual agreement, only a third (36%) knew that Berlin was not a party to the treaty. Bundestag acceptance was recommended by a majority of 57 per cent. Half the West Berliners were dissatisfied or only fairly satisfied with present relations with residents of West Germany, mainly due to the alleged failure of West Germany to keep its promises (12%) and inadequate economic aid (12%). Better relations were anticipated by the majority (57%). In contrast, the majority (65%) commended the assistance of the Western Powers. The British (60%) and the Americans (63%) received especially high commendation. Nevertheless, about a fifth of the respondents were dissatisfied and suggested that the Americans (24%) and the British (10%) take a firm stance in dealing with the Russians. As to French actions, half (51%) were not prepared to render judgment. Among those who did have an opinion, approval exceeded disapproval by three to one (35 to 11 per cent).

The Berlin mood remained relatively unchanged from December 1951 through June 1952. A large majority (75%) stated a preference to remain in Berlin and, if possible, start a business (39%) or make capital investments (33%). However, people who saw a worsening in the general state of mind of West Berliners were more inclined to attribute that change to political factors (21%) than had been the case before (10%).

PUBLIC OPINION IN SEMISOVEREIGN GERMANY

The HICOG Surveys, 1949-1955

edited by
Anna J. Merritt and Richard L. Merritt

How did postwar Germans feel about Hitler and their Nazi past? What price were they willing to pay for German reunification? What were they thinking as the military occupation of West Germany was transformed into a military alliance between the victors and vanquished of World War II?

These and other important questions are answered in the public opinion surveys conducted in West Germany for the civilian U.S. High Commission for Germany (HICOG), and which are summarized and analyzed in this volume. It completes the story begun by the Merritts in their 1970 book, in which they presented and interpreted the Office of Military Government, U.S. (OMGUS) surveys of occupied Germany.

This volume is the first comprehensive and readily accessible examination of HICOG's public opinion work. The Merritts' analysis will be particularly valuable for historians, political scientists, sociologists, communications specialists, and others interested in the interaction of policy and public perspectives.

ANNA J. MERRITT is editor and staff associate with the Institute of Government and Public Affairs at the University of Illinois. RICHARD L. MERRITT is research professor and head of the University's political science department. Together they have written extensively on postwar Germany.

379 pages. ISBN 0-252-00731-X.

UNIVERSITY OF ILLINOIS PRESS
Urbana Chicago London

Also by Anna J. and Richard L. Merritt ...

POLITICS, ECONOMICS, AND SOCIETY IN THE TWO GERMANIES, 1945-75
A Bibliography of English-language Works

This classified bibliography contains entries for nearly 8,550 books, articles, essays, and theses on the two Germanies since 1945. "... a major achievement, unique in its field, which most college, research, and larger public libraries should have." — Erwin K. Welsch, *Library Journal*. "... the best listing of English-language materials on the political and economic development of Germany." — Robert Lindsay, *Reference Quarterly*.
1978. 288 pages. $12.00.

PUBLIC OPINION IN OCCUPIED GERMANY
The OMGUS Surveys, 1945-1949

Contains summaries of 194 reports drawn from surveys conducted by the Office of Military Government, U.S. (OMGUS) and reflects the numerous problems arising from trying to govern and democratize an alien population." ... reveals considerable insight into the attitudes of the German people, and is a useful attempt to show what they really thought about the issues that confronted them during the occupation." — Aaron L. Goldman, *Social Science Quarterly*.
1970. 350 pages. $10.00.

Also on Germany ...

THE GERMAN REARMAMENT QUESTION
American Diplomacy and European Defense after World War II

Robert McGeehan
1971. 295 pages. $10.00.

POLITICAL DECADENCE IN IMPERIAL GERMANY
Personnel-Political Aspects of the German Government Crisis, 1894-97

Ekkehard-Teja P. W. Wilke
1976. 280 pages. $10.95.

UNIVERSITY OF ILLINOIS PRESS
Station A, Box 5081
Champaign, Illinois 61820

Report No. 147 (April 1952)

THE BASIC ECONOMIC ORIENTATIONS OF THE WEST GERMAN PEOPLE

I. General Views on Socialism, Capitalism, and Communism

Sample: 1,200 West Germans and 300 West Berliners.
Interviewing dates: 7 to 25 April 1952. (32 pp.)

Favorable orientations toward socialism were strong in West Germany (38%) and West Berlin (50%). Almost as many West Germans (35%) and West Berliners (46%) believed that socialism would grow stronger. What the German people appeared to be approving under the name of socialism were simply social welfare practices and economic policies, such as improvement of old age pensions and welfare (9 per cent in West Germany, 17 per cent in West Berlin) and improvement of living conditions (9 and 15 per cent respectively). When questioned directly, the West German populace (42%) manifested disapproval of industrial socialization--even if confined to heavy industries. A majority of 56 per cent (67 per cent in West Berlin) expressed the judgment that the worker would not be better off if industry were socialized. In no group, including both SPD political adherents and trade union members, did support for socialization of industry reliably exceed opposition.

Most Germans held distinctly negative attitudes toward capitalism as a concept. Disadvantages for the worker (23 per cent in West Germany and 18 per cent in West Berlin) and exploitation of the worker (7 and 6 per cent respectively) were cited as capitalism's major faults. Asked to label the present American economic system, the majority of West Germans (61%) had no answer at all. German youth were distinctly more favorable toward emulating the American economic system than were their elders, and respondents of SPD political persuasion did not appear to be any less favorable toward the American economic system than CDU and FDP sympathizers.

Most West Germans with opinions on the matter (55 per cent, 69 per cent in West Berlin) held socialism and communism to be fundamentally different. Almost one in five (17 and 22 per cent respectively), however, judged them to be about the same. Those who saw a fundamental difference argued that communism carried with it repression and totalitarianism (20 and 28 per cent respectively), while socialism did not. The large majority (65 and 69 per cent respectively) saw no good whatever in the communist philosophy--even leaving political considerations aside. But if we ignore no-opinion responses, as many as one in five remained who felt that, apart from political considerations, there was some good in communism.

Report No. 148 (7 August 1952)

THE BASIC ECONOMIC ORIENTATIONS OF THE WEST GERMAN PEOPLE

II. The Status of Trade Unions and the Question of Codetermination

Sample: 1,200 West Germans and 300 West Berliners.
Interviewing dates: 7 to 25 April 1952. (34 pp.)

The preponderant (52%) opinion in West Germany was that trade unions were a good influence. Only one in five (13%) among those with opinions believed that trade unions exerted a bad influence on the West German economy. Relatively few (7%), however, went so far as to state that trade unions were a *very* good influence. Conversely, only a negligible one per cent argued that their influence was *very* bad. Favorable appraisal of trade union influence centered on benefits to the workers: improved economy (13 per cent of West Germany, 20 per cent in West Berlin), fair wages and good working conditions (10 per cent in both), improved management-labor relations (9 and 14 per cent respectively), and protection of the workers (6 and 3 per cent respectively). Those opposed argued that trade unions interfered in the relationship between management and labor (2 and 3 per cent respectively) and that the unions were more interested in their own welfare than in that of their workers (2 and 3 per cent respectively).

Well over half (55%) of the West Germans judged that German trade unions did much to improve the living conditions of West German workers. A sixth (16%) voiced a contrary view, and a fractional 3 per cent argued that the trade unions generally accomplished nothing at all in improving the living conditions of the rank and file.

However favorable West Germans were toward union activity in general, only 29 per cent of them (39 per cent in West Berlin) approved of strikes. Those who opposed strikes for higher wages argued that wage increases only resulted in higher prices (13 and 11 per cent respectively), a strike meant a loss to the people and to the economy (11 and 18 per cent respectively), it would result in financial losses for the workers (11 and 13 per cent respectively), and negotiations were preferable (10 per cent in both).

In no group examined did more than a third label trade unions a bad influence on the West German economy. Approval of trade union influence appeared to be at its maximum among West German youth (61 per cent of whom thought it was a good influence). As to the effectiveness of trade unions, most believed that they did much rather than little. Even the unemployed and the lower income groups supported this view. Support for the right to strike was distinctly greater among West German youth (51%) than among their elders. The youth differed in this respect even from trade union members, among whom 52 per cent expressed the opinion that a strike for higher wages was basically wrong.

Opinions divided on whether the United States wanted to see trade unions occupy a strong or weak position in West Germany. Most (63 per cent in West Germany, 65 per cent in West Berlin) felt that labor should have a say in the decisions of plant management, although the majority of these (37 and 45 per cent respectively) thought the unions should have less voice than management.

Most West Germans (28%) who expressed an opinion on the matter believed that the United States did not want codetermination put into effect in West Germany. Only in Berlin did a similar proportion (38%) believe the contrary to be true. Those who thought that America would disapprove of such a move argued that industrial codetermination did not fit into the American economic system (7 and 9 per cent respectively), America feared labor would get too strong (6 and 3 per cent respectively), and America could manage more easily without industrial codetermination (5 and 3 per cent respectively). Those who felt that America approved codetermination countered that America used the system itself (3 and 10 per cent respectively), it would strengthen democracy and weaken communism (2 and 4 per cent respectively), and it would promote industrial harmony (2 and 9 per cent respectively).

Report No. 149 (8 August 1952)

A NOTE ON RECEPTIVITY AND RESISTANCE TO INTRODUCING AMERICAN WORKING METHODS INTO GERMAN INDUSTRY

Sample: 1,200 West Germans and 300 West Berliners.
Interviewing dates: 7 to 25 April 1952. (9 pp.)

A majority (38%) of West Germans with opinions felt that Germany's working methods were preferable to America's (35%). About half of the West Berlin sample, however, preferred American (51%) to German (33%) working methods. Only 19 per cent in West Germany (26 per cent in West Berlin) showed any interest in the introduction of American working methods; even fewer (17%) violently opposed the idea.

Those who opposed American working methods for Germany said that Germany did not need American methods (10 per cent in West Germany and 9 per cent in West Berlin) or that American methods were unsuitable for German conditions (6 and 8 per cent respectively).

Comparisons among population groups revealed that the better schooled, the more affluent, and German youth were more likely to prefer American methods. No more than a third of any population group expressed outright opposition to the proposal.

Report No. 150 (13 August 1952)

THE KOREAN RECORD IN GERMAN EYES
And Some Comparisons with British, French, Dutch, and Italian Views

Sample: 800 West Germans.
Interviewing dates: late July 1952. (34 pp.)

A large preponderance of the West German population (74%) had more or less detailed knowledge of the Korean situation, with a quarter (26%) actually specifying the truce negotiations as of primary importance at present. Widespread speculation that the communists were prolonging the armistice discussions to build up their military strength for a renewal of the conflict was subscribed to by 70 per cent of the sample. West Germans expressed confidence, however, that United Nations representatives were actually trying to end hostilities (57%), rather than stalling for time (21%). Two-thirds (67%) felt the U.N. wanted peace, while only 2 per cent were sure that the communists did.

Close to half (46%) felt the conflict would end in battle, not negotiations. Opposition to extending the conflict, should the talks fail, was the predominant opinion, with only 12 per cent advocating extension of the war into China. Complete withdrawal of U.N. forces from Korea was recommended by a fairly large minority (34%). Proponents of U.N. withdrawal were generally fearful that, if fighting continued, it would lead to another world war (19%). By way of contrast, advocates of extending the war into China not only believed that it could be contained in that area (6%) but also that this was the time and place to end the communist threat forever (3%).

Two-fifths (42%) of the West German people were aware of the communist charges that the U.N. was employing germ warfare in Korea, but 30 per cent added that they did not believe them.

Relatively few West Germans (22%) had much understanding of the details regarding the exchange of Korean prisoners of war, even though half (53%) claimed to have heard about it. The U.N. refusal to repatriate prisoners who did not wish to return to North Korea was almost unanimously approved by the informed minority.

The majority of West Germans (64%) knew that fighting was continuing during the peace negotiations. More specifically, a considerable segment (43%) was aware of the air raids on the North Korean power plants and 25 per cent of this group approved the raids. As to what course the U.N. should take to make the communists come to terms, some (39%) thought the U.N. should stop fighting entirely, while others (36%) recommended stepped-up military action.

The West German people largely accepted the decision of the U.N. to intervene in Korea, although approval of the action had declined from 56 per cent in 1951 to 46 per cent in 1952. The main argument against U.N. intervention in Korea was that it was a Korean affair, which the U.N.--especially

the United States--should have left to the Koreans to settle (12%).
A clear indication that the U.N. had lost some face with the German people was the finding that 39 per cent of the total population thought the U.N. had made a worse showing in Korea than expected. Only 15 per cent declared that it exceeded expectations.

Report No. 151 (25 August 1952)

WEST GERMAN RECEPTIVITY AND REACTIONS TO THE EXCHANGE OF PERSONS PROGRAM

Sample: 1,200 West Germans.
Interviewing dates: January-February 1952. (118 pp.)

Receptivity to the principle of the international exchange of ideas was widespread among West Germans. About seven in ten (72%) said Germans could profit from what other nations have to offer. Conversely, seven in eight (88%) stated that other nations could learn from Germany. As areas of German contribution, people named the technical-industrial areas (41%), practical traits such as diligence and efficiency (33%), and culture and education (21%). Germany could learn from other countries in the economic, technical, and industrial fields (21%), general way of living (17%), and politics (17%). Seventy-one per cent said that a German would be more valuable to Germany were he to live abroad for a year, while only 15 per cent thought his contribution would be greater if he stayed in Germany.

Germans thought that Germany could learn something from the United States (45%), England (6%), Switzerland (4%), Sweden (3%), and Russia (1%). Germans were receptive to Germany's learning from America in industrial development (68%) and agriculture (56%). Almost half (46%) said that the mass media in America had something or much to offer Germany by way of example. Nearly two-thirds felt that Germany could learn nothing from the United States in social welfare (62%) or the arts (60%).

Claimed awareness of the German-American exchange program was virtually the same in the American (43%) and British (39%) Zones, and somewhat less (33%) in the French Zone. The principal sources of information about the exchange program were newspapers (24%) and radio (21%). Over three-fourths of those who had heard of the program could define it correctly, and about a quarter knew that the United States paid for the program. About half felt that the American motive was to promote mutual understanding. Few felt America was merely exploiting Germany.

Special Flash Report No. 152 (2 September 1952)

WEST GERMAN PUBLIC OPINION IN RE THE LATEST RUSSIAN NOTE

Sample: 400 West Germans.
Interviewing dates: flash survey on 26 to 31 August 1952. (5 pp.)

The large majority (75%) of the West German people continued to favor a four-power conference, despite the fact that a waning minority (26%) considered such a conference as at all likely to result in advantages for West Germany. When presented as alternatives without indications of sponsorship, the Russian-sponsored agenda of peace negotiations before free elections was slightly more acceptable (44%) than the American-sponsored proposal of free elections before peace negotiations (41%). Many (46%) were unaware of the Russian proposal or supposed incorrectly that Russia supported free elections before peace negotiations (17%). On the other hand, nearly as many (38%) were ignorant of the American position or believed that America was in favor of peace negotiations prior to free elections (20%).

When the implications of choosing a peace treaty before holding free elections were clearly spelled out in the framework of the questioning, however, many respondents shifted to insistence upon free elections first. Eighty-two per cent of those sampled were aware that the leaders of East Germany had not been elected by the population in a free election. Almost three-quarters (73%) insisted that new East German representatives, elected by the people in a free election, should represent them in any peace negotiation.

Despite the recent note and continuous Soviet counterpropaganda, support for Bundestag ratification of the contractual agreement between the Federal Republic and the Western Powers rose from 33 per cent in early June to 40 per cent at the end of August. However, half of the latter (19%) indicated a desire for a four-power conference, even if it would delay the German treaty and integration with the West.

Report No. 153 (8 September 1952)

CURRENT WEST GERMAN VIEWS ON THE WAR CRIMINALS ISSUE

Sample: 400 West Germans.
Interviewing dates: flash survey on 26 to 31 August 1952. (19 pp.)

Only one in ten (10%) expressed approval of the way the Western Powers were handling the problem of German war criminals. Six times as many (59%) disapproved. In no population subgroup did approval of Western handling rise even to the status of an appreciable minority.

On the specific question of German generals held as war criminals, only one West German in eleven (9%) held that they were guilty. Seven times as many (63%) believed that most of these men were not guilty of the crimes for which they had been sentenced. Again, judgments that most of the imprisoned generals were not guilty tended to be most widespread among the more educated and informed population elements. The respondents felt the generals had been imprisoned as revenge against Germany (11%), out of fear of German military superiority (11%), or simply because Germany had lost the war (10%).

The predominant view among West Germans with opinions on the matter (42%) was that German generals held prisoner by the Western Powers should be permitted to hold important positions in the new West German army, primarily because of their experience (24%) and their military capabilities (17%).

Report No. 154 (15 September 1952)

WEST GERMAN EVALUATION OF THE U.S. AIR FORCE IN GERMANY

Sample: 1,200 West Germans and 200 West Berliners.
Interviewing dates: last two weeks of May 1952. (75 pp.)

Politico-military problems overshadowed all others in West German opinion. About two-thirds (63 per cent in West Germany, 67 per cent in West Berlin) indicated that these issues were the most pressing. For security reasons, the majority (58%) opposed any withdrawal of Allied troops from Germany. Germans who wanted the Allied forces to remain were of two minds as to whether those forces should be augmented (29%) or remain at their current strength (29%). West Berliners more frequently (57%) than others recommended additional forces. If additional armed forces were planned, most Germans recommended strengthening American air (37%) rather than ground (13%) forces. In West Berlin, 55 per cent chose the former.

Large majorities in West Germany (68%) and in West Berlin (71%) asserted that Germany too should have an air arm, the predominant view being that it was "very important" to have one. This was envisioned as an addition to American air support, not a substitute for it. Advocates of a German air corps (50%) more frequently than opponents (18%) recommended additional American air units.

Six in ten (58%) felt that an American air unit could be counted on to support German divisions. Over half (51%) believed that the Americans would give equal support to the Germans, while only 6 per cent felt the Germans would receive less support. Even among opponents of defense participation, as many as half believed the United States Air Force (USAF) would not fail to aid German troops.

West German evaluation of the quality of the USAF and airmen tended to be favorable, especially regarding the Air Force as a military organization without reference to its personnel. Americans were rated above the Luftwaffe (45 to 33 per cent) in World War II. Those rating the USAF best emphasized almost entirely its superiority in resources (7%), its huge number of planes (17%), and its equipment and technical facilities (10%). Well over half (57%) of the German public placed the American forces first, with Russia's air force rating second (5%). Over a third (35%) said they expected the United States to maintain this lead. West Berliners, who had personally experienced American air power as a foe in World War II and as a friend during the blockade, more frequently (80%) rated the USAF first than did West Germans (57%). In five years' time, West Berliners (68%) predicted, the American force would still be best.

A considerable percentage (30%) of West Germans asserted that the performance of the USAF in Korea had not come up to expectations. A similar number (29%) expressed surprise at what they considered to be the good showing of communist airmen.

As for the air force personnel, as opposed to the organization, six in ten (62%) West Germans rated the German airmen of World War II as superior fighters, while only 4 per cent gave the Americans this distinction. The relative superiority of the individual German airman was largely attributed to his greater courage and fighting spirit (33%), training (9%), superior discipline and sense of duty (7%), and perserverence (5%). The individual American airman, though not the equal of a Luftwaffe man, was rated above the American soldier in military qualities by those who felt competent to pass judgment.

The consensus of people living in the vicinity of an American air base was that it made no difference whatever to the community. The majority of West Germans (50%) not living near such a base, however, said they would have some objections to doing so. In West Berlin favorable responses (34%) outweighed negative ones (25%). People who objected to living near an air base stressed the noise and air traffic (22%) and the fear of bombing, should a war begin (19%). Only a small fraction based their objections on anti-Americanism (5%).

People who had been directly subjected to air attacks in the war did not differ from those who had not on any of the issues dealt with in this study.

Report No. 155 (22 September 1952)

PRESENT LEVEL OF WEST GERMAN POLITICAL AND ECONOMIC SATISFACTION

With Current Standings of the Major Political Parties

Sample: 1,200 West Germans.
Interviewing dates: 4 to 14 August 1952. (43 pp.)

The trend in satisfaction with personal economic circumstances was up considerably (59%) since it was last assessed in October 1951 (48%). Dissatisfaction was nonetheless still fairly high (40%). The majority of the West German public also expressed satisfaction with the Adenauer government. Favorable reactions greatly exceeded unfavorable opinions (58 to 23 per cent). On a more specific test of satisfaction and dissatisfaction--the government's stand vis-à-vis the Soviet Union--approval predominated by a three-to-one margin (50 to 16 per cent). The few who expressed dissatisfaction with the government's Soviet policy argued most frequently that it did not demonstrate sufficient readiness to negotiate and come to an understanding with the East (8%). And in almost equal measure West Germans agreed with the stand the Adenauer administration had taken regarding America, with 51 per cent approving the position and 18 per cent disapproving.

There was very limited support (15%) for immediate Bundestag elections, an idea occasionally voiced by the SPD. Well over half (56%) of the respondents felt it better to wait for the elections scheduled for fall 1953, and 29 per cent offered no opinion.

Party comparisons revealed that satisfaction with present economic conditions was greatest among CDU/CSU (71%) and FDP (66%) adherents. Seven of eight (88%) CDU/CSU adherents and 67 per cent of FDP affiliates also approved the current government's actions. Favorable opinions outnumbered unfavorable opinions among Social Democrats: 54 per cent indicated they were satisfied with their economic conditions and 49 per cent approved the Adenauer government.

The two major political contenders in West Germany--the Christian Democrats and the Social Democrats--appeared to be vying evenly for public support, with each eliciting adherence from 25 per cent of the West German population. Far back in third place, with 6 per cent support, was the Free Democratic party. A series of political preference soundings since March 1951, embracing fifteen surveys and over 15,000 cases, revealed a remarkably stable pattern. The SPD varied between 20 and 26 per cent support, the CDU/CSU between 15 and 25 per cent, and the FDP, exhibiting the most remarkable constancy, between 5 and 7 per cent.

Further study of the data revealed that, although the CDU/CSU and the SPD were attracting equal support, they were not attracting it in the same proportion from various groups in the West German population. In comparison with the SPD, the CDU/CSU attracted more women (56 to 45 per cent), more with higher educations (19 to 13 per cent), fewer with middle income levels (19 to 30 per cent), more of the affluent (17 to 10 per cent), fewer young voters (11 to 15 per cent), more of the old (25 to 18 per cent), considerably fewer skilled laborers (15 to 31 per cent), more farmers (17 to 4 per cent) and businessmen (13 to 6 per cent), considerably more Catholics (68 to 40 per cent), fewer refugees and expellees (12 to 17 per cent), and considerably fewer trade-union members (21 to 52 per cent). Compared to both CDU/CSU and SPD supporters, the FDP attracted (usually by a considerable margin) more high-income adherents, older people, businessmen or professionals, Protestants, and nonmembers of trade unions.

Asked which party (exclusive of the Communist party) they liked least, respondents listed the Socialist Reich party (11%), followed by the SPD and the CDU/CSU, each with 10 per cent.

Most West Germans with opinions on the matter believed that the SPD opposed West Germany's military participation in the West European defense army (48%). Only 10 per cent felt the government was bound to the contractual agreement with the Western Powers. Whatever their preferences in the matter, most West Germans (33%) believed that an SPD government would adhere to any defense arrangement that had been made.

Special Report No. 155-S (22 September 1952)

AN EXPERIMENTAL AUDIENCE REACTION STUDY ON THE "VOICE OF AMERICA"

Sample: 58 West Germans, selected from a larger sample of 164 radio listeners (in a survey of 179 respondents).
Interviewing dates: experimental study on 6 to 9 April and 5 to 9 May 1952. (53 pp.)

The first part of this study comprises a comparison of the 58 VOA listeners with the average radio listener, taking into consideration background characteristics, attitudes, and opinions.

The second part presents the results of evaluation sessions on four specific VOA programs. On the average, they received only a fair rating. A better rating was given by regular listeners of the VOA and by those who were more receptive to American ideas and methods.

Report No. 156 (3 October 1952)

WEST GERMAN REACTIONS TO VISIT OF EAST ZONE DELEGATION
With an Appraisal of Current Temper on the Unity Issue

Sample: 400 West Germans.
Interviewing dates: flash survey on 25 to 29 September 1952. (22 pp.)

The visit to Bonn of an East German governmental delegation on 18 to 20 September 1952 caught the attention of a very substantial portion of the West German citizenry. Six in ten

(61%) of the respondents claimed to have heard or read something about it. A similar proportion (64%) approved of the meeting. Approval was most widespread among the opinion-leading elements and especially among the young (74%). The single most frequent theme running through the comments of approving respondents was that no possibility for better understanding, however remote, should be overlooked (20%).

The majority of West Germans (65%) and all population subgroups supported negotiations on German unity between the Bonn and GDR governments, even though 60 per cent of the West Germans sampled stated flatly that the current leaders of the East German government had not been freely elected. Asked why the West insisted on free elections, most agreed that the conferees should be true representatives of the people (22%) and that elections would be indicative of the feelings of the East Germans (17%).

A majority (58 per cent, as against 47 per cent in April 1952) expressed certainty about American interest in German unity, while only one in five (19%) expressed doubt, and 23 per cent had no opinion. The more critical and informed population segments were more convinced of American sincerity. Nevertheless, almost half (33%) of the West Germans indicating they desired a four-power conference (70%) either were sure that America opposed, or were not sure that America approved, such a course. The majority of even those in doubt (20%) were still able to state with certainty that the United States wanted the reunification of Germany.

Among the one in four (23%) who demonstrated awareness of the latest Western move in the battle of notes, favorable reactions clearly outweighed unfavorable reactions (14 to 2 per cent), particularly among the opinion-leading elements.

Report No. 157 (13 October 1952)

ARE THE DIFFICULTIES OF RECENT EAST ZONE REFUGEES BREEDING DISAFFECTION WITH THE WEST?

Sample: 401 East German refugees from four temporary camps in West Berlin.
Interviewing dates: 4 to 12 September 1952. (24 pp.)

By their own admission, the large majority (75%) of refugees who came to West Berlin did not feel they had been specifically encouraged by the West to do so. Even among those denied refugee status, the number believing they had been encouraged by the West was only 27 per cent. The one in four minority (24%) who felt they had been encouraged by the West were often referring to encouragement from relatives and friends in the West (11%) rather than from more formal sources, such as radio programs (5%). The refugees reported fleeing because of persecution in response to their rejection of the communist system (39%), pressure to join the People's Police (24%), persecution for alleged offenses committed against the country's economy (16%), persecution for active opposition to the East German regime (10%), and pressure to become informers (5%).

Despite difficulties encountered in West Berlin, most refugees (72%) had not changed their opinions about the West. Among those reporting changes in attitude, shifts for the better (23%) clearly exceeded those for the worse (5%). Better-than-anticipated political (10%) and economic (10%) conditions were the reasons most frequently mentioned by refugees who reported an increase in favor toward the West as a result of their coming; another 8 per cent specifically complimented their treatment in the reception centers. The few refugees (5%) who spoke of worsened attitudes pointed to instances of alleged inequities in their processing (49%) or the West's lack of interest in their fate (1%). Virtually all refugees (97%) stated that they would choose the same course if they had it to do all over again. Even among those who were denied the status of political refugee, only a twentieth (6%) indicated that, if they had it to do all over again, they would have stayed in the East.

The large preponderance (74%) of refugees sampled agreed with the view broadcast by Jakob Kaiser, Minister of All-German Affairs, that East Germans should remain there unless their lives or freedom were in danger. Among the reasons advanced for agreeing with Kaiser were the disadvantages of having the West flooded with hordes of refugees (36%) and the advantages of having pro-West East Germans in the GDR (17%). The minority (21%), who felt that all East Germans should feel free to come to the West if they wanted to, argued mainly that everyone in the East was in danger (9%) and that flight to the West was the only way to escape that danger (5%).

Report No. 158 (14 October 1952)

WEST GERMANS APPRAISE THEIR PRESENT DAY PRESS
I. Newspaper Readership and Preferences

Sample: 1,198 West Germans and 200 West Berliners.
Interviewing dates: 12 February to 10 March 1952. (30 pp.)

Over half of all West Germans (56%) read newspapers at least six times a week and another quarter (23%) from two to five times weekly. Every sixth adult (16%) reads a newspaper less than once a week or not at all. Nearly a fifth (19%) of German readers read more than one paper, and another fifth (23%) said they would like to read more. However, the bulk of readers (57%) limited their reading to only one newspaper and indicated no desire to read more. Most (75%) German readers subscribed to the papers they read. Nine per cent bought them at newsstands and another 16 per cent got them in some other way. As might be expected, the elements in the population with higher status read newspapers regularly to a much greater extent than other groups. Men were more regular readers than women (63 to 50 per cent) and people living in cities more than those in small towns (78 to 65 per cent).

Readership of magazines and pictorials was more limited than that of newspapers. While 14 per cent of West Germans said they did not read newspapers at all, 38 per cent of them did not read magazines.

Three-fourths (72%) of West Germany's newspaper readers read "independent" publications, 15 per cent read SPD or near-SPD publications, and 14 per cent preferred CDU/CSU papers. Extreme rightist or extreme leftist papers were read by less than 2 per cent of the newspaper-reading population. Newspaper reading in Germany tended to be concentrated in mass circulation newspapers rather than spread out over a large number of smaller papers. Only 11 per cent read papers having 10,000 circulation or under, while 43 per cent read papers having a circulation of over 100,000.

Ranked in terms of popularity (regularity of readership) were local news (68%), crime and accident reports (48%), German political and economic news (40%), international news (36%), and editorials (33%). Local news was read regularly by all types and classes of Germans. Serious newspaper content was read particularly by men and the well-educated.

About the same proportion of West Germans listened to radio news at least daily (54%) as read a newspaper six times a week (56%), and 61 per cent of the former group were in the latter group as well. An additional 22 per cent tuned in their radios for news several times a week. The radio was named as primary news source by more people (51%) than the newspaper (37%). Generally, the newspaper was preferred by the better educated, while the radio was selected by those with a more limited education. Two out of five (39%) Germans listened to radio commentaries frequently. Again, men rather than women (72 to 47 per cent) and the better rather than the less educated (76 to 54 per cent) were most likely to listen to commentaries. Two-thirds of the regular commentary listeners (68%) also read German political and economic news most of the time. Fifty-eight per cent of them read editorials regularly, and 42 per cent read cultural news regularly.

Report No. 159 (15 October 1952)

WEST GERMANS APPRAISE THEIR PRESENT DAY PRESS
II. Evaluations and Recommendations

Sample: 1,198 West Germans and 200 West Berliners.
Interviewing dates: 12 February to 10 March 1952. (70 pp.)

About half (48%) of the respondents rated the German press favorably, a fourth (22%) considered it fair, and less than a tenth (8%) gave specifically unfavorable ratings. A majority (55%) felt that newspapers were more truthful in 1952 than they had been during the Third Reich. Six in ten (59%) of German reader-listeners were more likely to believe the version of the news presented over the radio than that in the newspapers.

Two-thirds (65%) said they relied on media other than the press as their chief means of forming opinions on current political and economic questions. Three in ten (31%) said they disagreed occasionally or frequently with the stand on current issues taken by the newspaper they read. Eight per cent read newspapers identified with one political party even though they personally supported another party.

Among the 53 per cent who opposed political affiliation in the press, 18 per cent stressed the importance of an objective and independent newspaper, while 15 per cent pointed to the need for diversification to appeal to a wide range of people.

Eleven per cent of German readers believed they read newspapers published in the interest of the CDU/CSU, and 7 per cent said their papers spoke for the SPD. But two-thirds (65%) believed their papers had no political affiliation at all. When the HICOG Press Branch's designation of political affiliation of newspapers was compared with the readers' image of the papers' political tone, there was considerable discrepancy. Four in ten (42%) readers of SPD newspapers and one-third (34%) of those who read CDU/CSU publications said their newspapers did not represent any group or party. Those who did attribute a party leaning or affiliation to their papers were likely to label them correctly.

More Germans (54%) believed that newspapers could freely publicize corruption (even if the reputation of the government was harmed by it) than believed they could not (23%). Seven in ten (70%) felt the press should attack and publicize corruption of all kinds. Twice as many adherents of the CDU/CSU (27%) as SPD members (13%) said the press should not publicize information injurious to the government's reputation.

A majority of West Germans (49%) believed that neo-Nazi activities should be reported in the newspapers. Of the quarter (23%) who said the papers should not do so, 30 per cent felt the German public should not be reminded of past times, and 28 per cent feared that people would only be alarmed unnecessarily.

Most adult West Germans were not sure that there was freedom of the press under the occupation. Only 20 per cent said that no control whatever was exerted by the occupation authorities over newspaper content, and only a third (32%) said that free criticism of the occupation powers was possible in the press. Fifty-seven per cent felt that the Western Powers exerted much or some control over the German press.

Over a third (37%) of the respondents said that German newspapers, in general, gave a favorable picture of Americans and their program in West Germany. Only 5 per cent thought the press presented them in an unfavorable light. Sixty per cent thought the portrayal was both favorable and true, while 29 per cent felt it was favorable and untrue.

There was no prevailing opinion that the postwar press licensing program was either useful or harmful. Most people did not realize the purpose of the program, and those who did were not convinced that it was successful in its purpose.

Report No. 160 (16 October 1952)

WEST GERMANS APPRAISE THEIR PRESENT DAY PRESS
III. Readership and Evaluations of the *Neue Zeitung*

Sample: 1,198 West Germans and 200 West Berliners.
Interviewing dates: 12 February to 10 March 1952. (20 pp.)

Seven per cent of the West Germans and nearly every third (29%) West Berliner claimed to be current readers of the American-sponsored *Neue Zeitung*. Three per cent said they read it at least weekly, and a somewhat larger additional group reported reading it several times a month.

Neue Zeitung readers had a good impression of the paper. Few (5%) actually disliked it, and the majority (55%) indicated that they liked it a lot. The *Neue Zeitung*'s features and cultural and literary sections were favorites (30%), followed closely by its political coverage (25%). What readers disliked most was what they perceived to be a tendency toward pro-American slanting and propaganda (13%) or else the political (12%) and cultural (10%) items.

Most *Neue Zeitung* readers (72%) found differences between that paper and the regular German press--nearly all the differences favorable to the *Neue Zeitung*. In particular, it was considered to have broader coverage (40%) and to be more objective (23%). Not unexpectedly, 42 per cent of *Neue Zeitung*'s readers rated the paper as a better news source for American affairs than German papers. Regarding general reliability of news, the *Neue Zeitung* ranked even with German papers in West Germany, with 35 per cent attributing equal reliability to both. Seventeen per cent felt the *Neue Zeitung* was more reliable; 18 per cent put more confidence in the German press.

Most *Neue Zeitung* readers were also radio listeners, and a majority of them (61%) listened to the "Voice of America." The readers divided fairly evenly on the subject of preference between the two as a source for the American viewpoint on important questions of the day, with 22 per cent choosing the *Neue Zeitung* and 31 per cent VOA. (In West Berlin, VOA was clearly favored.)

Well over half (58%) of the sample (87 per cent of West Berliners) accepted the idea of having an American-sponsored newspaper; actual opposition was displayed by 23 per cent (4 per cent in West Berlin). Opposition to the existence of the *Neue Zeitung* was not always indicative of anti-Americanism.

About half of those opposed (9%) simply stated that they saw no need for such a newspaper, since adequate German papers were available. Fewer (5%) expressed opposition to American propaganda or doubt about the truthfulness of such a paper.

Report No. 161 (30 October 1952)

THE IMPACT OF THE BDJ AFFAIR UPON AMERICAN PRESTIGE IN GERMANY

Sample: 400 West Germans.
Interviewing dates: flash survey on 20 to 23 October 1952.
(14 pp.)

Approximately two weeks after initial press reports about alleged American financing of guerrilla units of the League of German Youth (Bund Deutscher Jugend, or BDJ), almost six in ten (56%) West Germans had heard of them.

Two out of three (66%) rejected all of the BDJ's alleged objectives, and all but 2 per cent rejected the most extreme reported objective: the liquidation of SPD leaders in the event of Russian attack. As many as 16 per cent agreed with the BDJ's least extreme objective--offering resistance through guerrilla activity were such an attack to take place--but in no population group did more than a quarter agree with this aim. Only a small minority of West Germans (18%) were prepared to believe that America had supported or would support a group with aims like those of the BDJ.

Almost half stated that American prestige would suffer either seriously (18%) or slightly (28%) in their eyes if it were established that American authorities did, in fact, support the guerrilla groups--even if these authorities knew nothing about liquidation plans.

Report No. 162 (5 November 1952)

HAVE EAST ZONE CATHOLICS BEEN DEMORALIZED BY COMMUNIST PRESSURE?

Sample: 134 East German lay Catholics attending a convocation in West Berlin; see Special Report No. II/63-S on sampling problems and representativeness.
Interviewing dates: 19 to 24 August 1952. (20 pp.)

Only 17 per cent of the East German delegates to the Catholic convocation indicated that no hindrances had been placed in the way of the Catholic Church in their vicinity. Hindrances most frequently mentioned were officially sanctioned obstacles to finding facilities for church meetings (32%), difficulties in attending the convocation itself (27%), interference with the education of Catholic youth (25%), interference with Catholic youth meetings and activities (25%), and prevention of parish members from attending services by state imposition of competing duties (15%). Few respondents felt that the Catholic Church was in a position to take effective countermeasures against state-inspired anti-church activities. Approximately half of those questioned (30 per cent out of the 66 per cent of the total sample to whom the question was directed) stated that the Church could do nothing to counter such activity because of lack of power (13%) or fear of the consequences (11%). The other half (34%) stated that attempted countermeasures such as petitions and formal protests (15%), indirect warnings (7%), and side-stepping of hindrances (13%) met with little success.

Only a minority (18%) claimed personal difficulties because of their church membership. Over half (56%) felt that more rather than fewer young people participated in Catholic Church activities in 1952 than in 1950, primarily because of vigorous activities on the part of parish priests (25%) and a turning toward religion as a reaction to communist pressure (23%).

Two in five respondents (41%) felt that more East German youths openly acknowledged their faith than was true two years earlier. The youth showed their religion by participating in church activities and observing church rites (53%), acknowledging and defending their faith (24%), or wearing church symbols in public (22%).

Report No. 163 (15 November 1952)

WEST GERMAN REACTIONS TO THE AMERICAN PRESIDENTIAL ELECTIONS

Sample: 400 West Germans.
Interviewing dates: flash survey on 5 to 9 November 1952.
(20 pp.)

The American presidential election in 1952 attracted a large audience in West Germany. Eight in ten (82%) claimed to have heard or read something about the event, and three in four (74%) could substantiate this awareness by naming the victor. Almost half (47%) of the West German people were able to identify the winning party. Even among the usually ill-informed elements of the population--women, the less educated, the lower paid--half or more showed some awareness of the election outcome.

Among the respondents expressing an opinion on the matter, Eisenhower was preferred over Stevenson by a two-to-one margin (29 to 14 per cent.)

Results obtained in an earlier study revealed a favorable orientation toward Eisenhower, despite the large role he had played in the German defeat. More than a two-to-one preponderance in West Germany expressed confidence in Eisenhower as the leader of a common West German defense army (25 to 10 per cent) and their belief that he would not discriminate against German troops in any common defense setup (47 to 21 per cent).

Four in ten West Germans (39%) believed there would be changes in American policy as a consequence of Eisenhower's victory, with the largest proportion (29%) indicating that conditions would be changed somewhat, rather than considerably, and in a favorable direction (25%). Among the favorable anticipations cited, the most frequent theme was better understanding of Germany with consequent greater political and economic support (11%); others mentioned rearmament (5%), a united Europe (3%), and reunification of Germany (3%). Those who believed the changes would be unfavorable listed militarism (4%), the danger of war (4%), and economic disadvantages (2%).

Despite the sometimes rough-and-tumble aspects of American electoral campaigning, the large majority of West Germans (64%) was not in any way disturbed by it.

Report No. 164 (17 November 1952)

WEST GERMAN AUDIENCE POTENTIAL FOR A PROJECTED ATOMIC ENERGY EXHIBIT

Sample: 190 residents of Frankfurt.
Interviewing dates: November 1952. (6 pp.)

Respondents were chosen from among those who did not know that the atom could be put to nonmilitary uses, as well as those who did not know of American research on the peaceful application of atomic power. The final target group, then, represented 53 per cent of the residents of Frankfurt.

Only 7 per cent of this target group believed the United States used the atom solely for peaceful purposes (compared with 51 per cent of the total population), while 23 per cent felt the atom was used only for atomic bombs (compared with 12 per cent of the total population). Twenty-nine per cent (27 per cent of the total population) said they had heard of plans to place the atom under international control.

Report No. 165 (22 December 1952)

AN APPRAISAL OF PAMPHLETS AS A MEDIUM OF INFLUENCE IN WEST GERMANY

Sample: 1,200 West Germans and 200 West Berliners.
Interviewing dates: 12 to 27 November 1952. (14 pp.)

Only 39 per cent of the West Berlin population and even fewer West Germans (23%) professed any interest in reading pamphlets. Negative reactions rested on the feeling that pamphlets were of dubious origin, ambiguous, and worthless (15%) or that such booklets were issued by political parties for propagandistic purposes only (13%). In any case, only 25 per cent of West Germans recalled having seen any pamphlets during the entire previous year.

Report No. 166 (23 December 1952)

AN EVALUATION OF THE EFFECTIVENESS OF THE MARSHALLHAUS EXHIBIT

Sample: 108 persons interviewed at the exit of the Industrial Fairgrounds in West Berlin and 253 visitors to the Marshall House.
Interviewing dates: 19 September to 5 October 1952. (13 pp.)

The Office of the U.S. High Commission for Germany presented a special exhibit in the Marshall House--the American pavilion at the Industrial Fair. It took the form of a model house furnished with materials and finished products from all countries in the Atlantic community. The theme of the exhibit was that, through mutual cooperation, the high standard of living symbolized by the house could become a reality for the people of the Atlantic community.

Of the 108 persons interviewed at the fairgrounds' exit gate, only 25 per cent had visited the Marshall House, with most of the remainder (65%) saying that the pavilion was so crowded they did not want to wait. Those who visited the Marshall House were quite favorably impressed. In fact, more of them expressed approval of the Marshall House (96%) than of the fair as a whole (80%). The theme of the Marshall House exhibit was clearly evident to slightly less than half (44%) of the visitors. Another third (35%) seemed to have some grasp of the purpose of the showing.

Report No. 167 (12 January 1953)

A YEAR-END SURVEY OF RIGHTIST AND NATIONALIST SENTIMENTS IN WEST GERMANY

Sample: 1,200 West Germans.
Interviewing dates: 1 to 10 December 1952. (80 pp.)

Surveys during 1951-52 revealed that a preponderance of West Germans (44 per cent in December) believed there was more good than evil in National Socialism. This viewpoint was held by opinion leaders as well as the rest of the population. In 1952 there was a rise in pro-Nazi orientations among those aged 18 to 24 and FDP adherents. Only 24 per cent of the respondents said they would actively support such a movement. By their own admission, the large majority of the German people would not resist efforts by a Nazi-type group to return to power. West Germans were far less susceptible to communism, 53 per cent expressing a willingness to resist a communist movement to take over the country.

A substantial number of respondents (44%) approved the idea of a "single, strong national party." The idea was particularly popular with the youth (56%). A majority (58%) also approved unrestricted opportunities for former members of the Nazi party. This was especially true of opinion leaders. They argued that ability, not party membership, was the decisive factor (17%).

Well over half (56%) believed that General Ramcke, a former paratroop officer, was right when, speaking before a meeting of S.S. veterans, he called the Allies "war criminals" for bombing women and children. Only 25 per cent disagreed with his statement. In no population group did the number who disagreed with Ramcke exceed one in three. As for the plot of July 20 on Hitler's life, most Germans (58%) did not believe the plotters were traitors, arguing that they wanted to save Germany from ruin (23%). The minority who insisted these men were traitors felt that their action hastened German defeat (7%). The youth (16%) and FDP adherents (27%) were most inclined to see the attempt on Hitler's life as an act of treason.

Germans (54%) generally did not feel either guilty for what was done to the Jews during the Third Reich or responsible for compensating for these wrongs. West Berliners felt somewhat more responsible (50 to 45 per cent). In no population group did affirmation of German responsibility for Jewish restitution achieve preponderant status, although such an opinion was slightly more frequent among opinion leaders. It is not surprising then that West Germans voted two to one (49 to 26 per cent) against Bundestag acceptance of the Bonn-Israel restitution agreement of August 1952. And, when apprised that the Arab League had threatened to break off trade relations with West Germany after ratification, only one in eight (12%) felt the restitution agreement with Israel to be more important. To justify their opposition, Germans claimed that the sum being given as restitution was excessive (24%), Israel itself had not suffered during World War II (11%), or only the guilty should have to pay (7%).

Opposition to Jewish restitution was, to a significant extent, bound up with pro-Nazi attitudes. Respondents who saw more good than evil in National Socialism averaged almost 20 per cent greater incidence of opposition to restitution than did respondents who saw more evil than good. There was no indication of an appreciably greater economic squeeze on respondents who opposed the agreement with Israel than among those who approved. Evidence of anti-Jewish sentiments among West Germans emanated from the respondents' own comments: Jews were unscrupulous businessmen with deceitful business methods (15%), did not want to work (13%), were greedy (8%), and differed in outward appearance (6%). About as many unfavorable comments were made as indeterminate or favorable comments.

Results of the study suggested a notable rise in nationalism among the West German public from August 1951 (34%) to December 1952 (49%). Nationalist attitudes were most marked among those with a neo-Nazi bent (64%). As a further indication of nationalism, support for an integrated European army fell to 22 per cent, while approval of a national German army rose to 47 per cent. Sixty per cent of the neo-Nazis wanted a national army.

A majority of the German public (57%)--and particularly neo-Nazis (75%)--wanted to see West Germany as the "strongest country" in Western Europe. They justified German leadership by claiming that Germans were industrious, ambitious, and efficient (17%), and were technically and culturally superior (14%).

Report No. 168 (15 January 1953)

THE YEAR'S TRENDS IN WEST GERMAN THINKING ON THE PEACE CONTRACT AND POLITICAL PARTY PREFERENCES

Sample: 1,200 West Germans in the first survey, 800 in the second.
Interviewing dates: 2 to 10 and 12 to 20 December 1952. (43 pp.)

In mid-December 1952, three in ten (32%) West Germans declared themselves in favor of Bundestag ratification of the peace contract with the Western Powers. Less than two in ten (18%) were against it, and about as many (17%) were undecided. The remaining third of the population had not heard of the contractual agreement. These figures were about the same as those obtained following the initialing of the agreement in late May 1952. Personal preferences aside, most of those aware of the contractual agreement (47%) felt that the Bundestag would ratify it. A fraction (7%) argued that the parliament was faced with a choice of "ratify or else," with particular reference to the American position on the issue.

On the issue of German defense participation, the division of opinion was 50 per cent in favor and 40 per cent in opposition. This favorable picture was blurred by the finding that the group from which most recruits for a German army would have to come--those under 25 years of age--continued to be less enthusiastic about defense participation: fully half (53%) said they were opposed. Only 38 per cent favored the idea, the larger proportion (21%) of which was only somewhat in favor of the proposal. The higher status groups tended to be more in favor of participation than were their counterparts. Among supporters of the coalition parties, the trend was toward increased approval, while most socialist voters remained opposed.

Bundestag debates on the contract and its military corollary gained a fairly wide hearing among the West German public. Many (78%) were following the debates via the mass media. Forty per cent declared that they had listened to the broadcasts of the speeches. But the debates had little impact on opinions. Forty per cent of those who had heard or read about them asserted that the debates did not affect their views at all. Moreover, as many found their disapproval confirmed (4%) as were won over by the debates (5%).

The year-end picture of the internal West German situation, particularly regarding the position of the Adenauer government, was much brighter than the trends on foreign relations. A firm majority (64%) of the West German people declared themselves satisfied with the way their personal economic circumstances had developed during the year. Expressions of satisfaction about economic developments predominated in all population groups.

A disgruntled minority took issue with the Bonn government's perceived mismanagement of economic affairs, citing high prices, high taxes, unemployment, and low wages (13%), economic favoritism (11%), and remilitarization (4%) as reasons for their opinions.

As further evidence of the general mood of satisfaction with the government, most West Germans (56%) stated they were content to wait until the scheduled elections in the autumn of 1953. About half of the small minority (15%) advocating immediate elections based their arguments on issues related to the peace contract or the EDC agreement. The two major parties--the CDU and the SPD--enjoyed about equal support throughout West Germany as a whole.

On specific issues, as well as in overall appraisal, the Adenauer government appeared to have built up among the German public a considerable reservoir of confidence. On each of the following issues, the Adenauer government was considered more competent than a socialist government: German reunification (29 to 17 per cent), recovering the territories east of the Oder and Neisse rivers (21 to 14 per cent), the Saar issue (28 to 16 per cent), West Germany's security (35 to 14 per cent), and the solution of West German economic problems (37 to 16 per cent).

Report No. 169 (28 January 1953)

THE YEAR-END STATUS OF WEST GERMAN CONFIDENCE IN THE STRENGTH OF THE WESTERN POWERS

Sample: 791, 799, 791, and 786 West Germans respectively.
Interviewing dates: April 1951, September 1951, May 1952, and 12 to 20 December 1952. (14 pp.)

Throughout the period from April 1951 to December 1952 the preponderant view was that the Western Powers were stronger than the communists. The trend was quite stable, with the weight of opinion favoring the West by almost three to one on the average.

The December figures showed that 29 per cent of West Germans believed the Western Powers to be stronger. Two thirds of the West German public (66%) continued to predict that the Western Powers would ultimately win out over the communists. However, the West held only a very slight advantage (28%) over the East (24%) regarding dexterity in conducting the cold war. In fact, after September 1951, when the West's perceived success had been at its highest point (40%), the trend was downward for the West (32 and 28 per cent respectively in May and December 1952) with a corresponding upward trend for the communists' success (15 per cent in September 1951; 21 per cent in May 1952; 24 per cent in December 1952). These findings suggest that many West Germans predicted eventual victory for the West as a result of its power rather than its superior skill and strategy.

Special Report No. 169-S (January 1953)

PUBLIC OPINION IN WESTERN EUROPE
Attitudes toward Political, Economic, and Military Integration

Sample: 1,592 in West Germany, 1,503 in Great Britain, 1,380 in France, 1,505 in Italy, and 1,513 in the Netherlands, using a probability sample wherever possible.
Interviewing dates: September 1952. (237 pp.)

The study investigated popular reactions to the newly established European Coal and Steel Community (ECSC), as well as to the then projected defense parallel, the European Defense Community (EDC). Discussion of the responses is followed by a series of appendices comprising an account of the sampling technique and description of the national samples; in addition, there are detailed tabulations for each question, together with responses by population subgroups.

Majorities in all five countries approved the basic notion of Western European integration. There was somewhat greater support in West Germany and the Netherlands than in the others. When it was pointed out, however, that upon occasion the common interest might require decisions unfavorable to the respondent's own country, approval dropped sharply.

Despite claims by majorities in all the countries that they knew about the Schuman Plan, as few as 32 per cent (in Italy) actually knew which countries were involved in it. Among those who knew something of the plan, only one in three from the concerned countries was for it. Population breakdowns revealed that support for the Schuman Plan was greatest among manual workers.

When asked to name American activities which had made a favorable impression on them, majorities in the four ECSC countries mentioned the Marshall Plan. In Great Britain only 40 per cent mentioned it, while another 40 per cent responded that they could think of nothing positive. Unfavorable reactions to American behavior after the war varied markedly from one country to the other. Despite these criticisms, however, majorities in the ECSC countries and 43 per cent in Great Britain said that their net impression of America's policies was favorable.

That this generally favorable attitude by no means implied blanket approval of American aims is shown clearly by the fact that four out of ten Europeans used what must be regarded as negative terms in describing America's mission in the world. Cross-tabulations of the responses to the two questions suggest that there was a general distrust of diplomacy and power rather than a strong anti-American sentiment.

Outright hostility toward the Soviet Union, however, was rampant. An average of 62 per cent of the ECSC populations (ranging from 50 per cent in France to as many as 85 per cent in West Germany) could think of nothing positive that the Soviet Union had done since the war. Many could name specific unfavorable Soviet moves. More people blamed the Soviet Union for the tension between East and West than blamed the United States, but about a third blamed both sides equally. Cross-tabulations showed that, among those who blamed the Soviet Union for the tension, about three-quarters said their country should side with the West, while none chose the East. By way of contrast, those who blamed the United States favored neutrality; up to 39 per cent (in West Germany, with a low of 5 per cent in France) chose the West; and up to 37 per cent (in France, with a low of 2 per cent in Great Britain) chose the East. Among those blaming both sides equally, again almost no one chose the East; between 23 per cent (in France) and 61 per cent (in the Netherlands) chose the West; and between 32 per cent (in the Netherlands) and 68 per cent (in France) felt their country ought to remain neutral.

Sympathy with communist ideology was strongest in Italy (18%) and weakest in West Germany (5%). Outright hostility toward communism was strongest in Great Britain and the Netherlands. Population breakdowns indicated that sympathy with the communist cause was strongest among those evidencing higher levels of anti-American sentiment; also, about a third of the French, as well as the Italian, manual workers and farmhands expressed such sympathies. Even among the communist sympathizers, however, less than half said that America's postwar actions had made a basically unfavorable impression on them. Furthermore, an average of about a third of the communists in ECSC populations (ranging from 14 per cent in Italy to 67 per cent in West Germany) had unfavorable reactions to the Soviet Union's postwar actions.

Throughout the ECSC nations, all of which were projected participants in the European Defense Community, information about the West European army was rather low. Nonetheless, about a half (except in the Netherlands, where the figure was a high 63 per cent) favored participation in EDC by their country. Opinion-leading elements in all the countries tended to support EDC. Unlike opposition to the Schuman Plan, which seemed to rest on a lack of information, opposition to EDC appeared to stem from a basic dislike of the whole idea of Western defense. Support for EDC tended to rest on the feeling that the individual nations were relatively weak.

Trust in the various countries projected as EDC members or supporters ranged from very strong (in the case of the United States) to outright distrust (in the case of Italy). Almost without exception, complete lack of trust in any of the projected members meant opposition to membership in EDC. Absolute trust, however, was not necessary. The majority of those respondents who trusted various nations only "up to a point" still favored participation in EDC by their own country.

Fear of war was widespread throughout Western Europe in the fall of 1952. From one out of ten in the Netherlands to four out of ten in Italy said they worried a great deal about the possibility of a war breaking out. One-third of the people in the Netherlands and Great Britain, half the West Germans, and nearly two-thirds of the French and Italians worried at least somewhat about this eventuality. In the event that war really did come, about a fourth of the ECSC respondents (but as many as 57 per cent in Great Britain) thought the Soviet Union could be prevented from occupying their country. Cross-tabulations of the responses to these two questions revealed that in West Germany, France, and Italy there was a mood of fearfulness, while in the Netherlands the people tended to be fatalistic--convinced that the Russians could not be stopped--but nonetheless not very worried.

Most of the respondents said they felt their country was also involved in the East-West conflict, not just the Soviet Union and the United States. Nonetheless, in West Germany, France, and Italy, more than a third of the population could be regarded as out-and-out pacifist neutralists. This sentiment was strongest among women, lower socioeconomic groups, and members of political parties of the left. Regardless of their own feelings, most people thought their government had in fact already sided with the West.

Asked what they would do if the Soviet Union were to invade their country, nearly six out of ten in West Germany, France, and Italy said they would support resistance movements; two-thirds expressed this view in the Netherlands, and nine out of ten in Great Britain. If there were war between the Soviet Union and the United States, 70 per cent of the Dutch population, 58 per cent of the British, 52 per cent of the West Germans, and 36 per cent of both the French and the Italians thought their country ought to side with the United States. Relatively few would come to the aid of an invaded neighbor. Among those who favored fighting any Soviet aggression, nearly all had a great deal of confidence in the United States.

Report No. 170 (10 February 1953)

RIAS COVERAGE AND PROGRAMMING AS EVALUATED BY EAST ZONE LISTENERS

Sample: 201 young people and 306 adults in West Berlin refugee camps.
Interviewing dates: 9 October to 14 November 1953. (65 pp.)

Virtually all of those interviewed--the younger as well as the older refugees--said they had listened to RIAS when they were living in East Germany. Nearly four in ten said the programs were often difficult to hear because of interference. A third said the interference always occurred at the same time, while 45 per cent said it changed.
The most popular RIAS programs among adults were those dealing with news and politics. The young preferred light music and entertainment. Asked what they thought RIAS could do to improve its political programs, the largest percentage of respondents (40%) mentioned more news about East Germany.
For children up to ten years of age, both adults and young people said, RIAS ought to broadcast fairy tales, many of which were banned in the GDR or changed. Many also thought the station should broadcast political information for the very young: one suggestion was a story in which Stalin would be the wicked wolf. Comparisons between life in the East and West, as well as children's songs, were also mentioned.

Report No. 171 (11 February 1953)

HOW DO GERMANS FEEL ABOUT AN AMERICAN INFORMATIONAL OPERATION IN WEST GERMANY?

Sample: 1,595 West Germans in the first survey and 786 in the second.
Interviewing dates: July and 12 to 20 December 1952. (31 pp.)

An appendix to this report contains a list of public opinion studies in progress or already completed which deal with the general topic of American information programs and the media used to disseminate this information.
West German opinion was evenly divided on the question of whether or not it was a good idea for the Americans to carry on propaganda programs in West Germany: 34 per cent approved, 34 per cent disapproved, and 32 per cent were undecided. The situation was not completely clearcut, however, judging by the fact that 37 per cent reportedly did not think the United States was

using propaganda in West Germany. Furthermore, among those who knew that the United States sponsored the "Voice of America," 48 per cent were of the opinion that the Americans propagandized, while 35 per cent were not. It is probable that the term propaganda was the sticking point in these questions.

When the question was worded somewhat differently, the largest shift was in the percentage of those who thought American efforts were to Germany's disadvantage. Asked whether they had the impression that America's representation of its ideas and views in West Germany had been more to the Germans' advantage or disadvantage, 39 per cent replied the former, only 8 per cent felt it was to the Germans' disadvantage, but over half (53%) gave no response.

Most Germans (64%) said they thought propaganda was more effective if it stuck to the truth. By the same token, a larger percentage (34%) felt American propaganda would be less effective rather than more so (19%) if it used the same sort of methods as did the communists; 47 per cent, however, had no opinion. Nonetheless, 26 per cent thought the Soviet Union was more skillful in the propaganda field than the Americans, while only 2 per cent more (28%) put the Americans in this first position; 33 per cent had no opinion on the matter.

Almost half of the population (46%) also felt the Soviet Union was making a greater propaganda effort; in West Berlin, 83 per cent of the people put the Russians in top position on this score, while only 3 per cent ranked the Americans there. Asked whether the United States ought to carry on more propaganda in Eastern Europe, 32 per cent of the West Germans said yes; 13 per cent thought the right amount was being done, and 43 per cent had no opinion on the subject.

Even though West Germans accepted American views on communism, there was considerable skepticism about some of the information given regarding democracy in general and the United States in particular. A third (33%) thought the facts given about democracy were accurate, but almost as many (31%) felt the good aspects were exaggerated, and as many as 36 per cent had no view on the matter. Similarly, 35 per cent felt that Americans talked frankly about their country, but 31 per cent did not think they spoke frankly enough, and 32 per cent could give no opinion.

Report No. 172 (14 February 1953)

NOTE ON YEAR-END TRENDS IN WEST GERMAN ATTITUDES TOWARD THE UNITED NATIONS

Sample: 786 West Germans.
Interviewing dates: 12 to 20 December 1952. (12 pp.)

The extent of West German awareness of the United Nations

(66%) did not change substantially from the level of July 1951, when 69 per cent of the population said they had heard of the organization. West German conceptions of the main purposes of the U.N. focused on preservation of peace (23%), cooperation among nations (13%), and mediation of disputes (10%).

Since July 1951, confidence in the U.N.'s ability to prevent another world war had fallen from 29 per cent to 21 per cent, the most noticeable drop being in the French Zone, where the confidence level fell eleven percentage points. When questioned about whether U.N. influence had become stronger or weaker over the past year, West Germans were divided, with 19 per cent believing it to be stronger and 18 per cent weaker. Many (29%) expressed no opinion on the issue. As to the U.N.'s future, optimism outweighed pessimism (26 to 14 per cent) although, again, many (26%) were undecided.

Report No. 173 (24 February 1953)

SOME EARLY WEST GERMAN REACTIONS TO THE NEW AMERICAN ADMINISTRATION

Sample: 786 West Germans.
Interviewing dates: 12 to 20 December 1952. (20 pp.)

After the American presidential election, the West German public concluded that there would be no major shift in policy. Over half (55%) anticipated no change at all, and the quarter (23%) expecting change felt that it would be moderate. An appreciable proportion (30%) expressed the view that greater rather than less attention would be paid to Europe by the new administration.

A large preponderance (48%) of the respondents expected the new administration to be less conciliatory toward the USSR, and most of these welcomed the change. Upper status levels held this view more frequently than did others.

West Germans expected further American successes in world affairs. A quarter (25%) of the population declared that the Eisenhower administration would do a better job in world affairs. The President enjoyed considerable prestige among the West German public, with some mentioning his military reputation (28%), intelligence and vigor (15%), and great popularity (8%). When queried directly on the point, 80 per cent were unable to think of any possible weakness he might have.

Report No. 174 (5 March 1953)

THE AMERICAN SOLDIER AS APPRAISED BY THE WEST GERMAN PEOPLE
A Continuing Study of Civilian-Troop Relations

Sample: 1,600 West Germans.
Interviewing dates: January 1953. (126 pp.)

Efforts on the part of the United States Armed Forces and the High Commissioner's office to improve soldier-civilian relations in West Germany were largely effective. More than a third (36%) in West Germany as a whole and 44 per cent in the American Zone noted an improvement during 1952. The West Germans cited cordiality and friendliness (13%), joint entertainment (5%), and improved behavior (5%) in general, as well as Christmas parties (37%) and joint Christmas celebrations (22%) specifically, as instances of improvement. The reputation of the American soldier continued to remain at a high level, with most Germans believing the soldiers' behavior to be good.

Over two-fifths (43%) of the respondents felt that the Americans would fight well against the Russians. The reasons given by the 13 per cent who argued that the Americans would not fight as well as the Russians were that the former would not be defending their homeland (20%) and that they would rely too heavily on their superior war matériel (18%). By a ratio of five to two (26 to 10 per cent), West Germans declared that what they had heard about the Korean fighting gave them a better opinion of American soldiers. As in the past, however, the German soldier continued to be rated best (80%), with the Russian as runner-up. Russian soldiers were thought to be tougher and more brutal (17%) and more easily satisfied (11%) than American soldiers. The most frequently mentioned strength of the American soldier was his high-quality matériel and equipment (47%), although his character and intelligence (9%), physical health (9%), and high standard of living (9%) were also mentioned. But, at the same time, American soldiers were regarded as not particularly brave (12%), soft (12%), undisciplined (9%), pampered (6%), and poorly trained (5%).

Despite the fact that many West Germans criticized the combat qualities of the American soldier, they conceded that the soldiers did provide West Germany with internal and external security (57%) and some economic advantages (38%) in the form of additional jobs and increased dollar exchange. Although many Germans (41%) felt Germany was being occupied rather than protected, 67 per cent recommended that the troops remain, while only 19 per cent advocated their withdrawal. West Germans were less agreeable to an increase in Allied troop contingents. In contrast to the 30 per cent who would approve the move, 46 per cent would not, mainly because of the additional financial burden (19%).

There were few objections to the mode of American family life in Germany. Some criticized American extravagance (11%), but most (43%) did not object at all. Still, 37 per cent did not think American servicemen should be allowed to bring their families to Germany because of the burden of costs to the German people (25%) and the housing shortage (18%). The 45 per cent who favored having American families in Germany felt it important to maintain family life (16%).

Although more Germans (39%) thought the care given American troops was just as it should be, many (32%) thought American forces were coddled, and criticized their extravagance (10%) and high pay (7%). About three in ten respondents (29%) thought the U.S. Army no longer requisitioned property and 57 per cent felt it made every effort to derequisition as much as possible. Past experience, however, had left a bad impression with many (34%), notably in the American Zone (44%). The three leading complaints were that more housing was taken than was necessary (15%), furniture was damaged or stolen (13%), and requisitioning was arbitrary and inconsiderate (11%).

Report No. 175 (20 March 1953)

A GERMAN AUDIENCE EVALUATION OF THE FILM *WITHOUT FEAR*

Sample: 147 filmgoers in Königswinter (of 400 who attended the showing at a regular commercial theater of *Don Camillo and Peppone*, which the short film *Ohne Furcht* followed).
Interviewing dates: March 1953. (20 pp.)

According to 86 per cent of the viewers, films such as *Ohne Furcht (Without Fear)* needed to be shown to enlighten the people (24%), to warn them of the dangers from the East (22%), and to defeat indifference (20%). The majority of viewers found the film informative (52%) and convincing (33%). A few in the audience thought it was too propagandistic (16%) or "strange" (15%). After seeing the film, 62 per cent of the viewers agreed with the theme that only in a free and unified Europe could people live happily.

Report No. 176 (27 March 1953)

GREEN WEEK VISITORS APPRAISE THE MARSHALL HOUSE EXHIBIT "AGRICULTURE IN THE FREE WORLD"

Sample: 179 West Germans and 387 East Germans.
Interviewing dates: 30 January to 7 February 1953. (18 pp.)

The theme of the exhibit was that a farmer operating as a private individual in a free economy can and does produce more and live better than farmers under any other system. Nearly a score of American farm implements, a model American farm complete with buildings, fields, and machinery, and related displays of farm produce and the American farmer's way of life were featured in the exhibit.

Many respondents were not convinced that American methods would work in Germany. Among West Germans visitors, opinions divided evenly: 45 per cent agreed that such methods were feasible in Germany and 45 per cent thought not. East Germans were more inclined to take the affirmative view, with 62 per cent saying American methods could work in Germany while only 32 per cent disagreed. Opposition rested on the feeling that German farms were too small for mechanization (29 and 21 per cent respectively). Other reasons given were overpopulation (12 and 6 per cent respectively), the expense of the machinery (8 and 4 per cent respectively), and German conservatism (4 and 2 per cent respectively).

Report No. 177 (20 April 1953)

CURRENT APPRAISAL OF WEST BERLIN MORALE, WITH REACTIONS TO THE REFUGEE INFLUX

Sample: 400 West Berliners.
Interviewing dates: 23 February to 3 March 1953. (82 pp.)

West Berliners were optimistic about future American policy toward their city under the Eisenhower administration. Almost half (46%) expected a change and 40 per cent thought the change would be favorable. A firmer hand against the Russians (17%), increased economic aid (11%), and better support (6%) were among the anticipated favorable changes. The large majority expected (80%) and approved (77%) a less conciliatory policy toward Russia.

Most West Berliners (85%) were certain that the United States wanted German unity. Nine out of ten (89%) urged West Germany to take its stand with the West in the East-West conflict. A large majority (79%) advocated German integration with the West. Three-quarters (76%) of the West Berlin public continued to believe that, even if it were to their advantage, the Americans would not leave Germany.

Eight in ten Berlin residents (80%) knew of the peace contracts with the Western Allies, and most (60%) approved Bundestag ratification. West Berliners (97%) turned thumbs down on the withdrawal of occupation forces, mainly due to their distrust of the Russians (54%) and satisfaction with the present Berlin Senate (20%). Six in ten (58%) declared that West Berlin would be worse off if all four occupiers, including the Russians, left. The minority (22%) which thought West Berlin would gain from such a move cited a united Germany (9%) and normal trade relations (9%) as beneficial results. Opponents argued mainly that West Berlin would then be at the mercy of the Russians (33%).

Many (60%) were alarmed by the stream of refugees, saying it was having a disastrous effect on the economy (29%) and allowed for the influx of criminal types (15%). Many West Berliners (52%) suspected that Soviet authorities were deliberately encouraging these flights to the West to get rid of politically undesirable elements (15%) and to hurt the West Berlin economy (15%). Over half (53%) of the respondents recommended that more efforts should be made to induce East Germans to stay in the East. Most of the remainder (44%), however, felt refugees should be permitted to enter West Berlin, mainly because of a moral obligation.

According to a two-thirds majority (67%), the influx of refugees would continue indefinitely, and most (83%) were satisfied with the Berlin Senate's handling of the problem. Only 51 per cent expressed approval of Bonn's approach to the problem. Well over half (57%) thought that the United States was doing enough, but the doubtful few (17%) suggested more financial aid (7%) and more emigration to the United States (4%). Half (50%) of the West Berlin population said the West should solve the refugee problem, mainly because the Potsdam Agreement made the West coresponsible for it.

Almost as many West Berliners (44%) believed the move to erect barriers was only another gambit in the war of nerves as believed the intentions of the East German authorities were serious (51%). Thirty per cent believed such efforts would not harm West Berlin because it was not dependent on the East.

In the face of renewed Soviet threats, most Berliners (76%) were unwilling to leave their city. For many (38%) it was simply because Berlin was "home." The public was convinced that Berlin was a concrete symbol of the struggle for freedom against communism (35%). Compared with a two-thirds (63%) vote of confidence in 1952, three-quarters (74%) in early 1953 expressed satisfaction with the West Berlin Senate. As a further indication of good morale, fewer said their personal situation had worsened during the year (26%) and more (25%) that the city's mood was better than it had been a year earlier. According to 78 per cent of its people, West Berlin could hold out indefinitely.

Special Report No. 177-S (30 April 1953)

WEST GERMAN PUBLIC OPINION IN THE WAKE OF STALIN'S DEATH AND THE SOVIET "PEACE OFFENSIVE"

Sample: 764 West Germans and 299 West Berliners in the first survey, and 376 West Germans and 191 West Berliners in the second.
Interviewing dates: representative probability sample on 13 to 21 April, and flash survey on 23 to 28 April 1953. (32 pp.)

Nearly all respondents (98 per cent in West Germany, 100 per cent in West Berlin) were aware of the death of Josef Stalin. Many West Germans (40%) felt that political prospects had improved as a result of his death, with only a few (5%) expressing the contrary opinion. Respondents, seeing gains for the West, believed that the new Russian government showed a readiness to negotiate (27%), the removal of Stalin's hostility was beneficial (6%), or the resulting political crisis would lead to Russian disunity (5%). On the specific issue of another world war, close to half (44%) explicitly asserted that the chances of avoiding another war had improved, with supporting reasons focusing most prominently on alleged changes in Russian attitudes as a result of Stalin's death (26%).

Stalin's death also accounted for some increased hope for German reunification: over half (54%) in West Germany and 70 per cent in West Berlin judged the chances for reunification to be good to very good.

West German support for the contractual agreement (46%), German military participation in Western defense (63%), and German allegiance to the West (71%) rose to new highs following Stalin's death. From May 1952 to April 1953 the proportion who felt the Western Powers had scored the greatest successes in the cold war rose fifteen percentage points in West Germany (from 32 to 47 per cent) and a remarkable forty percentage points (from 32 to 72 per cent) in West Berlin. Success in welding Western defenses (15%), attracting followers (14%), and checking communist expansion in Korea (7%) were the most frequently mentioned reasons for this change in attitude. General satisfaction with American policy toward the Soviet Union rose seven percentage points in West Germany (from 36 to 43 per cent) and twelve percentage points in West Berlin (from 41 to 53 per cent). Confidence that America was really for German unity also showed a steady increase to 65 per cent in West Germany.

Satisfaction with the activities of the current German government was also on the rise. In the latest survey, an unprecedented proportion of West Germans (71%) registered satisfaction with the Bonn government, an increase of thirteen percentage points over December 1952. Complaints from the dissatisfied (18%) only infrequently referred to considerations of Western policy. More people were concerned with the low living standard (5%), economic and social policy (4%), and tax policy (3%) than with the European Defense Community treaty, the German treaty, or remilitarization (3%).

Group comparisons revealed that the recent gain in satisfaction with the federal government was general among population groups, the biggest change occurring among Social Democrats. Though indication of party preference continued to be relatively stable, there was a slight rise in preferences for the CDU, from 21 per cent in April 1952 to 28 per cent in April 1953.

West Germans continued to support a four-power conference by an overwhelming majority (72 to 9 per cent). An appreciably greater proportion (growing from 43 per cent in September 1952 to 56 per cent in April 1953) believed that the United States subscribed to the idea of holding such a conference. The earlier Russian proposal regarding the reunification of Germany was still rejected (83 to 14 per cent). Finally, an increased proportion (from 33 per cent in June 1952 to 43 per cent in April 1953) expressed the opinion that a four-power conference would be advantageous for West Germany.

Report No. 178 (14 May 1953)

GERMAN IMPACT AND EVALUATIONS OF PRESIDENT EISENHOWER'S FOREIGN POLICY ADDRESS

Sample: 376 West Germans and 191 West Berliners.
Interviewing dates: flash survey on 23 to 28 April 1953. (23 pp.)

A week following its delivery, President Eisenhower's foreign policy address had achieved scant notice, with but a third (37%) in West Germany and half (50%) in West Berlin claiming awareness, and only a quarter (27%) in West Germany and 38 per cent in West Berlin demonstrating familiarity with its contents.

Among those respondents claiming familiarity with the speech, the reactions were almost wholly favorable (25 per cent in West Germany; 41 per cent in West Berlin) with only a minuscule one per cent in West Germany and no one in West Berlin voicing an unfavorable impression. As reasons for their approval of the speech, West Germans cited its hopefulness (7%), sincerity (3%), and goodwill (3%).

All respondents were asked to read a copy of Eisenhower's speech. Over half (52%) of the West Germans and 72 per cent of the West Berliners reacted favorably, with many (21 and 28 per cent respectively) giving their unqualified approval. Some (31 and 26 per cent) reacted favorably to the speech but were skeptical as to the possibility of realizing its objectives. The minority (6 and 1 per cent) who voiced unfavorable reactions felt the speech to be dishonest and propagandistic. A few West German respondents would have liked more attention to German problems, such as reunification (4%), the Oder-Neisse line (2%), and the Saar issue (2%).

Most West German respondents (63%) judged the speech to be an earnest step on the part of the American government to resolve problems of the cold war. Only a few (13%) felt the speech was a mere tactical maneuver, and still fewer (6%) thought that it made excessive demands on the Russians in its proposals for peace. On the contrary, a large majority (70%) believed American demands to be reasonable, arguing that Russia could fulfill them without losing prestige (34%) and that Eisenhower had not made demands but offered suggestions proposing cooperation (6%).

Report No. 179 (15 June 1953)

CURRENT WEST GERMAN POLITICAL TRENDS AND PROJECTED REACTIONS TO POSSIBLE RUSSIAN PROPOSALS

Sample: 740 West Germans.
Interviewing dates: early June 1953. (27 pp.)

By early June 1953 satisfaction with the Adenauer government had risen to 69 per cent in West Germany, an increase of 11 per cent since August 1952. Seventy per cent of the respondents said they were from fairly to very satisfied with their economic progress. The CDU was clearly preferred (28%) to the SPD (21%).

Optimism about Russian peace intentions following Stalin's death fell off from 52 per cent in April 1953 to 28 per cent. At the same time, there was less inclination to ascribe gains to the West in the East-West struggle (from 47 per cent in April to 40 per cent in June) or to look approvingly upon American policy toward the Soviet Union (from 50 per cent to 31 per cent). Accordingly, there was a rather marked drop in approval of Bundestag ratification of the German treaty (from 46 to 39 per cent).

Desire for a four-power conference on German problems continued to be widespread (71%), and approximately a quarter (23%) of the respondents believed the new Soviet régime was more desirous of reaching an agreement. The majority (56%), however, did not want a conference so badly that they would approve Western acceptance of a Russian proposal that was unacceptable to Germany. The minority (19%) who favored discussion of even unacceptable proposals argued that negotiations might result in advantages for Germany (11%) and that, in any event, a discussion would do no harm (6%). The majority expressing disapproval countered that such a discussion would be useless (25%) and harmful to German interests (12%).

Given the opportunity to accept or reject Russian proposals for a neutral, reunified Germany (with the Oder-Neisse issue open to compromise), 38 per cent supported and 41 per cent rejected such a notion. Comments of those who would have accepted even a completely unarmed Germany made it clear that few (1%) explicitly welcomed such a prospect. Gains from a presumed peace treaty and German reunification overshadowed the possible absence of any German defense force. Further questioning of the 64 per cent who indicated that they would go along with a Germany possessing no or limited armaments revealed evidence of wishful thinking regarding Soviet respect for German neutrality. Almost a third (31%) did not think it would be respected, but a quarter of these (8%) indicated that it was worth a try, a fifth (6%) that the West could guarantee German security, and still others (4%) that all avenues toward peace should be explored. Those who felt the Russians would not violate German neutrality (21%) contended that fear of a new war (11%) and respect for treaties (3%) would force Russia to accept such a situation.

Report No. 180 (6 July 1953)

GERMAN POLITICAL TRENDS FOLLOWING RECENT SOVIET CONCESSIONS AND SUBSEQUENT EAST ZONE RIOTS

Sample: 761 West Germans and 186 West Berliners.
Interviewing dates: 22 June to 2 July 1953. (40 pp.)

Despite rioting in the GDR in June 1953, West Germans continued to be impressed by conciliatory gestures on the part of the East toward the West. Almost half (46%) of the West Germans and 61 per cent of the West Berliners expressed this view. About the same percentage of West Germans (44%) thought the demonstrations were a good thing for Germany, but only 17 per cent expected substantial improvements for the East Germans to result from them. West Berliners, by contrast, gave widespread approval (87%) to the demonstrations, and many felt they would be useful (43%).

A great many Germans (47 per cent in West Germany; 78 per cent in West Berlin) felt the Soviet concessions had come as a result of the Western policy of strength. Similar numbers (51 and 69 per cent) felt that the concessions were either partly or completely due to the "firm and determined" policy of the West. Despite the Soviet concessions, most Germans (74 and 92 per cent) continued to distrust Russian motives.

Satisfaction with the Adenauer administration was higher than ever (76 and 88 per cent). Substantial numbers (58 and 74 per cent) were satisfied with the way Adenauer was approaching German reunification, and only a minority (20 per cent in both) wished Adenauer would change his policy toward the Soviet Union. Only 12 per cent of the West Germans and 11 per cent of West Berliners thought the SPD would do a better job if it were in power.

Support for Western allegiance remained high (69 and 92 per cent), as did support for the army (56 and 84 per cent) and the contractual agreement with the West (42 and 69 per cent). The West was seen as having made more political gains than the East (41 and 71 per cent), and most people (50 and 51 per cent) felt that the West should continue with the same policy.

Desire for a four-power conference had increased slightly to 84 per cent in West Germany and to 94 per cent in West Berlin. The preponderance of respondents (46 and 64 per cent) saw German advantages likely in such a conference. Despite the riots, most Germans (55 and 74 per cent) continued to believe that the chances for reunification were fairly good to very good. In West Germany 38 per cent felt that the Russians would be prepared to grant a reunified Germany at the price of neutrality. Nearly as many (35%), however, felt that such a development was unlikely. In West Berlin half again as many (57%) felt that Russia would agree to a reunification of Germany with free elections if Germany were to remain neutral as felt that Russia would never agree to such a proposal (38%).

Report No. 181 (17 July 1953)

THE AMERICA HOUSE EVALUATED
A Study of the Effectiveness of the U.S. Information Centers in West Germany

> *Sample:* in the first set of interviews, 2,000 respondents (15 years of age and over) residing within the official city limits surrounding America House installations in 46 cities; in the second set, 200 persons interviewed as they left America Houses in each of eight different cities.
> *Interviewing dates:* Service area study on 12 February to 15 March 1953; visitors' study on 7 to 24 April 1953. (132 pp.)

Well over half (61%) of those West Germans living near an America House had visited one during the preceding year, and almost half of these were in fact fairly frequent visitors. More men than women were visitors, and the young tended to visit the centers more than the old. Residents of small cities were more likely to visit America Houses than were residents of large cities. For instance, 16 per cent of the residents of a large city like Hamburg or Munich had been to one, while in towns with populations under 90,000 as many as 30 per cent had been visitors. America House visitors tended to be regular churchgoers and politically conservative.

Among those who were interviewed as they left an America House, 15 per cent said they were there for the first time. Newcomers tended also to be young people with a better than average education; six in ten were under thirty.

Of the frequent visitors, 75 per cent used the library, 73 per cent attended film showings, 62 per cent lectures, 56 per cent concerts, and 52 per cent the exhibits. As for audience ratings of the specific America House facilities, films ranked highest, at 4.3 on a scale ranging from +5 to -5; discussions ranked lowest, with +3.4.

The overwhelming majority of visitors to America Houses regarded these information centers in a positive light. Many (82%) had spoken about them to friends or recommended their going to one (78%). Asked whether they thought the centers tried to show America as it really is or gave a more favorable picture than was warranted, 58 per cent said they felt it was realistic.

Report No. 182 (31 July 1953)

THE CURRENT STANDING OF RIAS AMONG WEST BERLIN RADIO LISTENERS

I. Reactions and Evaluations

Sample: 286 West Berliners.
Interviewing dates: 11 to 31 May 1953. (30 pp.)

A large majority (69%) of the West Berlin radio audience concurred in the opinion that RIAS had done much or very much for West Berlin, citing as illustrations its enlightenment of the public (37%), moral support of West Berliners (11%), furtherance of their interests (10%), entertainment (10%), and material help through charities (10%). In evaluating the effectiveness of RIAS in refuting Eastern propaganda, 78 per cent expressed the judgment that it had been effective, with 49 per cent of these finding RIAS very effective. Reasons for considering RIAS effective were that East German residents regularly listened to the station and believed its statements (27%), RIAS reported truthfully and objectively about conditions in East and West Germany (23%), and RIAS succeeded in refuting arguments put forth by Eastern propagandists (10%). The 9 per cent who saw little or no effectiveness listed weak propaganda (2%), exaggeration (2%), and Eastern propaganda (2%) as reasons for their doubts.

Despite widespread acknowledgment of its contributions, the popularity of RIAS was less (53%) than in 1949 (76%). In a comparison with other radio stations, 29 per cent of the listeners said they preferred RIAS, and 26 per cent selected Northwest German Radio (NWDR). NWDR owed its popularity to its better musical programs (15%), its variety (10%), and its small number of political programs (7%). Most West Berliners who rated RIAS over NWDR said it had better entertainment (17%), was specifically directed at Berliners (13%), and had the best news programs (11%).

Report No. 183 (14 August 1953)

SOME CLUES TO THE EFFECTIVENESS OF A PRODUCTIVITY FILM PROGRAM AMONG GERMAN FACTORY WORKERS

Sample: 173 workers in a West German factory.
Interviewing dates: June 1953. (36 pp.)

The survey was undertaken to ascertain the impact of an

audiovisual aids program being conducted in selected plants and factories. Interviews were done in a factory that made machines for dyeing and bleaching. It had about 250 employees, a relatively large proportion of whom were machinists, that is, highly skilled workers. In all, eight films were shown on three different days: 24 January, 2 February, and 18 April.

At least half of those interviewed remembered seeing each of the films; only 19 per cent did not see any or did not remember doing so. There were more favorable comments about the films than unfavorable ones. Most referred to their instructive value. Seven in ten also liked the talks accompanying the films. The overwhelming majority (86%) said they would like to see more such films on other aspects of production. Just over half (51%) also said they had talked about the films with their co-workers.

Special Report 183-S (24 August 1953)

GERMAN THINKING ON A FOUR-POWER CONFERENCE

Sample: 625 West Germans and 199 West Berliners.
Interviewing dates: late July 1953. (19 pp.)

As expected in the light of earlier trends, the Western proposal for a four-power conference met with the overwhelming approval of both the West German (83%) and West Berlin (95%) citizenry. Strong majorities in both West Germany (75%) and West Berlin (90%) expressed their conviction that, in the event of a four-power conference, America could be relied upon to push for German reunification. Confidence in the British was substantially less (47 and 70 per cent). Traditional German-French suspicion was more than a little indicated by the fact that only 13 per cent (27 per cent in West Berlin) expressed any confidence in French support for German unity.

Although many (40 and 60 per cent) felt that advantages for West Germany were likely to come from a four-power conference, only a minority (26 and 41 per cent) were so optimistic as to anticipate agreement on reunification. Nevertheless, 48 per cent of the West Germans and 72 per cent of the West Berliners wanted to continue EDC efforts. Western insistence on free elections prior to any negotiations with East German representatives was approved by many respondents who argued that it was necessary to determine the real opinion of the GDR's people (25 per cent in both), weaken communist influence (20 and 25 per cent), and have a representative government (19 and 40 per cent). Upon direct inquiry, 68 per cent of the West Germans and 93 per cent of the West Berliners concurred with the Western thesis. But, if insistence on free elections meant a delay in possible reunification, support fell off to 42 per cent in West Germany and 68 per cent in West Berlin.

Corroborating earlier indications, a majority (55%) of West Germans leaned toward German neutrality if it would lead to reunification. In West Berlin the weight of opinion (52%) opposed this course (42 per cent in favor). Although few (18 and 22 per cent) believed that the Western Powers would go along with a neutral Germany, more (43 and 68 per cent) felt that they would not. But without a Western guarantee of security, neutrality was not as acceptable (28 and 25 per cent).

Whatever attitudes respondents might have had about the acceptability or nonacceptability of neutrality as a price for reunification, the preponderant opinion (38 and 61 per cent) was that within five years a neutral Germany would side with the West.

Should a four-power conference fail, continued conciliation outweighed more forceful recommendations among West Germans (39 to 21 per cent). West Berliners, however, elected tough reactions (47 to 34 per cent).

Report No. 184 (27 August 1953)

WEST BERLIN SUBSCRIBERS APPRAISE THE *NEUE ZEITUNG*

Sample: 335 West Berlin subscribers to the *Neue Zeitung*.
Interviewing dates: 17 to 29 March 1953. (58 pp.)

Neue Zeitung subscribers were unlike most West Berliners in their amount of formal education, income, age, and occupation. Three times as many *NZ* subscribers as nonsubscribers had attended university (17 to 5 per cent). Over half (54%) made at least DM 400 per month, compared with 22 per cent in the general population. In addition, *Neue Zeitung* subscribers tended to be professionals and to be older rather than younger.

Over half (56%) of the *NZ*'s Berlin subscribers read the *NZ* only, and most of those who read other papers as well considered the *NZ* to be their favorite paper. Objectivity and reliability were the main reasons (33%) for preferring the *NZ*. Other reasons were its variety and extensive coverage (25%), higher standards and superior style (25%), and informativeness (20%).

Report No. 185 (27 August 1953)

EAST ZONE VIEWS ON THE JUNE RIOTS, FOOD AID, AND CURRENT POLITICAL ISSUES

Sample: 876 East Germans at food distribution points in West Berlin.
Interviewing dates: a series of three surveys between 6 August and 15 August 1953. (41 pp.)

East Germans gave strong majority endorsement (77%) to the Western handling of the June 17th demonstrations. A disgruntled minority (13%) commented that the West should have intervened with military force (7%), that they should have given the people more moral support (5%), and that the U.N. should have exerted more pressure on the Russians to keep them from interfering (4%).

Over two-thirds (68%) felt that the June riots had been at least partially successful. The gains mentioned most frequently were that the GDR government had come to realize that the people were not behind it (14%), the people had become more outspoken and bolder (14%), the government had become more yielding (10%), or Eastern residents could buy more food (8%). The minority (25%) who saw no favorable consequences commented that the demonstrations were suppressed by force of arms (13%), they were not well-organized (4%), or the GDR government was still too severe (2%). In fact, in the view of some, since the riots there was less freedom (12%); travel restrictions had been renewed (10%); police controls had become more severe (7%); and food supplies were worse (4%). The majority (61%) nonetheless felt that there had been a definite improvement in morale as a result of the riots.

In the worldwide East-West struggle, the majority (75%) regarded the West as more successful, with the Korean armistice (21%), the unity, stength, and peaceful policies of the West (16%), Western freedom (10%), and the Western standard of living mentioned as indications of this success. Only 3 per cent felt the communists had achieved more success.

A majority (54%) registered satisfaction with American policy toward the Soviet Union, singling out American firmness (15%), conciliatory policies (14%), and "right" course (7%). The quarter (25%) who were either dissatisfied or partly dissatisfied mentioned that the United States was not tough enough with Russia (21%) and that Americans were too trusting (2%).

The majority opinion (68%) among the East Germans was that efforts toward a European Defense Community (EDC) should go on unabated rather than be postponed for fear it would block German reunification.

Most East Germans approved of the West's insistence on free elections in the GDR before any German reunification. They cited the necessity of ascertaining the real opinion of the people (25%), negotiating power of an elected government

(19%), and unrepresentativeness of the present government, which they saw as having been appointed by the Russians (15%).

As in the West, the majority of East Germans (52%) would accept a neutral Germany if the USSR insisted on such a condition as a basis for German reunification. Of the 39 per cent who opposed neutrality, 23 per cent felt that the danger of a Russian invasion would be increased (23%).

Awareness of a food relief program was most generally obtained through listening to RIAS (68%). Almost three-quarters (72%) of the East German food recipients tested were aware that America was the source of the food aid. Most (64%) believed America was motivated primarily by humanitarian considerations. Only a minority (8%) focused on political considerations and, more often than not, in terms that indicated approval.

Report No. 186 (18 September 1953)

FURTHER SOUNDINGS OF EAST GERMAN OPINIONS ON CURRENT POLITICAL ISSUES

Sample: 448 East Germans (excluding East Berliners) at seven food distribution points in West Berlin.
Interviewing dates: two surveys on 29 August to 2 September and 3 to 7 September 1953. (33 pp.)

In line with their general expression of satisfaction (86%) with the activities of the Adenauer government, the East Germans interviewed in this survey strongly endorsed (66%) West German participation in European defense. Prior to the Bonn election of September 1953, the preponderance of East Germans (45%) expressed a preference for a CDU victory. In the event of free all-German elections, the CDU was again preferred by most (45%). This situation marked a distinct change from a July 1952 survey that had indicated strong SPD support (38 per cent, in contrast with 23 per cent for the CDU). Among the reasons advanced for preferring the CDU were that it was successful in West Germany (12%), was the best party (12%), had a Christian and democratic attitude (11%), or stood up for the East Germans (5%). Supporters of the SPD commented that the SPD was a workers' party (16%), supported German reunification (2%), or opposed war (1%).

The idea of a four-power conference was very widely endorsed (97%). However, most East Germans (72%) stated that free elections of East German representatives must precede such a conference, even at the expense of delaying reunification. The majority (75%) nonetheless felt that any agreement on reunification as a result of such a conference was highly unlikely. If the conference failed to achieve reunification, half the respondents (50%) recommended the use of more forceful measures, up to and including war. Nearly as many (38%) urged the continuation of negotiations and avoidance of war. But if reunification could not be achieved by any other means, 62 per cent advocated the use of force.

Over three in five (62%) of the East Germans in the sample

felt that further demonstrations were likely, citing as reasons for their opinions the discontent and unrest (20%), unkept promises made by the government (19%), and intolerable political pressures (9%). Opinions were divided as to whether additional demonstrations would benefit the East German population. Nearly half (49%) felt that the outcome of future demonstrations would be good, because the weight of public opinion would force Russia to make concessions (27%), the government might be overthrown (13%), or reunification might become a reality (8%). Those who feared new demonstrations pointed out that any demonstrations would be immediately quelled by the police (20%), more rigid suppression would result (10%), or new demonstrations would be just as useless as the previous ones (4%).

Report No. 187 (7 October 1953)

AN EVALUATION OF AUDIENCE REACTIONS TO THE U.S.I.A. FILM *MAGIC STREETCAR*

Sample: 442 West Germans drawn from audiences of three movie theaters in Königswinter.
Interviewing dates: October 1953. (49 pp.)

Slightly over half (55%) of the interviewed audience said they liked the film *Magic Streetcar*, but as many as 44 per cent were critical. (In comparison, another short film on the same subject, *Without Fear*, was liked by 77 per cent of the viewers.) Almost everyone who saw the film considered its aim to be serious. Half (51%) mentioned that *Magic Streetcar* was designed to show differences between East and West. Only 2 per cent mentioned its romantic aspect. Over two-thirds (69%) felt it important to show such films in Germany because of their general information (26%) and specific information about the poor conditions in the East (19%). A quarter (26%) felt the film was unimportant, mainly because it did not tell the audience anything it did not already know (10%), and because it failed as propaganda (9%).

Report No. 188 (29 October 1953)

THE CURRENT STANDING OF RIAS AMONG WEST BERLIN RADIO LISTENERS

II. Comparative Indices of Station and Program Popularity

Sample: 289 completed radio-listening diaries were analyzed.
Interviewing dates: 4 to 10 May 1953. (61 pp.)

Almost everyone who listened to the radio at all in West Berlin listened to RIAS. Furthermore, each listener tuned it in for an average of 17.8 hours per week, which meant that the station received 65 per cent of the attention given radio programs in the city. Second in popularity was the Northwest German Radio (NWDR), with one-third of the total listening volume. Very few people said they listened to the American Forces Network (AFN). The same was true of East German stations. News and light and popular music seemed to be the most popular fare.

Report No. 189 (30 October 1953)

EAST ZONE RADIO LISTENING
Trend and Current Evaluations of RIAS

> *Sample:* 586 East Germans interviewed at food distribution points set up in West Berlin as part of second phase of food program.
> *Interviewing dates:* 3 September to 9 October 1953. (27 pp.)

Between June 1951 and September 1953, RIAS appeared to have lost some of its regular listeners, primarily to another Western station, NWDR. The most frequently given reason for no longer listening to RIAS was bad reception (29%) due to jamming.

Very few respondents had any criticisms to make about RIAS. In fact, over half (56%) said that RIAS had done very much for East Germans in the course of the year; another 37 per cent said the station had done much. Asked for examples of this help, 35 per cent mentioned the news and information programs, 25 per cent said that RIAS had issued warnings and information on informers as well as directives about behavior, and 23 per cent spoke of the information programs. The station was given even higher ratings for effectiveness against Eastern propaganda.

Report No. 190 (16 November 1953)

THE MARSHALL HOUSE EXHIBIT AT THE 1953 BERLIN INDUSTRIAL FAIR
An Evaluation of West Berlin and East German Reactions

> *Sample:* 612 respondents at the Marshall House, where the United States exhibit was held; and 623 respondents at the two main exits to the fairgrounds.
> *Interviewing dates:* from 29 September through 11 October 1953. (69 pp.)

One-half of all respondents said they had visited the Marshall House exhibit. Of those who had not done so, most said it was because of a lack of time or because the exhibit had been too crowded. A solid majority of those asked were able to give a reasonable definition of the theme of the exhibit: industrial research and production can, with the consent and participation of the individual, continue to raise the standard of living throughout the free world. Among those interviewed at the exits of the Marshall House and who had visited at least one other pavilion, 30 per cent of the West Berliners and 22 per cent of the East Germans said they had liked the Marshall House exhibit best. Within the exhibit, the section dealing with the Tennessee Valley Authority was given the highest rating.

Report No. 191 (11 December 1953)

A SURVEY ANALYSIS OF THE FACTORS UNDERLYING THE OUTCOME OF THE 1953 GERMAN FEDERAL ELECTIONS

Sample: 664, 1,270, and 904 West Germans over the age of 21.
Interviewing dates: 22 August to 3 September 1953, 14 to 27 September 1953, and 22 October to 2 November 1953. (72 pp.)

Preelection trends based on twenty-four surveys from March 1951 to September 1953 revealed that the SPD's greater popularity throughout 1951 gradually gave way to a dominant position for the CDU/CSU, a position maintained after April 1953. Polls throughout the two months before the election showed that the parties most likely to join in a coalition government under Adenauer would receive an overwhelming majority of the votes and that the CDU/CSU by itself would outpoll the Social Democratic party by somewhere between a quarter and a third of the latter's votes. On the day before the election, HICOG analysts circulated a report predicting both that the CDU/CSU alone would get 46.0 per cent of the vote (it actually got 45.2 per cent) and that the coalition governing the First Bundestag--that is, the CDU/CSU, FDP, and DP--would obtain 60.9 per cent (somewhat above its actual total of 57.9 per cent).

Postelection surveys sought to determine why respondents voted as they had. Political issues in any specific sense were not overwhelmingly salient to them. CDU/CSU voters stressed general feelings about the way things were going: Adenauer's personality and prestige in the world (mentioned by 30 per cent), religious reasons (21%), the economic gains of the years previous (19%), and satisfaction with the achievements of the CDU (17%), or simply their belief that the CDU/CSU "is the best party" (9%). Those who said they had voted for the SPD were only slightly more oriented to specific issues. The top three reasons volunteered to explain why ballots had been cast for the Social Democrats were: the belief that the SPD advocates the cause of workers (69%), economic and social gains that could be expected from an SPD government (9%), and in third place (with 7 per cent) the issues named by most observers as having been the key factors in the election--SPD opposition to German remilitarization and the European Defense Community.

Neither did many German voters worry about the special political circumstances that were said to have favored the Christian Union parties. Only 6 per cent of all voters attributed the party's success to its more effective election campaign, and only 4 per cent cited poor propaganda as a cause of the SPD's relatively poor showing. Asked whether they had anything to criticize about the parties' campaigns, two-thirds (66%) responded negatively, and a quarter (24%) offered criticisms. Half of the latter group complained in general about the mudslinging tactics (7%) or the waste of money in campaigning (5%), but many of the remaining respondents focused more narrowly on the propaganda of one party or the other. The charges were directed in roughly equal proportions at the two major parties.

Another such special circumstance, Secretary of State John Foster Dulles's preelection remarks, which were widely interpreted as an overt indication of American backing for Chancellor Adenauer and the CDU/CSU, seemed to have had some but not an overwhelming effect on German voters. Whereas in July only one in six (16%) felt the United States supported the CDU/CSU, the postelection survey in September found that 28 per cent held this view. Among the electorate as a whole, 40 per cent felt that America did not support any particular party. No one among the 1,270 respondents in the nationwide poll seems to have responded to an open-ended question about the reason for the CDU/CSU's success with the charge that it was due to American intervention.

Among different social groupings, the CDU/CSU emerged from the election with a nearly clean sweep. HICOG analysts divided respondents into 33 categories according to sex, level of education, age, income, occupation, origin (natives vs. expellees or refugees from the East), and religion. In only four of these--two of them (nineteen persons professing a religion other than Protestantism or Catholicism, and forty-one professing no religion at all) comprising too few respondents for the results to be considered statistically significant--did the number of SPD voters outweigh those who reported having voted for the CDU/CSU. The two clearly deviant categories were semi-skilled workers (34 per cent for the CDU/CSU, 37 per cent for the SPD) and skilled workers (35 and 36 per cent respectively). Others above average in supporting the SPD were lower-middle income groups, persons aged 35 to 54 years, Protestants, those with only an elementary education, and men. (The questions asked in the survey do not permit an assessment of the importance of party identification.)

The electoral outcome was satisfactory to a majority (58%) of West Germans. Only 14 per cent of those questioned were at all disturbed by it. Most of this concern centered on fears of remilitarization and the possibility that the CDU/CSU would become dictatorial. Respondents also thought that democracy had become stronger in West Germany during the previous few years (44 per cent, as opposed to 5 per cent who termed it weaker, and 33 per cent who had no opinion on the question). Interest in politics, too, had risen, from 43 per cent in November 1951 to 49 per cent in late September 1953.

Report No. 192 (28 December 1953)

WEST GERMAN REACTIONS TO U.N. AIRING OF KOREA ATROCITIES

Sample: 635 West Germans and 227 West Berliners.
Interviewing dates: 20 November to 1 December 1953. (18 pp.)

A scant majority (52%) of the West German respondents, but as many as 78 per cent of the West Berliners, had heard or read of atrocities allegedly being committed in Korea. In both groups, it should be added, most people said they had heard that atrocities were being committed by both sides, not just by the communists. In West Germany, 32 per cent of the population had heard of and believed the reports about communist atrocities, while 10 per cent had heard and also believed the same about U.N. troops. In West Berlin far more respondents (64%) believed stories about communist atrocities, but only 7 per cent believed such stories about U.N. troops.

Questioned more specifically about communist charges that U.N. troops were using germ warfare, four in ten West Germans and three in four West Berliners indicated awareness of these allegations, but almost all either did not believe the stories or reserved judgment.

Slightly more than half (52%) of the West Germans and a solid majority (77%) of West Berliners approved the American proposal to bring North Korean and Chinese atrocities before the U.N. In addition, there was a large no-opinion group on this question, especially in West Germany.

Special Report No. 192-S

INTERNATIONAL SURVEY ON PRESIDENT EISENHOWER'S U.N. SPEECH

(German Results)

Sample: not given.
Interviewing dates: not given. (26 pp.)

A majority (57%) of West Germans had not heard or read about President Eisenhower's speech of 8 December 1953 before the United Nations. Of the 43 per cent who had read or heard of it, most (24%) also claimed to remember some aspect of it in detail.

All respondents were told that the speech called for those nations with atomic materials to contribute to a stockpile to be controlled by an international agency under the jurisdiction of the United Nations. Asked whether or not they considered this a sincere proposal, most (70%) thought it was. Opinion was split, however, on the question of whether or not such an agency would in fact be created (39% to 38%).

Report No. 193 (18 January 1954)

GERMAN PUBLIC OPINION ON THE FOUR-POWER CONFERENCE
With Latest Trends in EDC Thinking

Sample: 601 West Germans and 207 West Berliners.
Interviewing dates: late December 1953 (with reference to surveys in mid- and late April 1953, late June 1953, and July 1953). (38 pp.)

Before the decision was finally made to hold a four-power conference, confidence in positive results from such a meeting declined among both West Germans and West Berliners. Even after the decision, confidence continued to decline. While vast majorities (85 per cent in West Germany, with multiple responses) approved of what they thought American aims in such a conference would be, low percentages approved of what they considered the French (9%) and Soviet (15%) intentions to be. In addition, over two-thirds of the respondents in both West Germany and West Berlin believed that, if the United States had to choose between supporting French or German interests, it would side with the latter. The reasons most frequently put forward for this belief were Germany's stability, reliability, and maturity.

Large majorities in both West Germany (73%) and West Berlin (91%) agreed that free elections had to be held before there could be any negotiations with East German representatives on the question of reunification. However, if the conference were threatened by an impasse on this issue, far fewer people (45 and 62 per cent) said they would insist on such elections.

Neutrality as a price for reunification was widely acceptable (47 per cent in West Germany, with 33 per cent opposed), although in West Berlin its acceptability had declined from 42 per cent in July 1953 to only 25 per cent by December. In contrast, solid majorities in both West Germany (69%) and West Berlin (82%) opposed recognition of the Oder-Neisse line as a price for reunification. Most respondents supported this view with statements like "What is German cannot be given away." Furthermore, 70 per cent of the West Germans and as many as 88 per cent of the West Berliners also felt that the United States would be in favor of restoring the Eastern territories to Germany. They were far more skeptical of French intentions on this score: only 9 per cent of the West Germans and 20 per cent of the West Berliners thought France would approve such a restoration.

Starting as early as June 1952, more West Germans favored than opposed their country's participation in the defense of Western Europe. Indeed, by late December 1953, 57 per cent were in favor, 31 per cent opposed, and 12 per cent had no opinion. In West Berlin the supportive figure was, as always, far higher (83%). Not quite half the West Germans (48%) and almost three-quarters (74%) of the West Berliners even felt that plans for EDC should proceed despite the projected four-power conference. This large support for EDC notwithstanding, more Germans favored a national army than a general European army. Most of the arguments made on this point centered on the fear that German soldiers would be exploited and misused in an integrated command.

Report No. 194-I (24 January 1954)

PUBLIC OPINION DURING THE FOUR-POWER CONFERENCE

I. West German Views on Eve of Four-Power Conference

Sample: 300 West Germans and 150 West Berliners.
Interviewing dates: 20 to 22 January 1954. (13 pp.)

On the eve of the four-power conference among the United States, Great Britain, France, and the Soviet Union, 77 per cent of the West German population, as well as 92 per cent of West Berliners, knew that such a conference was to take place. In West Germany less than half (46%), and in West Berlin somewhat over half (55%), of those interviewed thought the conference would result in advantages for Germany; the West Berlin figure represented a large drop from the April 1953 high of 69 per cent, when a similar question was asked.

In both West Germany and West Berlin, respondents felt that reunification was the greatest problem facing the country, although large minorities cited other problems. Asked whether they were generally satisfied or dissatisfied with the way Chancellor Adenauer was handling the issue of reunification, 72 per cent in West Germany and 82 per cent in West Berlin expressed satisfaction; both figures represented a rise from the June 1953 survey.

Solid majorities in both West Germany (62%) and West Berlin (84%) knew that a preliminary conference had taken place in Berlin. However, while more West Berliners thought it had gone well (42%) than badly (30%), the reverse was true in West Germany, where 27 per cent felt it had gone badly and only 20 per cent considered it successful. In both areas almost all people who thought it had gone badly placed the blame on the Soviets.

In a survey conducted some six months earlier, respondents were asked, "Supposing Russia would agree to a reunification of Germany through free elections only on condition that Germany would remain neutral and would not be allowed to enter into an alliance with either West or East: Would you on that condition be more for or more against a reunification?" At that time 55 per cent of the West Germans said they would favor reunification, 21 per cent opposed, and 24 per cent had no opinion. In West Berlin the picture looked somewhat different: 42 per cent were in favor, 52 per cent opposed, and only 6 per cent had no opinion. During the ensuing months the percentage of those favoring reunification under these conditions declined, but by January 1954 the trend seemed to reverse itself. In West Germany the percentage of those favoring reunification had once again risen to 50 per cent, while in West Berlin the figure stood at 40 per cent. Reunification along lines of the settlement made for Austria was opposed by almost half (48%) of the West German respondents and over half (58%) of the West Berliners.

Finally, half of both the West Germans and the West Berliners were of the opinion that the Soviet Union did not fear an attack by the West. In West Germany 34 per cent felt Russia did have such fears, while in West Berlin the figure was 45 per cent. Very few respondents, however, felt these fears were justified.

Report No. 194-II (31 January 1954)

PUBLIC OPINION DURING THE FOUR-POWER CONFERENCE
II. West German Reactions to Initial Developments

Sample: 324 West Germans and 147 West Berliners.
Interviewing dates: 28 to 30 January 1954. (11 pp.)

In West Germany the percentage of persons aware that a four-power conference was being held, as well as where it was being held, rose astonishingly in the one-month period between late December 1953 (53%) and the end of January 1954 (91%). In West Berlin the percentage rose from an already fairly high 82 per cent to an even higher 98 per cent.

Slightly over half the population (51%) thought the conference might result in advantages for West Germany. Very few (26%) thought an agreement on reunification might be reached. On the general question of how they thought the conference had gone up to that point, respondents were extremely careful. In West Germany, 23 per cent said it had gone fairly well, 22 per cent said "so-so," and 27 per cent withheld their opinion.

In West Germany more people (60%) had not heard or read about Secretary of State Dulles's first major speech at the conference than had (40%). In West Berlin, however, more people

(56%) had heard of it than had not (44%). Majorities in both West Germany (58%) and West Berlin (75%) disapproved of the proposed Soviet agenda for the conference. Nonetheless, three-quarters (75%) felt the West was right in accepting it in order not to delay the actual negotiations.

Increasing numbers of people hoped for immediate reunification regardless of the possible difficulties and dangers involved. However, in West Germany, there were decreasing numbers (55 per cent in July 1953, 47 per cent in late January 1954) in favor of reunification if the price involved were to be neutrality; in West Berlin, the figure stood at 40 per cent, as it had in the previous survey one week earlier and only two percentage points lower than in the first survey on this question in July 1953.

Report No. 194-III (3 February 1954)

PUBLIC OPINION DURING THE FOUR-POWER CONFERENCE
III. Flash Reactions to Eden and Molotov Plans

Sample: 200 residents of West German cities with populations of 50,000 or more, and 200 West Berliners.
Interviewing dates: flash survey on 2 February 1954. (6 pp.)

Asked about the Eden Plan calling for reunification of Germany and free elections throughout the country, 72 per cent of the urban West Germans and 89 per cent of the West Berliners had heard of it. At the same time, 68 per cent of the urban West German respondents and 79 per cent of the West Berliners had heard of the Soviet reunification proposal (the Molotov Plan). Whereas 73 per cent of the West Germans approved the Eden Plan, only 19 per cent approved the Molotov Plan.

Concerning specific aspects of the Molotov Plan, 78 per cent of the urban West German respondents and even more West Berliners (89%) said they would be against reunification if acceptance of the Oder-Neisse line were set as a precondition.

For 33 per cent of West Germans the two reunification plans permitted a compromise acceptable to Germany; 43 per cent, however, saw no possibility for compromise. In addition, 42 per cent felt the West ought to stick to its plan and not necessarily try to compromise. Although 66 per cent of the population thought the West was doing all it could to achieve reunification, only 16 per cent thought it would succeed.

Report No. 194-IV (7 February 1954)

PUBLIC OPINION DURING THE FOUR-POWER CONFERENCE
IV. West German Reactions to Western versus Soviet Proposals

Sample: 309 West Germans and 139 West Berliners.
Interviewing dates: 4 to 6 February 1954. (16 pp.)

Although the first days of the four-power conference seemed to elicit optimistic feelings about Germany's future-- 51 per cent in West Germany and 60 per cent in West Berlin had said the conference would bring advantages for their country-- by the end of the first week in February strong doubts had already set in. In West Germany only one-third of the population felt it would bring advantages, while 52 per cent thought such advantages were unlikely. In West Berlin the January figures were completely reversed: where 60 per cent had said then there would be advantages, now only 37 per cent thought so; and where 37 per cent had said in January there would be no advantages, 61 per cent felt this way in February. In addition, the percentage of people considering agreement on reunification as a likely result of the conference continued its downward trend from previous surveys. Both West Germans and West Berliners were also far less enthusiastic about how the conference was actually going. Whereas in January only 8 per cent of the West Germans thought it was going badly, in early February the figure jumped to 17 per cent; and in West Berlin it had gone from 10 to 14 per cent. Nonetheless, very few people thought the Russians had the upper hand in the negotiations; in fact, 29 per cent of the West Germans felt the Western Powers had been more successful up to that point; but 39 per cent felt both sides were equally successful; and 24 per cent had no opinion. At the same time, vast majorities in both West Germany (82%) and West Berlin (92%) thought the Western Powers were doing all they could to achieve reunification on terms acceptable to the Germans.

At this point in the conference, two proposals had been made for Germany's reunification: one by the Western Powers, the other by the Soviet Union. Of the 57 per cent of the West German population who knew about a Western proposal, 50 per cent approved of it. Of the 56 per cent of the West German population who knew about the Soviet proposal, only 5 per cent approved the plan. In fact, asked whether or not they would consider the Soviet proposal if the Soviets should flatly refuse the Western idea, 37 per cent of the West German population preferred to have things remain as they were. Less than half (46%) would accept neutrality as a condition, and only 14 per cent would favor reunification if the prerequisite were recognition of the Oder-Neisse line.

Asked about France's attitude with regard to Germany during the conference, 52 per cent of the West Germans and 76 per cent of the West Berliners said France had been more favorable than they had expected. Asked about the Soviet Union, 47 per cent of the West Germans and 52 per cent of the West Berliners said the USSR had behaved as expected, while 25 and 34 per cent respectively felt the Russians had acted more favorably than anticipated.

Report No. 194-V (8 February 1954)

PUBLIC OPINION DURING THE FOUR-POWER CONFERENCE
V. East German Reactions to Western versus Soviet Proposals

Sample: 200 East Berliners, 200 East German residents, 309 West Germans, and 139 West Berliners.

Interviewing dates: survey of East German and East Berlin residents 4 to 8 February 1954; West German and West Berlin survey on 4 to 6 February 1954. (13 pp.)

It should be noted at the outset that the East German respondents were a special rather than representative sample, since interviews were conducted with visitors to the annual "Green Week" (a West Berlin exhibit dealing primarily with agriculture and agricultural products).

Somewhat greater percentages of East Germans (49%) and East Berliners (46%) than West Germans (33%) and West Berliners (37%) thought the four-power conference would result in advantages for Germany. Solid majorities throughout Germany, with even higher figures in the two halves of Berlin, did not, however, think agreement was in fact likely. Most East Germans thought the Western Powers had been more successful up to that point in the conference, while only about a third of the West Germans and West Berliners felt this way; about a fourth of the East Berliners felt that both sides had been equally succussful, while as many as 45 per cent of the West Berliners did. The overwhelming majority of all respondents felt the Western Powers were doing all they could to achieve reunification.

Although a solid majority of East German visitors (as many as 73 per cent in East Berlin) and 55 per cent of the West Berliners had heard of the Eden Plan for German reunification, only 36 per cent of West German exhibit visitors had heard of it. Likewise, 85 per cent of the East Germans, 83 per cent of the East Berliners, and 67 per cent of the West Berliners--but only 56 per cent of the West Germans--had heard of the Molotov Plan. Very few anywhere approved of the latter plan. Also, only between 10 and 16 per cent said they would exchange acceptance of the Oder-Neisse line as a permanent border for reunification. Over 80 per cent of the visitors from the East regarded Molotov's proposal for a plebiscite on a peace treaty or the EDC treaty as a diversionary maneuver; just as great a percentage felt it ought to be rejected.

While over three-quarters of the visitors from the East thought that France was displaying a more favorable attitude toward Germany than expected, only half of the West Germans thought so. Between 5 and 12 per cent felt that Russia's behavior was more favorable than expected, and about half thought it was as expected.

Report No. 194-VI (15 February 1954)

PUBLIC OPINION DURING THE FOUR-POWER CONFERENCE
VI. West German Opinion on Molotov's European Security Proposal and Other Late Conference Developments

Sample: 305 West Germans and 137 West Berliners.
Interviewing dates: 12 to 14 February 1954. (20 pp.)

Decreasing percentages of the West German population were of the opinion that the Western Powers were doing all they could to achieve reunification under conditions acceptable to the Germans. And, although at the end of the second week of the conference there were increasing numbers of persons who felt the Western Powers agreed among themselves about their policy toward the Soviet Union, by the end of the third week this optimism, too, had receded. In both West Germany and West Berlin, decreasing percentages felt the Western Powers had been more successful in attaining their aims than the Russians; in fact, in both areas the percentage of those who thought the Soviet Union had met with greater success increased.

Of the 50 per cent of the West German population who had heard of Soviet Foreign Minister Molotov's proposal for the neutralization of Germany within the framework of a European security pact (which would exclude the United States), only 4 per cent approved the plan; even fewer (3%) approved the security pact. The compromise suggested by French Foreign Minister Bidault, calling for a committee to supervise free elections throughout Germany and comprising representatives from the GDR, the West German federal government, and neutral governments, was approved by 42 per cent of the West German respondents and 65 per cent of the West Berliners. Respondents were then asked whether the West ought to negotiate with the GDR about interzonal trade and removal of interzonal borders if it should happen that the Soviet Union and the Western Powers were unable to come to an agreement on reunification. In West Germany 48 per cent said the West ought to negotiate in such circumstances, 32 per cent said no, and a fifth (20%) had no opinion. In West Berlin almost as many (45%) agreed, while 50 per cent responded negatively. Half the West German population and 77 per cent of the West Berliners continued to favor British Foreign Minister Eden's plan for reunification.

Another alternative calling for an interim solution similar to one being discussed for Austria received about as many positive (37%) as negative (38%) votes in West Germany; in West Berlin, however, 60 per cent approved, 33 per cent opposed, and only 7 per cent reserved judgment. In the event that this conference should fail, only 39 per cent of the West Germans, compared with over half (51%) of the West Berliners, would have preferred to see another conference begun immediately rather than wait for the West to strengthen its position before embarking on new negotiations.

Report No. 195 (11 March 1954)

WHO WON THE FOUR-POWER CONFERENCE?
The West German Public State Their Views

Sample: 634 West Germans and 200 West Berliners.
Interviewing dates: 26 February to 3 March 1954. (25 pp.)

Although the four-power conference did not result in the means to achieve German reunification, the West's handling of the situation seemed to impress the West German and West Berlin populations. Among West Germans, 19 per cent felt the West had gained substantially in prestige, 20 per cent thought they had gained somewhat, and 42 per cent felt there had been no change. In West Berlin, 39 per cent felt they had gained substantially, 20 per cent somewhat, and 33 per cent thought there had been no change. In contrast, when asked the same question about the Soviet Union, very few respondents mentioned either substantial or even limited gains; most (48 per cent in West Germany and 64 per cent in West Berlin) felt there had been no change, and somewhat over a quarter said they thought the Russians had lost substantially.

Large majorities continued to feel that the Western Powers had done all they could to achieve German reunification. In fact, three-quarters (75%) of the West German population and seven in eight (88%) West Berliners thought the Soviet Union was chiefly to blame for the fact that no agreement had been reached on this point.

Although 39 per cent of the West German respondents and 33 per cent of the West Berliners felt that the conference had been of no value, more people (40 per cent in West Germany and 57 per cent in West Berlin) felt the West had achieved some favorable results than thought the Soviet Union had (9 per cent in both areas); almost a quarter felt that both nations had achieved about the same favorable results. Nonetheless, Molotov's tactical skill did not go unnoticed. Large minorities in both West Germany (20%) and West Berlin (21%) expressed the view that the Russians had been more successful in pursuing their aims.

A particularly interesting point about the aftermath of the four-power conference was the sharp drop in opposition to the European Defense Community (EDC). Whereas opposition to German participation in EDC had stood at 31 per cent in December 1953, by early March 1954 it had decreased to 23 per cent, with the result that support (57%) outweighed opposition by two and a half to one. While just as many West Germans felt that EDC would further as hinder reunification (24%), there were almost three times as many (49%) West Berliners who thought EDC would further reunification as thought it would be a hindrance (17%).

Chancellor Konrad Adenauer enjoyed rather widespread popularity among the German people. Solid majorities said this prestige had not changed as a result of the conference.

With absolutely no progress having been made on the reunification question, it is perhaps not surprising that 46 per cent of the West Germans and 49 per cent of the West Berliners felt that, if the Soviet Union should insist they deal directly with the East, the West ought to go ahead and negotiate with the GDR on questions relating to interzonal traffic and trade. Despite the failure of the conference on this question, however, 43 per cent of the West Germans and 54 per cent of the West Berliners thought there would be reunification within the next five years.

The final three sections of the report consist of attitudes toward selected issues on the part of four different population groups: supporters of various political parties, refugees, religious groups, and the young. Of particular interest among the political groups was the SPD. Even among SPD adherents, Adenauer's prestige, if anything, had risen rather than fallen; and, although a far higher percentage of SPD members opposed EDC, about the same percentage of this group (19%) and CDU/CSU members (21%) felt that EDC was hindering reunification. Refugees and Protestants tended to be more satisfied with the course of the conference and the Western Powers' handling of it than were natives and Catholics. A higher percentage of refugees and Protestants also claimed that Adenauer's prestige had risen in their view; and, although more Catholics (70%) than Protestants expressed satisfaction with Adenauer's handling of the reunification issue, there was only a one-point difference. Finally, West German youth seemed far less impressed with Western efforts at the four-power conference than were their elders; at the same time, however, they displayed similar disenchantment with the Soviet efforts.

Report No. 196 (12 April 1954)

CURRENT WEST GERMAN POLITICAL OPINIONS AND REACTIONS TO RECENT DEVELOPMENTS

Sample: 801 and 659 West Germans respectively.
Interviewing dates: 15 to 27 March and 2 to 7 April 1954.
(14 pp.)

One week after the Soviet Union proclaimed the German Democratic Republic to be a sovereign state, 60 per cent of the West German population had neither heard nor read of the event. After those who were unaware of this proclamation were given more information and all respondents were asked which country, East or West Germany, was politically more independent, 82 per cent responded that the West German government was more independent, 3 per cent cited the East German government, and 15 per cent withheld judgment. Just over a third (35%) of the West Germans asked felt that the Federal Republic had relatively great freedom, 19 per cent termed it great, and 6 per cent very great. Almost no one thought the prestige of either the Western Powers or Chancellor Adenauer had been lowered as a result of the Soviet move.

While the percentage of West Germans approving German participation in EDC remained at about the 60 per cent level (29 per cent very much in favor, 33 per cent somewhat in favor), it is interesting to note that in late March the bulk of the population thought it very likely (31%) or likely (30%) that EDC would come into being; a quarter as many thought it somewhat unlikely (10%) or very unlikely (6%); and 23 per cent had no opinion. At the same time, as many as 28 per cent felt that, in the event EDC could not in fact be established, the advantages would balance the disadvantages for Germany; and another 11 per cent thought that it would be advantageous for Germany.

Opinion on the establishment of a West German army followed a somewhat erratic course after February 1952 when the question was first asked. At that time the percentage of those in favor of a West German national army that would participate in the defense of West Europe stood at 43 per cent, and in December 1952 at 47 per cent, only to drop to 42 per cent by June 1953, rise again in November 1953 to 49 per cent, and drop sharply once more--this time all the way down to 40 per cent--in late March 1954. Those preferring that West German divisions be integrated in a general West European army comprised 25 per cent of the sample in February 1952, 22 per cent in December 1952, 28 per cent in June 1953, 24 per cent in November 1953, and 30 per cent in March 1954.

Asked whether or not they would be in favor of concessions by Chancellor Adenauer on the Saar issue to induce France to agree to EDC, roughly half (48%) opposed such a move, only a quarter approved, and 27 per cent had no opinion.

Compared with the previous survey of 26 February to 3 March, a larger percentage (49 per cent, as compared with 46 per cent) of West Germans felt that the West ought to negotiate directly with the East German government on interzonal traffic and trade in the event that the Soviet Union indicated an unwillingness to do so. Finally, 22 per cent of those asked said that recognition of the GDR as the official--although not necessarily legitimate--government of East Germany was necessary, 38 per cent felt that such recognition was not necessary, and 40 per cent expressed no viewpoint on this issue. Only 22 per cent thought that de jure recognition of the GDR would ultimately be necessary.

Special Report No. 196-S1 (17 May 1954)

THE STATUS OF RED-WHITE-RED AMONG AUSTRIAN RADIO LISTENERS
I. Preliminary Report For Vienna and Lower Austria

Sample: 379 residents of Vienna and environs.
Interviewing dates: April 1954. (38 pp.)

Among the three radio stations in the Vienna area which had a large number of listeners, the "Red-White-Red" station was clearly the favorite: 82 per cent of the respondents said they valued it most, whereas only 8 per cent mentioned RAVAG (Radio Vienna), and 5 per cent "Alpenland." Respondents also gave RWR newscasting a high rating for reliability: 47 per cent called it very reliable, another 47 per cent termed it fairly reliable, only 2 per cent felt it was not at all reliable, and no one denied having heard one of the station's newscasts.

Special Report No. 196-S2 (25 May 1954)

THE AMERICAN AND WEST GERMAN AID PROGRAM IN THE EYES OF WEST BERLINERS
With General Indications of Current West Berlin Morale

Sample: 415 West Berliners.
Interviewing dates: 5 to 15 April 1954. (94 pp.)

Almost a quarter (24%) of the city's population felt that West Berlin's economic situation was bad; 57 per cent termed it fair. Disregarding the political situation, 57 per cent said they thought the most important problem facing the city was unemployment, while 18 per cent cited the economic situation. Of the 84 per cent who thought the unemployment problem was serious, very serious, or dangerously serious, 19 per cent explained that unemployment was producing discontent. Fully 60 per cent of the city's population felt that Berlin's economic situation was an international rather than purely national problem. In addition, 95 per cent of the people said that West Berlin needed outside economic aid. Of these, 33 per cent argued that Berlin was too poor to handle the task alone, another 33 per cent cited the city's island position, and 20 per cent mentioned the unemployment problem. Most West Berliners (44%) looked to West Germany for this aid, but over a third (35%) said that the United States should provide assistance, mainly because it was felt that America was best able to help.

Only a small fraction (6%) said that West Berlin was receiving no help from West Germany, although opinion varied widely on its extent. At the same time, although 58 per cent thought West Germany was doing its share in helping the city, about half as many (31%) felt it was doing less than its share. As far as American aid was concerned, 16 per cent rated it as very much, 38 per cent called it much aid, and as many as 37 per cent had no opinion on the matter. The vast majority of respondents said that America's motives in giving the aid were good. Almost three-quarters (74%) felt that the flow of aid would continue, while only 7 per cent thought it would be decreased. In fact, 36 per cent felt it was highly necessary and 32 per cent termed it very necessary, while only one per cent said it was not so necessary. Furthermore, a solid majority (64%) did not think West Germany could take on the extra burden if American aid were discontinued, although 15 per cent thought Bonn would certainly try to do so.

Most West Berliners did not feel that their incomes were adequate, nor did they feel economically secure. Just over a quarter (29%) said they were better off then than they had been a year earlier, 26 per cent viewed their situation as worse, 29 per cent just as good, 15 per cent just as bad, and one per cent had no opinion on the question. However, a solid majority (53%) saw the economic situation developing favorably, while only 12 per cent saw it in an unfavorable light. At the same time, 64 per cent thought their own financial prospects for the coming year would remain the same, 14 per cent anticipated higher incomes, 7 per cent anticipated lower incomes, and 14 per cent said it would depend on various factors. Long-range expectations were far higher: 38 per cent felt their situation would be better in five years, while only 5 per cent said they felt it would be worse.

A high proportion of West Berliners continued to feel that the residents of the city would accept a continuation of their troubled situation even if it went on for twenty years. In February 1953, 78 per cent had voiced this opinion; by April 1954 the figure had dropped by only six percentage points. Moreover, 75 per cent still insisted that they would not leave Berlin even if they had the opportunity to do so.

Report No. 197 (14 June 1954)

THE IMPACT OF AMERICAN COMMERCIAL FILMS IN WEST GERMANY

Sample: 2,000 West Germans.
Interviewing dates: late spring 1953. (56 pp.)

Although fairly sizable minorities reported going to the movies once a week (13%), two to three times a week (14%), or about once a month (14%), almost the same percentage (12%) said they had never been to a movie at all. Not surprisingly, most West Germans (78%) said they liked German films best. The number of films from the United States far exceeded the number from any other country.

Almost half (45%) of those who had seen several American films thought these films had mainly a favorable influence on the German population. Interestingly enough, among those who had seen only one or two, somewhat fewer (29%) saw so favorable an influence. Unfavorable influences were also mentioned: chief among the concerns were westerns and gangster films.

Given a list of eleven aspects of the American way of life (listed in order of favorable ranking: standard of living, police, outlook on life, men, upbringing and behavior of children, role of women, businessmen and business life, interest in religious affairs, family and married life, treatment of Negroes, crime and gangsterism), in all but the last three instances more people said that American films gave a favorable impression of this aspect of life than said the opposite. A further tabulation revealed that, in each of the eleven areas investigated, the primary effect of American commercial films on West German viewers was a reinforcement of beliefs already held.

Report No. 198 (15 June 1954)

TRENDS IN WEST GERMAN APPRAISAL OF THE UNITED STATES FORCES IN GERMANY

Sample: 1,596 West Germans and 462 residents from Rhineland Palatinate.
Interviewing dates: Spring 1954. (111 pp.)

From December 1951 to late spring 1954 there was an upward trend in every aspect of German-U.S. troop relations for which data were collected. The same was true of German esteem for the combat qualities of the American forces stationed in Germany.

The 1954 survey revealed that about six in ten Germans felt that relations with American armed forces had improved (compared with about four in ten who had held this opinion one year earlier). Much of this goodwill seemed to stem from the German-American Christmas program, which increasing numbers of persons had heard of and considered a real contribution to mutual understanding. Approximately one-third of the population thought relations between Germans and Americans would not be affected if Germany had soldiers of its own; almost as many, however, had no opinion on the subject.

While a clear majority of Germans said there was nothing in particular that they did not like about the American soldiers, some felt differently (17 per cent in West Germany, 19 per cent in AMZON, and 24 per cent in Rhineland Palatinate). The most frequently voiced complaints dealt with lack of discipline, overly casual manners, sloppiness, and loudness.

Cross-tabulations of responses to some of the questions discussed above revealed that the more contact West Germans had with American soldiers, the more likely they were to note improved relations. Even among those who said the troops behaved badly and those who found nothing pleasing about the soldiers' appearance or manners, majorities said that rapport between the two groups had improved.

Although West Germans consistently ranked their own men ahead of all others in combat qualities, during the three years under consideration the percentage of West Germans rating American soldiers in second place doubled (from 12 to 24 per cent). However, the Russians drew still more support for second place: in each of the three surveys, 31 per cent of the West German population said they were second best. Most of the reasons given for this high regard emphasized the Russians' endurance, simplicity of demands, the discipline invoked by communism, and their disregard for life. West Germans regarded the American soldier as a healthy, nice person, strongly supported by technological achievements, but lacking in toughness and aggressiveness.

In 1954 a sizable minority (30%) of the West German population continued to regard the American soldiers chiefly as occupation troops. Far more (45%) regarded them as protection for Western Europe, however, and 13 per cent felt they performed both functions. Asked what the main advantage of the United States troop presence was, 45 per cent mentioned external security. The most frequently mentioned disadvantage was the cost of maintaining them.

Hand in hand with this growing approval of the presence of American troops in Germany, increasing numbers of Germans also approved of the presence of military families. Most of those who disapproved retracted this opinion when asked how they would feel on this subject if the United States would provide housing rather than using available German homes.

Report No. 199 (18 June 1954)

WEST GERMANS STATE THEIR VIEWS ON THE ROLE OF ATOMIC WEAPONS IN WESTERN DEFENSE

Sample: 618 West Germans and 263 West Berliners.
Interviewing dates: 26 April to 10 May 1954. (77 pp.)

Solid majorities of West Germans were aware that both the United States (84%) and the Soviet Union (71%) possessed the hydrogen bomb. Most (80%) also knew that hydrogen bomb tests had recently been conducted. Although almost as many were opposed to such tests (35%) as favored them (37%), the opinion-leading elements in the population tended to be in the latter group.

In the event of another world war, 33 per cent felt that atomic and hydrogen bombs would be used, while 49 per cent did not think so. If bombs of even greater destructive power were to be produced, 31 per cent thought this would increase the danger of another war, 28 per cent felt it would reduce the danger, and 25 per cent could give no opinion on the matter.

Asked which country they thought would be the most likely target for atomic weapons, 41 per cent replied Germany. A solid majority (67%) believed the United States would use the weapons only in an extreme emergency.

Only one in seven (14%) was unconditionally opposed to America's use of atomic weapons. A quarter (26%) saw such use justified only if someone else used them first; 32 per cent felt their use was justified only in certain circumstances; and 28 per cent expressed no opinion. If the Soviet Union were to attack West Germany without using atomic weapons, 22 per cent would agree to their use by the Americans, while 60 per cent would not. Virtually all population groups showed majority opposition on this question.

Along with this negative attitude toward atomic weapons, decreasing percentages of West Germans favored participation in EDC. Between early March and May of 1954, the share of those very much for such a move dropped from 30 to 27 per cent, and those somewhat for it from 33 to 26 per cent. The proportion somewhat opposed dropped from 13 to 10 per cent, but those very much against it increased from 13 to 17 per cent. A question designed to test whether West Germans thought the new atomic weapons had decreased the importance of the EDC revealed that 21 per cent shared this view, while 45 per cent felt EDC had not diminished in importance. It should be noted that opinion leaders were more inclined both to support EDC and to feel its importance was undiminished.

Close to half of the West German population (46%) said they approved of America's recently announced intention to use massive retaliation in the event of an attack on any of the Western nations. Opinion was nonetheless divided on what exactly such retaliatory measures might entail: 42 per cent thought they meant the use of atomic weapons, while 33 per cent did not interpret the term in this way. In any case, majorities in both opinion groups felt that the Americans would in fact carry out the threat if necessary.

A majority of the respondents (63%) was unaware that the United States had made efforts to prevent the use of atomic energy for war purposes. Almost a quarter (24%) thought America should have done more to reach an agreement banning atomic weapons. Furthermore, 40 per cent felt that the United States ought to do more about the peaceful uses of atomic energy.

Report No. 200 (28 June 1954)

CURRENT TRENDS IN WEST GERMAN OPINIONS ON MAJOR POLITICAL ISSUES
With Reactions to Bonn-Moscow Overtures and the Geneva Conference

Sample: 599 West Germans.
Interviewing dates: 7 to 16 June 1954. (71 pp.)

Recent Bonn-Moscow overtures. Over half (58%) of the West German population favored the establishment of diplomatic relations between the Soviet Union and West Germany. Of these, well over half (35%) said they too would be against the move if the price were recognition for the GDR.

Geneva Conference. Somewhat over half of the West German population (54%) was aware of the international conference taking place at Geneva, and another 12 per cent had heard of the meeting but did not know where it was taking place. Most of these aware respondents felt the meeting had some degree of importance for Germany, but 12 per cent attached no importance to it at all.

Desirability of a further conference with the Russians. Most West Germans (67%) said they would like to see another conference on Germany, although very few thought the reunification issue could be settled. Even when several arguments against holding further meetings with the Soviet Union were listed, 55 per cent said they wanted more negotiations to take place.

American prestige. Although the percentage of those ranking American prestige as high to very high had dropped between January 1954 (55%) and June 1954 (48%), it was still higher than it had been six months earlier, when it had stood at 42 per cent. Those considered the opinion-leading elements in the society tended to rank American prestige highest. Furthermore, 77 per cent of the population ranked the United States as the political leader of the Western world, and most thought it either well or very well fitted for this role.

Communist vs. Western strength, neutralism, and fear of war. Except in November 1953--following Stalin's death, the East German uprisings, and the Korean armistice--when the Western Powers were clearly ahead, opinion was always fairly evenly divided on whether the communists or the Western Powers had been more successful in the political arena during the previous few months. A decreasing percentage (from 66 per cent in November 1953 to 58 per cent in June 1954) thought the Western Powers had the better chance to win ultimately in the East-West struggle. Increasing percentages felt that West Germany ought to remain neutral, even in the event of war. In the early summer of 1954, twice as many people (22%) thought there would be another world war within three or four years as had thought so six months earlier (10%).

EDC support and national army preference. Although slightly over half continued to be either somewhat or very much for participation in EDC, the trend was definitely downward. Support for such a move was highest among the opinion leaders. More people favored a national army to an integrated European army. If France decided to turn down EDC, then 41 per cent felt that West Germany ought to plan its rearmament with the United States and other Western European countries without regard to France.

A solid majority (about 75 per cent in each of three surveys taken in 1952 and 1954) favored efforts at uniting Western Europe. Support was highest among opinion leaders.

Satisfaction with the present régime and Chancellor Adenauer's handling of the Saar issue. While the percentage of those fairly satisfied with Chancellor Adenauer dropped somewhat between 1952 (47%) and 1954 (37%), the percentage of those very satisfied rose dramatically, from 11 to 36 per cent. About one-third (30%) were satisfied with Adenauer's handling of the Saar issue, and 23 per cent were dissatisfied

Recognition of the East German régime. Increasing percentages of West Germans felt that it would not be necessary to recognize the GDR; by June 1954, fully 50 per cent were of this opinion. A somewhat higher percentage favored recognition if it would result in better interzonal traffic and trade conditions. A majority of 60 per cent said they would be for recognition if it would substantially improve conditions for the East German population.

Report No. 201 (20 August 1954)

ESTIMATES OF SOVIET ZONE AUDIENCES OF RIAS PROGRAM FEATURES

Sample: not indicated.
Interviewing dates: not indicated. (42 pp.)

The report consists of the complete RIAS program for each day of the week, together with the percentage of listenership for each time slot broken down according to sex, age, and education.

Report No. 202 (8 September 1954)

GERMAN REACTIONS TO THE JOHN AFFAIR AND OTHER RECENT POLITICAL EVENTS
With Trends on EDC, Further European Conferences, and Related Issues

Sample: 902 West Germans and 305 West Berliners.
Interviewing dates: 19 to 27 August 1954. (79 pp.)

An overwhelming majority of West Germans (82%) and West

Berliners (92%) knew that Dr. Otto John, head of the Federal Office for the Protection of the Constitution, had defected to East Germany earlier in the summer. Most thought the defection had lowered West German prestige, but a sizable minority of West Germans (25%) were undecided on this question. Adenauer's prestige, however, was less affected by the John affair. Although 29 per cent felt his prestige had gone down, 43 per cent did not think so.

Relatively few people knew that the Soviet Union had recently sent two notes to the Western Powers regarding Germany as well as the general European situation. After being informed that one of the notes called for a new conference with the Soviet Union, 59 per cent of the respondents said they favored such a meeting; 14 per cent said they did not care. Opinion leaders tended to be more in favor than others. Almost no one, however, thought the chances were good that such a meeting would result in reunification. The percentage of persons who thought "these never-ending negotiations with the communists" ought to be stopped because they led nowhere dropped between June and late August 1954 from 55 to 48 per cent; in West Berlin it was already as low as 29 per cent. At the same time, only 43 per cent were willing to accept neutrality as the price for reunification, a drop of twelve percentage points since July 1953.

Although increasing percentages of West Germans were aware of EDC (by late August 1954 the figure was up to 83 per cent), the percentage of those very much in favor of it was dropping (23%), and less than a third (31%) continued to be somewhat for it; decreasing percentages were opposed, but increasing percentages were uncertain. Support for EDC was highest among the opinion leaders. The question of a national versus European army continued to cause uncertainty. The trend showed that in late August 1954 somewhat fewer (38%) favored a national army; the percentage of those favoring a European army had settled at about one-fourth (26 per cent, having fluctuated from 22 up to 30 per cent in earlier surveys); and the percentage of those expressing no opinion had jumped rather dramatically (from 29 per cent in June to 36 per cent in August). However, in the event that France refused to ratify EDC, over three in five (62%) thought West Germany ought to try to achieve an agreement with America and other West European countries without regard to France.

Over half (55%) of the population favored immediate and complete sovereignty for West Germany. A sizable minority (13%) nonetheless had some misgivings about this prospect, and fully 25 per cent were undecided. The percentage of persons foreseeing difficulties if Germany were granted full sovereignty rose to about one-fourth when specific issues such as reunification or American aid were brought into the picture.

By late August 1954 the communists had recovered their strength in the international political arena, at least in the eyes of the West German public (having risen from the low of 8 per cent registered in November 1953 to 38 per cent). In fact, they outranked the Western Powers for the first time. The West had dropped in prestige from its high point of 46 per cent in November 1953 to a new low of 17 per cent. Most of the changes seemed due to events in Indochina and Korea.

Most West Germans continued to be either very (21%) or fairly (51%) satisfied with the activities of the Adenauer government. Only 15 per cent expressed dissatisfaction, while almost no one (3%) was greatly dissatisfied.

Special Report No. 202-S (2 November 1954)

POST-EDC CLIMATE OF WEST EUROPEAN OPINION
With Reactions to the London Conference

Sample: 800 adults (21 years of age and over) in West Germany, France, Italy, and Great Britain.
Interviewing dates: 15 to 28 October 1954. (22 pp.)

Majorities in West Germany (70%), France (63%), and Great Britain (61%), but only 44 per cent in Italy, had heard of the recent nine-power conference held in London. Of these, very few favored the old plan for a European Defense Community. In West Germany 27 per cent preferred the London Conference decision on German rearmament; in France it was only 22 per cent and in Great Britain 21 per cent.

Between September 1952 and October 1954 increasing majorities in all four countries were in favor of a Western European Union. Among those aware of the London Conference, most respondents viewed it as a step toward such a union.

Very large minorities in each country had no opinion on political leaders from other than their own country. However, more Italians and Britons had a good opinion of Chancellor Konrad Adenauer than had a bad one, as was true in France, Italy, and Great Britain with regard to Secretary of State John Foster Dulles.

Asked whether they approved or disapproved of America's attitude toward France regarding Europe and European defense, 34 per cent of the West Germans, but only 18 per cent of the French themselves, said they approved; in both countries the "don't knows" received a majority of the responses (55 and 57 per cent respectively). With respect to Germany, almost half of the French respondents (46%) thought American treatment too favorable, while 73 per cent of the West Germans, 30 per cent of the Italians, and 48 per cent of the British felt it to be about right.

In both West Germany and Great Britain, approximately 60 per cent of the population felt their government ought to side with the West. In France and Italy, however, only about 40 per cent held this view. If it came to war between the United States and the Soviet Union, about half the populations of West Germany, France, and Italy said their countries should not take sides; in Great Britain, 52 per cent said they should side with the United States. Asked which side they thought had the better chance to win ultimately in the East-West struggle, about half the West Germans and British thought the Western Powers did, while 52 per cent of the French and 45 per cent of the Italians said they didn't know.

If Russia were to suggest an East-West conference on the German problem, a solid majority of West Germans (64%), French (56%), and British (54%) said they thought the West ought to accept it; in Italy only 46 per cent thought so. Very few people in any of the countries, however, thought there was much chance for a solution to the problem at such a conference.

Asked whether the United States or the Soviet Union was more to blame for the conflict between the two nations, 53 per cent of the West Germans pointed to the Soviet Union. Very few in any of the countries surveyed singled out the United States, but over a fourth (in France the figure was as high as 40 per cent) blamed both sides.

In all four countries solid majorities were unaware of any proposal for the international use of atomic energy for peaceful purposes. Of the minority who had heard of such a proposal, almost all knew that the suggestion had come from the United States.

Less than half the respondents (in France the figure was as low as 29 per cent) felt that the United States should increase its efforts to counter communism in the Far East; large minorities gave no answer to the question. Opinion was split on whether or not the United States ought to oppose the move by force of arms if China were to attack Formosa. One-fourth of the West Germans and Italians, 35 per cent of the British, and 37 per cent of the French felt that Communist China ought to be admitted to the United Nations.

Most West Germans (69%) considered reunification to be a more pressing problem than European union. About the same number (62%) were satisfied with the way Chancellor Adenauer was dealing with the issue.

Report No. 203 (10 November 1954)

EAST ZONE REFUGEES REPORT ON THEIR RADIO LISTENING HABITS

Sample: 1,027 refugees from East Germany and 377 refugees respectively.
Interviewing dates: May to June 1954 and late May 1954. (24 pp.)

Whereas in June 1951, 78 per cent of a group of refugees and visitors from the East had said they listened mainly to RIAS while in the GDR, some three years later this figure had dropped sharply to 31 per cent; another 33 per cent claimed to listen sometimes. By way of contrast, RIAS's closest rival, NWDR, had gained in popularity with a jump from 6 per cent to 37 per cent. East German stations were also more popular: 23 per cent said they listened to them mainly, while another 58 per cent said they listened sometimes.

As for the VOA program, 62 per cent reported listening to it at some time during the year before their flight to the West. Most who had stopped listening said it was due to poor reception, to jamming.

Among VOA listeners, 30 per cent said they also listened to BBC, while 43 per cent said they listened only to VOA. However, in the event of a serious political crisis, more people said they would tune in VOA than BBC.

Report No. 204 (29 November 1954)

RADIO DIARY STUDY IN WEST GERMANY AND WEST BERLIN, MAY 1954

Sample: 1,013 listeners in West Germany and 488 in West Berlin.
Interviewing dates: 17 to 23 May 1954. (179 pp.)

The most popular station in West Germany was clearly NWDR, with 60 per cent of the radio audience. Radio Munich was second, with 27 per cent of the respondents saying they listened to it; while Frankfurt and Süd-West Funk were third (25%). It should be noted, however, that each station was the most popular in its own particular region.

Almost all radio listeners in West Berlin listened to RIAS. The average amount of time spent listening to the station was 17.7 hours per week. The second most frequently listened-to station was NWDR, with 75 per cent. In addition, 14 per cent of the radio audience said they listened to East German stations.

Report No. 205 (1 December 1954)

THE BERLIN ATOMIC ENERGY EXHIBIT
West and East German Reactions

Sample: a total of 998 people 15 years of age and over: 398 general visitors from West Berlin and West Germany, 223 East Berliners, 177 East German visitors, and 200 members of special groups from West Berlin touring the exhibit.
Interviewing dates: 15 October to 15 November 1954. (54 pp.)

The vast majority (87%) of visitors to the exhibit accepted the idea that atomic energy would bring benefits to mankind. No one described the exhibit in negative terms, and only one per cent described it as merely fair.

A solid majority (ranging from 79 per cent of the invited visitors to 91 per cent of the general West Berlin and West German visitors) felt that the exhibit gave an honest picture of the efforts being made by the United States in the field of atomic energy. Most of those who disagreed thought the military purposes ought to have been shown as well, to balance the picture.

A great many people said they had learned something from the exhibit; in fact, only 17 per cent said they had learned nothing. Most (37%) mentioned applications of atomic energy in the field of medicine.

Report No. 206 (6 December 1954)

CURRENT GERMAN OPINION ON THE SAAR
(Following the Paris Agreement)

Sample: 654 West Germans.
Interviewing dates: 9 to 20 November 1954. (55 pp.)

While a solid majority (70%) continued to feel that reunification was the most important task facing the federal government at that time, a sizable minority (16%) also mentioned the Saar issue. Despite this relatively low level of salience, 53 per cent knew that a Saar agreement had recently been signed; of these, 31 per cent were aware that it was not a final settlement, and 20 per cent were opposed to it. Among those who had to be told what the agreement was, more people favored (16%) than opposed it (8%), and 23 per cent had no opinion on the matter. Among all those opposed to the agreement, over half (19%) continued to express opposition even if asked to suppose that the Saar agreement was necessary to get France's approval for increased German sovereignty and for armament. Asked how they thought the people of the Saar themselves would respond to the agreement, 27 per cent thought they would approve it, 28 per cent thought it would be rejected, and 45 per cent were uncertain. In any case, 52 per cent said they did not think it would have been possible to reach a better agreement.

Only somewhat more than a third (37%) of the respondents said they could see why France was making certain demands regarding the Saar. And over half (53%) did not think the demands were in any way justified. Asked to consider the fact of Germany's involvement in the last two wars, 80 per cent of the respondents nonetheless said they thought Germany had the greater claim to the Saar. However, only 37 per cent thought the region would in fact belong to Germany once again at some future date; 18 per cent thought it would come under West European control, 12 per cent felt it would become a sovereign state, and 29 per cent were uncertain.

By way of contrast, 42 per cent were certain that the Oder-Neisse territories would be returned eventually to Germany. Furthermore, 72 per cent felt that Germany ought not to resign itself to their loss, even if this could be made the price of reunification.

The percentage of persons ranking Adenauer's prestige as high to very high--never below the 50 per cent level--stood at 60 per cent in mid-November 1954. Most people were also either very satisfied (34%) or fairly satisfied (41%) with the chancellor's government. There were nonetheless four specific issue areas in which a sizable minority expressed dissatisfaction with Adenauer or reserved judgment: independence, reunification, remilitarization, and the Saar. Regarding the last of these, 38 per cent said they thought Mendes-France had accomplished more for his side during the Saar Agreement negotiations than had Adenauer; in fact, 25 per cent felt the chancellor's prestige had been either markedly or at least somewhat lowered through these negotiations.

The prestige of the four major powers--the United States, Great Britain, France, and the Soviet Union--all rose somewhat compared to the results of a survey conducted some two months earlier, but none scored very high. The Soviet Union was given a high to very high ranking by only 4 per cent of the population; 73 per cent ranked it low to very low. The United States ranked high to very high with 42 per cent of the West Germans; however, while this was higher than the 38 per cent registered in early September 1954, it was much lower than the 55 per cent attained in mid-January of the same year.

Special Report No. 206-S (4 February 1955)

THE CURRENT STATE OF MORALE AMONG YOUTH IN WEST BERLIN

Sample: 313 West Berliners and 137 refugees from East Germany, all between the ages of 14 and 24.
Interviewing dates: mid-January 1955. (56 pp.)

Almost all the young West Berliners interviewed conceded that there had been some degree of economic recovery in their city. Among the young East German refugees, too, the majority said they had received better treatment economically than expected during their first month in the West, and many more (78%) said they were satisfied with the way their economic situation had developed since then. Both groups saw Berlin's economic future in a bright light, the refugees being more optimistic than the West Berliners.

Asked whether or not they thought young people were getting their fair share of West Berlin's recovery, majorities in all groups responded positively. West Berliners between the ages of 18 and 24 were less happy (64%) than those from 14 to 17 (74%), and both of these groups said they thought West Berlin authorities were concerned with their welfare. Most were aware of special institutions and programs for the young in the city.

Very few belonged to any youth organizations, but those who did belong felt they gained a great deal from their membership.

Unemployment was regarded as a problem by most West Berlin youth but only a minority of the refugees. In fact, whereas only 3 per cent of the West Berliners viewed the situation as "not serious at all," 23 per cent of those from the East held this view. Furthermore, whereas 91 per cent of the West Berliners thought the city needed outside economic aid, only 75 per cent of the refugees thought this necessary.

A majority (61%) of the West Berlin youth and even more (77%) of the young East German refugees were in favor of West German rearmament. Very small percentages had no opinion on this subject. Among the fairly small percentage (about 33 per cent) of respondents who knew that there had been anti-rearmament demonstrations in West Germany, almost all opposed them.

Although over three-quarters of the respondents felt that the democratic form of government then in existence in West Berlin was the best form to have for the city, about 16 per cent expressed no opinion on this matter. Among the small percentage opposed, the single major point made was the need for a strong leader, a unitary authority.

During the preceding twelve-month period, only 37 per cent of the West Berliners interviewed had not been to East Berlin. Quite a few had been there for extensive visits, up to two weeks. Most had noticed sharp differences between the two halves of the city, primarily in the higher standard of living in the West. Despite what they themselves had seen, 28 per cent in both groups said they knew of people who had gone to the East to live, and another 40 per cent of the East German refugee group said they knew of people who had fled to the West and then returned to the East. Most of the young people interviewed did not think the East was better than the West in any way; but about a third in both groups thought it was, with most of these mentioning military strength.

Asked whether they thought the West did as much for the younger generation as the East, 52 per cent of the young West Berliners between the ages of 14 and 17 said they thought the West did more, while only 41 per cent of those between the ages of 18 and 24 held this view. Among East German youth the figure stood at 51 per cent. At the same time, 28 per cent of the 18- to 24-year olds in the West felt the West did less than the East, 19 per cent of those from 14 to 17 years old did also, and only 14 per cent of all the East German refugees did.

Only 45 per cent of the refugees had never watched or visited one of the Communist youth rallies in East Berlin. Among those who had, most had been either unfavorably (17%) or very unfavorably (22%) impressed.

Report No. 207 (4 February 1955)

PUBLIC OPINION IN WESTERN GERMANY ON THE REESTABLISH—MENT OF MILITARY FORCES

Sample: 1,867 West Germans, including 206 between the ages of 18 and 24.
Interviewing dates: 6 to 22 January 1955. (42 pp.)

In late 1954 and early 1955, rearmament was without a doubt the hottest issue of the day in West Germany. On 5 May 1955, some three months after completion of the survey, Germany formally joined NATO, and rearmament was in fact begun.

Support for the idea of West German participation in the defense of Western Europe had decreased steadily since reaching its high point in June 1953, when almost three out of five were for it. By January 1955 the figure had dropped to 45 per cent. Among those of draft age the figure was even lower (41%). Despite this opposition, only 34 per cent of the population was aware of the anti-rearmament demonstrations which had taken place in several West German cities shortly before the interviews. Most of those who did know about them disapproved of them.

Fully 60 per cent of the population said that, regardless of their personal feeling, they thought an army was in fact necessary, primarily to protect the country. In addition, 41 per cent were in favor of compulsory service (although only 30 per cent of the draft-age respondents held this view). Among the male population, only 7 per cent said they would like to become soldiers, 20 per cent said they would not mind being drafted for a limited period, and 27 per cent said they would not like being drafted but would be willing to serve. About three in ten said they would try to evade the draft (18%) or refuse to serve (11%). Among the female respondents, 34 per cent felt that young men should not mind being drafted for a limited time; 11 per cent thought all men ought to refuse to serve. Breakdowns according to age revealed that draft-age men were more willing to serve than the male population in general.

Although the SPD leadership was strongly opposed to rearmament, adherents of the party were only somewhat more opposed than members of other parties.

Report No. 208 (15 February 1955)

FRANKFURT VISITORS APPRAISE THE ATOMIC ENERGY EXHIBIT "ATOMS FOR PEACE"

Sample: 400 exhibit visitors, 15 years of age and over.
Interviewing dates: 10 to 29 January 1955. (33 pp.)

The survey was conducted for comparison with an earlier survey (Report No. 205) of visitors to this exhibit when it was shown in West Berlin. The findings suggested that the enthusiasm of the Frankfurt visitors was no less than that of Berliners.

Although the figure was not as high as in Berlin (85%), a solid majority of the Frankfurt visitors (77%) rated the exhibit very good or even excellent. No one rated it bad.

Far more visitors to the exhibit in Berlin (91%) felt that it showed a valid picture of America's efforts to exploit the peaceful uses of atomic energy than was true among the Frankfurt visitors (71%). Of the 17 per cent in Frankfurt who thought it showed too favorable a picture, most mentioned that the military uses had been overlooked.

Report No. 209 (11 March 1955)

GERMAN ATTITUDES TOWARD FRANCE AND THE FRENCH
A Program Guidance Study on Franco-German Rapprochement

Sample: 1,529 West Germans and 198 West Berliners.
Interviewing dates: December 1954. (138 pp.)

Less than a fourth (24%) of the West German population had ever been in France, and of these about half had been there as soldiers. Almost no one had lost a very close relative in France during World War II. A sizable minority knew some French people, and about the same percentage said they were interested in getting to know France and the French people better. The same percentage (14%) said they could speak French as said they could speak English.

Only one in five (21%) considered the country one of Germany's enemies.

Between 1952 and 1954 increasing percentages of West Germans said they liked the French as a people (from 36 per cent to 42 per cent). The rate of decrease for those disliking the French was even stronger (from 37 per cent to 12 per cent). Asked what in turn they thought French opinion of Germany was, more people thought it was good (10%) or fair (35%) than bad (33%) or very bad (5%). (These figures were quite close to the actual ones obtained in France in a survey conducted in mid-October 1954.)

Although there were almost twice as many people who thought relations between France and Germany were good in December 1954 as had thought so one year earlier, the percentage of those describing these relations as not too good also rose; there was a large decrease in the no-opinion group. Almost six in ten (59%) felt the antagonism toward Germany in France was stronger than that in Germany toward France. Over a third could see some justification for this.

Franco-German rapprochement was viewed favorably by a large majority of West Germans (75%) and even more West Berliners (93%). Almost as many thought such an understanding would in fact come about, and approximately the same percentage felt it to be necessary. As for what they thought each side was actually doing toward this end, only about a third felt France was doing anything, while almost three-quarters

(74%) thought their own country was doing something. Asked what they thought stood in the way of a rapprochement between the two countries, 60 per cent mentioned specific issues, primarily the Saar issue and German rearmament. Far more West Germans felt that France ought to make some concessions (57%) than felt their own country ought to (22%); in fact, 38 per cent said they did not think Germany should make any concessions. Again, the issue mentioned most frequently was the Saar territory.

Asked in what areas they thought the Germans and the French were superior to each other, 41 per cent said they felt the Germans were superior in morals, general character, and attitudes toward work; another 41 per cent mentioned business, technology, and agriculture. The areas mentioned for French superiority were not mentioned at all for Germany: fashion and cosmetics (16%), the art of living (13%), and human relations (6%). Regarding various other aspects of French life, a majority had a favorable opinion of French culture, while pluralities viewed favorably their religious life, general outlook on life, and family life. French politics, as well as the business and industrial spheres, tended to be regarded unfavorably.

Special Report No. 209-S (23 March 1955)

WEST EUROPEAN PUBLIC OPINION ON CURRENT ISSUES

Sample: 800 adults 21 years of age and over in West Germany, France, Italy, and Great Britain.
Interviewing dates: 3 to 17 February 1955. (24 pp.)

Between September 1952 and February 1955, increasing majorities in the populations of West Germany and Great Britain favored greater efforts toward a united Europe, with Great Britain included; in France and Italy the percentages dropped. As for the establishment of a West European defense organization, majorities in all the countries except France felt it to be necessary; France had the highest percentage of "don't knows" on this question (35%). Half the British population and almost that many in Italy (48%) favored German participation in the defense of Europe; in France the figure was as low as 29 per cent, while 43 per cent opposed such participation.

Asked how they thought relations between their country and the United States were at that time, the only country in which less than a majority thought they were good was France; again the no-opinion category was large in France (24%). Responses to the same question regarding the Soviet Union were far more varied. In Italy, for instance, 10 per cent termed relations with the USSR fair, 40 per cent poor, 19 per cent very poor, and 29 per cent had no opinion; in Great Britain, by contrast 46 per cent rated them fair, 18 per cent poor, 8 per cent very poor, and 13 per cent had no opinion.

Decreasing percentages in all four countries between 1952 and 1955 felt that their country ought to side with the West. In West Germany, Italy, and Great Britain, increasing minorities said they thought their country ought to remain neutral;

while in France the greatest jump was in the no-opinion group. Even if war should break out, increasing percentages of the populations (reaching as high as 54 per cent in France in October 1954) felt their country ought to remain neutral. Many of these, however, did not think it would in fact be possible to do so. Only the British population showed some optimism about the outcome of an East-West conference, but even there only 21 per cent thought the chances were good for achieving some beneficial results. The predominent opinion was that the chances were poor, and up to 38 per cent (in France) had no opinion on the matter.

Opinions varied markedly on the question of whether or not there would be a war within the next three or four years. In Great Britain, 60 per cent (up from 47 per cent in October 1954) thought war would be avoided, while 10 per cent (down from 28 per cent) said it would be avoided only in certain circumstances, and 21 per cent did not know. During the same period in France, however, decreasing percentages thought war would be avoided (55 per cent down to 44 per cent), the percentage of those thinking there would be a war almost doubled (from 7 per cent to 13 per cent), and a somewhat greater percentage had no opinion. As many as 40 per cent (in France) did not think the United States was doing all it could to prevent war. A fairly large minority in each of the four countries continued to blame both sides rather than any single country for the tension between the two great powers.

Except in France, where the percentage stood at a very low 37 per cent, solid majorities (with a high of 71 per cent in Great Britain) had heard or read of the North Atlantic Treaty Organization. Even greater majorities (including the French) said they would favor an East-West agreement prohibiting the manufacture of all atomic weapons. But less than a third felt that such an agreement was a real possibility. Except in France, where the question was not asked, overwhelming majorities opposed the use of atomic weapons. Somewhat over half (except in Italy, with only 47 per cent) had heard of peaceful uses of atomic energy. Far fewer knew that an actual proposal had been made for the international use of atomic energy or that it was the United States that had made the proposal.

Asked their opinion of specific political leaders in various countries, the West Germans had the lowest percentage of "don't knows." Secretary of State John Foster Dulles received the highest vote of confidence (in Great Britain and West Germany) followed by Eden (in West Germany). For most of the leaders, the percentages centered on the "good" or "fair" opinion groups, with substantial "don't knows" throughout. The same was true of opinions concerning each other as well as Communist China and the Soviet Union.

Relatively few people had heard the expression "peaceful coexistence." Of the 29 per cent in West Germany who had heard it, 19 per cent felt it was idealistic, 2 per cent regarded it as propaganda, and 8 per cent had no opinion. Again in West Germany, 13 per cent (of the 29 per cent who had heard the phrase) thought the Soviet Union had also used it, 5 per cent did not think so, and 11 per cent did not know.

Opinion split sharply on the question of whether or not the United States acts the way it talks. The highest rating for the United States in this regard came from West Germany (49%), the lowest from France (20%). In both France and Italy about half had no opinion on this question. As for the Soviet Union, 63 per cent of the West Germans, 42 per cent of the British, 32 per cent of the French, and 30 per cent of the Italians felt its actions differed too often from its words.

Asked about the Communist party in their own country, 60 per cent of the West German respondents felt it was losing ground, while in Great Britain 46 per cent held this view, in France 27 per cent, and in Italy 23 per cent. Only in Italy did a sizable minority (22%) feel it was gaining. About a fourth in all the countries surveyed felt it was staying the same.

Report No. 210 (15 April 1955)

AN APPRAISAL OF THE AMERICA HOUSES IN GERMANY
A Program Guidance Study on Effectiveness of the U.S. Information Centers

Sample: 1,611 West Germans 18 years of age and over, as well as 4,383 visitors to America Houses in West Germany and West Berlin 15 years of age and over.
Interviewing dates: general survey conducted in October 1954; visitors survey conducted on 8 to 20 November 1954.
(369 pp.)

In late 1954 about half the population of West Germany was aware of the existence of the America Houses, with the greatest percentage of knowledgeable residents in AMZON (60%) and the lowest percentage in the British Zone (34%). Between February 1948 and October 1954 there had been a steady increase (from 4 per cent to 84 per cent) in the percentage of AMZON residents able to give specific information about what an America House offered. The library facilities were mentioned most frequently. In AMZON, 12 per cent of the population said they had visited an America House at some time; in the French Zone, the figure stood at only 4 per cent.

Only 13 per cent of the West Germans interviewed had ever heard of the bookmobiles and German-American reading rooms situated in places where there were no America Houses, and almost no one had ever been to one or the other.

It was estimated that a total of 35.9 million visits to America Houses had been made during the previous year by about three and a quarter million individuals. About half had done so upon the personal recommendation of a friend or relative. Among the visitors interviewed, 9 per cent were at the center for the first time. Over half (53%) had been going since before 1952.

The general appraisal of the America Houses by their visitors was extremely favorable. As many as 68 per cent rated the offerings as very good or even excellent, while another 29 per cent termed them good. Most frequent mention was made of the libraries. Most people (51%) were satisfied with the fact that the United States financed and ran the America Houses, but 43 per cent felt they ought to be financed and directed jointly by Americans and Germans.

Report No. 211 (9 May 1955)

REUNIFICATION

West German Aspirations and Expectations

Sample: 843 West Germans and 302 West Berliners.
Interviewing dates: 28 March to 12 April 1955. (107 pp.)

When asked what they considered to be the most important problem facing Germany at that time, 37 per cent--the highest percentage mentioning any single issue--cited reunification. This represented a considerable drop from the 75 per cent who had mentioned this issue one year earlier. Most people hoped for reunification either for economic reasons (primarily the hope that the situation in the East might be improved) or for national and traditional reasons (that Germany should once again be a single nation).

Whereas in January 1954 half (50%) of the population thought the chances for reunification were either good or very good, only 27 per cent still felt this way in early spring 1955. Moreover, there had been a considerable shift over the course of the preceding six months in ascribing blame for the situation. Whereas in October 1954 61 per cent blamed the East and 24 per cent blamed both sides, in April 1955 only 43 per cent blamed the East, and nearly as many (38%) blamed both sides.

A solid majority (55%) felt that the United States should step in and do something about the situation. Most of those taking this position explained that America ought to adopt a more reasonable attitude, especially toward the Soviet Union, and should try to get the Russians to negotiate. Very few recommended a get-tough policy. Almost half (47%) felt that Germany itself ought to do something, but as many as 30 per cent did not think it could do anything.

Asked whether or not they could see any disadvantages to reunification, 16 per cent replied yes, with most of these pointing to economic problems. However, 62 per cent saw advantages, again mostly economic.

Only 30 per cent saw the chances for reunification as being good or very good. Most of those with an opinion on the subject felt that the Soviet Union would demand political, economic, and military concessions in return for reunification; most rejected the idea of such concessions.

Compared with October 1954, fewer people liked the idea of German participation in a Western defense system (with support dropping from 44 per cent to 40 per cent), but even fewer chose the Soviet proposal for reunification on the condition that Germany not join any alliances; the percentage of those who were undecided rose from 23 per cent to 29 per cent. The vast majority (72%) opposed recognizing the Oder-Neisse line as the permanent eastern frontier in exchange for reunification. Given a list of possible prices for reunification, 68 per cent rejected the idea of elections that would not be as free as those known in West Germany, while 53 per cent would accept withdrawal of NATO forces from Germany if Russian troops were also removed. Germans were certain that the communists would exert greater influence in a reunited Germany, but 32 per cent felt it would be easy to counter this influence; 42 per cent thought it would be difficult, and 3 per cent thought it would be impossible.

Since the high of 72 per cent in January 1954, the percentage of those expressing satisfaction with Chancellor Adenauer's handling of the reunification problem had dropped to 48 per cent. In addition, his general prestige, while quite high (69%), had also slipped since June 1953 when it stood at 76 per cent.

Report No. 212 (13 May 1955)

WEST GERMAN RADIO LISTENING DURING FEBRUARY 1955

Sample: 1,950 West Germans.
Interviewing dates: 14 to 16 February 1955. (29 pp.)

Almost all West Germans (89%) listened to the radio, and the same high percentage owned radios. The average number of hours listened per week was 19.8; 82 per cent listened every day. Three-quarters of the population generally listened to NWDR, which had recently been split into two stations, one for Hamburg and the other for Cologne.

Just under half the respondents said they used the radio as their main source of information about news in Germany and the world at large. This represented a drop since February 1952, when just over half made this claim. At the same time, those relying on newspapers rose from 37 per cent in 1952 to 43 per cent in 1955.

Despite the fact that the Western Powers had not done so for some time, more than a fourth (27%) thought they continued to exercise some measure of control over what was broadcast.

Report No. 213 (1 July 1955)

SOVEREIGN GERMANY SPEAKS
Reactions to Sovereignty, Austria Solution, and Coming Four-Power Conference

Sample: 626 West Germans and 297 West Berliners.
Interviewing dates: 1 to 11 June 1955. (128 pp.)

One month after Germany had regained its sovereignty--accorded by the Paris agreements, which went into effect on 5 May 1955--77 per cent of the population had heard of the event, while 23 per cent were unaware of it. Sixty per cent were aware that the Western Powers had reserved certain rights for themselves, and for this reason some West Germans were not overwhelmingly enthusiastic about their new status. While more West Germans mentioned reunification than any other issue when asked what the most important problem facing their country was, still only 34 per cent listed it; in West Berlin it was mentioned by 68 per cent.

Following a high of 72 per cent registered in May 1953, decreasing percentages of West Germans reported thinking that their country ought to side with the West in the cold war. In June 1955, 52 per cent advocated such a course; 33 per cent said Germany should choose neither side; and 14 per cent offered no opinion on the matter. Even if there should be a war between the Soviet Union and the United States, over half (52%) the population did not feel that the FRG should take sides; 35 per cent said they would want to side with the United States.

Given their new sovereign status, very few West Germans (17%) felt their country ought to assume a new attitude toward the Western Powers. A large minority (34%) nonetheless thought a change necessary vis-à-vis the Soviet Union, most particularly through the establishment of diplomatic relations. Almost four in five (79%) basically favored such a step; but if the price for FRG-Soviet relations were to be recognition of the GDR, then this figure dropped to 24 per cent. Three in ten (30%) felt the acquisition of sovereignty had improved chances for reunification, 39 per cent thought the situation remained unchanged, and 22 per cent had no view on the matter.

Less than three weeks after the signing of the Austrian Treaty on 15 May 1955, 70 per cent of the West Germans and 80 per cent of the West Berliners were aware of the event. Almost half the West Berliners (47%) but only 23 per cent of the West Germans felt it might be viewed as a success for Western policies. Furthermore, if Chancellor Adenauer were to be invited to Moscow to discuss reunification, as many as 77 per cent of the West Germans and 81 per cent of the West Berliners felt he ought to accept. A rather large minority (41%) thought it might be possible to arrange an "Austrian solution" for Germany, 27 per cent did not think so, and 32 per cent had no opinion.

The majority (70%) of West Germans and even more West Berliners (84%) were aware that a four-power conference was being planned to discuss the future of Germany. During the preceding year, increasing percentages of Germans were hopeful that something would be achieved at such a meeting. But opinion was divided on the question of whether Germany could achieve more through independent negotiations with the East (29%) or not (32%); 39 per cent had no opinion.

Although a sizable minority had always preferred a hypothetical Soviet proposal for a reunited but neutral Germany rather than the Western offer of incorporation into the Western defense system, in June 1955 for the first time more people chose the former (36%) than the latter (34%). Opinion split on whether the Western Powers would give a guarantee of security to an armed but neutral and reunited Germany, with 31 per cent saying they thought the West would and 32 per cent saying it would not. Regardless of what they felt on the issue, however, very few West Germans (22%) thought the four-power conference would result in an agreement on reunification.

APPENDIX: LIST OF U.S. EMBASSY SURVEY REPORTS

UNITED STATES EMBASSY STUDIES, SERIES 2 (continuation of HICOG Series 2)

214. Written Media in West Germany: A Study of Public Reactions and Extent of Penetration (15 August 1955)
214-S. West German Views on Vital Questions (Atomic Energy, NATO, and the Far East) (6 September 1955)
215. German Reactions to the Geneva Conference on Peaceful Use of Atomic Energy (21 September 1955)
216. German Reactions to Atomic Weapons (23 September 1955)
217. Appraising the Adenauer Moscow Agreements (11 October 1955)
218. The U.S. Exhibit at the Berlin Trade Fair 1955 (25 October 1955)
219. Some East Zone Radio Listening Habits--As Revealed by Visitors to the Berlin Trade Fair (September 24 to October 9, 1955) (28 October 1955)
220. East Zoners Appraise the Adenauer and GDR Moscow Agreements (2 November 1955)
221. A Study of the Extent and Nature of Exchangee's Contacts with the German Population (22 November 1955)
222. A Study of Audience Reactions to *Tom Schuler*, a U.S.I.S. Short Feature Film (7 December 1955)
223. The Relative Influence of U.S.I.S., Informal, and American Commercial Media in West Germany (27 December 1955)
224. Study of U.S. Impression and Dissemination in Germany by Participants in the Information Specialist and in the Students' Exchange Program (30 December 1955)
225. Visitors' Reactions to the Family of Man Exhibit (23 January 1956)
226. West German Attitudes Concerning the New German Army (10 February 1956)
227. The American Soldier Reappraised: A Further Study of Civilian-Troop Relations (21 February 1956)
228. President Eisenhower's Mutual Aerial Inspection Plan as Seen by the West German Public (6 March 1956)
229. Public Opinion in the Saar (19 March 1956)
230. Gauging West German Susceptibility to Authoritarianism (16 April 1956)
231. Public Confidence in Chancellor Adenauer Following the North Rhine-Westphalian Episode (25 April 1956)
232. A West German Perspective of U.S. Politics and Culture (with separate appendix) (7 May 1956)
233. West German Thoughts on U.S. and German Economic Life: I. Knowledge of U.S. and German Economy (with separate appendix) (21 May 1956)
234. Appraisal of "The Hour of Choice" by a Group of Hessian Civil Servants (28 May 1956)
235. Radio Diary Study 1955 (15 June 1956)

236. West German Thoughts on U.S. and German Economic Life: II. Conception of the U.S. and German Economics (with appendix) (19 June 1956)
237. West German Thoughts on U.S. and German Economic Life: III. Comparison of U.S. and German Economic Life (with separate appendix) (10 July 1956)

UNITED STATES EMBASSY STUDIES, SERIES 3 (A AND C)

A-1. A Working Class Audience Appraisal of the U.S.I.S. Film *Maker of Abundance* (23 July 1956)
A-2. Methodological Problems of the Radio Diary and Coincidental Interview Methods (30 July 1956)
C-1. Assessment of Troop Community Relations (in light of a newspaper campaign) (15 August 1956)
C-2. Current Political Issues (22 August 1956)
C-3. West German Susceptibility to Soviet Moves: I. General Reactions (with separate appendix) (10 September 1956)
A-3. The U.S. Space Unlimited Exhibit at the Berlin Fair 1956 (24 October 1956)
A-4. A Study of East Zone Radio and TV Habits (26 October 1956)
C-4. East German Opinions as of September 1956 (7 November 1956)
A-5. Political Attitudes of West Germans Exposed to U.S.I.S., Informal, and American Commercial Media (20 November 1956)
C-5. Basic Orientation and Political Thinking of West German Youth and Their Leaders--1956 (15 December 1956)
A-6. Reactions to "Die Schildburger"--A Pre-Release Study of a U.S.I.S. Film (15 January 1957)
A-7. West German Reactions to President Eisenhower's Middle-East Doctrine (28 January 1957)
C-6. West German Editors Assess the Press (with separate appendix) (21 February 1957)
A-8. The Frankfurt Showing of the Space Unlimited Exhibit (27 January 1957)
A-9. East Zone Opinion of RIAS Programming (6 March 1957)
C-7. Further Information on East German Political Opinions (20 March 1957)
A-10. A Study of the Effects of Time on Visitors' Reactions to the Space Unlimited Exhibit (28 March 1957)
A-11. The Amerika-Haus Bookmobile Program--Part I: Who Are the Bookmobile Users? (12 June 1957)
A-12. The Amerika-Haus Bookmobile Program--Part II: Pattern of Bookmobile Use (12 June 1957)
A-13. The Amerika-Haus Bookmobile Program--Part III: Appendix (12 June 1957)
C-8. Use of Amerika-Dienst Material by West German Editors (12 June 1957)

Appendix: U.S. Embassy Survey Reports/261

A-14. Current Awareness of and Opinions Concerning the Mutual Aerial Inspection Plan (with separate appendix) (26 August 1957)
C-9. The Degree of Interest in Features of American Life Expressed by Possible Target Groups (11 September 1957)
A-15. A Study of *Ost-Probleme* Subscribers (with separate appendix) (23 September 1957)
C-10. West German Confidence in NATO (10 October 1957)
A-16. A Study of the Nature and Operation of U.S.I.S.'s Film Committees (22 October 1957)
C-11. Extent of Western Influence on the East German Population (with separate appendix) (4 November 1957)
A-17. Visitors' Reactions to "America Builds," the U.S. Exhibit at the Berlin Industrial Fair 1957 (13 November 1957)
A-18. Radio Listening in the GDR (with separate appendix) (19 December 1957)
C-12. East Zone Political Opinion (in Relation to U.S.I.S. Exposure) (with separate appendix) (27 December 1957)
C-13. Sputnik's Influence on West German Confidence in the U.S. (22 January 1958)
A-19. The Net Effect of Having British-American Libraries in Duesseldorf and Oldenburg (28 January 1958)
A-20. Recipients Evaluate U.S.I.S. Vienna Press Products (20 February 1958)
C-14. First Reactions to the "Explorer" (27 February 1958)
C-15. Factors in West Berlin Morale--Part I: Economic Factors (with separate appendix) (7 April 1958)
C-16. Factors in West Berlin Morale--Part II: Political Factors (with separate appendix) (21 April 1958)
C-17. A Short Appraisal of NATO (1 May 1958)
C-18. German Reunification and a Summit Conference (8 May 1958)
C-19. A-Bomb Test Suspension and a Summit Conference (3 June 1958)
C-20. Atomic Weapons for the Bundeswehr (6 June 1958)
C-21. The Influence of the Nagy-Maleter Executions on West German Expectations Concerning a Summit Conference (1 August 1958)
C-22. East Zone Germans Assess Their Current Situation (22 October 1958)
A-21. "Kalamazoo Comes to Berlin"--The 1958 Berlin Industrial Fair Exhibit (10 November 1958)
A-22. Station Popularity and Reception Conditions within East Germany (17 November 1958)
C-23. Assessment of NATO and American Forces in West Germany (before the Berlin Crisis) (15 December 1958)
C-24. West Germany Views the Berlin Crisis (10 February 1959)
A-23. The Role of "Culture" in West German Assessment of U.S. Foreign Policies (with separate appendix) (2 April 1959)

C-25. West German and Berlin Confidence in NATO (6 July 1959)
-- Post Geneva Opinions on Eisenhower-Khrushchev Visits and Related Issues (September 1959)
-- East Zone Opinions toward Current Issues (A Study among East Zone Visitors to the Berlin Industrial Fair 1959 (September 1959)
-- Radio Listening and TV Viewing in East Germany (27 October 1959)
-- East Zone Radio Listening and TV Viewing (March 1960)
-- German Opinion
-- East Zone Radio and TV Viewing Habits (and some Data about the RIAS Image) (November 1960)
-- Sources of Information about the U.S. (January 1961)
-- East Zone Radio Listening and TV Viewing Habits (March 1961)
-- RIAS Program Reaction Survey (June 1962)
-- Interaction Survey on President Eisenhower's U.S. Speech (German Results)

INDEX

(Note: The numbers listed after each entry refer to report numbers rather than to page numbers.)

Adenauer, Chancellor Konrad: and Franco-German union, 21; satisfaction with, 28, 56, 155, 168, 179, 180, 196, 200, 202, 206, 211; popular awareness of as Chancellor, 28, 106; and young people, 50; and East German offer to discuss reunification, 55, 58, 60, 64, 71-S; economic policies of, 81; East Germany, 186; personality of as factor in 1953 election, 191; and reunification issue, 194-I; support for after four-power conference, 195; attitude of other Europeans toward, 202-S, 209-S. See also FRG

Adult education: and German youth, 54

Agricultural exhibit: American, 176

Air force: need for, 154

Allied powers: right of intervention in FRG, 99; withdrawal of troops, 211. See also Western Powers

America. See United States

Amerika Haus: and young people, 17, 42; general awareness of, 31, 76; effectiveness of, 181, 210

Amerikanische Rundschau (U.S. sponsored magazine), 2; and young readers, 43

Anti-Semitism, 1, 113, 167

Armaments production in FRG, 94

Army: establishment of, 9, 33, 34-S, 36, 45, 46, 47, 180, 196; national vs. European, 20, 117, 131, 167, 193, 202; and former Nazis, 57; willingness to serve in, 61, 88; role of former generals in, 153; reaction to new, 226. See also European Defense and Remilitarization

Asia: U.S. efforts to counter communism in, 202-S. See also Korean War

Atlantic Pact: views on participation in, 17-S, 20, 36, 45, 46, 47, 48, 51, 52, 53, 55, 58, 60, 61, 64, 69, 70-S, 80, 88, 94, 117, 120, 131, 207; reasons for opposition to, 48, 52, 130; and 1950 local elections, 56; and lessons of Nuremberg, 57; effect of participation in on reunification, 60, 115; and Spain, 93; agreement with American views on purpose of, 107; attitude toward in West Berlin, 128; Bundestag debate on, 129, 130, 131; awareness of in Western Europe, 209-S. See also European army, European defense, European Defense Community, and NATO

Atomic energy: exhibition, 164; peaceful uses of, 192-S, 205, 208, 209-S

Atomic stockpiles: President Eisenhower's speech before U.N. dealing with, 192-S

Atomic weapons: prospect of in Korea, 53; first use, 91; and defense of Europe, 199; attitude toward in Western Europe, 209-S

264/Index

Austria: radio listenership, 196-S1
Austrian treaty: as model for Germany, 213

Bavaria: student attitude toward government of, 17; unemployment in, 23
BHE: refugees' support for, 136
Blockade: recommended moves in case of second, 142, 145, 146
Bonn: as capital, 3
Bund Deutscher Jugend (West German youth group), 161

Capitalism, 147
CARE, 7
Catholics: East German, 162
CDU/CSU: reasons for voting for in 1950 local elections, 56; types of support for, 155; preference for in East Zone, 186; and 1953 federal elections, 191
China: People's Republic, 209-S
Church: Catholic, in GDR, 162
Civil liberties: vs. economic security, 17, 17-S, 50; for KPD members, 59
Codetermination, 75, 148
Cold war, 18; West German allegiance in, 143, 213; and Western European populations, 169-S; responsibility for, 209-S. See also East-West conflict
Collective guilt, 113, 167
Collectivization: of GDR farmers, 133
Communications. See Films, Magazines, Newspapers, Radio listening
Communism: vs. reunification, 1; and unemployment, 22, 23; appeal of in West Germany, 59; general views on, 147; in Western Europe, 169-S, 209-S
Communist newspapers, 35
Communist Party of Germany (KPD), 18, 209-S; ban on, 59; civil liberties for members, 59
Contractual agreement, 99, 135, 137, 138, 141, 144, 168, 179, 180; GDR citizens' attitude toward, 138; attitude toward in West Berlin, 142, 146, 177; support for, 152, 169; effect of Stalin's death on attitude toward, 177-S
Currency reform: effect of, 17-S

Danzig: as part of Germany, 1
Decartelization, 75
Democracy: definition of, 15
Democratization: U.S. efforts at in Germany, 11, 40
Denazification, Wuerttemberg-Baden scandal, 8; as viewed by SRP adherents, 87
Der Monat (U.S. sponsored magazine), 2; and young readers, 43
Disarmament, 123
Draft: attitude toward possibility of, 47, 120, 207; willingness to serve if called, 88. See also Army and Military service
DRP: in 1953 election, 191
Dulles, John Foster, Secretary of State: remarks by, and 1953 German election, 191; speech at four-power conference, 194-II; West European attitude toward, 202-S, 209-S

East Berlin: visits to by West Berliners, 206-S
East Berlin Youth Festival: knowledge of beforehand, 79; evaluation of during, 101; effects on East German population, 110
Eastern territories: claim to, 1, 143, 168. See also Oder-Neisse territories
East-West conflict, 55, 91, 169, 180, 202; assessed by East Germans, 63-S, 185;

as viewed by SRP adherents, 87; West Berlin attitude toward, 128, 146; comparative strength, 18, 169-S, 200, 202; and four-power conference, 195; responsibility for, 202-S

East-West trade: West Germany and, 86, 143

East Zone. See German Democratic Republic

Economic integration: hopes for, 98

Economic security vs. civil liberties, 17-S; among students, 17; among the young, 50

Economic situation, 17-S, 22, 23, 122; in West Berlin, 5, 125, 134, 196-S2, 206-S; of East Germans, 63-S; and Bonn government, 81; as major problem, 91; preference for reconstruction over rearmament, 130; in West and East Berlin, 134

EDC. See European Defense Community

Eden: views of, 209-S

Eden Plan (for reunification), 194-III, 194-IV, 194-V, 194-VI

Education: East German youth attitudes toward, 116. See also Adult education

Eisenhower, Dwight D.: as Supreme Commander of European Army, 58, 60, 61, 120; as presidential candidate, 163; attitude toward after 1952 election, 173; foreign policy address, 178; speech before U.N. on atomic stockpiles, 192-S

Elections: 1950 local, 56; need for federal, 56, 106, 168; in East Germany, 63-S, 185; in lower Saxony, 87; federal in 1953, 191

Employment: opportunities for East German youth, 38; refugees, 136. See also Unemployment

Enterprise: freedom of, 75

Erlangen: attitude of students at University of, 17

ERP. See Marshall Plan

Europa Train: reactions to in Mainz, 85; reactions to in Berlin, 98

European army: Germany and, 20, 45, 46, 47, 48, 51, 52, 53, 55, 58, 60, 61, 62, 64, 69, 70-S, 80, 88, 94, 111, 120, 135, 137, 138, 141, 144, 168, 213; vs. national army, 20, 117; and 1950 local elections, 56; and views on Nazism, 57; and reunification, 115, 211; and French Saar policy, 124; West Berlin attitudes on, 142. See also Army, European defense, and Remilitarization

European Coal and Steel Community, 169-S

European defense: Germany and, 17-S, 20, 36, 45, 46, 47, 51, 52, 53, 55, 58, 60, 61, 62, 64, 69, 70-S, 80, 88, 94, 111, 117, 120, 129, 130, 131, 135, 137, 138, 141, 144, 168, 169-S, 177-S, 180, 193, 195, 196, 199, 200, 202, 202-S, 207, 209-S, 211, 213; national vs. European army, 20, 117, 131, 167, 193, 196, 202; plans for, 33, 36; reasons for opposition to, 48, 52, 130; and 1950 local elections, 56; and views on Nazism, 57; and reunification, 60, 115, 211; agreement with Americans on need for, 107; and French Saar policy, 124; West Berlin attitudes toward, 128, 142; Bundestag debate on, 129, 130, 131; views of those who had experienced air raids, 154; West European views of, 209-S. See also Atlantic Pact, European Defense Community, NATO, Neutrality,

266/Index

and Remilitarization
European Defense Community, 169-S, 183-S, 196, 199; attitude toward in East Germany, 185; as election issue in 1953, 191; support for, 193, 200, 202; drop in opposition to following four-power conference, 195; attitude toward in Germany, France, Italy, and Great Britain, 202-S. *See also* European defense
European unity: attitude toward among students, 17; East German attitude toward, 71-S; and reunification, 111; as issue in 1953 election, 191; support for, 200
Exchange program with U.S., 12, 44, 151
Expellees, 17-S, 22, 23. *See also* Refugees

Farmers, East German: and RIAS, 132; and collectivization, 133
FDJ. *See* Free German Youth
FDP: and 1950 local elections, 56; types of support for, 155
Films: *Races of Mankind,* 23-S; *Welt im Film* (newsreel), 29; American documentary, 43; *Ohne Furcht* (short film), 175, 187; use of in factories to increase production, 183; *Magic Streetcar* (U.S.I.A. film), 187; U.S. commercial in West Germany, 197
Four-power discussions, 51, 53, 61, 64, 74, 82, 194-I, 194-II, 194-III, 194-IV, 194-V, 194-VI; usefulness of, 58, 60, 61, 64, 69; city mayors' attitudes toward, 68; East German attitude toward, 71-S, 186, 194-V; agreement with Americans on reasons for failure of, 107; interest in, 144, 152, 177-S, 179, 180, 183-S, 193; Molotov Plan, 194-III, 194-IV, 194-V, 194-VI; Eden Plan, 194-III, 194-IV, 194-V, 194-VI; reaction to results, 195; and future of Germany, 200, 213
Four-power withdrawal: East German attitude toward, 71-S
France: and Schuman Plan, 71; dependability of, 88; appointment of ambassador to Saar from, 124; and FRG defense contribution, 130; and reunification, 139; policy on trade between East and West Germany, 140; and EDC, 169-S, 202-S, 209-S; attitude toward, 193, 209
Franco-German relations, 21, 62, 124, 209
Freedom of the press, 59, 159
Free German Youth: and Whitsuntide March (May 1950), 16, 25, 63-S; attitude toward among young East German men, 79; reasons for membership in, 108, 116
FRG
  Economic policy: unemployment, 23, living conditions, 91; satisfaction with, 155
  Foreign policy: and Western Powers, 28; relations with France, 62, 124; and GDR, 86; and U.S., 103; and GDR youth, 121; and reunification, 139; and USSR, 213
  Political system: attitude toward, 3, 17-S, 28, 106, 122, 144, 179, 191; as a democracy, 15; and young people, 17, 50; and West Berlin, 125, 146, 177-S, 196-S2
  Security of: 46, 48, 52, 55, 58, 94, 99, 143,

Index/267

167; after Korean War, 32, 33, 36, 37; Western contribution to, 62; and occupation troops, 72, 119; and ERP funds, 84; Soviet threat to, 130, 145, 177-S; policies, 168; and U.S. troops, 174; confidence in U.S. support, 177

GDR
  Army, 20
  Catholic church in, 162
  Economic situation, 63-S
  Farmers: RIAS broadcasts for, 132; collectivization of, 133; at U.S. agricultural exhibit, 176
  Four-power conference and, 194-V
  FRG-GDR relations: West German awareness of GDR, 3, 28, 156, 196; reunification, 55, 58, 69, 71-S, 115; trade, 86, 140, 196; West Berlin and, 134; contractual agreements, 138; Oder-Neisse territories, 138; refugees from GDR, 157, 177; defection by Dr. Otto John, 202
  People's Police: West German and American views of, 107; East German views of, 108
  Political situation: elections, 63-S; information level and attitudes, 108; 17 June 1953 riots, 180, 185, 186
  Radio listeners, 90, 203; young, 109; and RIAS, 189
  Recognition of, 196, 200
  Youth: employment opportunities for, 38; attitudes among young men, 79; impressions of West Berlin, 101; and hypothetical questions for McCloy, 102; views on world politics, 108; and propaganda to the East, 108; and radio listening, 109; schools and, 116; morale, 121; and Western media, 126

Geneva Conference on Vietnam, 200
Great Britain: dependability of, 88; and reunification, 139; policy on trade between East and West Germany, 140; popular support for communism in, 169-S; attitude toward EDC, 202-S; attitude toward European defense, 209-S
Grotewohl, Otto (GDR Prime Minister), 55, 58, 60, 64, 71-S

H-Bomb: attitude toward development of, 13
Heute (U.S. sponsored magazine), 2, 14; and young readers, 43
HICOG: local representatives of, 78
Hitler: attitude toward plotters in assassination plot against, 113, 114, 167
Housing: for miners, 66; for refugees, 136

Industry: socialization of, 27; codetermination, 75; decartelization, 75; American vs. German working methods in, 149
Information vs. propaganda, 171
Integration: in Western Europe, 169-S
Internationalism-nationalism scale, 71, 111
Israel: restitution agreement with, 167
Italy: dependability of, 88; and EDC, 169-S, 202-S; popular support for communism in, 169-S; and European defense, 209-S

Jewish restitution, 113, 114

268/Index

John, Dr. Otto (defector to East Germany), 202
Jugend in der Freien Welt (youth magazine), 24
July 20th plot, 113, 114, 167

Kaiser, Jakob (minister of All-German Affairs), 157
Kemritz, Dr. Hans: scandal surrounding, 89
Korean War, 32, 33, 34-S, 37, 55, 107; rumors about, 28-S1, 28-S2; and increased possibility for world war, 47, 53; and opposition to Atlantic Pact participation, 48; attitude on withdrawal from, 61; dismissal of General MacArthur 77, 83; cease fire negotiations, 92, 150; effect on European defense, 94; U.N. role in, 150; U.S. Air Force in, 154; U.N. investigation of atrocities in, 192
KPD. *See* Communist Party of Germany
Kreis Resident Officers (local HICOG representatives), 78
Krupp, Alfried: and Landsberg decision, 63; assessed by mayors, 67

Landsberg decisions, 63, 70; evaluated by mayors, 67; views of among SRP adherents, 87
Law for the Equalization of Burdens, 136
League of German Youth, 161
London conference: nine-power, 202-S
Luftwaffe: assessment of, 154

MacArthur, Gen. Douglas: relieved of duties in Far East, 77, 83
Magazines: reading of, 2, 14; *Amerikanische Rundschau*, 2; *Der Monat*, 2; *Neue Auslese*, 2; *Heute*, 2, 14; *Quick*, 14; *Jugend in der Freien Welt*, 24; among young people, 43

Magic Streetcar, U.S.I.A. film, 187
Marshall House: at Berlin Industrial Fair, 166, 190
Marshall Plan, 17-S, 39; and West Berlin, 5; attitude toward among students, 17; housing project for Ruhr miners, 66; use of funds, 84; knowledge of in Mainz, 85; agreement with American view on, 107; East German views of, 108; GDR youth views on, 116; Western European views of, 169-S
Massive retaliation: U.S. doctrine of, 199
McCloy, John J. (U.S. High Commissioner for Germany), 103; and East German youth, 102
Military service, 1, 9, 17. *See also* Draft
Miners: housing problems of, 66
Molotov Plan (for reunification), 194-III, 194-IV, 194-V, 194-VI
Morale: of West Berliners, 146, 177
Munich: attitude of students at University of, 17

Nationalism: attitudes characterizing, 1, 143; and FRG-GDR trade, 86; SRP and, 87; vs. internationalism, 111; extreme, 118; and rightist sentiments, 167
Nationalism-internationalism scale, 71
National Socialism: as being more good or evil, 11, 118, 167; student attitudes, 17; evaluation of, 17-S, 113; and employment, 22, 23; and SRP, 87;
NATO: Germany and, 20; Spain and, 93; evaluation of, 120; and new army, 57. *See also* European defense *and* Remilitarization
Negro soldiers: and German public, 119

Neo-Nazism, 118; press reports of, 159; attitude toward revival of, 167
Netherlands: and EDC, 169-S; communism in, 169-S
Neue Auslese (U.S. sponsored magazine), 2; and young readers, 43
Neue Zeitung (American-sponsored newspaper in West Berlin), 160, 184
Neutralism, 61, 88, 94, 137, 200, 213; in East-West conflict, 18, 55, 58, 60, 69; in case of war, 33, 37; and opposition to Atlantic Pact, 48; as advocated in magazine article, 49; as price for reunification, 61, 64, 183-S, 193, 194-I, 194-II; and FRG-GDR trade, 86; in Western Europe, 169-S, 209-S; and East German residents, 185
Newspaper reading, 17-S, 158, 160; among East German youth, 109
Newspapers: Communist party, 35; Western, read in East, 79; as unbiased news source, 159; *Neue Zeitung*, 160, 184
News sources, 158, 159, 160, 165. See also Magazines, Newspapers, Radio
Nuclear power: peaceful uses, 199, 202-S
Nuremberg Trials: articles about, 49; fairness of, 57; and Atlantic Pact, 57. See also Landsberg decisions

Occupation: feelings on continuation of, 103; costs of, 72, 174, 198
Occupation powers: relations with West Germany, 103; intervention into FRG politics, 106
Occupation statute: revised, 74
Occupation troops: views of, 1, 103, 119; withdrawal of, 19, 119, 177

Oder-Neisse boundary, 136, 137, 138, 211; and reunification, 193, 194-III, 194-IV
Oder-Neisse territories, 143, 206
Ohne Furcht (U.S. short film), 175, 187
Opinion leaders: views on Landsberg decision, 67; views on four-power conference, 68
Organizations: youth, unified vs. decentralized, 73; veterans, 112

Pacifism, 57
Pamphlets: as information sources, 165
Paris agreements, 209-S, 213
Parties: multiparty vs. single-party system, 15; rightwing in 1953 election, 191. See also CDU/CSU, SPD etc.
Peaceful coexistence, 209-S
Politics: popular attitude toward, 17-S; and young people, 50
Population problem in FRG, 143
Press. See Newspapers
Press freedom, 35; and Allied occupation, 159
Production: use of films to increase, 183
Propaganda vs. information from America, 171

Quick (illustrated periodical), 14; and young readers, 43

Races of Mankind (film), 23-S
Racism, 1
Radio Leipzig (East German station), 90
Radio listening, 17-S, 95, 100, 204, 212; in West Berlin, 4, 34; among young people, 41; Western stations listened to in East, 79; in GDR, 90, 170, 203; among East German youth, 108, 109; for news, 158, 159; RIAS, 182; RIAS and West Berliners, 188; RIAS and East Germans, 189; in Vienna, 196-S1

Rearmament: opposition to, 48, 206, 207; East German views on, 108; and danger of war, 120; need for air force, 154; views on in West Berlin, 206-S
Reconstruction: and the U.S., 1, 17-S, 39; and Western Powers, 30
Refugees: agreement with American views on, 107; motives for flight, 121; housing for, 136; integration of, 136; political views of, 136; effect on West Germany, 143; difficulties of, 157; attitude toward RIAS, 170; effect on West Berlin morale, 177; radio listening habits, 203. See also BHE
Religion: Catholics in GDR, 162
Remer, General Otto (head of SRP), 114
Remilitarization, 9, 20, 45, 46, 47, 51, 52, 53, 55, 57, 58, 69, 80, 94, 107; opposition to, 48, 52, 206, 207; proposed East German plebiscite on, 70-S, 80; East German views on, 108; and danger of war, 120; need for air force, 154; views on in West Berlin, 206-S. See also Army, Draft, European defense, European Defense Community, NATO, and Neutrality
Reorientation program, 10, 11, 12, 40, 41, 42, 43, 44
Restitution to victims of Nazism, 167
Retaliation: U.S. doctrine of massive, 199
Reunification, 1, 17-S, 143, 206, 211, 213; and creation of GDR, 3; attitude toward among students, 17; East German offer to discuss, 55, 58, 60, 64, 115; and participation in Atlantic Pact, 60; neutrality as price for, 61, 64, 69, 193, 194-I; East German attitudes toward Grotewohl negotiation offer, 71-S; Western Powers' view of, 71-S; and West European unity, 98, 111; GDR youth views on, 102; responsibility for continued division, 107; attitude toward Soviet proposal for, 135, 137, 138, 141, 152, 179; France and, 139; Great Britain and, 139; U.S. position on, 139, 156, 177; contractual agreement and, 144; and GDR delegation to Bonn, 156; FRG policy, 168; Stalin's death and, 177-S; and East German riots, 180; and four-power conference, 183-S, 194-I, 194-II, 194-III, 194-IV, 194-V, 194-VI, 195; East German attitudes, 185, 186; as election issue in 1953, 191; and free elections, 193; and Adenauer government, 194-I; Oder-Neisse boundary and, 194-III, 194-IV; Eden Plan, 194-III, 194-IV, 194-V, 194-VI; Molotov Plan, 194-III, 194-IV, 194-V, 194-VI; Austrian treaty as model for, 213
Reuter, Ernst (mayor of West Berlin), 63-S
RIAS (Radio in the American Sector), 4, 34, 182, 204; East German listeners, 90, 185, 189, 201, 203; and East German youth, 109; broadcasts for farmers in East Germany, 132; and East German refugees, 170; popularity of in West Berlin; 188
Rightwing parties in 1953 election, 191
Riots of 17 June 1953 in East Germany, 185, 186
Ruhr statute, 1
Rumors, 28-S1, 28-S2, 34-S

Saar: as part of Germany, 1; appointment of French ambassador to, 124; FRG policy, 168, 196, 200; Paris agreement on, 206
Schools: and *Eight Great Americans* pamphlet, 65; East German and young males, 79; U.S. history in 96
Schumacher, Kurt (head of SPD), 106; opposition to Schuman Plan, 81; and remilitarization, 88
Schuman Plan, 51, 71, 143, 169-S; publicity campaign for, 81; knowledge of in Mainz, 85; and French Saar policy, 124
Security of FRG, 207; Soviet threat to, 138
Silesia: as part of Germany, 1
Socialism: general views on, 147
Socialization of industry, 27, 147
Soldiers: rank-ordering of effectiveness by nationality, 119; German attitude toward American, 174
Sovereignty for FRG, 202, 202-S, 206, 213
Soviet Union: harassment of West Berlin, 5, 25, 141, 142, 145, 146; threat to FRG, 9, 55, 58, 108, 117, 130, 138, 145; influence on world affairs, 17-S, 18; relations with United States, 25, 58, 173, 185; relative military strength, 91, 154, 174; peace proposals, 152; attitudes toward postwar policies, 169-S; Western European views of, 169-S, 209-S; effect of Stalin's death on policies, 177-S; GDR view of U.S.-USSR relations, 185; negotiations with, 200; proposal for four-power conference, 202
Spain: and NATO, 93
SPD: and 1950 local elections, 56; types of support for, 155; and 1953 federal elections, 191

SRP, 87, 118, 155; views on plot to assassinate Hitler, 114
Stalin: death of, 177-S, 179
Standard of living: and Atlantic community cooperation, 166
Stevenson, Adlai (U.S. presidential candidate), 163
Strikes: public attitude toward, 148
Students: attitudes of those at Erlangen and Munich, 17

Third Reich, 114; labor service plans during, 38; magazine articles on, 49; and Jews, 113
Trade between East and West Germany, 86, 140, 143, 196
Trade unions: influence on economy, 148
Truman, President Harry S.: and H-Bomb, 13; and General MacArthur, 77, 83

Unemployment: as major problem, 22, 23; among the young, 38; in West Berlin, 125
United Nations: knowledge of, 91, 172; role in Korean conflict, 150; investigation of Korean atrocities, 192; President Eisenhower's speech on atomic stockpiles, 192-S
United States, 197, 208, 209-S, 210; soldiers, 1, 6, 174, 198; prestige in West Berlin, 5, 128; reorientation program, 10, 11, 12, 40, 41, 42, 43, 44; influence on Bonn, 17-S; influence on world affairs, 17-S, 18; confidence in, 19, 88, 200, 206, 209-S; and reconstruction of FRG, 30, 39; and possible aggression from East, 53, 55, 60; foreign policy debate in, 83; and Kemritz scandal, 89; stronger than Soviet Union, 91; military and economic pact with Spain, 93; interest in

history of among children, 96; GDR youth views on, 102; relations with FRG, 103, 128; and German reunification, 139, 211; policy on trade between East and West Germany, 140; view of trade unions and codetermination, 148; industrial working methods, 149; areas in which Germans could learn from, 151; peace proposals, 152; sponsorship of *Neue Zeitung*, 160; and Bund Deutscher Jugend, 161; presidential elections in, 163, 173; atomic energy exhibit, 164, 208; Western European views of, 169-S; information programs in Germany, 171, 210; agricultural exhibit, 176; cold war and, 178; support for CDU in 1953 election, 191; and West Berlin morale, 196-S2 films, 197; and European defense, 202-S

United States Information Centers. See *Amerika Haus*

Veterans' organizations, 112, 167
Vienna: radio listening in, 196-S1
VOA. See "Voice of America"
"Voice of America," 26, 95, 97, 104, 105, 155-S; and young people, 41, 109; and East German listeners, 90, 203; letters to, 108-S; and East German youth, 109; and East German farmers, 132; as news source, 160

War: chances of, 13, 16, 18, 47, 48, 125, 200, 209-S; and Korean conflict, 32, 37, 53; danger of increased by rearmament, 120; fear of in Western Europe, 169-S
War criminals: attitude toward Western Powers' handling of, 153. See also Nuremberg Trials *and* Landsberg decisions
Welt im Film (newsreel), 29
West Berlin: American prestige in, 5; Marshall Plan aid to, 5; morale in, 5, 16, 25, 125, 128, 146, 177, 196-S2, 206-S; economic situation, 5, 125, 177; reaction to Free German Youth rally at Whitsuntide (1950), 16, 25; expectation of war, 16; radio listening in, 34, 182; and East German youth, 101, 110; cultural festival in (September 1951), 127; attitudes on East-West conflict, 128; attitude toward East Berlin, 134; attitudes toward defense participation, 142; attitudes toward contractual agreement, 142, 146; reaction to Soviet pressures, 142, 146; attitude of West Germany toward, 146; and EDC, 146; refugees and, 177; *Neue Zeitung* readership, 184; as depicted in film *Magic Streetcar,* 187; Marshall House exhibit at Industrial Fair, 166, 190
Western European Union, 17-S, 21, 143, 202-S; and young people, 50
Western Powers: influence on Bonn, 3, 28; and reconstruction, 30, 39; and West German security, 32, 33, 37, 46, 48; and world situation, 58; stronger than communists, 83, 169; West Berlin confidence in, 128; sovereign Germany and, 213
West European unity, 85; and Schuman Plan, 71; and reunification, 98
West vs. East in world politics: East German estimates of, 63-S
Whitsuntide march (May 1950), 16, 25; and FDJ members, 63-S; and young East German men, 79

World War II: responsibility for, 1; Allied decision to end state of, 92-S

Young people: magazine reading among, 24, 43; and unemployment, 38; opportunities for in East vs. West Germany, 38; and American reorientation program, 40, 41, 42, 43, 44; radio listening among, 41; and Amerika Haus, 42; and American documentaries, 43; and German-American exchange program, 44; attitude toward politics, 50; and Bonn government, 50; and Chancellor Konrad Adenauer, 50; and economic security vs. civil liberties, 50; and Western European Union, 50; and adult education, 54; East German, and hypothetical questions for McCloy, 102; East German, and Western propaganda, 108; East German, and Western media, 109, 126; East German, on world politics, 116; morale among East German youth, 121; in West Berlin, 206-S

Youth Festival: held in East Berlin, 101, 116, 121, 126, 206-S; effect on GDR population, 110

Youth organizations, 25; centralized vs. diversified, 38, 73; East German, 79. *See also* Bund Deutscher Jugend

A NOTE ON THE AUTHORS

Anna J. Merritt, editor and staff associate at the Institute of Government and Public Affairs at the University of Illinois at Urbana-Champaign, received her B.A. from Smith College. She has worked extensively and published in the fields of education and public perspectives, and held a number of community offices related to education.

Richard L. Merritt is professor of political science and research professor of communications at the University of Illinois at Urbana-Champaign. He is currently head of the department of political science. He received his B.A. from the University of Southern California and his Ph.D. from Yale University. He has held teaching positions at Yale University and the Free University of Berlin, served as program chairman for the 1970 Annual Meeting of the American Political Science Association and the 1979 World Congress of the International Political Science Association (in Moscow), and has been a consultant to the United Nations as well as government agencies and universities in the United States and Germany.

The Merritts have focused much of their research activity on postwar Germany. Among their publications are *Public Opinion in Occupied Germany; West Germany Enters the Seventies; Politics, Economics and Society in the Two Germanies, 1945-1975;* and numerous scholarly articles on education, public opinion, and political life in Berlin and West Germany.